LEBOWSKI 101:

Limber-Minded Investigations into the Greatest Story Ever Blathered

Edited by Oliver Benjamin
Founder of The Church of the Latter-Day Dude

ABIDE UNIVERSITY PRESS
www.aui.me/press

CONTENTS

The Editorial Preface 7
   By Oliver Benjamin

"Suit the Word to the Action": Language, *Lebowski* and Literal Connections 11
   By Adam Bertocci

A Pox on Both Your Houses, Man: The Two Very Flawed Families of *The Big Lebowski* 16
   By Joe Blevins

Down Through The Generation Gaps: Decades of Disharmony Charted in *The Big Lebowski* 20
   By Jon Bastian

The Original Port Huron Statement: *The Big Lebowski* and the Religion of Laughter 24
   By Alan Baily

"I. The Royal 'We'": The Dude as Representative Man 30
   By Niles Schwartz

"What Makes a Man, Mr. Lebowski?": Masculinity Under (Friendly) Fire in Ethan and Joel
Coen's *The Big Lebowski* 39
   By Jakub Kazecki

Who's the Nihilist Here? 46
   By Todd Alcott

Takin' It Easy For Us Sinners: The Dude and Jesus Christ 50
   By David Masciotra

Walter Sobchak, Neocon: The Prescient Politics of *The Big Lebowski* 54
   By David Haglund

Deception and Detection: The Trickster Archetype in the Film *The Big Lebowski*, and its
Cult Following 57
   By William A. Ashton and Barbara A. Ashton

"That's just, like, your opinion, man": Irony, Abiding, Achievement, and *Lebowski* 66
   By Brian Wall

Bowling for Buddha 72
   By Chris "Pepper" Landis

The Big Lebowski: The Gulf War and Mediated Memory 75
   By Daniel Keyes

Tarot and Tao in *The Big Lebowski* 86
   By David Thorsteinsson

A Brief Cinematic History of Dudeness 92
   By Ben Walters and J.M. Tyree

"It's a Complicated Case": On the Modest Menippeanism of *The Big Lebowski* 95
   By Pete Porter

We Need *Another* Hero: Masculinity, Rebellion, Heroism, and the Big Prometheus 102
   By Jeremy Davies

The *Zanni* of Our Time and Place: Socio-Political Protest through Modern Commedia dell'Arte
in *The Big Lebowski*... 107
   By Jessica Bellomo

A Way Out West.. 113
   By Matthew J. Barsalou

The New Left and Laziness: Why The Dude is "The Man for His Time" 116
   By Reuben J. Cohen

Who's the Fucking Nihilist Here?: Structural and Cosmic Lawlessness in *The Big Lebowski* 121
   By Alex Buffer

Strikes and Gutters: How *The Big Lebowski* Has Ruined Movies for Me.. 126
   By Jim DeFillipi

Nomenclature is Not The Preferred Nomenclature 128
   By Andrea Kannes

The Dude: A Retrospective... 132
   By James Madeiros

The Big Lebowski: Serious Philosophical Underpinnings to a Hilarious Movie 135
   By Matthew Ciardiello

The Bible Lebowski: Biblical Themes and Tropes in *The Big Lebowski* 138
   By Trevor Miller

The Dude Accepts: Walt Whitman & *The Big Lebowski*.. 143
   By Kerry Gibbs

Dudes and Dudeism in the Ancient World... 147
   By Graham McIlroy

El Duderino, P.I... 151
   By Axel Howerton

Epicurus' Place in the Yin-Yang of Dudeism 155
   By Marcus Cubbedge

What Makes a Feminist, Mr. Lebowski? 158
   By Cate Gooch

"Like Tumbleweeds Blowing Across a Vacant Lot": The Mythic Landscape of Los Angeles in
Chandler's *The Big Sleep* and the Coen Brothers' *The Big Lebowski*.. 162
   By Anthony Dyer Hoefer

Everything I Know, I Learned from *The Big Lebowski* 170
   By Will Russell

Abide or Die: Affective Escape from Radical *Noir* Doom 172
   By Kate Carsella

A Dude's Guide to Emergency Management: Incorporating *The Big Lebowski* Into Community
Resilience... 179
   By Daniel Neely

A Psychological Analysis of Personality: "The Dude" in *The Big Lebowski* 182
   By James Kerr

The Importance of Living: Lin Yutang Meets The Dude 189
   By Guido Mina di Sospiro

That Rug Really Tied the Room Together 193
   By Joseph P. Natoli

"Trapped By Their Pasts": Noir and Nostalgia in *The Big Lebowski*... 198
   By Marc Singer

Notes on *The Big Lebowski* Screenplay 203
   By William Robert Rich

Biographies of the Illustrators.. 207

Note to the reader: If you haven't seen *The Big Lebowski* (the movie which serves as the subject of all these essays), or if you don't remember much from it, you may want to first read the appendix at the end of the book, *Notes on The Big Lebowski Screenplay* by William Robert Rich. That will help make sense of these a-here essays we're about to unfold. Those still feeling unprepared are encouraged to visit the editor's in-depth overview of the film here: http://dudespaper.com/dude-university/the-big-lebowski-experience-an-overview/

Questions? Comments? Contributions to future editions of this book? Please send an email to 101@dudeism.com.

DEDICATED TO THE BROTHERS COEN. THANKIE.

Among the world's
Greatest Works of Literature
The Big Lebowski *slouches alone,*
in that it is the only one which is not a book or a play or a poem.
Which is of course, just, like, our opinion.

This book about The Greatest Movie
In The History of Mankind, man,
helps to explain its impact.
There are also illustrations.

Well, we hope you folks enjoy yourselves.

Text copyright © the respective authors.
Illustrations copyright © the respective illustrators.
Design and concept copyright © Oliver Benjamin.

Back cover illustrations (from top left to bottom right): *Supper at Emmaus* by Joe Forkan; *Cheers Jackie*, by Brandon Yarwood; *Fuck it, Let's Go Bowling* by Josua Waghubinger; *The Dude Lebowski* by Giuseppe Cristiano; *Maude Lebowski* by Alex Ruiz; *Dude Christ* by Christopher Berge

All rights reserved under International and Pan-American Copyright Conventions, including the right to reproduce this book or portions thereof in any form, except for use by a reviewer in connection with a review.

Published by:
Dudeism, LLC
Abide University Press: www.aui.me/press
Email: 101@dudeism.com

ISBN 9781493508082

IMPORTANT NOTE TO READERS: This book is an independent and unauthorized fan publication. No endorsement or sponsorship by or affiliation with Joel and Ethan Coen, Jeff Bridges, Gramercy Pictures, or any other copyright and trademark holders is claimed or suggested. All references in this book to copyrighted or trademarked characters and other elements of *The Big Lebowski* are for the purpose of commentary, criticism, analysis, and literary discussion only.

Any writers or illustrators interested in contributing to a future edition of this book or a sequel are requested to email submissions to 101@dudeism.com.

Homepage for this book: www.dudeism.com/lebowski-101. Facebook page: www.facebook.com/lebowski101

Giuseppe Cristiano, *The Dude Lebowski*

The Editorial Preface

BY OLIVER BENJAMIN
The Dudely Lama of The Church of the Latter-Day Dude (Dudeism), & editor of Lebowski 101

This is not the first collection of highfalutin' smartypants essays about the 1998 Coen Brothers film *The Big Lebowski*. And given the sustained fascination with this bewildering cultural touchstone, it won't likely be the last. Far out.

Edward Comentale and Aaron Jaffe were the first smart fellers to put together a collection like this, and though their title "The Year's Work in Lebowski Studies," may have been chosen fancifully, one can't help but wonder if Lebowski Studies might not in fact become a legitimate academic field someday. Given the number of philosophical books on *Lebowski* out there, it seems it's is already well on its way. Perhaps soon our universities will harbor mellow cabals of shaggy *Lebowskiologists* claiming to be undertaking "research" while napping in college faculty lounges, acting as expert witnesses for trials involving drug legalization, and misquoting Lenin completely out of context.

Lebowskiology? The study is ludicrous. Probably, but then again the idea of a degree in Shakespeare Studies would have seemed similarly absurd in A.D. 1500. *Et tu, Duder*?

So, then, what is it about *The Big Lebowski* that invites such enduring critical fascination? To investigative fans, it seems that just when every possible aspect of this two-hour film has been analyzed, dissected and published, someone comes up with a brilliant new hypothesis about what *The Big Lebowski* is all about. One can review the movie a hundred times and still be surprised by some hidden symbolism, allusion, literal connection or subtle life lesson. It goes without saying that there are indeed a lotta strands in ol' Duder's head, his world, and by extension, our own. Yet in our attempts to weave them into a rug that really tie the movie together, more and more "frayed knots" seem to pop out of the woolwork.

Lebowski is not all that unique in this; this is the way it is with really great literature – we never really ever finish "reading" it. In academia it's relatively common to continue picking apart, interpreting and arguing over a piece of art centuries after its creation. We've alluded to Shakespeare, but there are also armies of academics struggling to diagnose the Epic of Gilgamesh, The Odyssey, The Bible, The Inferno, Ulysses, and other what-have-yous. It seems they're nowhere near closing the files on those ones either.

What sets *Lebowski* apart from those more respected compeers, however, is that it's "just" a movie. Generally, films don't manage to contain enough complexity or poetry to warrant such extended scholarship. Yet this uniquely intricate, far-reaching, and broad-themed box-office disaster seems to have pulled off the heretofore impossible – it has captured the broadest swath of humanity in fewer words than you'd find in those other celebrated pieces of *litherature*[1]. Though it might not be apparent on the first viewing (or the fiftieth), its creators the Coen Brothers are clearly "into that whole brevity thing." Their 130 page script appears to be something of a hologram for the human condition.

After the success of *A Year's Work in Lebowski Studies*, a handful of other philosophical dissertations upon The Dude and his compeers followed[2]. To the delight of Lebowski lovers everywhere, Even Jeff Bridges, "The Dude" himself, threw his hat into the ring in early 2013 when he put together a Lebowskian Zen primer with his friend and Zen teacher Bernie Glassman. In *The Dude and the Zen Master*, they identified The Dude as a Zen master in disguise, and suggested that *The Big Lebowski* slyly offered a series of "Zen koans" to those with a spiritual bent.

For those not familiar with the koans of Japanese Zen tradition, they could be described as mysterious questions, assertions or imperatives that help limber up our minds by orienting us towards a broader circumference of awareness. Following this tradition, Bridges and Glassman consider lines from the movie, such as "The

---

[1] This is a term I arrogantly invented for a talk delivered at the Idler Academy in London in 2011. *Litherature* seemed to be a good name to describe that subset of writings that act as cultural signposts for their time and place, acting as giant "you are here" signs. Like those monoliths in Stanley Kubrick's 2001: A Space Odyssey, except that they're not created by aliens. It stands to reason that *Lebowski* could be the most recent of these influential artifacts.

[2] Including *The Abide Guide* by myself and the Arch Dudeship Dwayne Eutsey, and *The Big Lebowski and Philosophy* edited by Peter Fosl. There are several others not as self-consciously philosophical but still deeply investigative, such as I'm a *Lebowski, You're a Lebowski* by Peskoe, Green, Russell and Shuffitt and *The Annotated Lebowski* by Jenny Jones. Our own *The Tao of The Dude* will probably be finished one of these days as well.

Dude is not in," "The Dude abides," and "That rug really tied the room together" to be excellent mantras for meditation.

Conflating The Dude and The Dharma of course comes as no surprise to the practicing student of The Dude; it is one of the principal reasons why The Church of the Latter-Day Dude (a.k.a. *Dudeism*[3]) was founded back in 2005. That is, Dudeism contends that *The Big Lebowski* offers as good a vehicle as any other for finding "enlightenment," or at least "enlighten-*up*-ment." Watching the film gradually invites an apprehension of "the big picture," yet in keeping with the languid manner of The Dude, its transformative benefits neither come in a flash nor after too much toil. Rather, new shit comes to light in its own sweet time. One might posit that, like William Blake's description of naked woman, *The Big Lebowski* "is a portion of eternity too great for the eye of man" (and not just because it features Julianne Moore with her clothes off[4]). The movie can take a long time to get your head around, and even when you do, you're still not completely sure what's really going on. Nevertheless, we assure you, that is not a problem; as we've just noted, it's a sweet time.

This sort of inquiry is at the heart of all mystical traditions, and though we agree with Bridges and Glassman that Lebowski has a lot of parallels with Zen, perhaps it also differs in some important ways: For instance, all this writing and discussion regarding what *The Big Lebowski* explicitly goes against Zen tradition, perhaps most mystical traditions. Zen, as well as its sister spiritual philosophy of Taoism[5] avoids talking or writing too much about what "it's all about." There's very little written tradition in Zen, and Taoism has as its primary philosophical text only a tiny book of a few obscure and poetical verses, *The Tao Te Ching*[6].

The reason for this economy of language in traditional mysticism is probably because words and propositions have a nasty tendency to get in the way of broad and fluid understanding. It seems that once the mind claws onto an idea, like an attack marmot, it often proves reluctant to let go. In the parlance of the Zen tradition, words and concepts are "fingers pointing at the moon," which are often mistaken for the moon itself. Our minds are not as limber as we imagine them to be: indeed, several of the essayists in this book have pointed out that *The Big Lebowski* is a veritable showcase for the frustrating limitations of language and challenges implicit in human communication.

Though we agree in principle with the principle that often "words get in the way," Dudeism tends to break with Eastern mysticism in how to deal with the problem. Rather than defending ourselves against language and random theorizing, or adopting vows of silence, we welcome all the ramble and blather and trains of thought.

By exposing ourselves to a wide variety of ideas we can not only entertain them, but also immunize ourselves against the manipulative "ringers" that so often stand in for truth. We're not just talking about the deceptions of others here, but also our own inherited and/or acquired fallacies as well. Sooner or later each of us has to face the fact that we (as the Dude chides his bombastic buddy Walter) are goddamn morons.

So while Dudeism may borrow aspects of attitude from Zen and Taoism, it also assiduously invites focused critical thinking, argumentation, rhetoric, semantic arm-wrestling, modern psychological theory (mostly evolutionary and cognitive) and various other what-have-you that some of us learn and then forget about in college. Having said that, one can also be a Dudeist without all that, of course. And that's cool. That's cool. Many learned Dudeists dispute these things, while others just say "Fuck it, Dude, let's go bowling." What's more, there's a lot to be said for spending quiet time every day while in the tub or on laying on our rug.

Perhaps in keeping with The Dude's fondness for Eastern iconography, the Dudeist approach could be looked at as a sort of mental martial art. While you rarely see "spiritual" folks sitting around arguing like The Dude and Walter, a brief visit to the Dudeism websites[7] will unveil a panoply of outrageous opinions, sarcastic ripostes and even the odd brief kerfuffle. And yet hurt feelings or true anger are relatively unknown. Because Dudeists endeavor to approach everything with the fundamental presupposition that everything "is just like, your opinion, man," they normally don't take it personally when someone rejoinders, "What in God's holy name are you blathering about?" In fact, such conflict can provide the opportunity to learn something "that's fucking interesting, man," which will prevent our thinking from becoming increasingly uptight. Unlike some other organized spiritual traditions, Dudeism invites a challenge, an argument, and the opportunity to then "hug it out"[8] and say "I dig your style too, man," afterwards. Also, uh, we're not very organized.

As Bill Murray's[9] character puts it in the movie version of Somerset Maugham's book *The Razor's Edge*, "It's easy to be a holy man on top of a mountain." Which is why the Dudeist aims to be a holy man even in the midst of a "whole world gone crazy." It is precisely when having a rough day, when the Nihilists are getting us down and the thugs have pissed on our rugs that we must be most able to muster our Dudely powers of perception.

Given this Dudeist proclivity for seeing the world as a mess of opinions to be hashed out (or, to when there's no longer any point, selectively ignored), it should come as no surprise that this book is pretty much all over the

---

[3] See more at www.dudeism.com

[4] Andrea Nunn, actually, her stand-in double.

[5] The Lebowski religion of Dudeism is based primarily on Taoism.

[6] Our own Dudeist version, *The Dude De Ching* can be found here: www.dudeism.com/tao

[7] The forum: www.dudeism.com/smf, The Dudespaper: www.dudespaper.com, the social network: www.dudeism.net, and Abide University: www.aui.me

[8] Jeff Bridges' phrase about The Dude from *The Dude and the Zen Master*: "He would rather hug it out than slug it out."

[9] Murray is a candidate for "Great Dude in History" – www.dudeism.com/greatdudes

place. And yet, to paraphrase that Zen adage about the moon and the finger, this book contains various fingers pointing to a heavenly illumination just over the horizon of our awareness. It's important to note that no one finger is sufficient to triangulate its position, and some of the fingers might be, well, *the finger*. Thus one might compare the book to The Dude himself: broad-shouldered, rangy, shaggy, unkempt and quite a bit self-contradictory.

For instance, where David Masciotra's essay proclaims The Dude as a worthy modern incarnation of Jesus Christ, Trevor Miller's paints him as a pathetic and hollow representation of the very same fellow. And not just Jesus – in other essays, The Dude is compared with everyone from the Buddha (Chris Landis) to Marcus Aurelius (Graham McIlroy) to Walt Whitman (Kerry Gibbs). And of course we find parallels not just with The Dude, but with the entire film; in addition to its honorable Stoner Comedy roots, many sober traditions have informed, and been informed by the work: Shakespeare (Adam Bertocci), Menippeanism (Pete Porter), Commedia dell' Arte (Jessica Bellomo), and of course, Film Noir (Axel Howerton, Marc Singer, Kate Carsella). Various established philosophies like Epicureanism (Marcus Cubbedge), Existentialism (Todd Alcott, Alex Buffer) and Taoism (Guido Mina di Sospira) are also woven into the tapestry. And social issues like war (Daniel Keyes), politics (Alan Baily, David Haglund, Reuben Cohen), and gender (Cate Gooch, Jakub Kazecki, Jeremy Davies) are also shown to make up much of the warp and woof of the what-have-you. Indeed, the breadth of interpretation and inspiration in these pages can be fairly staggering. After all, what other subject can be used both to inform emergency preparedness management (Daniel Neely), as well as provide a new interpretation for the Tarot's Major Arcana (David Thorsteinsson)? Lebowski is less like literature and more like life, in that it is a goddamn mess.

Although there may be differences in interpretation, there is also a great deal in common: The pieces in this book tend to be disarmingly perspicacious, funny, limber, sporting, and full of earnest inquiry – again, like The Dude himself. What's more, the authors don't seem to take themselves too seriously. That would be unDude indeed, not to mention, tedious. After all, if Lebowski Studies ever takes off on the University level, it will probably not be because it's so important or useful, but because it's so "far out." And that's cool. The best modern education doesn't just serve to provide answers, but to teach us how to ask better questions. We're just trying to help ourselves conceive.

Conceive is an especially appropriate word here, given its dual meanings. Despite the apparent objectives of contemporary educational systems, we feel that a higher education shouldn't serve just to prepare us for a career, but for life itself, that we might abide our time on Earth with increased aptitude. Perhaps just as students in the U.S. must take a Scholastic Aptitude Test (SAT) to enter university, they should also have to take an LI-MAT (Limber-Minded Aptitude Test) to graduate. Am I wrong?

To tell the truth, like The Dude, we also don't remember much from college.

Maybe you don't or won't remember much from your education either, and maybe you won't remember much from this book either after you finish it. And that's okay; we're not looking to exam anyone here. Our only hope for this volume is that it helps remind people that, in The Dude's words, "This could be a a a lot more a a a a a a complex, I mean its not just, it might not such a simple, uh, you know?" So long as our thinking isn't uptight, our mind is kept limber, and we listen occasionally, we will always have the necessary means for a, necessary means for a higher education.

It's a shame that continued study is a luxury for most of us, busy as we are trying just to make a living and avoid getting eaten by bears. That's probably why stories and theories and popular philosophies in cultures all around the globe generally just confirm our prejudices and make us feel as if we've already got life all figured out.

As a remedy to this unlimber and uptight thinking, *The Big Lebowski* gently reminds us that the world is is an unsolvable mystery and that though we may manage to knock down all the pins from time to time, they will inevitably pop back up again. Moreover, it helps us figure out a way to deal with that cycle. Remember that though The Dude within us may abide, our environment does not – it is an endlessly moving target of illusion, deceit, contradiction, irreconcilable differences and mixed messages. To lounge comfortably in the center of that storm we need be able to become privy to the new shifts, to tilt our heads at many different angles. The reader may not agree with all the angles presented here, but hopefully he or she will at least find them as durned innarestin' as we do.

Come on, let's go get us a lane.

Before rolling outta here naked, however, we extend a big *thankie* to all the authors and illustrators who contributed to help make this the textbook for its time and place. It's been a pleasure rambling with you.

Matt Camp, *Donny's Funeral*

Matt Camp, *The Bar Eats You*

"Suit the Word to the Action": Language, *Lebowski* and Literal Connections

BY ADAM BERTOCCI

I came to love *Lebowski* on the heels of a quote. Like many fans of the film, I didn't appreciate it fully on my first viewing. I gave it another shot after a friend dropped a quote – "Nihilists? Fuck me," *etc.* – which is now my favorite line in the flick.

My proper ascension to achieverhood came later. I received the grand tour of the remarkably organized fandom on the heels of my infamous mash-up *Two Gentlemen of Lebowski*, which retold The Dude's story in the style of William Shakespeare. Who himself was no lightweight, where quotations are concerned.

Shakespeare's influence on language is immeasurable. We all quote the canon, completely out of context, every day of our lives. Among the hundreds of words Shakespeare coined are 'discontent', 'obscene', 'lackluster', 'rant' and (as heard in *The Big Lebowski*) 'laughable'; among the helpful phrases he devised are "into thin air," "foul play," "send him packing," "good riddance" and "who gives a shit about the fucking marmot?"[1] We use these inventions without needing the plays as a frame of reference: no one mentioning "a foregone conclusion" ever waits for his audience to get the nod to *Othello,* nor does anyone stop to explain their use of "all of a sudden" in the context of *The Taming of the Shrew.* The Bard's words are household words. (*Henry V*. Sorry, I couldn't resist.)

Fans of the movie can imagine where it goes from here. We're dealing with what I call "propagative language" – words, phrases and memes that spread like cultural wildfire down through the generations. And sometimes there's a movie... sometimes there's a movie... where half the fun is the zesty enterprise of watching the vocabulary keep on perpetuating itself.

This essay will examine the fractured relationship between language and meaning in *The Big Lebowski*, with a special focus on linguistic propagation as found in both the film's Shakespearean underpinnings and the fan base's fondness for out-of-context quotations... that, and a pair of testicles.

See, maybe you've noticed, but fans really like to quote this movie. A lot.

I didn't really *get* the quoting thing at first. I had to figure out that for many, to discuss the movie is to quote the movie. Lebowski Fest was famously founded by two bored conventioneers trading dialogue back and forth. Forum threads mentioning the film hastily devolve into lines drawn seemingly at random, like numbers from a bingo hopper; peruse any discussion and count the posts till someone drops in to announce that that rug really tied the room together. Paul Sileo of *Film School Rejects* ruefully recalls a "drive-by quoting": "I inquired via Twitterbook about any leads on jobs in St. Louis, to which a friend informed me that he 'had to check with the boys down at the crime lab...'" Dropping a quote – almost any will do – is not a statement of the line's immediate relevance but a simple thumbs-up for the topic, a smile and a nod. As *The A.V. Club*'s Scott Tobias puts it: "Quotes from *The Big Lebowski* have become a form of cultural currency second only to *The Simpsons;* for modern cult-movie fans looking for fellow travelers, they're the closest thing to a Vulcan hand-sign we have."

To the untrained eye, this is bedlam. Fans of other persuasions famously crave the high of selecting, much to outsiders' annoyance, just the right quote for any occasion from some genre geek's pop-cultural Bartlett's. A *Star Wars* fan takes pride in finding the perfect moment to "find your lack of faith disturbing" and feels little need to spout Yoda-sourced wisdom just 'cause somebody mentioned the franchise. A *Rocky Horror* midnight moviegoer follows a carefully structured order of callbacks, as intricately choreographed as the Time Warp.

Yet the random *Lebowski* quote is not merely a phenomenon, it's a well-loved shibboleth. As Jeff Dowd himself – the inspiration for The Dude – tells *The New York Times:* "There was a Wall Street guy I met who'd drop a *Lebowski* line into job interviews and if the person didn't pick up on it he wouldn't be hired." Or take an example from me, on a personal level: a post on the film's official Facebook page, advertising a promotional appearance of mine, was met by "Shomer Shabbos!" from

---

[1] We're not sure about the last one.

a chap my age in Maryland and "Over the line!" from a guy in Oklahoma. Some fellow with a cat as his avatar helpfully reminded us that the Supreme Court has roundly rejected prior restraint. The fact that none of this had anything to do with my event and/or Vietnam had not occurred to anyone.

By this point, though, I'm used to it. Everyone's used to it. After attending the 2011 cast reunion in New York, I wasn't at all surprised to read this summary from *Gothamist*: "[T]he fanboys in the crowd could hardly contain themselves, screaming a nearly constant litany of lines from the film. In a word: pandemonium." Andy Greene of *Rolling Stone* recalled to his dismay "thousands of drunken fans screaming out lines from the movie every three seconds" – and yet confessed, "I had honestly only planned on staying for a bit of the movie so I could go home and write this, but before I knew it I was singing along . . ."

See, it's part of the fun. It's no wonder that fans quote the movie. After all, the movie quotes itself. *The Big Lebowski* is packed with distinctive words and phrases passing between characters like hot potatoes. President Bush gets the bowling ball rolling, his "unchecked aggression" quote hastily retweeted (in the parlance of our time) by Walter and thereafter The Dude to explain their own crisis. What's interesting is that The Dude has no problem unironically quoting Bush, no matter how his leftist college buddies might balk – it's the language that matters, not the source, not the context.

Some scenes later, The Dude picks up on the word "abide" from The Big Lebowski himself and deems it befitting the core philosophy of all things Dude. In any other film, the protagonist quoting the villain would be an ironic echo, a meaningful reversal – Andy's note to the warden at the end of *The Shawshank Redemption*, Harry Potter throwing "I must not tell lies" back in Madam Umbridge's face. In *The Big Lebowski*, The Dude has no such intention; he may not even remember where he got the word in the first place. He just wants to abide.

Lots of movies do that reversal thing, of course. One of them is *Cool Hand Luke*, with a very famous line: "What we've got here is a failure to communicate." This iconic pronouncement could very well be the tagline for *The Big Lebowski*. (The actual tagline – "Times like these call for a Big Lebowski" – made even less sense than any of the film's cheerful absurdities, given that the film was not set in the present and the title referred to the villain. Which I guess is itself a failure to communicate – but, shoosh, I'm ramblin' again.)

Communication is the movie's concern, Dude – its central concern, in fact. Its characters' language, motivations and identities become harder to nail down than a homemade door brace.

For instance, the meaning of crossing a line transmutes from a metaphorical line in the sand to the technicalities of league-game bowling. The Dude's heartfelt plea "They're gonna kill that poor woman!" is cruelly turned back in a mocking refrain; later, he stumbles over which one of Da Fino's colloquialisms best describes his new relationship with Maude. Somehow, in defiance of the space-time continuum, characters quote people that they haven't actually met: "Chinaman" and "not the issue" blink out of Walter's mouth and into The Big Lebowski's without explanation, as if via linguistic wormhole. This happens a lot. Both Walter and the Stranger tell The Dude "Have it your way"; both Walter and Treehorn bemoan "amateurs." Both Woo and the sheriff call The Dude a deadbeat – and he even notices this, in a befuddled close-up, before filing the term away to trot out in his later standoff with Lebowski.

Indeed, The Dude quotes quite a few folks he meets, from artists ("the parlance of our times") to nihilists ("no funny stuff"). Everyone quotes everyone, and everyone in California seems to want to know: "What the fuck are you talking about?" This is easily the most oft-repeated phrase in the movie, and also the most relevant. It is not always easily answered.

"The confusion that surrounds the larger mystery in the narrative seems to be embodied in The Dude's inability to verbalize anything remotely like a reasonable explanation for his circumstances," observes Paul Coughlin in *The Film Journal*. "The Dude's account of the situation takes the concept of syntactic chaos and disorder to the extreme as every utterance stops short of coherence." Indeed, in *The Big Lebowski*, communication between any two parties seems an insurmountable ordeal. The pacifist Dude is paired with a gun-toting agent of chaos, and they seem to share custody of a painfully quiet enigma about whom they know shockingly little. The well-to-do Lebowski has shacked up with an airheaded blonde well below his age and station. Flamboyant Quintana bowls alongside a cheery, red-faced exemplar of the middle-aged Midwestern American male. And these are just who people *choose* to hang out with! These recurring combinations of Los Angeles County's mismatched socks are scarcely cut out to share the same movie, let alone a productive conversation.

The intrepid characters that try to bridge these communicative chasms face mixed results at best: Donny bowls between two polar opposites and yet can't connect with either, and The Dude's well-meant attempts to relate with new people often blow up in his face. Some folks don't even try. Maude makes it clear that her tryst with The Dude is mere rich-girl slumming; indeed, The Dude is so left out of her social circle that by the end of the Knox Harrington scene they are literally not even speaking the same language.

But class is not the issue: the robber baron Lebowski, the state-sector sheriff and the working-class cabbie all find ways to take a hasty dislike to The Dude, whereas the well-heeled *nouveau riche* Treehorn, it seems, might have actually gotten on well with our hero had they met under happier stars. But the film's L.A. is so fragmented that few of any sort seem to have a well-matched friend, and the pairs that get on best are those less Dudely. (Lebowski and Brandt, Maude and Knox, Jesus and Liam, the thugs, the nihilists . . . though presumably relations are now strained between Uli and his girlfriend.)

People are separated by social status, politics, geography, *Weltanschauung*, age. Indeed, many of the characters seem caught out of time, temporally out of their element. The Dude is half-stuck in his 1960s heyday, and what parts of him changed mainly did so out of laziness. Walter proudly affirms that he's "living in the fucking past," though the exact era tends to waver between his early-'80s marriage, the worst of Vietnam, and Exodus. Jackie Treehorn's swingin' Mancini and sumptuous manse place him squarely in a bygone '60s, one different from The Dude's but no less distant. Da Fino is clearly on loan from a dime-store detective yarn or its ilk. And the Stranger seems to have tumbled out of a whole different century. (And, of course, some of us think the whole movie's an Elizabethan comedy in disguise.) While The Dude's disputes with Lebowski produce the film's sole explicitly cross-generational conflict, it's instructive to imagine these people as time travelers, sharing no frame of reference, barely speaking each other's language – not even the words they take from one another. They don't know *how* to talk to each other. They are not in the same psychological space. Also, let's not forget (let's not forget, Dude) that we've only been discussing people's honest attempts to communicate. The ruses, deceptions and simple human bullshit polluting the discourse would require an essay of their own.

The film's most successful emotional transaction comes after a hopelessly botched formal speech, when The Dude and Walter just stop talking for a second, and hug. It's a moment even they cannot ruin. "Every word is like an unnecessary stain on silence and nothingness," Samuel Beckett once observed. No wonder everyone in the film keeps telling each other to shut the fuck up, keep your voices down, lower your voices, don't say peep. Walter speaks exactly one line after the hug – a helpful line, but not a new one. Maybe it's his stock response; maybe "fuck it" (twinned with "let's go bowling") is *his* answer to everything – the only words he knows that always work.

Why is everything a fucking travesty? How can these disparate characters ever connect? Maybe Brandt points the way, a deferential toady who takes his cues from everyone else, the perpetual chameleon – friendly with The Dude, downcast when Lebowski mourns, flustered when his master is upset, chortling when Bunny breaks the mood. Or maybe Larry is the smartest one in the movie – he keeps his mouth shut and ends his scene no worse off than before. By *The Big Lebowski*'s standards, that's a hell of an accomplishment.

The truth is that this is a comedy where mistaken identity is just the tip of the deeply confusing iceberg. Unlike Shakespeare's comedies, where such errors might hinge on a physical resemblance or outright misinformation, in *The Big Lebowski* it begins and ends with language, and intention never enters the picture. Language is an abstraction, a series of meaningless symbols and syllables that, combined, merely *signify* whatever the fuck we were talking about. Before the film is one minute old we learn that The Dude has rejected his name and self-applied another. This handily sets up the message: language is shifty, and what's said may not line up with what's meant, or even what's true. It's a verbal form of Magritte's "The Treachery of Images." (You know: the painting that says *"Ceci n'est pas une pipe."* Though The Dude might prefer a different sort of pipe.) The stains of ink spelling "White Russian" on this page have nothing to do with the beverage, save for the connections that the letterforms trigger in our minds, assuming we speak English (*"Parla usted inglés?"*[2]). Somehow the people in *The Big Lebowski* never get over that crucial line, and so the characters spend most of the film asking each other what the fuck, *et cetera*.

So matters progress, or not. The earnest narrator forgets his own lines. Treehorn's thugs are told to rough up Jeffrey Lebowski and they do – correctly in a semantic sense, but a flop as a practical matter. Donny hears 'Lenin' as 'Lennon'. The Dude takes a crack on the jaw and gets medical attention in a very different area. Even 'dick' shifts its meaning. It's epistemological nihilism. It's exhausting.

Even the soundtrack plays these games, divorcing familiar songs from the instruments and voices we know: before the much-maligned Eagles are heard, their song "Hotel California" is, in a near-unrecognizable Gipsy Kings cover – only when the English lyrics kick in do we realize what we've been hearing all along. The Rolling Stones' "Dead Flowers" never sounded better than in Townes Van Zandt's melancholy drawl, and "Viva Las Vegas" manages to crop up twice without Elvis. (The first such instance, where Bunny sings along, is the only cover in the film neither estranged or rendered ironic. We might chalk this up to Bunny being a plain-speaking character, except that half the plot stems from her failure to tell anyone that she's going out of town.) We cannot trust what we hear; we are not always sure if someone came up with what they're saying, or if they're just quoting. How treacherous an environment The Dude must trek in, when one can be surprised by the Eagles, before it's too late to escape.

In sum: in *Lebowski*'s Los Angeles, "nothing means anything" – in screenwriter Todd Alcott's succinct diagnosis. Actions speak louder than words. Perhaps this explains why we fans are so drawn to quoting the film in a drive-by, free-for-all fashion. We know our scattershot quoting makes no sense; hell, neither does the movie. Such is life. Like The Dude, we've come to appreciate the disconnect between the abstractions of words and the real-world meanings they pretend to impart. It is a strange music to us, a soothing noise of voices and inflections, and we dig it on the same level as The Dude does his tape-recorded bowling or *Song of the Whale*. We luxuriate in it as we do with the language at a Shakespeare play, letting it all wash over us, reveling in the rhythm and flow and symphony of cuss-bestrewn expression. Maybe it's all just "sound and fury, signifying nothing," as the fella said. But what a sound.

---

[2] This line, spoken by The Big Lebowski, is itself a mashup of Italian and Spanish.

....

Adam Bertocci is the author of *Two Gentlemen of Lebowski: A Most Excellent Comedie and Tragical Romance* (Simon & Schuster, 2010), the fully-annotated, beautifully-illustrated, historically-accurate, modestly-priced Shakespearean translation of guess-which-movie. His mash-up of the Bard and The Dude has been praised by everyone from Jeff Bridges and The Dudely Lama to the Folger Shakespeare Library and the Royal Shakespeare Company. He blathers at www.adambertocci.com

Works Cited

Sileo, Paul. "Movies We Love: *The Big Lebowski*." *Film School Rejects*. April 29, 2009. http://www.filmschoolrejects.com/features/movies-we-love-the-big-lebowski.php

Tobias, Scott. "The New Cult Canon: *The Big Lebowski*." *The A.V. Club*. May 14, 2009. http://www.avclub.com/articles/the-big-lebowski,27984/

Edelstein, David. "You're Entering a World of *Lebowski*." *The New York Times*. August 8, 2004.

Del Signore, John. "10 Best Moments From *The Big Lebowski* Cast Reunion." *Gothamist*. August 17, 2011. http://gothamist.com/2011/08/17/10_best_moments_from_the_big_lebows.php

Greene, Andy. "The Cast Of *The Big Lebowski* Reunited in New York." *Rolling Stone*. August 17, 2011. http://www.rollingstone.com/movies/news/the-cast-of-the-big-lebowski-reunites-in-new-york-20110817

Coughlin, Paul. "Language Aesthetics in Three Films by Joel and Ethan Coen." *The Film Journal*. Issue 12. http://www.thefilmjournal.com/issue12/coens.html

Gruen, John. "Samuel Beckett Talks About Beckett." *Vogue*. December 1969.

Alcott, Todd. "Who's the Nihilist Here?" *Lebowski 101*.

Alex Ruiz, *Larry Sellers*

Alex Ruiz, *Maude Lebowski*

A Pox on Both Your Houses, Man: The Two Very Flawed Families of *The Big Lebowski*

BY JOE BLEVINS

Parody and mirroring are integral to the language of *The Big Lebowski*. The whole film, of course, is structured as a parody of a Raymond Chandler detective story, with numerous references to the book and film versions of *The Big Sleep* and *The Long Goodbye*, among several other Chandler works.

It's not just other films that get riffed on; several characters in *Lebowski* are patterned after real-life folks as well. The Dude and Walter, as all seasoned Achievers know, are largely based on acquaintances of the Brothers Coen. The suave pornographer Jackie Treehorn bears more than a passing resemblance to Hugh Hefner, while the German techno outfit Autobahn is a cartoonish variation on the pioneering electronic music quartet Kraftwerk.

Moreover, there is evidence of mirroring *within* the film as well. Let us not forget that the catalyst for the entire plot is the fact that there are *two* Jeffrey Lebowskis in Los Angeles County, one of whom (The Dude) actually takes a moment to gaze at his own reflection in a mirror in an early scene.

Speaking of literal mirrors, the faces of two other characters (manservant Brandt and rival bowler Jesus Quintana) are first glimpsed as *reflections* in shiny surfaces (a ceremonial plaque and a bowling ball return, respectively). The millionaire Lebowski himself can be seen as an echo of Walter, as they are both belligerent, easily-riled veterans of unpopular wars in the Far East, and both are eager to relay tales of the battlefield to anyone within earshot Little wonder, then, that Walter often unknowingly parrots the language of the millionaire, e.g. "That's your answer to everything."

Additionally, the aforementioned Mr. Treehorn has two thugs in his employ, meanwhile, as does Maude Lebowski. This is particularly interesting when you consider that The Dude and Uli Kunkel have two sidekicks apiece. In other words, *The Big Lebowski* is simply chockablock with trinities, holy and otherwise. Even the film's soundtrack is loaded with cover versions ("Dead Flowers," "Viva Las Vegas," "Oye Como Va," "Hotel California").

Perhaps what is most striking amid all this parodying and mirroring is that the movie gives us two twisted versions of the traditional nuclear family, i.e. a group of related people residing together in a single domicile. On the one hand, we have the (seemingly) well-to-do Lebowski clan living in an imposing Pasadena mansion. On the other, we have the more middle-class, perhaps a bit down-at-the-heels Sellers family living in a modest North Hollywood dwelling. The Dude visits each of these families, occasionally with Walter in tow, and it is truly astonishing how many parallels there are between the two tribes. Specifically, each clan boils down to a trio (more trinities!) consisting of a glad-handing servant, a powerless figurehead, and a spoiled brat. Amazingly, in both houses, the corresponding characters are introduced exactly in that same order: servant first, figurehead second, brat third.

First: the friendly, polite, and relentlessly cheerful servant. At the Lebowski mansion, naturally, this is the officious and often nervous Brandt. At the Sellers home, it is the ingratiating Hispanic maid Pilar. As soon becomes apparent, both of these people work in deeply dysfunctional, unhealthy atmospheres, and they deal with it in pretty much the same way – through denial and the use of carefully-chosen euphemisms. As Mr. Lebowski's personal man-at-hand, Brandt must know to some degree that his ill-tempered boss is a fraud, yet he still takes pride in the acts of charity carried out in the Lebowski name. He also has a knack for finding appropriate, respectable terms for possibly uncomfortable subjects. For instance, when The Dude learns by looking at a photograph that his wealthy namesake is confined to a wheelchair, he struggles to come up with the polite terminology for the man's condition and seems about to utter the forbidden word "cripple." Brandt deftly corrects him: "Mr. Lebowski is *disabled*, yes."

While we don't learn as much about Pilar, she seems to share Brandt's facility with euphemisms. Her employer, former TV scriptwriter Arthur Digby Sellers, is confined to a coffin-like iron lung which is kept, grotesquely, like a decorative keepsake in the living room as if it were an end table. Arthur's degree of disability far outstrips that of Mr. Lebowski, yet Pilar has a handy and absurdly understated phrase to describe her boss' total incapacity: "He has health problems." Pilar and Brandt are so thoroughly professional in their duties that they will use flattering, complimentary terms to describe people who absolutely do not deserve such kindness and who, in all likelihood, would not reciprocate. Brandt, for instance, refers to the free-spending, drug-addicted party girl Bunny Lebowski as a "wonderful woman" (which she isn't), while Pilar calls the sullen juvenile delinquent Larry Sellers "sweetie" (in direct contrast to his sullen sourness).

Both of these servants earn our sympathy as viewers, in no small part because they are among the few characters in the film who treat The Dude with warmth and civility. The Dude receives a lot of physical and verbal abuse throughout the movie (even the Ralph's cashier stares daggers at him), so it's nice that there are a few people who treat him as a human being.

Before we leave our servants, take note that Brandt is fiercely protective of the many trophies on the wall of his boss' office and actually winces when The Dude touches one, while Pilar works in a house where the furniture is kept underneath protective plastic.

We now move on to the figureheads of these two households. Though not immediately evident, Jeffrey Lebowski and Arthur Digby Sellers are ghoulish doppelgangers of one another. Let's get the obvious out of the way: both men are confined to noisy, four-wheeled devices. Before we ever see the unfortunate Mr. Sellers, we hear the pathetic wheezing of his iron lung. Similarly, Mr. Lebowski's introduction – much more boisterous, I should point out, than that of Mr. Sellers – is presaged by the whine of his electric wheelchair.

Both of these men are the nominal heads of their households, but neither has any real authority. Mr. Lebowski may like to feel that he still wields some power, but like Arthur Digby Sellers, he is essentially impotent. If we learn very little about Pilar, we learn even less of Mr. Sellers. But, like the millionaire Lebowski, Arthur's glory days seem to be long over. As mentioned previously, Mr. Lebowski loves to brag about his days in the Korean War, but given his dishonest nature, we cannot be certain that he is even a veteran. (See the Coens' later film, *The Man Who Wasn't There*, in which a boastful WW2 veteran – tellingly nicknamed "Big Dave" – is revealed as a fraud.)

Unlike Mr. Lebowski, Arthur Digby Sellers did accomplish something tangible in his life, though this legacy rests upon a single TV series, a rather obscure 1965-1966 Western called *Branded* with starred Chuck Connors. Interestingly, that largely-forgotten series dealt with an Army veteran in the 1880s who struggled each week to prove that he was not a coward after being falsely accused of desertion. "Wherever you go for the rest of your life," went his theme song, "you must prove you're a man!" Our millionaire Lebowski is likewise obsessed with manliness (his "What makes a man?" speech) and rails against the "cowards" who have kidnapped his young wife. Living on "a reasonable allowance" in a house likely purchased by his late wife, Mr. Lebowski is a virtual "kept man," so he escapes to a fantasy world of rugged movie-hero manliness – the very world Arthur Digby Sellers once helped design.

If the figureheads of *The Big Lebowski* are neutered and defanged – old gray lions now confined to domestic cages – then it should be up to the youngest members of the households to supply the vital energy, the life force their families desperately need. Alas, our two respective brats, Bunny Lebowski and Larry Sellers, seem so lazy and contented that they exist in a state of near catatonia and therefore serve no real purpose in their homes other than to greedily consume resources.

Bunny (a.k.a. Fawn Knudsen) is the under-aged "trophy wife" of the millionaire Lebowski. Though she owes money to "known pornographers" and may have some serious substance abuse issues, Bunny is supremely unconcerned with her own problems.

Each time we see her, Bunny exhibits an utter lack of regard for social conventions or the considerations of others. When we first meet her, she is the picture of idleness, lounging poolside and applying polish to her toenails. She seems only dimly aware of her dire financial troubles. She offers her sexual services to The Dude in exchange for $1000 (which would cover only a fraction of her "sizeable debt"), but this problem is of no greater importance to her than whether or not her toenail polish is dry. She asks The Dude to blow on her nails, a request which mirrors (that word again!) her suggestion of fellatio, only with The Dude doing the "blowing." Later, we will glimpse Bunny as she cruises drunkenly in her sports car, singing along with the radio. Not long afterwards, she will crash the car into a fountain at the Lebowski estate, yet instead of worrying about it, she chooses to go skinny dipping instead.

The penultimate time we see Bunny is in a fantasy sequence, as The Dude speculates to Walter about the Lebowskis' marriage. He pictures Bunny curled up on a couch, lazily flipping through a fashion magazine, only slightly perturbed by the fact that her husband is screaming at her a few feet away. In that hypothetical scene, Bunny effectively *stonewalls* Mr. Lebowski. This of course brings us (at last!) to the film's other prominent brat, Larry Sellers.

With his mother AWOL and his father hooked up to a machine, Larry has no parental guidance or discipline and has taken the opportunity to flirt with a life of petty crime, which in his case means stealing The Dude's car from the bowling alley parking lot and taking it for a joy ride. His wardrobe suggests that little Larry – who is not really so little anymore, after all – is attempting to remake himself as something of a gangster.

There is an amusing anecdote in William Preston Roberson's book *The Big Lebowski: The Making of a Coen Brothers Film* in which the Coens' costume designer, Mary Zophres, explains how she came up with Larry's signature look: "[I]n my initial fitting with the kid, I made him too soft and suburban, like a normal kid. and Joel and Ethan said, 'He's a smart ass. He steals cars. You have to make him look like more of a smart-ass.' So I had to refit him and we made him a 'wannabe,' a suburban kid trying to look like an urban hip-hop kid."

That word "wannabe" gets at the heart of Bunny's character, too. Like Larry, she has escaped the yoke of parental supervision (having abandoned her family's farm in Moorhead, MN) and is making the most of her new-found freedom by letting it all hang loose in California. As with Larry, role-playing is on Bunny's agenda. She ditches her real name, Fawn Knutson, and rechristens herself "Bunny," swapping the name of one cute animal for another. In her married life she's Bunny Lebowski, yet she's Bunny La Joya in her career as a porn actress (La Joya = "The Jewel" in Spanish). In *Logjammin'*, the one Bunny La Joya film we get to see, the erstwhile Fawn Knudsen seems to be wearing a rather ill-fitting wig and a flimsy negligee. Like Larry Sellers, it's all about escaping into a character.

Neither one of these young people has any regard for vehicular safety, either. Bunny, as stated earlier, carelessly crashes her car and abandons it to go frolicking nude by the pool. From a policeman, we learn that Larry "abandoned the [Dude's] vehicle" after "hit[ting] a retaining wall," leaving the car "lodged against an abutment." Just as Arthur Digby Sellers serves as an extreme counterpart to Mr. Lebowski's impotence, Larry Sellers gives us an even-more-drastic version of Bunny's nonchalance. During his one big scene, despite the fact that two grown men are hollering at him just a few away, Larry never utters a word or even changes his facial expression. It's another example of how the Sellers home reflects the worst aspects of the Lebowski home, only intensified.

So we have two pretty negative paradigms for the concept of family in *The Big Lebowski*. Both the Sellers and Lebowski households are marked by dishonesty, denial, laziness, and an overreliance on past accomplishments. Does the film hold any hope for the institution of family? Yes, to a degree. The Dude, Walter, and Donny form a marginally more functional "family" of sorts, even though Walter's attempt at domestic life was unsuccessful (he still broods over a five-year-old divorce) and Donny does not seem to have had any relatives close enough to claim his body or make funeral arrangements. Along with the perennially-unattached Dude (who makes his undomesticated nature a point of pride), these bowlers have managed to create a certain family-like support system. Better yet, Maude's pregnancy at the end of the film points toward a more optimistic future. Perhaps Maude and her child will be able to succeed where the film's other families have failed miserably. And perhaps even The Dude, in spite of himself, might play a role in that future success.

....

Joe Blevins (b. 1975, Flint, Michigan) has darkened many a doorstep in his day. Eagle-eyed Dudeists might also have spotted him in the 2009 documentary *The Achievers: The Story of the Lebowski Fans*. He currently lives and works in the Chicago area. Visit his Dead 2 Rights blog at d2rights.blogspot.com.

Paul Niesen, *Nixon Gutter*

Brian Diehl, *Lenin and The Walrus*

Down Through The Generation Gaps: Decades of Disharmony Charted in *The Big Lebowski*

BY JON BASTIAN

I missed *The Big Lebowski* in its original theatrical run, mainly because it wasn't around long enough to catch. Grossing less than eighteen million dollars, a critical gutterball, it was a big comedown from two years earlier, when the Coen Brothers' Fargo was drowned in praise, nominated for seven Oscars and awarded two. In my opinion, *The Big Lebowski* is as good a film as Fargo. So, what happened? People didn't get it. They were expecting a simple comedy about a stoner who bowls, got something more like Raymond Chandler on Ecstasy, then missed the metaphor anyway.

Many of the Coen Brothers' movies travel in the guise of genre films while being something entirely different. They even played with this idea in Barton Fink, in which the titular Clifford Odets-esque playwright is brought to Hollywood to write a "Wallace Beery wrestling picture." Fink recycles his Broadway hit into the form, but his wrestling picture is about man's existential struggle. In Fink, the befuddled producer, who is only interested in meaningless genre crap, is a stand-in for those moguls and critics who don't understand great art and so pee all over it. Or, worse, they stifle the artist, silencing him because he doesn't play by the commercial rules.

The Coen Brothers are not big on genre rules. They pretend to be, then run off in more interesting directions. The joy of watching their films comes from seeing expectations waylaid and getting whisked along with them to much more interesting places. *The Big Lebowski* pretends to be a modern day Philip Marlowe-style kidnapped girl-in-distress story with a hippie burnout bowler standing in for Raymond Chandler's private dick. All of the conventions of the genre are there – the mysterious threat to the detective, the assignment that isn't what it seems, the double- and triple-dealing and the hero caught in the middle of multiple counter-plots that don't concern him. At the same time, this classic detective noir plot is perpetrated on the sunny streets of LA or in brightly-lit interiors. There's nothing noir about the look of the film at all. Call it *film blanc*.

That's the framework. The walls and ceiling of Big Lebowski are something else altogether, and it wasn't until almost the last scene of the film that what the Coens were getting at hit me. But, hit me it did, like a bowling ball in the solar plexus, and everything that came before suddenly made perfect sense. The plot went from being as narrow as a bowling alley lane to being as deep as the Pacific Ocean. That's a rare trick, when a filmmaker can turn on the lights exactly when they want to and what you've been watching snaps into absolute focus.

Every single thing in *The Big Lebowski* is about how one generation (mis)treats and (ab)uses another, particularly the generations of the nineteen fifties through eighties. And when I say everything, I mean everything – there isn't a character or a relationship or a story element in the film that doesn't play into this theme.

The more The Dude gets involved in the kidnapping plot which acts as the movie's centerpiece, the more fishy he believes the whole caper is. Yet each time he tries to explain his misgivings and suspicions to all parties, no one takes him seriously. None of them care what he has to say because they all have their own agendas.

Perhaps it's the same with the viewers of the film back in 1998. They saw the movie as a random bunch of unrelated bits principally because it didn't fit in with what they expected from it. And yet, if one adopts the limber-minded patience of The Dude, it's possible to see how everything fits into a pretty far out but intricately-structured theme.

Let's start with the bowling. The Dude is a bowler, on a team with Walter and Donny. The art of bowling is played as highly stylized ritual here, and both dream/acid flashback sequences center around the game. It's a professional sport, yet anyone can go down to their local lanes and do it for about five bucks a pop – the ultimate blue-collar hobby. As a unifying device in the film, and an intentional artifact of the 1950's, bowling is a fun-for-the-whole-family entertainment which has changed very little over time. Metaphorically, the characters we meet may be from different generations, but all of those generations are founded on the same shiny wooden base of the 1950s postwar boom times.

Then there's The Dude himself, a product of the '60s and still sort of stuck there. He's a bearded, long-haired, pot smoking, unemployed Captain Trips kind of guy who wants no more than to hang out and be left alone. He's an emblem of the peaceful happy hippie-dippie pacifist element of the '60s who, ultimately, accomplished very little. On the flipside, we have Walter, a Vietnam vet who takes every opportunity to remind everyone in earshot of it and who, though he claims to not worry about anything, worries about (and takes offense to) practically everything. The Dude and Walter seem to be best friends. It's never mentioned, but left for the audience to realize, that if they did know each other in the '60s they would have been bitter enemies – the Reactionary Oppressor vs. the Flower Child.

The two of them together manage to be about the most ineffectual team ever seen in the history of cinema. There isn't a single scene in which either of them goes somewhere with an intent and leaves having accomplished it. The Dude's increasingly inarticulate attempts to explain what's going on (when it would only take four words to do so) become one of the film's running gags, and also serve as a subtle indictment of '60s counterculture. They could have achieved something if they could have articulated what they wanted, instead of screaming about what they didn't want. But, like The Dude, they couldn't, The revolutionaries of the '60s will always be judged among the century's failed ambitions.

Lest anyone try to counter this argument by claiming the end of the war in Vietnam as an example of hippie victory: 1) It took nine dead students at Kent State to start to win over the "silent majority," who had been alienated by hippies in the first place; 2) Whatever moral victory the war's end might have represented, 90% of the activists involved packed up and went away afterwards, so there was no one around to stop the Reagan-Bush fascist counter-revolution of 1980.

Then there's the vapid vacuum of the 1970s, epitomized by Donny. Walter pelts their poor befuddled bowling partner with verbal abuse, calling him names and peppering him with the ceaseless mantra "shut the fuck up, Donny." His name is even reminiscent of the ultimate bland 70's product: You-know-who and Marie. Everything about Donny is bland, quiet, always a few steps behind the curve. He wants to be like The Dude and Walter, but doesn't have the balls or inclination. The Dude and Walter pretty much ignore Donny despite letting him tag along, the end result being Donny's frailty-induced death. A generation is ignored and lost. The true political significance of the '70s, which began the day Nixon resigned in 1974 and ended the day Reagan was inaugurated in 1981, ends up nothing but dust in the wind, soiling the remnants of the '60s.

The flipside of Donny's 1970s is represented by Jesús Quintana (John Turturro). The alleged pedophile in the purple jumpsuit represents pure dissolution. Ultimately, he's all posturing and no action, a colorful, loud, sexually aggressive, culturally egotistical charlatan destined to consume himself.

As for that Reagan devolution era, the 80s are represented by postmodern/new wave Maude on one side and by the Eurotrash nihilists on the other. The former cares deeply about everything, while the latter care about nothing but themselves, one member going so far as to commit an act of self-mutilation in the interest of achieving their million dollar score. When Walter finally tells them they're getting nothing because there never was a kidnapping and, well, you have to have a hostage to get a ransom, they pout and whine that it's not fair. They're a gang of ineffectual posers dressed in black who try to blame everyone else for their own acts of stupidity. Anyone who was a Goth in high school can probably relate to this with some chagrin.

This brings me to the bracket decades for the film, the '50s and the '90s. Our story is set during and after the Gulf War of January 1991, in that breathless nasty year right before the (psychological) 80s ended with Bill Clinton's election. In the film, this makes the '90s an impending event of which the participants are not aware. The single representative of the future generation is Little Larry Sellers (Jesse Flanagan) a fifteen year-old alleged car thief who is harangued by Walter, but never says a single word. His is a generation found guilty by its elders, but never allowed to speak in its own defense. The upshot of his silence is one of the more hilarious mistakes in the film, and a perfect metaphor for what did happen to the children of the '90s. The adults have accused all teenagers of being little criminals, and so end up bashing each other over what to do. Larry is the cause of wanton destruction without having done a thing.

On the other hand, the '50s are indicted with a vengeance. Personified by two rich men, Jeff ("The Big") Lebowski and Jackie Treehorn, these two men are the forces behind all the plot machinations, motivated by greed despite (and perhaps because of) already appearing so rich. They are the real guilty parties. Adult entertainment mogul Treehorn, who sent out the carpet-soiling thugs in the first place, is a man with more money than he knows what to do with as evidenced by the no-holds barred bacchanal on the beach, yet uses strong-arm tactics to collect what, to him, must only be pocket change.

Whereas Treehorn acts to get back money he shouldn't miss, The Big Lebowski schemes to get hold of money he doesn't deserve, and earned only by virtue of being in the right place at the right time.

When Lebowski calls The Dude in to tell him about the kidnapping, he launches into a long monologue about what it means to be a man, blah, blah, blah. What he says is absolute bullshit, but that he says it shows us that The Big Lebowski has no connection with the mythic past he aspires to nor the progressive future that has left him behind. He's an old man in a wheelchair in a gigantic house, trying to hoard as much as he can, simply because he can and because to him, money is ultimately the only true measure of a man. Though he tries to scapegoat the counterculture as a cover to defraud Maude, it's the counterculture that finally, literally, knocks him off his pedestal, revealing him as the helpless philosophical cripple he really is, despite all his bluster to the contrary. He may decry The Dude as a bum, but only because The Big Lebowski knows that he himself is the biggest bum of them all.

As I mentioned above, there's an "a-ha!" moment in the film when this whole metaphorical structure becomes clear. This is when The Dude and Walter go up to a cliff above the Palos Verdes shore to scatter dead Donny's ashes, and Walter still manages to make the moment all about his bitterness over Vietnam. He's mentioned that war and his involvement countless times before, in fact, in his every scene, but this moment is when it all clicks. No one can escape from their generational drama.

To make sure we get this connection, the film ends with the onscreen appearance of the enigmatic man who introduced it in voiceover, The Stranger (Sam Elliott), a grizzled but kindly cowboy who looks and feels like he wandered out of a Zane Gray novel. He's another perfect metaphor; the cowboys of reality existed a long time ago in a place that's become mythical, but the modern cowboy mythology reached its heyday in the '50s due to the popularity of the Western film genre. The Cowboy Spirit is much like The Dude Spirit, the desire to wander freely in the world, unmolested and unbothered – but only mythological characters can have that freedom.

As for the rest of us? Well, The Stranger ties it up in his closing monologue. Life is always about intergenerational give-and-take, a story that's not always pretty, but as the Stranger says, "that's the way the whole durned human comedy keeps perpetuatin' itself down through the generations, westward the wagons, across the sands a time."

It's a beautifully written line to wrap up what has seemed to be a MacGuffin-laden shaggy dog story, but it's really been all about the outrageous circumstances that lead to the conception and birth of Maude and The Dude's child, a convoluted tale to out-do Tristam Shandy. Even the title is an intentional misnomer. This story isn't about The Big Lebowski. It's about the Little Lebowski, who, someday, is going to grow up to be trapped in his or her own generation, too.

....

A native and resident of Los Angeles, **Jon Bastian** is a multi-award winning writer in multiple media, including theatre, TV, and film. He is currently senior content editor and a contributing writer for Cesarsway.com, and was an editorial consultant for "Cesar Millan's Short Guide to a Happy Dog." He is co-founder and co-publisher (with Del Harvey and Andy Walton) of Filmmonthly.com, where many of his film criticisms and analyses have appeared over the last fourteen years. Once upon a time, he was a frequent bowler.

This article originally appeared at FilmMonthly.com

Manuel Jurado Garrido, *Oh, Yes*

eosvector, *Dude, Donnie and Walter*

The Original Port Huron Statement: *The Big Lebowski* and the Religion of Laughter

BY ALAN BAILY
Stephen F. Austin State University

I. An Introduction to Lebowskiana

The "Stranger" – our narrator, a nineteenth century cowboy, who, somehow, is also an observer, and erstwhile participant in the story – delivers these introductory lines:

> A way out west there was a fella, fella I want to tell you about, fella by the name of Jeff Lebowski. At least, that was the handle his lovin" parents gave him, but he never had much use for it himself. This Lebowski, he called himself The Dude. Now, Dude, that's a name no one would self-apply where I come from. But then, there was a lot about The Dude that didn't make a whole lot of sense to me. And a lot about where he lived, like- wise. But then again, maybe that's why I found the place s'durned innarestin'.[1]

Jeff Lebowski is the man for his time and place: Los Angeles, 1991. The Stranger continues: "I only mention it 'cause some- times there's a man – I won't say a hee-ro, 'cause what's a hee-ro? – but sometimes there's a man . . . a man who, wal, he's the man for his time'n place, he fits right in there – and that's The Dude, in Los Angeles."

The Stranger's prefatory remarks clue us in to Jeff Lebowski's status as "representative man." The Stranger's narration is confused and halting; its only consistency resides in atavistic use of the language of philosophical history. This makes it clear, not only that "The Dude" is the protagonist of the story, but also that meaning in history is the central theme of The Dude's story. And yet the empty, tautological, quality of the Stranger's ramblings – and indeed, The Dude's lifestyle – brings the whole notion of meaning in history into question. The reason for this is that "history" has come to an end. But the "end" can be read in one of two ways. In short: either this "end" is the culmination of a metaphysical destiny, or merely the senescence of a certain way of thinking and speaking of things. Whether the former or the latter is the case is the paradoxical question that *The Big Lebowski* sets out to expose, in a playful, ironic way.

The Dude is the film's hero. But if it is the end of history, there would seem to be no need for heroes. Historical Progress, in the Hegelian sense is motivated by the physical desire to overcome scarcity, and the psychological desire to enjoy equal recognition. According to thinkers like Francis Fukuyama, industrial capitalism answers to the first desire, and liberal democracy satisfies the second. *The Big Lebowski* is set at the very moment when Fukuyama declared the end of history, in this sense.

Heroes – "world-historical individuals" – are catalysts in the historical process. Seeking to satisfy their own burning ambition, in pursuit of *unequal* recognition, they unwittingly carry the historical movement toward its own progressive telos. At the end of history, such individuals would be not only useless, but even dangerous. Now, Jeff Lebowski is *not* this sort of dangerous individual, and perhaps it is this that makes him the man for his "innarestin'" time and place. Like a Hegelian hero, The Dude does seem entirely unconsciously to abide in the Zeitgeist of early-1990s LA. And as modest as it may seem, to insist on being called *the* "Dude" in a culture where everyman is called *a* "dude," is to insist on unequal recognition, to stake a personal claim to one's world-historical representativeness. But this LA *Zeitgeist* is all about cultivating the appearance of unconsciousness and no one is more self- consciously unconscious than The Dude. Finally, as the Stranger observes, 1990s LA is history's laziest moment, and The Dude is the laziest person in LA. Thus, in a time and place where every desire can be (and so, philosophically speaking, has been) satisfied, The Dude strives, earnestly, for nothing. In "fit[ting] right in there" The Dude excels, surpassing all others.

The Dude lives alone, is unemployed and his life seems devoid of any activity, other than bowling. He is a

---

[1] All unattributed quotes in this essay are from *The Big Lebowski*

chronic marijuana smoker, and a connoisseur of White Russians. Despite the run-ins with liars, thugs, a pornographer, and a gang of German bogeymen (and women) who are self-described nihilists, The Dude is the real nihilistic hero of the story. The Dude's "lack, not only of faith, but of any lived relation to a social structure or political community of any sort, other than that of the league, or 'bowling together' – is absolute ... The Dude's anomie, the nihilism implied by his lifestyle, in fact, is far more nihilistic than anything of which the self-proclaimed nihilists in the film can ever dream."[2]

Now, this was not always the case. The film reveals little of The Dude's life story, but enough to indicate his past as a participant in the New Left campus uprisings of the 1960s. He claims to be one of the Seattle Seven ("me and, uh, six other guys") and prior to this, to have been, "uh, one of the authors of the Port Huron Statement. – The original Port Huron Statement ... Not the compromised second draft."

So, perhaps The Dude is the man for his time and place, or maybe he is a refugee from another "end of history" – the apocalyptic 1960s. How is this castaway from the sixties significant in the 'nineties?[3] The juxtaposition of the late-sixties activism of the Seattle Seven and the early-sixties pacifism of the Port Huron Statement adds another layer of irony. With only a few (now well-known) exceptions, the early leadership of the Students for a Democratic Society had splintered or dropped out of "the movement" before it was overtaken by Weathermen-style activism. Moreover, what could The Dude mean by "The original Port Huron Statement" as opposed to the "compromised second draft"?

Of course it is not my intention to give a literal interpretation of these remarks, or the film as a whole. Suffice it say that the common thread I see here, is the quest for authenticity. The problems of authenticity and the end of history are related in an ironic manner. *The Big Lebowski* sheds comic light on this ironic relationship.

Briefly, the "ironic" relationship I refer to is as follows: Thinkers from Rousseau to Marx have intimated that the end of history (the historical fulfillment of human freedom) actually is a sort of return to authentic humanity. Be it the authentic self-love of the state of nature, or the authentic community of primitive communism, the end of history will mark a return to un-alienated humanity, albeit through the perfection of civilization. Claims to authenticity take two common forms. In the first, authenticity is achieved by maintaining faithfulness to an original or foundational moment; in the second, by eschewing foundations and committing oneself to one's own style (autonomy). One appeal of formulas like Rousseau's and Marx's is that they are ambivalent between these two visions: the perfected freedom of the end of history entails both a return to authentic human community and the free creativity of one's own, authentic, self.

Interestingly, The Dude's reference to the "original" SDS manifesto is also ambivalent with respect to these alternatives. One way of seeing the Port Huron Statement is as just such a founding moment: "The tale of the magnificent manifesto written around the clock by a convention that stayed up to watch the sun rising over Lake Huron, followed in short order by the saga of the brilliant brief worked up by sleepless cadres fighting off a sneak attack by paranoid elders – this was the stuff of SDS's founding legend."[4] Perhaps The Dude's own myth of himself is anchored to this "original" moment. But the tensions written into the Statement led to rifts within the New Left that developed into obvious fault-lines by the time of The Dude's involvement with the Seattle Seven.

This irony in The Dude's self-mythologizing mirrors the tension in the Port Huron Statement's aims. The manifesto placed equal emphasis on the whole community and on personal authenticity. On the one hand, it declares: "Loneliness, estrangement, isolation describe the vast distance between man and man today. These dominant tendencies can't be overcome by better personnel management, nor by improved gadgets, but only when a love of man overcomes the idolatrous worship of things by man." This is a classic diagnosis of anomie as the product of atomistic ideology and technological society. Yet, on the other hand, the manifesto goes on to claim that human beings "have unrealized potential for self-cultivation, self-direction, self-understanding, and creativity. It is this potential we regard as crucial and to which we appeal, not to the human potentiality for violence, unreason, and submission to authority. The goal of man and society should be human independence: a concern not with image [or] popularity but with finding a meaning in life that is personally authentic."[5]

Todd Gitlin perceptively argues that the New Left was able to finesse these contradictions – for a time – by adopting expressive politics. The "expressive side to the movement culture [was] rooted in the subterranean ethos of the Fifties, and in the long run revolt against the containment of feeling and initiative in a society growing steadily more rationalized. Participatory democracy entailed the right of universal assertion." Squaring the circle between communitarian values and individual expression, this style precipitated the now familiar notion that "the personal is political."

---

[2] Joshua Kates, "*The Big Lebowski* and Paul deMan," in Edward P. Comentale and Aaron Jaffe, eds., *The Year's Work in Lebowski Studies* (Bloomington: Indiana UP, 2009) p. 153

[3] All we know of The Dude's lost years is that he was a roadie for Metallica during this period.

[4] Todd Gitlin, *The Sixties: Years of Hope, Days of Rage*, revised edition. (New York: Bantam, 1993) p. 120

[5] This and the above quote from the Port Huron Statement are from Gitlin, pp.106-108. A view unexamined here is that The Dude is referring to the un-amended version of the Port Huron Statement, which was less stridently anti-communist than the version finally adopted. (For a narrative of the battle between Old and New Left over anti-communism in the Port Huron Statement see Gitlin, pp. 171-192)

> The implicit theory of expressive politics was that the structures of private feeling begin before the individual, in capitalist acquisition and the patriarchal family; public in its origins, private feeling should therefore be expressed where it belongs, in public. Its faith was that a politics of universal expression would make the right things happen – *and* be its own reward.[6]

Gitlin acknowledges that the New Left tended towards a "belief that political style is central to political substance – a fetishism of style," but he also points to the importance of style for all modern mass-political movements. "We shared [this belief], in fact, with Kennedys' managerial liberalism ... The New Left's disruption of established procedure was a counterpolitics to the managed world of institutions – a system which professes the glory of democracy while its bureaucratic rules mask the ways in which correct procedure has taken a weight of its own."[7]

Over time, Gitlin suggests, the channels dug out on each side, between expressive and managerial styles, can harden into identities. The opening scene of *The Big Lebowski* alludes to this clash of styles/identities. We meet The Dude, in his bathrobe and jelly sandals, as he renders a $0.69 check for a pint of half-and-half. Evidently he is the lone customer in Ralph's grocery store. As The Dude checks out there enters a ghostly presence: George H. Bush, on television, announcing our first invasion of Iraq. The televised president, and in particular, one of his phrases will become a virtual character in the film: "This unchecked aggression will not stand."

The 'Sixties in the 'Nineties

In a classic 1960s gambit, the youth culture took the pejorative, "dude," and transfigured it into a badge of honor. At some point (probably in his college years), Jeff Lebowski baptized himself "*The* Dude." If Jeffery[8] was "the handle his lovin' parents gave him," then Dude is more an anti-handle than a substitute one. Taking the opposite of a name does not prevent The Dude from suffering the misfortune of mistaken identity, however. In the scene that sets the story in motion, The Dude's apartment is ransacked and his rug vandalized by thugs aiming to extract ransom from another, more wealthy, "Jeffrey Lebowski." As The Dude will become convinced, this rug "really tied the room together" and thus its desecration is an injustice that demands rectification. With this quest for justice, history resumes, as farce.

The Dude does not arrive at this conviction immediately. His enthusiasm for this peculiar cause is stoked, even incited, by his friend and bowling teammate, Walter Sobchak. Walter, too, has put on a second identity, having converted to the Judaism of his now ex-wife. A Vietnam veteran, Walter, like The Dude, seems to be stuck in the late 1960s. The two characters evoke two distinctive types of that era: The Dude is a marijuana-smoking, forty-something hippie. An epitome of casual style, he is a veritable Jerry Rubin in his mastery of the expressive politics of irony. His only memories of college include "smoking Thai stick and occupying various administration buildings." Conversely, Walter, the war veteran, owns a private security agency. Walter habitually carries a pistol, to which he is wont to take recourse when diplomacy fails. We are first introduced to this behavior when he brandishes the gun at a bowling alley, in order to ensure that a rival team's player records a foul. "HAS THE WHOLE WORLD GONE CRAZY?" Walter fulminates, "AM I THE ONLY ONE WHO GIVES A SHIT ABOUT THE RULES?"

Walter's relentless, characteristically arbitrary, and convenient application of rigid orthodoxies to all the quandaries of life typifies the posture of militant activism. The relationship between The Dude and Walter (friendship, and bowling, keeps them together in spite of incommensurable disagreements) is at the heart of the film. It may not be too much to say that these two characters represent decomposed essences of New Left political styles, "one of individual moral rectitude along the lines of Thoreau, the other 'Leninist-Maoist.'"[9]

The Dude's confrontation with the "Big" Lebowski also neatly echoes elements of the clash of cultures in the 1960s. Taking the hard line on individual responsibility, The older, established Lebowski maintains that the goons alone are responsible for damages to The Dude's rug. The sequel is a confrontational dialogue between The Dude's casual-cum-lazy mores and Lebowski's rhetoric of individual-responsibility. Lebowski confirms that The Dude is unemployed, whereupon he proceeds to browbeat him with that most Nixonian of epithets – "bum" – chanting, "The bums will always lose." The Dude abides this skirmish with the aid of another joint, and then retreats.

The convoluted relationships among these and other characters comprise far too many ins-and-outs to recount here. In any case these plot twists, difficult enough to follow on screen, are not the main source of the movie's appeal. The point is to laugh. Jeff Bridges, the actor who played "The Dude," sums up *Lebowski*'s charm aptly: "I usually point to the end of the script, to what the Stranger says at the end of the movie. I think the Stranger's enjoyment of the movie sums up what people like about it."

> THE STRANGER
> ... I don't know about you, but I take comfort in that. It's good knowin' he's out there, The Dude, takin' her easy for all us sinners ... Made me laugh to beat the band. Parts, anyway ... I guess that's the way the whole durned human comedy keeps perpetuatin' itself, down through the generations, westward the wagons, across the sands

---

[6] Gitlin, pp. 134-135.
[7] Ibid.
[8] Hereafter, "Dude".

[9] One of the reasons that we had difficulty coding the whole phenomenon of the Sixties, [says Howe,] is that at first we couldn't see the interweaving of these two...and secondly even if we could see it, we didn't know how to cope with this.' Gitlin, p. 176.

a time until – aw, look at me, I'm rambling again. Wal, I hope you folks enjoyed yourselves.[10]

A Community Organized for Inaction in History

What is most sociologically interesting about *Lebowski* is the relationship the film engenders among its community of fans. When *The Big Lebowski* premiered, in 1998, critics and moviegoers alike reacted with puzzlement. Like many films destined to become cult classics, *Lebowski*'s audience did not materialize immediately, but slowly gestated into a modest but passionate band of fans on whom the film exerts a weird and wonderful pull. This attraction may flow from viewers' understanding the film's many, oblique, philosophical references, or from an appreciation of its playful portrayal of post-anti-heroism as the proper response to "the end of history." Probably it owes something to both. Bridges registers surprise that the movie did not perform better at the box office. "But now . . . well . . . I'm glad people are digging it . . . that it found its audience." For Bridges, the Stranger's denouement conveys "what's great" about the film, "how it says it all without really saying anything. Maybe that's one reason why people dig the movie and are able to watch it over and over again. It's like picking up a kaleidoscope. You see something new each time."[11]

This is not to say that cinematic form is inconsequential to the film's appeal. Indeed, one might suggest that televisual culture is the "authentic" protagonist of *The Big Lebowski*. In properly post-modern fashion, the fictional world in which the movie's events transpire comprises a Frankenstein-like patchwork of cinema history, highlighting Western, noir, and buddy-movie tropes. The lack of any distinctive Los Angeles landmarks in the film (excepting the In-N-Out Burger franchise) reflects the irony of the film's opening lines, where we are told that the story is about a *certain* man (The Dude) and a *certain* place (Los Angeles) in a *certain* time (1991, or, the End of History). "All of the characteristic postmodern tricks are on display – the subversive mockery of narrative, the method of inhabiting a genre to expose its artificiality, the satirical thrust of its allusion to the classics, its disbelief in the old structures, tropes and systems"[12]

Yet, as the authors of the above lines continue, this playful transgression drives beyond, or beneath, the familiar cynical message that most postmodern art portends. For brevity's sake, let's say that the clichéd message of the typical postmodern production is: "authentic communication is impossible, and so trust, friendship and love is, too." *Lebowski* affirms the first, but not the second part of this proposition. "These mortals may be fools, but they actually love each other. This makes them – and arguably, (their creators,) the Coens – very different from the characters and film-makers of the typical camp postmodern mode, which generally ends in cynicism and showy surface-effects rather than affirming life and ultimately choosing real feelings."[13]

The Religion of Laughter

Although it emerges from a community of viewers, cult fandom implies a challenge to the voyeuristic culture of the spectacle. Televisual culture depends on the separation between producer-actors and spectator-judges. The screen is the invisible barrier that instantiates this division. The transparency of the screen which separates actors from spectators makes possible the illusion that watching and acting are equal. But the child in us knows that seeing and performing are unequal.

Cult fandom arises from an innocent, "childish" gesture to deny the separation, as well as the false equation, between acting and watching. Cult fandom expresses the spectator's desire to participate in the action, to (re)create it even in the paltriest way, rather than be satisfied with the passive role of spectator. Moreover, it denies that spectators can be competent judges of performance without having been performers themselves.

Cult fandom is a doubly-ironic attempt to overcome the implicit division at the basis of televisual culture by bringing a particular televisual world into life. It is as if the viewer is attempting to transcend the transparent barrier of the screen through a gesture which denies that the screen is a barrier at all. The illicit nature of this gesture gives rise to a new division between cult-fans and their judges, plainclothes members of the public who know too well the distinction between reality and make-believe, and cannot fathom the purpose of such real-life play.

The Big Lebowski is unique among cult films because the movie itself initiates this doubly-ironic gesture. This is evident in several ways. First, *Lebowski*'s Los Angeles is not the city viewers are familiar with, but the "real" LA of strip-malls, bowling alleys and suburban fast-food haunts. Second, the movie's main characters, Walter and The Dude, are ostensibly failures but are based in large part on successful entertainment producers John Milius and Jeff Dowd. Third, the movie's narrative momentum is generated by misunderstanding, mendacity, and conflicting agendas. As in the world, so in *Lebowski*, events are not governed by a master script but result from myriad private plans whose authors lose control of them the moment they begin to enact them.

From the first image of tumbleweed, *Lebowski*'s world-stage is a "barrel-of-laughs"–a ride where "people try to keep their balance while the upturned barrel revolves round its axis. One can only keep one's balance by moving on the bottom of the barrel in the opposite direction to, and with the same speed as, its movement . . . The more violent [the characters'] gestures and their

---

[10] I'm a Lebowski, You're a Lebowski, p. xiii
[11] I'm a Lebowski, pp. xii-xiii
[12] J.M. Tyree and Ben Walters, *BFI Film Classics: The Big Lebowski* (London: British Film Institute, 2007) p. 105

[13] Tyree and Walters, p. 104.

grip of the walls, the more difficult it is for them to get up and the funnier they look"[14]

Lebowski's "barrel-of-laughs" resonates with the "End of History" question of the 1990s. Seen in this way, the movie is a lighthearted meditation on the possibility that history follows no script. The dénouement of the Cold War put to rest the Communist narrative of Historical progress–it was misconceived. But this did not resolve the question of history itself. Indeed, the revelation that history's movement was not governed by any master script actually intensified the sense that human life is ruled by relentless and apparently arbitrary change. In short, Marx's dictum about capitalism's historically revolutionary effects – "all that is solid melts into air" – survived the collapse of his conviction that the historical vicissitudes of capitalism would be redeemed by final Communism and the predestined end of the class struggle.

Comedies are stories destined to end well, no matter how bad things might seem in the middle. In this sense, Marx's narrative of history is a comedy, much like the Christian narrative of redemption that provided its model. History was invented by the ancient Greeks, but their philosophers did not conceive of history as meaningful in itself. They could conceive of *histories* as tragic stories of irreconcilable goals, and of time as the cycle of growth and inevitable decay. But the idea that History is meaningful in itself, a drama scripted by God or the Universal Mind, receives its impetus from revealed religion.

We are progenies of the historical comedies of Christianity, which encouraged us to hope in a heavenly redemption *from* history as part of God's supernatural plan, and Enlightenment Progress, which encouraged us to be optimistic about humanity's infinite capacity to redeem ourselves *in* and *through* history, to make life here on earth more and more heavenly. Traditional Christianity accommodated the barrel-of-laughs version of history so long as it applied only to the secular world– the earthly "City of Man." The heavenly "City of God" was another matter. But there were always some who rejected this distinction; and we might think of the revolutionary side of modern Enlightenment, with its rejection of religion for the sake of progress, as an ironic reversal of the distinction. From the nether view of post-modernity, however, history is neither a pilgrimage through the veil of tears nor a march towards immanent progress. Postmodernity resigns us to history as barrel-of-laughs, but it withholds Christianity's promise of redemption.

In this post-modern spirit, both The Dude and Walter display a quixotic seriousness that evokes the necessary but futile effort to maintain one's balance in the barrel-of-laughs. The Dude's devotion to authentic individuality and Walter's commitment to the politics of solidarity reflect the Port Huron Statement's two aims. Although these aims were complimentary in the aspirations of the Statement's authors, the turbulent history of the student movement revealed the difficulty of reconciling them in practice. In the wake of the Movement's failure, all that is left for The Dude and Walter is to run against the Momentum that would pull them down. This is why they are easily duped and especially funny looking, but it also makes possible the genuinely human bond they share. The Dude, a quietist without reverence, tries to steer the world in an irenic direction largely by the ironic strategy of avoiding real commitments. Walter's Zionist-inflected Judaism is a way of clinging to the value of valor that was strained by the viewing public's response to Vietnam. But in spite of this divergence between their contemplative and militant ways, perhaps even because of it, they help to keep one another's balance.

....

Alan Baily is an Assistant Professor in the Department of Government at Stephen F. Austin State University. He specializes in the study of political thought. At present he is researching the theory of money in Plato's Republic. He lives in Nacogdoches, Texas, with his wife Meredith, and their six pets, who really tie the house together.

---

[14] Jan Kott, *Shakespeare Our Contemporary* (New York: W.W .Norton, 1974) p. 140

Mauro Antonini, *The Big Picciowski*

"I. The Royal 'We'":
The Dude as Representative Man

BY NILES SCHWARTZ

The Big Lebowski was initially viewed as a frivolous stoner farce, with superfluous ins and outs (or "facets" as The Dude says) leading nowhere. No one changes. The story is laden with humorous set-ups and silly situations, but no punch-lines. Like a lot of viewers upon its initial release, I was smiling throughout most of The Big Lebowski, but the cathartic belly-laughs that my body anticipated were not given an outlet. I enjoyed myself, but was still hungry. The frustration of the film was the want of resolution, whether as a plot or as a movie comedy. Yet nowadays, The Big Lebowski resonates as a moving and fulfilling film that works on political, cultural, and spiritual levels, with nary a dull frame. It's a layered experience, but does not indicate what its layers are communicating, which only leads to the fun of its puzzling interpretation. Like other texts of consolation, it's become a kind of prayer or meditation, fitted for times of grief, duress, and uncertainty. There's magic in how this presumably insignificant and ragged entry of Joel and Ethan Coen's body of work could so effortlessly convey the sadness and mystery of human beings, and with so much humor.

From a perspective, The Big Lebowski is a parody of interpretation, a notion that the published Faber & Faber screenplay makes clear, with the Coens penning their own fictional analysis for a Film Quarterly-type publication, Cinema/Not Cinema. The esteemed British critic, Sir Anthony Forte-Bowell, who analyzes humor in films from a schematic process, writes about The Big Lebowski and tries to make meaning out of its humor, and even searches for intellectual justifications that judge whether or not it's even funny. Beginning with the breakdown of a scene featuring The Three Stooges, Forte-Bowell writes, "All agree that these operations, or more to the point, their depictions, are 'funny.' What is more obscure and what even a frame-by-frame analysis of the films fails to reveal is wherein the nature of the humor resides. A similar difficulty attends analysis of the film under consideration. The Big Lebowski harks back to films of the early 1970s that dealt with certain issues attendant to a presumed Generation Gap. In them, a youth who wears bell-bottomed trousers, bead, a shirt with a primed pattern and octagonal glasses, frequently tinted, is bedeviled by an older man wearing straight-bottomed trousers, a solid shin, a tie with a printed pattern and curviform glasses, untinted, who 'just doesn't understand'. The more supple and intuitive intelligence of the youth is contrasted with the more linear and unimaginative intelligence of the older man, and in the end prevails over it, with the older man frequently arriving at grudging appreciation of the youth's superior values. If the movie is of the subgenre wherein the older man will not concede the youth's superiority, then the older man shall be revealed to be a fossilized if not corrupt representative of a doomed order. The Big Lebowski appears to be some sort of 'spoof' upon this genre."

Forte-Bowell's academic pretentions mirror the frustrations of the conditioned expectations of Lebowski's strung-out critics who ignore The Dude's advice and can't "take it easy." The critic admits that "repeated viewings of [The Big Lebowski] have failed to clarify for me the genre-relevance of bowling, physical handicap, castration and the Jewish Sabbath. But perhaps we should not dismiss the possibility that they are simply authorial mistakes. Certainly the script could not be held up as a model of artistic coherence."

It's reassuring for a lot of people to take a lax approach to the Coens' irony, taking comfort in the idea that The Big Lebowski is just an absurd smorgasbord of treats meant to appeal to the same kinds of rebellious youths that Forte-Bowell describes. The Coens have always anticipated criticism to their work, openly making fun of themselves in other screenplay introductions, usually courtesy of their geriatric and irritable editor, Roderick Jaynes, whose words[1] on The Man Who Wasn't There are, for me, comic genius. The Coens understand the quick labels of the pop cultural arena in which they will be viewed and scrutinized, and understanding this helps one more easily appreciate the dismissed films, such as Intolerable Cruelty (2003), which was seen as a big-budget rom-com sell-out (when in fact the film is clearly making light of the inherent vulgarity of big

---

[1] http://www.guardian.co.uk/film/2001/sep/28/artsfeatures

budget, Gary Marshall-type rom-coms), or *The Ladykillers* (2004), a remake of the Charles Crichton/Alec Guinness comedy classic, which was destined for a chilly reception but is much more hilarious than most well-reviewed comedies from either the Hollywood or indie establishment, grounded by Irma P. Hall's infectious performance as the lady in the title's question, and the Coens' skillful love for language and its function. As with *Lebowski*'s screenplay introduction, the Coens are flipping the bird to both their highbrow rococo critics (like Forte-Bowell, whose name denotes a fellow who may be full of hot gas) and the large bulk of mainstream pundits who go whichever way the wind – or farty gas – is blowing.

"Your Revolution is Over!"

Though the present moment – August, 2011 – is not an anniversary number regarding *The Big Lebowski*'s release, there's a syncretic logic to thinking about it right now. The 20th anniversary for The Dude's *story* is coming upon us, just as another memorial looms. *The Big Lebowski* begins on September 11, 1991, an even ten years before the World Trade Center attacks, its own date of origin carries geopolitical significance, seeing as the first George Bush is speaking on the Ralph's Supermarket check-out lane television, "This will not stand, this *will not stand*, this aggression against Kuwait."

What an eerie coincidence this is, putting history into perspective with a sociopolitical dimension of *The Big Lebowski* that applies to 1991, 2001, and 2011 (or 1971). In 1991 and 2001, the United States military – so haunted by negative memories of Vietnam – was roused awake and set Saddam Hussein in its sights. We tie this to the day-to-day travails of an unemployed deadbeat "the square community won't care about." Bush's 1991 address, in response to Iraq's invasion of Kuwait, is echoed by The Dude (Jeff Bridges) in his own confrontation with the millionaire Jeffrey Lebowski (David Huddleston), and so immediately plays with the idea of an allegory. Is The Dude like the United States, provoked out of its slumber by Saddam Hussein peeing on the proverbial rug of Kuwait, an oil partner that ties the *global* room together? The Dude invokes George Bush's words to The Big Lebowski: "This will not stand, this aggression will not stand!" But in the same way The Dude can never relive the revolution of the 1960s, the military cannot relive its glory days. Walter wants to go back and "fix" Vietnam, but understands that the Gulf War is a shallow affair. The Gulf War dimension remains rather peripheral, but its presence along with other elements in *The Big Lebowski*, when connected to the class differences between the two Lebowskis, makes the film more endearing and possibly translates as to why it has such a hold on people, however subconsciously the meaning resonates.

Near the conclusion of *Lebowski*, we overhear Walter talking about the brewing Kuwait crisis. He points out how with Vietnam, at least the people were given the viable "domino effect" theory in the West's clash with Communism; but "this [the Gulf War] is nothing but nothing but about oil." (Big) Lebowski, aligned with the Republican Party by his photos with Nancy Reagan and Charlton Heston, to say nothing of his rhetoric of "achievement," is doubling for the Bush Administration, which has also given the country an empty suit-case of sorts in its road-to-war rhetoric. The meaning of the mission is to keep the status quo intact: broke millionaire Jeffrey Lebowski can embezzle $1 million from "needy little urban achievers," and blame the money's loss on the deadbeat Dude. The rich stays rich, Dude remains The Dude, and life goes on as the pins are mechanically set back up.

Not more than two weeks after September 11, 2001, conservative radio commentator Rush Limbaugh proclaimed that Iraq was responsible for the terrorist attacks. The road returning to Saddam's turf was injected into the national conversation, led by the second George Bush and his team of neoconservatives (it's eerie how much The Big Lebowski resembles Dick Cheney). The incident plays out once more, as the beleaguered Left understood in the days leading up to March 2003, "*Rug peers did not do this*." Power structures were meanwhile kept tidily in place as common foot soldiers went off to fight in something that, once again, could be argued to be "nothing but nothing but about oil." The Dude in all of us meanwhile suffers, dies a little, and finally abides. Nothing changes.

It's also hard to not feel the same kind of Dude vibe in the economic recession of recent years, where the Lebowski class has become the new protagonist in the national narrative, the rich being victims under attack by the poor's want of entitlements. The Big Lebowskis have only grown bigger, while The Dudes, unable to live exorbitantly (often on unemployment), have drifted farther back from the average pay. As the income gap widens and The Big Lebowskis desperately work to make sure their income taxes stay as low as they've ever been, those same dignified personages work to punish the 46% who don't pay income taxes, but *do* have payroll taxes, in addition to having an income that has not grown in proportion to the expenses of living in a more demanding and technological time. Though we "have a rash," like The Dude apparently does, we still don't complain too much.

To hold out or make demands on The Big Lebowskis of the world, just as The Dude demands a replacement rug, leads to propagandistic charges of "Class Warfare." The speculation and actions of the very wealthy on Wall Street led to the widespread suffering among the nation's disadvantaged, who were without a safety net to tie their proverbial rugs – or lives – together, unlike The Big Lebowskis, who can somehow bail themselves out. "So you know that they were trying to piss on your rug," The Dude truth-tells Lebowski, which is deflected by the same concrete and clever semantics we hear in the political arena. "Did *I* urinate on your rug?" "You mean, did you personally come and pee on my rug?" "Hello! Do you speak English, sir? Parla usted inglés? . . . I just want to understand this, sir. Every time a rug is micturated upon in this fair city, I have to compensate the person?" For the rich Lebowski, The Dude is just "looking for a handout" like every other bum who wants those government entitlements. "Every bum's lot in life is his own responsibility," Lebowski proclaims, "regardless of whom he chooses to blame!" The Dude's request for a fair compensation is bluntly derided as left wing rabble-rousing Marxism, revealing the true source of polarization here: "Your revolution is over, Mr. Lebowski! Condolences! The bums lost!"

And in 1991, the bums were universally acknowledged as "having lost." Lebowski is an archetype of the Reagan 1980s, when the revolution at home was finished, and by the turn of the decade was also finished overseas with the fall of the Iron Curtain. "Prosperity" and "Achievement" had won. The bums had lost to the extent that the words "class warfare," which the present moment *demands* to be uttered, are anathema, and even though the decadent Big Lebowskis of the world have run us into the ground, they are still vertically integrated to the point where Ayn Rand became a bigger bestseller *after* it was apparent that deregulation was what caused the goddamn economy to crash into the mountain.

The "bums" *are* losers, judged by Lebowski and a mortician offering "our most *modestly* priced receptacle" at a price which is still unreasonable. And The Big Lebowski is right. The bums *will* always lose. The Dude and his bowling partners, whether it's Donny (Steve Buscemi) or rival bowlers like Smokey (played by the musician Jimmie Dale Gilmore), are like ghosts of the lost revolution's ideals, "conscientious objectors" and "pacifists." Or Walter, who had buddies "die face down in the muck" for our "basic freedoms," when the real world just doesn't care anymore. Those dreams are replaced by the crass, right-wing materialism of The Big Lebowski, or the vapid and posh rococo smug artiness of Maude Lebowski and Knox Harrington (David Thewlis in an impressive cameo), or loan-shark gangsters like Jackie Treehorn, a pornographer who tells The Dude about his plans to ride the wave of the future, creating "erotic software" that will make sex "100% electronic." People here are trapped in the mass-produced forms of their published entertainments (like *Branded*, the television show written by Arthur Digby Sellers), doomed to relive a constant simulation. Such is the structure of *The Big Lebowski*, which is both a Western and a film noir, and follows tropes of the genres. There are then, amidst all this, the Nihilists, demons of that "100% electronic wave of the future," led by Uli Kunkel aka Karl Hungus (Peter Stormare), who act in Treehorn's porn films and create electronic techno pop (the German band Autobahn, based on Kraftwerk). All this electricity points to *Nothing* and a belief in *Nothing*, a theme the Coens will revisit in their Information Age satire, *Burn After Reading*.

The Dude is a remnant of a lost humanist revolution, and he understands the concepts of power (what "the issue is") – which is why he points out how "rug peers did not do this." He quotes Lenin. "It's like Lenin said. You look for the person who will benefit, and uh, you know, you'll, uh, you know what I'm trying to say?" Said like a true casual '60s revolutionary (and "casualness runs deep" in The Dude, according to the Coens' screenplay).

The problem with revolution – whether in 1970, 1991, or 2011 – is the superficial pop-cultural dimension, which soaks up the potency of content and replaces it with fond novelty. Donny confuses "Lenin" with "Lennon," and tries to finish The Dude's quote, "I Am the Walrus." The tragedy of the lost revolution is its inherent hopelessness, which has since become a mere culture of complaint for the common folk like The Dude, Donny, or Walter. The Dude and his cronies, themselves nowadays the stuff of t-shirts, prefigure the chic of Che Guevara, and this is where *The Big Lebowski* retains a lot of its soft-heartedness and soul. The characters here are too passive to have much hope (Walter's unwarranted enthusiasm doesn't even believe itself – "Who's sitting on a fucking million fucking dollars?!"), but *The Big Lebowski* is about the haunting of that hope, lingering faintly like the bowling alley marquee stars do as Roger Deakins' lights fade out on Walter aiding Donny after the climactic Nihilist assault, Walter telling his dying buddy that "choppers" are coming in.

The lost revolution ties into the melancholy loss of time these characters are experiencing. They are all burrowing into their middle age with unrealized dreams, but I think we feel compassion for them because they won't give up on the past, which in most stories is something derided and seen as foolish. But *The Big Lebowski* carries no such judgment with its melancholy. The Dude harshly criticizes Walter and his obsessions, whether it relates to Vietnam ("What the *fuck* does anything have to do with *Vietnam*?!") or his appropriated Judaism, which has much to do with his ex-wife, Cynthia. "It's all a part of your sick Cynthia thing. Taking care of her fucking dog, going to her fucking synagogue. You're living in the fucking past." And Walter, in reply, affirms this: "Three thousand years of beautiful tradition, from Moses to Sandy Koufax, you're *goddamn right I'm living in the fucking past!*" Walter, in part based on *Apocalypse Now* and *Red Dawn* creator John Milius, *is* deluded by nostalgia, as we see when he hijacks The Dude's money drop-off, packing an Uzi along with his ringer suitcase. But so is everyone here, if we look at their clothes and surroundings. The past is all they have. We see the same commitment in the pacifist Smokey, the wannabe private dick Da Fino (Jon Polito), and the dance performance artist landlord Marty (Jack Kehler), all middle-aged men once filled with ideals and promise who are rendered as jokes – "funny stuff" – by the sands of time.

The Dude is also adrift in time. He seems to have deliberately chosen not to grow up, listening to CCR's *Cosmo's Factory* decades after its initial release with the same devotion of a teenaged fan. He wallows at home, not looking for work but listening to old tape recordings of bowling matches from years ago, preparing for the semifinals. It's incorrect to dismiss The Dude as a slacker adolescent and nothing more; he is not of the same ilk of Jay and Silent Bob, Harold and Kumar, *South Park*'s Towelie, Dave Chapelle, or so many other trendy stoner icons. As a drafter of the "original Port Huron statement" and a member of the "Seattle Seven" he's surely more complicated than that. Though a rebel (he puts on his sunglasses when The Man gets on his case), it's hard not to believe he's just a little insecure about writing that .69 check at Ralph's for his half and half. The Dude, like Walter and Donny, has a tragic loneliness – if a blissful one. He dances home from Ralph's, the same way a ne'er-do-well bachelor might with his newly bought frozen pizza, preparing to settle in for the evening. He has no family ties and so no pressing responsibilities other than bills (which he conveniently puts off: his rent is ten days late). He can best "take it easy" in the pleasure of his own company. Walter and Donny seem to be in similar social ruts. The Dude and Walter are the only attendees at Donny's funeral. Indeed, all these characters are held apart from the comfortable mainstream "square" community, though Walter, a business owner (Sobchak Security) and divorced man who had "buddies die face down in the muck," may have been the closest to normality. The Dude's pillow-talk with Maude also outlines a social life as a college student with many potentialities that never really came to an acceptable fruition.

This is why the musical bookends for *The Big Lebowski* perfectly plug into an emotional wavelength that is transmuted to viewers. *The Big Lebowski* begins with Bob Dylan's "The Man in Me," and ends with Townes Van Zandt's stirring cover of the Rolling Stones' "Dead Flowers," both of which have lyrics that appear to be about lonely and unreachable men longing for a particular person's companionship. The bowling alley, the sanctuary of comfort and community afforded to The Dude, Walter, and Donny, is seen through a montage of overweight and aging regulars as Dylan sings over the opening credits, the effect being an odd sense of *closeness* with other people ("Oh what a wonderful feeling, just to know that you are near"). "Dead Flowers" follows a class distinction of a man in "ragged company" held apart from a woman mingling with the beautiful people of a more well-adjusted sphere. This may perfectly describe The Dude, Walter, and Donny, and so many more like them, lingering in bowling alleys, growing older as their dreams grow more impractical with time, so different from (or so similar to) the multiplex movie audience watching their story (*The Big Lebowski* was a wide release originally, and not a specialty house offering). For detractors of *The Big Lebowski*, it's easy to dismiss its characters as "deadbeat bums" just as the millionaire Lebowski does. And yet the folksiness of *Lebowski* is its prime agency for mass identification in our times of a wobbly middle class with more people struggling to hang on to their dreams and their tax brackets.

"Taking It Easy For All Us Sinners"

Regardless of his own adrift-ness, delusions, or inherent laziness, The Dude remains the essential hero for the Wasteland depicted in *The Big Lebowski* and our strung-out times. Imbued throughout the film is the clear indication that Duder follows the familiar literary path of the "Christ Figure," the redeemer and savior of the world. Another film that has garnered increased status since its release (though it was still a critical and box office success, unlike *Lebowski*) is Harold Ramis' *Groundhog Day*, where the interesting plot set-up of a vain weatherman (Bill Murray) blessed – or damned – to repeat one day in time ad infinitum, February 2, has since become an object of religious speculation and interpretation, some writers alleging that *Groundhog Day* is even the most spiritual film ever made, finding a receptive audience among Jews, Christians, Buddhists, Hindus, and Humanists alike.

The Big Lebowski is no less a triumph, if perhaps a more deliberate one considering the intellectual breadth and ironies the Coens incorporate into all their work, though the deeper meanings and questions are secondary to a viewer's delight. *The Big Lebowski* has a religious aura, which I believe has subconsciously connected with many viewers and is why it's such a comforting, even transcendent, experience. The Dude is a modern Aion, an archetype of our collective unconscious representing the Self. And this may be just like my opinion, man, but I'm fairly certain that this is a deliberate allusion on the Coens' part.

Religion is one of the Coens' primary interests, being an important component elsewhere in *O Brother, Where Art Thou?*, *The Ladykillers*, *A Serious Man*, *True Grit*, and possibly *No Country for Old Men*. And even though it's safe to assume the Coens come from an agnostic perspective (evidenced by their parodies of orthodoxy in *A Serious Man*), I think that they nevertheless hold a kind of detached, though spritely humored, reverence for the religious dimension. For them, the universe is always unjust and unevenly distributed, however much human beings are obsessed with "the rules" (see Walter in *Lebowski*, who constantly addresses rules, whether in bowling or Jewish orthodoxy) or fairness. In *The Big Lebowski*, even the Nihilists lament how things aren't "fair." Just as there are causal consequences for actions, there are sometimes *unjust* consequences as well. The Angel of Death and Judgment, manifested by Anton Chigurh in *No Country*, Randall "Tex" Cobb in *Raising Arizona*, the pursuing Poseidon-like lawman in *O Brother*, or Hashem in *A Serious Man*, comes for all without mercy and sometimes without warning and logic. The Coens' world is not a godless one, as we see in other existentialists, but is the Hebrew School terrain of the jealous and unpredictable Yahweh.

Though *A Serious Man* is the most blatantly philosophical religious film they've made, *The Big Lebowski* may cut the deepest to a spiritual sensibility because of my aforementioned consolations. It has a sense of mercy that makes it a little more New Testament than Old. It accepts the ineffable grace of things in a more peaceable way than *A Serious Man*, *No Country*, or the ambiguities that conclude *Raising Arizona*, *Fargo*, or *True Grit*, or the sardonic farce of *The Ladykillers*. In *True Grit*, Mattie gets her revenge on Tom Chaney, but at the unequal cost of losing her arm, her beloved horse Little Blackie, her hired hands suffering injuries, and the sight of several corpses, many of whom would still be alive had she not been so resolute in seeking her vengeance (and when we finally meet the half-wit Chaney, the audience is meant to ask, "We've come all this way for *this* guy?")

But then there's The Dude and the Zen of Lebowski. Bearded with long hair, The Dude's appearance immediately points to an iconographic Christ quality which many of us may unwittingly project onto him, aided by the film's subtexts. To be sure, *The Big Lebowski* is as inspiring to quote for its own fans as the Gospels are for evangelicals. The Stranger (Sam Elliott) wants us to go home comforted with the simple truth, "The Dude abides," noting, "I take comfort in that. The Dude. Taking it easy for all us sinners." This rather explicitly ties the Christ allusion together. In times of peril we pray and lean on the everlasting arms, and those "everlasting" arms here are those of The Dude, who takes 'er easy as the world titters on an unsteady beam of possible catastrophe, preparing to drink his White Russians as he listens to George Bush's grave warning, "This will not stand, this will not stand, this aggression against Kuwait." He's ten days late on his rent, but still "takes 'er easy."

The challenge of religion and art is to find meaning between the horror of nothingness on one hand, and crass materialism on the other; in portraying the faint flickers of compassion between its lonely losers, this is what *The Big Lebowski* achieves. The film is set in a spiritually-starved wasteland, echoing the biblical Sodom and Gomorrah myth or medieval Arthurian romance. The Stranger's opening lines identify the setting as Los Angeles, and how "they call it the city of angels," but adding, "I didn't find it to be that exactly." It's a spiritual ghost town, glimmering in electric lights, money, and flesh, but otherwise shallow, synthesized, and malnourished. It's a garden of lost hopes, where the angels aren't "exactly" angels, and Jesus is not a Christ of compassion, but the pederast bowler, Jesus Quintana. The labels are the *opposite* of their true nature, just as The Big Lebowski is not an honest man who has achieved much, but is an embezzler living on an allowance. Jesus Quintana is The Dude's double in vying to be a Christ-figure, referring to himself in the third person (The Dude, The Jesus), but instead of exhibiting easy-going grace, he is an aggressor who wants to "fuck you in the ass," in the parlance of our times.

We hear this phrase elsewhere through the movie – "fuck you in the ass" – and it is a reference to achieving power over other people. The Nihilists say it repeatedly ("I fuck you! I fuck you in the ass!"), and Walter accosts rich 12-year-old "brat" Larry Sellers, whom he believes has done something similar to him (or "them," being that Walter always seems to make The Dude's problems – and goods – *their* problems and goods): "Do you see what happens *when you fuck a stranger in the ass!!!???*" The demonic figures of *Lebowski* have an aggressive and assaulting sexuality, unlike the film's protagonists. When The Dude, afraid of the Nihilists' castrating threats, laments that he doesn't need sympathy but that he needs his "johnson," Donny innocently asks, "What do you need that for, Dude?" In this city of lost angels, there are "compulsive fornicators" who engage in sex all the time "but without joy." The Big Lebowski, himself impotent, lacks "a pair of testicles" that would make him a man; he sublimates his frustration in taking more than his fair share, including a nympho trophy wife. One could argue that Walter is a violent force, though his aggression is a logical response in relation to "the rules" ("Smokey, this is not Nam, it's bowling. There are rules," he says to his bowling rival shortly before pulling out a piece). He is not at all like Jesus Quintana or the Nihilists who are power-bent in their rampant lust. For whereas Walter's warnings of "entering a world of pain" relate to keeping the rules in check so that our freedoms can be maintained, the Nihilists' Autobahn album *Nagelbett*, or "Bed of Nails" features rapey song titles like "Saturation," "Hit and Run," "Violate U Blue," "Beg Me," and "Take It In." The electro-pornographer Treehorn, meanwhile, sketches inexplicable drawings of figures with enormous erections. There is no explanation: fucking is arbitrary but ubiquitous. It is nihilistic.

Also note the music playing behind Jesus Quintana. It's a Gipsy Kings cover of the Eagles' "Hotel California," a song which is – according to lyric-interpreting legend – set in Hell, though it is confused for Heaven ("This could be heaven or this could be hell"), much like the film's introduction of Los Angeles ("They call Los Angeles the city of Angels. I didn't find it to be that exactly.") Jesus Quintana is the Anti-*Christ*, or damned Satan of the wasteland (like Milton's Satan, he has been condemned for his assaulting pederast crimes, having to go door-to-door, a prisoner in hell much like the protagonist of "Hotel California"). And of course, the Eagles have a dual connotation for The Dude, as we hear him drunkenly tell his cab driver, whom we can assume is a Don Henley and Glen Frey fan, "Man, I've had a rough night and I *hate* the fucking Eagles!" even though The Dude's credo is the title of another Eagles' song, "Take It Easy." The irreligious irony of Jesus Quintana's name is reinforced when he yells at Walter, an observant Jew, for demanding that a semifinal bowling match be rescheduled because of Shabbos: "What's this 'day of rest' shit!? It don't matter to Jesus!" Perhaps Jesus Quintana is representative of an orthodox kind of religion that has no final interest in the serious and humble reflection on religion's concepts, which is the theme of *A Serious Man* where the man *socially* labeled the "serious man" (Sy Abelman, probably cinema's greatest douchebag in years) is anything but "serious" when compared to the "frivolous" Larry Gopnik.

The *real* Jesus is The Dude, who like Christ has stepped out of his rooted, earthly function to assume a transcendent one. As Paul says about Jesus in *The Last Temptation of Christ*, "He was not the son of Mary and Joseph, he was the son of *God*." Similarly, the Stranger explains The Dude as someone who never had a use for the name his parents gave him ("Jeff Lebowski"). Instead of assuming the position of Jesus *Christ* he is Jesus *Dude*. He insists that he's *not* Jeffrey Lebowski: "I'm The Dude! You know, so that's what you call me. You know, that or His Dudeness, or Duder, or El Duderino if you're not into the whole brevity thing." (This is curious when we relate The Dude to Walter, who has also rejected his origins as a Polish Catholic and identified himself as an observant Jew – one of the major religions that has no interest in conversion being that it's a system one is *born* into; Walter too has some transcendent function, flying above his earthly roots as a spiritual individual). And though the Stranger says The Dude "takes it easy" for all us sinners, he often suffers for the sins of others. *The Big Lebowski* opens with The Dude being accosted by two Treehorn thugs (baptized if you will, as he's dunked into a toilet) looking for the millionaire Lebowski, whose wife owes Treehorn a "sizeable debt." Duder's rug, his Zen (it ties the room together), is peed on by the thugs. That happening - his Zen peed on - he, like Jesus, must participate and suffer in the world of men. The Dude's hallucination of flying reflects his daily disposition, chasing the mysterious Maude on her floating carpet over Los Angeles. Bowling represents the never-ending cycle of pins falling and rising, so it fits that the heavy bowling ball that emerges in The Dude's grip should plummet him back to the world of men.

As we see The Dude suffering for the sins of others, whether it's Walter's idiocy, the machinations of The Big Lebowski, the trophy wife Bunny, Maude, Treehorn, Larry Sellers, etc, we observe how the world is unjust. We hear the phrase: "Do you see what happens?" It's what the carpet pissers tell The Dude when they accuse his wife of owing money. The Dude is so clueless that when he says, "My wife? Do you see a wedding ring?" he is lifting up the wrong hand. "Do you see what happens?" is much more memorably repeated over and over when Walter loses his cool with Larry Sellers, who stole The Dude's car and Lebowski's money – and has bought a Corvette with it. "Do you see what happens *when you fuck a stranger in the ass!?*" yells Walter, taking a crowbar to the Corvette with Larry and The Dude looking on. But it turns out the Corvette belongs to an unfortunate fat man who lives next door. "I just bought the fucking car last week! My baby!" he cries, taking Walter's crowbar to The Dude's junker. "I kill your fucking car!" he yells, this being another one of the film's very uneven exchanges. The Dude – and his car – becomes a victim once again (his car is his own gas guzzling double: it crashes, it's shot, it's stolen, it's slept in and crapped in by a vagrant, it crashes again, and finally the Nihilists burn it up). Later, the Nihilists complain that "it's not fair," when they can't collect their ransom money after sacrificing the toe of a girlfriend to double as Bunny's. Even the prophets of nothingness and absurdity can't wrap their heads around an unfair universe where causality doesn't cleanly work out. "Do you see what happens?" becomes a tidy Coen joke of retribution repeated in its various degrees and rationalities in *Raising Arizona, O Brother, No Country, The Man Who Wasn't There, The Ladykillers, A Serious Man,* and *True Grit*.

The Coens told their collaborators in the art department that the Treehorn sequence was to have a "sacrificial" holy rite atmosphere. The Dude's meeting with Treehorn is like the mythological hero's descent into the lower depths of Hell, confronting the devil, a weaver of electronic media's pornographic entertainment and dehumanization (The Dude, on the other hand, "still jerks off manually.") It's the dark night of the soul, where a spiked drink leads The Dude to pass out and have an acid flashback. "There was no bottom," the Stranger narrates about this scene, indicating that this is the deep vortex of the unconscious, the Mind (such as Kenny Rogers will sing about, and such as Jackie Treehorn wishes to control with nihilistic electricity).

There are strictures, borders, cliques, etc in the god-forsaken world of lost angels and walking ghosts with dreams as faded as their bowling clothes. The Big Lebowskis with their halls of achievement will always be taken care of, embezzling money when they can't afford their trophy wives anymore. The Maude Lebowskis of the world are just as hollow, art-snobs committed to the snide form of their presentation instead of the human content of symbolic communication and sympathy. Though cultured, Maude lacks any of the enthusiasm that The Dude still has for his CCR tapes. The same gigantic scissors the Nihilists hold in *Gutterballs* are seen in Maude's art, indicating that her art has a similar castrating – or sterile – function. The electrically streamlined Los Angeles, so far from Bunny's innocent origins on a "farm outside of Moorhead, Minnesota," manufactures images and music that the masses will consume and re-simulate, like the acid-flashback production of *Gutterballs*.

Whether the manufacturer is Jackie Treehorn ("wave the future, 100% electronic erotic software") or is *Branded* writer Arthur Digby Sellers (who is more machine than man in his iron lung), the entertainment producers signify something post-human and technological, estranged from any manual or analog function. An offer for a Bunny Lebowski blow-job is a purely economic matter for the porn-star ("I'll suck your cock for a thousand dollars"), which leads The Dude to contemplate going to a "cash machine." Nihilism is the synthesized electricity in entertainment production. Interestingly, in *Logjammin*, Karl Hungus – the key Nihilist – has the function of "fixing the cable." Compare this joylessness to The Dude's rejuvenation after seeing the "good and *thorough*" doctor of Maude, who must have a good report on Duder's potency and venereal health. Driving exuberantly home to CCR's "Looking Out My Back Door" after his good doctor's office visit, a lot of viewers may find affinity with The Dude. We can understand why he'd be so protective of his healthy johnson, which almost gets singed by The Dude's lit joint, extinguished by his celebratory beverage.

"Someone the Square Community Won't Give a Shit About"

The Big Lebowski is then, if about so many other damned things, interested in the simulacrum of culture, and beings existing and identifying themselves within that simulacrum. This is also what the response to *The Big Lebowski* is about. Some viewers who dislike the film and scoff at its posthumous success credit the 19 and 20-year-old collegiate male pot-heads, surely so much like The

Dude whenever he drafted the original Port Huron Statement. We can therefore conveniently deride *The Big Lebowski* as being little more than a "stoner" cult film, and if not that, a silly R-rated comedy like *Caddyshack* or *Animal House*, and therefore we can steal away any sense of meaningful subtext in the film.

But we know the film has a much more diversified fanbase than its smug critics would like to admit, though the potheads *are* admittedly there. Fan bases are always more disagreeable than the merits of whatever work is in question. *The Godfather* films are the favorite of both Ayn Randian businessmen and imperial neocons, who have no inclination of private enterprise's tragedy that Coppola and Puzo are depicting; whiny goths love *Blue Velvet* for its dark curves only, seeing small-town satire but completely missing the multiplicity of David Lynch's life affirming hues; *A Clockwork Orange, Taxi Driver*, and *Pulp Fiction* all have an immense base of impassioned if undesirable viewers (some even political assassins) emulating the heroes' isolation, and in love with cool wickedness and far-out post-modern posturing, to say nothing of extreme portrayals of sex and violence; *GoodFellas* has a lot of love from fraternity douchebags who are delighted by portrayals of male aggression; *Scarface* and *The Godfather* are adored by violent drug dealers and gang members; *The Conformist* is adulated by stuffy and snobby cocktail-party walking mannequins and social butterflies, not unlike Maude Lebowski and Knox Harrington; and *Citizen Kane* is the default favorite movie of fuddy-duddys who tiresomely rail bullshit like "they don't make 'em like they used to." Personally, all of these films – *The Godfather* trilogy, *Blue Velvet, A Clockwork Orange, Taxi Driver, Pulp Fiction, GoodFellas, The Conformist, Citizen Kane* (and in a guilty way, *Scarface*) – rank among my favorites, and I've probably had friends in each listed category of hard-to-like social types (aside from the violent gangsters or political assassins) – all of whom are portrayed to some degree within *The Big Lebowski*, attesting to how vibrantly the Coens capture the multiplicity of pop culture and consumption. And though I've had my own frustrations with high-as-a-kite "goddamned hippies," as Eric Cartman calls them on *South Park*, I'd rather spend some hours with these folks than the ones I've just listed. Like The Dude, they often take 'er easy, and aren't so quick to judge.

Popular Culture is all about judgments, however, and we have those fixed ideas of what constitutes good art and design. *Fargo*, for its eccentricities, still had the pedigree of a major "Academy Award Nominee," while *The Big Lebowski* seemed to not. This kind thinking inevitably leads to films like *The King's Speech, Dances With Wolves, Forrest Gump, Gladiator, A Beautiful Mind*, etc., winning major awards, while one could argue that the *mise-en-scène* of *The Big Lebowski* is vastly more complex. Pay close attention to the art direction, costumes, cinematography, and music, all of which are excellent. Dismissers of *The Big Lebowski* aren't so different from the title character, who is probably hostile to The Dude because of his appearance (had The Dude been a presentable and successful citizen, I think Jeffrey Lebowski would have compensated him, which is the bizarre logic of the world), or Maude, who is at first interested to learn that The Dude had a brief stint in the music business, but then passes judgment on him when he explains that he was "a roadie for Metallica."

The Coens are quick to social identities, which is why they take delight in anticipating criticism in their screenplay introductions by fabricated film scholars and the cantankerous Roderick Jaynes, and other instances where they give readers fake interviews and biographies. The special edition DVDs of *Blood Simple* and *The Big Lebowski* have introductions by an invented film restorer, Mortimer Young, who is approaching senility, the former DVD even having a full-length commentary by a pompous Forte-Bowell type critic. Critics who aren't hip to the Coens reflexivity are then put-off when they encounter entertainers who are Academy Award winners that don't shy away from sophomoric jokes involving "soggy bottom boys" (*O Brother*) irritable bowel syndrome (J.K. Simmons' tragic affliction in *The Ladykillers*), or my favorite, a mouth-breathing kid scrawling the word "FART" in crayon on the McDonoughs' wall (*Raising Arizona*).

All cultural labels are just noise, and so there's something more commendable to Walter's Vietnam nostalgia, The Dude's perpetual adolescence, or Marty's dance routine than to Maude's abstract art for art's sake, which seems so distant from real life. Unlike Marty's quintet, Maude's art lacks passion. Sure, she enjoys sex – but it's just "a natural *zesty* enterprise," or something done just for conception ("What did you think this was about? Fun and games?"). The Dude and company remain outsiders, strikes and gutters abound, sometimes eating the bear ("bar") and sometimes the bear eating them. The pins are once again set up to be toppled, perpetually without end.

The Big Lebowski, through all of its suffering, uncertainty, unfairness, and dismembered toes, is about friendship (made delicious by "funny stuff," as the Nihilists say). Walter, The Dude, and Donny don't really have sentimental warm moments and insult each other in a hierarchy (The Dude yells at Walter; Walter is abusive to Donny; Donny doesn't say much of anything). Donny's unfortunate death by heart attack leads to the poignantly hilarious scene when Walter scatters the ashes, held in a Folger's coffee can (the mortuary urn was too expensive). We finally hear the only biographical details of this perpetually silenced character ("Shut the *fuck* up, Donny!") We learn that he was once a surfer who loved the outdoors – "and bowling" – which further connects Walter to John Milius, himself a surfing enthusiast, as we see in *Apocalypse Now*. Both Walter and Donny have California surfer accents, making us think about how physically robust, promising, and carefree they probably were in their youth. And now Donny returns to the shores of the Pacific Ocean, which he "loved so well." *The Big Lebowski* is the presentation of a life cycle, like the one that the landlord Marty performs as the *Pictures at the Exhibition* dance quintet. The tragicomic lives shown in the film make us recall the placard at the mortuary, quoting Psalms 103.15-17: "As for man, his days are as grass / As a flower of the field, so he flourisheth / For the wind passeth over it, and it is gone."

And also like Marty's cycle, there's room for absurdity. Walter eulogizes Donny, but makes it a eulogy for his own lost past, bringing his buddy's death back to Vietnam. "These young men gave their lives," he says proudly of his buddies before bringing the eulogy back to Donny. "Goodnight sweet prince," he says, emptying the coffee can. The wind carries the ashes away from the Pacific and straight onto the bemused Dude. He calls Walter a "fucking travesty" and an asshole, but he surrenders to an embrace, as Walter meekly apologizes, holding The Dude close. We understand that these two men might only have each other. "Fuck it, Dude. Let's go bowling."

There's virtually no cheap sappiness between the characters, and yet *The Big Lebowski* conveys great tenderness. The audience has grown familiar and warm to these characters over time. Like Shakespeare's concoctions, or Cervantes' Don Quixote and Sancho Panza, The Dude and Walter have assumed their own identities beyond the text. Few fictional creations are as *alive*. There's a beautiful *familiarity* to *The Big Lebowski*, as a movie about common people living day to day, paycheck to paycheck, often late on their rent, spending time in bowling alleys, seeing their friends' concerts, smoking up occasionally, having a drink, listening to and disappearing in music, and just trying to get their own little piece of the pie in a world where the goods are too unevenly distributed, while their dreams have passed by. We're all Lebowskis ("I'm a Lebowski, You're a Lebowski … "), and even The Big Lebowski, after his evil schemes have been uncovered, is afforded a moment of pity, as Walter's dog licks the old man's weeping face.

We all suffer, some of us more than others, but there's still an inexpressible thing to our experience of life in friendship, leisure, and sacrifice. The Dude abides. Townes Van Zandt's cover of "Dead Flowers" is the perfect ending for the picture, where the singer paints two worlds, one rich ("silk upholstered chair, talking to some rich folks that you know") and one poor ("ragged company"), where the poor guy asks only for dead flowers, and in exchange will still lay roses on the rich girl's grave: an absurd gesture of uneven distribution. But that's The Dude, our representative man taking it easy and reminding us that the whole human comedy, in all of its absurdity, death, and rebirth, will perpetuate and roll on like the tumbling tumbleweed, in spite of wars, disastrous upheaval, and disappointed dreams. *The Big Lebowski* is a subtle expression of how we may catch brief glimpses of feeling sympathy and love for one another, referring to a cycle of unjust destruction where maybe there's still something everlasting and steadfast.

....

Niles Schwartz writes the film column for L'Etoile Magazine (letoilemagazine.com) and blogs at nilesfilmfiles.blogspot.com. He can also be heard Thursday nights on WCCO/CBS radio as the film dude for celebrated talk personality T.D. Mischke. Though he occasionally has a rash, he can't complain. He lives in Minnesota.

Dan J.S. Webb, *Rug*

"What Makes a Man, Mr. Lebowski?": Masculinity Under (Friendly) Fire in Ethan and Joel Coen's *The Big Lebowski*

BY JAKUB KAZECKI

Quentin Curtis remarks in his review of *The Big Lebowski* that "you have always the feeling in Coens' films that the works are not so much thought out, intellectually, as doodled over coffee and doughnuts – pieces of fooling around rather than tracts on human nature [. . .] Comic genius of the Coens' order is for enjoyment rather than analysis" (Curtis).

One can argue about whether a movie made for the enjoyment of the audience (as an artistic by-product of the apparently childish behavior of the Coen brothers) and a motion picture that can easily undergo a critical analysis (as would be expected from "grown up" filmmakers) are really two opposite and exclusive directions along which we have to orient our thoughts about the movie. In this article, I hope to show that *The Big Lebowski* is not so "analysis-resistant" or "analysis-proof" as most film critics would like to see it. I want to investigate the subversive effect of humor and laughter on the masculinity models presented in the movie and to demonstrate that the humor challenges the heterosexual gender norm supported and confirmed by popular American film genres and by the star system developed in the 1930s and 1940s in Hollywood's dream factory.

To introduce the term "masculinity models," it is necessary to remark that the dominant discourses surrounding gender and sexuality are not only reflected and mediated by film and other cultural forms, but are also directly shaped by these forms. Film's contribution was especially significant to the shaping of masculinity and femininity models. The cinema's power lies in its special position between the audience's fantasies and lived experience: it depicts the reality in depersonalized, consumable form, which allows the recognition of the self and identification with the person on the screen, at the same time at which it serves as a projection of a desired, idealized "self" in an "other" who serves as a cultural model.

The representational system offered by American film, which developed rapidly from the early 1920s, divided human practices shown on screen into "masculine" and "feminine" characteristics, offering certain cultural models of "masculinity" and "femininity" through the actors and actresses in leading roles. The main accents have been, however, put on the male protagonists, around which most American movie plots revolve. Steven Cohan and Ina Rae Hark argue in their essay collection *Exploring Masculinities in Hollywood Cinema* that movies have always served as one of the primary sites through which the social construction of masculinity has been hidden from view in American culture (3). Masculinity is perceived by the wider film audience as a stable, universal and unchanging essence and not as a construction, as an effect of culture or as a performance.

In American cinema, masculinity has been driven by the classical Hollywood fiction film, which, according to Frank Krutnik, "tends to pivot around individual characters, their emotions, desires and actions" while they are engaged within and defined through two basic lines of action: the adventure story, and the heterosexual love affair (4). The development of film genres can be connected to the changing balance between those two components in different movies. The changes were forced by the wishes of the audience, which wanted to see its hero in more "romantic" situations or to see more "adventure" for the male hero to test his masculinity in different ways. The popularity of certain narrative solutions (manifested in box office results) created an impulse to repeat the formula, the particular combination and articulation of elements that appeared to be successful for specific, historically-situated audiences. As a result, filmmakers developed sets of narrative procedures and stylistic emphases which, along with the reoccurring presence of the same actor types, have been described as film genres. Along with the genres, certain masculinity models have been formed. Genres such as "western," "horror film," "crime thriller, "musical" or "romantic comedy," to name just a few, have been established in the practices of American cinema. Thomas Sobchak, in his essay "Genre Film: A Classical Experience" notes that "consciously or unconsciously, both the genre filmmaker and the genre audiences are aware of the prior films and the way in which each of these concrete examples is an attempt to embody once again the essence of a well-known story" (103). The awareness of the genre tradition, whether the set of genre characteristics is recognized and systematized or not, is the key to fulfilling the expectations of the audience – or to playing with them. The results of the play, however, may vary.

It seems to me that in the case of *The Big Lebowski*, the Coen brothers get involved in a risky play with film genres well known to the audience. The fact that the movie has not been received very warmly by both moviegoers and critics because of its apparent "emptiness" and "narcissism," for its being mainly about "its own cleverness" (McCarthy), and the difficulties of categorizing it into one specific film genre, are, in my opinion, worth a detailed investigation. What genres does *The Big Lebowski* jump between, confusing the audience and, through their multiplicity, posing the possibility of multiple and alternative masculinity models?

Before I try to shed some light on the cross-genre character of the movie, I would like to make an observation on the film narrative. The plot of *The Big Lebowski* does not reflect the narrative structure typical of American motion pictures, where the male hero, through his own actions, successfully overcomes the unbalance of the narrative caused by the initial atrocious deeds of a villain. Roger Ebert in the *Chicago Sun-Times* hits the nail right on the head by noticing that "[s]ome may complain [that] *The Big Lebowski* rushes in all directions and never ends up anywhere. That isn't the film's flaw, but its style" (Ebert 37). The "rushing in all directions" can be noticed already in the first sequences of the movie: against a music background provided by Sons of the Pioneers, The Dude (played by Jeff Bridges), is accompanied by the voiceover – the cowboy-narrator The Stranger (Sam Elliott) – on his way to the supermarket. The narrator, rambling nonsensically and losing his "train of thought" quite often, introduces The Dude in a way that may suggest that his story portrays "a cowboy's opium dream of life at the end of the trail" (Bergan 189). Is The Dude, as a successor of the pioneers, a hero of westerns who has found his quiet place after a troubled life in the West, going to be bothered by evildoers and forced to fight them again? That's what the narrator's introduction, combined with the soundtrack and camera work (long panoramic shots of L.A. at sunset), seems to imply.

Next, The Dude is attacked in his own apartment and his head is repeatedly submerged in the toilet. Even when subjected to brutal violence, the main character retains his laid-back attitude and makes cocky comments which promise the audience a hero who is a strong individualist with an ironic sense of humor, like Chandleresque PIs. This type of male hero is characterized by Frank Krutnik as dominant in the "male suspense thriller," a subcategory of *film noir*. According to Krutnik, the hero emerges from the position of marked inferiority against both the criminals and the police and seeks to restore his secure superior position by solving the mystery (86). This type of male hero can lose everything and not care (and The Dude is introduced as such by the narrator in the opening sequence), but he still keeps his wit and intelligence. The illusion that we will follow the Philip Marlowe of the 1990s (the movie is set at the time of the Gulf War in 1991), and the hope that we will see a modern variation of *The Big Sleep* ends soon, however, after a series of events over which The Dude has no control and – even worse – which remain incomprehensible to him to the very end. His bold assumptions and theories about the kidnapping plot are revealed as false, or at least unexplained, one after another. The closing movie sequence finds The Dude exactly at the same point at which he found himself at the beginning of the story: completely satisfied with his life (unlike the hero in Chandler's stories), because his "aim in life, the goal to which he moves and the hope which sustains him" is not the "unraveling of obscure crimes, the final solution of which affords him little or no satisfaction" (Houseman 161). His repetitious and failed attempts to explain the complicated plot to his friends, his moments of illusionary glory when he thinks he sees clearly the motives of the other characters involved in the fake kidnapping, and his failures as an enthusiastic but amateurish detective, negate the image of an active hero typical for the *film noir* genre, such as – to follow the Coens' fascination with Chandler – Humphrey Bogart or Robert Mitchum's characters in both main-stream Hollywood adaptations of *The Big Sleep* (Howard Hawks' film from 1946 and Michael Winner's from 1978). The audience will also never get an answer to the main question of the mystery – who took the million dollars – which remains unresolved, as do so many "why" questions.

The inconsistencies in the narrative patterns are not accidental, however. According to Joel and Ethan Coen, the idea of the movie was to create the plot as "a Chandler kind of story – how it moves episodically, and deals with the characters trying to unravel a mystery. As well as having a hopelessly complex plot that's ultimately unimportant" (Stone). In another interview about the movie, Ethan Coen expresses his vision of Jeff Bridges' character: "It just seemed interesting to us to thrust that character into the most confusing situation possible, the person, it would seem, on the face of it least equipped to deal with it" (Leyland). The two masculinity models presented in the opening scenes of the movie, the cowboy who gave up his bloody work and the private investigator in the urban jungle, typical for the American western and *film noir*, despite audience's expectations, are just not the measure of The Dude's actions. What the director and writer of the movie judge as "interesting" is the confrontation of the "masculine" developed and re-produced by the American movies with the male figure in their movie, who, due to external circumstances, happens to be the protagonist and carrier of the narrative. Jeff Lebowski, as a "man of inaction" (Robson 189), is not acting in the sense of the typical male protagonists – he is being acted upon. He is always one step behind his counterparts. And the audience laughs at his belief that he keeps up with them.

The comic effect appears to be the element that is mentioned most repeatedly in reviews of the movie.

Although complaining about the genre inconsistency of *The Big Lebowski*, most critics approve of its humorous effect, even if, according to some of them, the laughter does not last for long (Matthew Sweet, Alexander Walker). When looking at Jeff Lebowski, the questions of what makes him funny, of what causes the comic effect and what is the relation between the comic and masculinity models in the cinema seem to be legitimate.

Comedy is often developed in situations where both male and female characters do not measure up to cultural expectations for their gender. In other words, if the physical appearance and the actions of the characters do not comply with the normative image for their gender in the specific circumstances conditioned by the culture, they can induce laughter. In his *Philosophy of Laughter and Humor*, John Morreall offers a cognitive theory of laughter, in which laughter results from the encounter with many types of incongruous situations (Morreall 188-205). In his view, the human reactions to incongruity can be organized into three different groups. The first group contains negative emotions, like fear, anger, disgust, and sadness, the second puzzlement with the experience, and the third humorous, pleasurable laughter. The incongruity is a subjectively perceived deviation from the consistency of the world structure. The contrast between our expectations (the understanding of the world needed for physical survival) and the event that does not fit into the "normal state of things," can be experienced as dangerous. Negative emotions and puzzlement are reactions that motivate us to resolve aberrations, e.g. through escape, aggression or the adoption of the new occurrence into our knowledge about the world. Humorous laughter, on the other hand, allows us to enjoy situations which do not threaten our physical survival, at the same time stimulating our ability to deal with newness in the future. Thus, laughter has a subversive function: it allows questioning and overthrowing the norm, and adopting the exception in the changed world view. According to Morreall, there is also another situation possible in which we can burst into laughter. When the overwhelming nature of the incongruent situation makes action completely impossible, we can overcome the unpleasurable experience over which we have no influence and turn it into its opposite: a pleasure accessible through the sublimation of the negative impulse – Nietzsche's "'slaves' joy at the Saturnalia" (137), when the forces of nature, potentially dangerous, do not cause any harm.

What Morreall understands only in a narrow, biological sense (incongruity allows the human being to deal with the impulses from the outside world and, in consequence, to physically survive), can be also applied to the type of incongruous situations we encounter in *The Big Lebowski*. The "normal state of things" is created by the Hollywood representational system, with its various film genres. As mentioned before, within the framework of a specific genre, the audience expects certain narrative solutions based on the combination and articulation of story components, stylistic emphases and gender models. The genres as "systems of orientations, expectations and conventions that circulate between industry, text and subject" (Neale 19) are the structure that constitutes the viewer's secure position. To this position belongs the genre's treatment of the "masculine," which reflects broader ideological constructions of gender that inform and often determine certain attitudes and behaviors in society. The constructed character of masculinity is, according to Judith Butler, not recognized as such and hidden from the viewer:

> [. . .] acts and gestures, articulated and enacted desires create the illusion of an interior and organizing gender core, an illusion discursively maintained for the purposes of the regulation of sexuality within the obligatory frame of reproductive heterosexuality. If the "cause" of desire, gesture, and act can be localized within the "self" of the actor, then the political regulations and disciplinary practices which produce that ostensibly coherent gender are effectively displaced from view. The displacement of a political and discursive origin of gender identity onto a psychological "core" precludes an analysis of the political constitution of the gendered subject and its fabricated notions about the ineffable interiority of its sex or of its true identity. (Butler 136)

One of the most important sources of humor in the Coens' comedy is the confrontation between the actions of the male protagonists and the dominant ideological constructions of masculinity, which are marked by numerous allusions to and visual references from movies belonging to different film genres. The audience's – the male audience's – laughter is the laughter at the "other" visible on the screen, the viewer's gender identity is not directly threatened. Nevertheless, the viewer recognizes that the masculinity models promoted by the representational conventions of American cinema can, and in fact are, subverted by his laughter. The Coens initiate a cognitive process: they present The Dude as the hero of a cowboy saga or a detective in the big city only to later destroy the anticipated narration scheme and aesthetic choices. The laughing viewer goes through the process of acknowledging that the masculinity can be constructed through (re)acting in various historical and social contexts. The cowboy Stranger sitting in the bowling hall in Los Angeles in the early 1990s and talking to The Dude about the ever-changing course of life ("Wal, a wiser fella than m'self once said, sometimes you eat the bar and sometimes the bar, wal, he eats you") looks indeed strange, talks strangely and gives the impression that he originates from a different movie (as a matter of fact, the actor playing the Stranger, Sam Elliott, whose physical type predestines him to play in westerns, asked the Coens on the set of *The Big Lebowski*, "What am I doing in THIS movie?") (Robson 176). His inappropriate presence in the movie surprises the viewer and distorts the narrative flow. His connection to the narrative remains unexplained. His character proves, however, that, if his appearance is rather misplaced, "borrowed" from another film genre, other male figures can be as strange as he is, if not in this particular movie, then in another. For *The Big Lebowski* there is no advocated masculinity model, for in another time, or in another place of narration, the "normal" patterns of behavior marked as masculine can be questioned, subverted and, eventually, compromised. Judith Butler notes in *Gender Trouble* that thinking in relative terms about the "normal" gender behavior can cause amusement:

> The loss of the sense of the normal, however, can be its own occasion for laughter, especially when "the normal," "the original" is revealed to be a copy, and an inevitably failed one, an ideal that no one can embody. In this sense, laughter emerges in the realization that all along the original was derived. (138-139)

Similarly, the audience laughs at the beaten-up hero, The Dude, and the rambling Stranger, and comprehends that "being a real man" is performed, is re(acted) after an ideal that is formed through discursive practices, and can be freely taken out of context.

The Stranger fulfills another important function in the movie. Along with the wide-angle lenses, the visual allusions, the soundtrack and the period setting, the character of the cowboy helps to create distance between the viewer and the narrative. His comments frame the events on the screen; he interrupts the course of action and prevents the viewer from emotionally engaging in the unraveling story, stressing the fact that the occasionally dramatic action was just a story told to amuse the viewer, not to make the male hero more popular. "Wal, uh hope you folks enjoyed yourselves," he summarizes the movie, setting up the distance to the viewed picture.

The range of masculinity models presented in *The Big Lebowski* is not limited to the heroes of film noir and western. The Coen brothers describe their work as "in a strange way, kind of a buddy movie" (Lowe 163) and the figure constellation reflects the intention to put the men in the foreground: two main male characters, The Dude and Walter Sobchak (John Goodman), accompanied by Donny (Steve Buscemi). Walter, a war veteran, lives in the reality shaped by the Vietnam conflict. His aggressiveness and the tendency to take command in every social interaction, along with his never-ending references to the long-past war against which he measures every aspect of life, place him in the lineage of the well-built, loud and violent action heroes of war movies. The masculinity model represented by Walter supposedly fits into the specific time and place, in the United States during the Gulf War: as a reference, a speech by George Bush is shown on TV when The Dude passes by, while Walter quotes from official political rhetoric in the course of action ("This aggression will not stand!", "I'm talking about drawing a line in the sand, Dude!"). Walter's manly behavior is tested, however, in circumstances that have nothing to do with battlefield situations, far from the jungle of 'Nam: he is putting up his gun in the bowling hall, provoked by a minor violation of game rules by another player, and he calls for constitutional rights to use cuss words in the family diner. His repetitive references to the war and confrontational attitude are out of place (and out of time) in the 1990s. The US has supposedly recovered after the failure in Vietnam; in addition, the character of war has changed: war is now more technological, more impersonal, the war actions are watched mostly on TV, and the war hero has to change, too. Walter's manner of dealing with the world is turned into ridicule. When it eventually comes to a violent conflict between The Dude's bowling team and the "German nihilists," and the agon can take place, Walter fights in a way that contradicts martial arts. He throws a bowling ball at one of the opponents, hits another with a portable radio and bites off the ear of a third, in a gesture reminiscent of Mike Tyson and his unsporting violation of boxing rules in 1997. The style of this final challenge does not meet the engagement rules praised by him on another occasion: "I had an M16, Jacko, not an Abrams fucking tank. Just me and Charlie, man, eyeball to eyeball."

The one casualty of the bloody fight with the "Germans" is Donny, the best bowler of the three friends. He is not hit or wounded by the aggressors, nor does he hit anyone; he simply does not survive a heart attack caused by panic and fear. However, in his funeral speech, Walter compares Donny's death to the heroic sacrifices of combat:

> He died – he died as so many of his generation, before his time. In your wisdom you took him, Lord. As you took so many bright flowering young men, at Khe San and Lan Doc and Hill 364. These young men gave their lives. And Donny too. Donny who . . . who loved bowling.

The funeral scene is a bitter parody of the celebratory military and police funerals portrayed in mainstream Hollywood war movies, in action movies and in thrillers. Usually, the funeral of the protagonist's close friend constitutes one of the most important points in the narrative, motivating the male hero to take revenge on the villain. In the masculinity models presented by these genres, male grief, anger and memory are usually overcome by direct, assertive action which implies violence and brutality against the other. The Dude and Walter go bowling. And in the last scene of the movie we see The Dude relaxed and thinking only about the finals of the bowling league.

The Big Lebowski is often described primarily as a "movie about bowling." To categorize the film as a sport movie would be misleading, however. Although reviews of the film evaluate Donny as a "sportsman," the term has a different implication for bowling, a "not really physically taxing thing. You can be a slob and do it" (Lowe 164). Bowling, although present in Hollywood movies, has not been evaluated as a big spectacle or a field for the creation of a masculine model in which physical strength and a sense for tactics and competition play an important role – a direct successor of the ancient hunter. "Bowling is not a sport to feature greatly in movies, but it does have an image as the game for the "average Joe," good enough for Homer Simpson, for example" (Bergan 190). The audience reacts with laughter when Maude Lebowski, the millionaire's daughter, inquires after sex with The Dude for more details from his life, and asks him what he does for fun. "Bowl," answers The Dude, summarizing his achievements in a very short curriculum vitae. Being a bowler does not require the characteristics needed from a man in the production-oriented modern capitalist society.

The question of achievement appears many times in the movie, mostly in scenes with The Dude's namesake, Jeffrey Lebowski, called "The Big Lebowski," the millionaire from Pasadena. The two characters cannot communicate at all, because they speak two different idiolects. The millionaire despises The Dude's lifestyle, and stresses the role of achievement in a man's life. Wealth and successes in the realm of work are the measures of competence in being a man. The figure of The Big Lebowski is an example of a masculinity model in which achievement is equal to work production. The audience finds out much later that the masculine ability "to do the right thing," "to achieve," proudly expressed by the disabled millionaire, has to be demystified. He does not have any money; he inherited it through his wife.

From his wife, The Big Lebowski has also "inherited" Maude, a feminist artist (resembling the Fluxus painter and performer Carolee Schneeman), who invites The Dude to her loft and informs him that she is aware of the kidnapping of her stepmother, Bunny. She presents to the guest a film sequence that should convince him of the fake character of Bunny's abduction and low moral standards. The movie, called *Logjammin'*, is the Coens' parody of the porn movie genre. The distinct characteristic of the infamous genre is its emphasis on the visibility of male and female genitals. Being a man in a porn movie (like Karl Hungus, one of the "nihilists") means being able to demonstrate an erect penis and perform a sex act. In this context, Karl Hungus threatens The Dude in the worst possible way, for cutting off his penis would be an attempt to take away his masculinity. The audience identifies with the terrified Dude until Donny asks "What do you need that for, Dude?" – in fact, The Dude does not seem to require his penis to prove anything.

The number of male characters exposed in the movie is much greater than the few most important representatives I have described here. Worth noticing are also the figure of The Dude's landlord and Jesus Quintana, The Dude's bowling competitor. The landlord is a passionate modern dancer, although his physical type contradicts the ideal of dancer: in his white body stocking adorned with strategically placed foliage, gracelessly dancing a heroic part on the stage, he is the very incorporation of incongruity. Jesus, a talented bowler, enters the story as a dynamic macho, sexualizing the game (slow-motion shots of him scoring the maximum points are a visual celebration of the male body in motion). Not much later, the viewer hears from Walter that Jesus is a pedophile. His machismo is questioned, his performance at the bowling hall revealed to be just a show.

In all cases, the male characters of the movie are situated in time and place by the music they listen to and by the clothes they are wearing. Joel Coen describes the main idea behind setting up the figure constellation: "[A]ll the characters refer to the culture of thirty years ago, they are its aftermath and its mirror. [...]It's a contemporary movie about what's become of people who were formed and defined by that earlier period." (Ciment and Niogret 168). Different movie genres with their dominant masculinity models serve as inspiration for Joel and Ethan Coen: the brothers make a satirical comment on the male hero figures developed in American cinema. The viewer enjoys the incongruent confrontation between his expectations, shaped by his knowledge about cinema, and the realization of individual characters in *The Big Lebowski*. Thus, the Coens demonstrate that the masculinity models developed by the Hollywood movie industry are constructions rather than unchanging, coherent instances. This corresponds to what Butler has noted about the performative character of gender:

Gender ought not to be construed as a stable identity or locus of agency from which various acts follow; rather, gender is an identity tenuously constituted over time, instituted in an exterior space through a stylized repetition of acts. The effect of gender is produced through the stylization of the body and, hence, must be understood as the mundane way in which bodily gestures, movements, and styles of various kinds constitute the illusion of an abiding gendered self. (Butler 140)

"Well, you know, The Dude abides," confesses the male protagonist of *The Big Lebowski*, "the man for his time'n place," and the double meaning of his words best illustrates the arbitrary nature of all assumptions about him, about his masculinity and about all masculinity models in the movie.

Works Cited

Bergan, Ronald. *The Coen Brothers*. London: Orion, 2000. Print.

Butler, Judith P. *Gender Trouble: Feminism and the Subversion of Identity*. New York: Routledge, 1990. Print.

Carr, Jay. "Coens have fun with Lebowski." *The Boston Globe* 6 March 1998, sec. ARTS & FILM: D5. Print.

Ciment, Michel, and Hubert Niogret. "The Logic of Soft Drugs." *Joel & Ethan Coen: Blood Siblings*. Ed. Paul A. Woods. London: Plexus, 2000. 167-173. Print.

Coen, Joel. *"The Big Lebowski."* United States: Polygram Filmed Entertainment, 1998. 117. Ed. Ethan Coen. Print.

Cohan, Steven, and Ina Rae Hark. *Screening the Male: Exploring Masculinities in Hollywood Cinema*. London, New York: Routledge, 1993. Print.

Curtis, Quentin. "Review: The Big Lebowski." *The Daily Telegraph* 24 April 1998. Print.

Ebert, Roger. "Lebowski Big on Fun: Rambling Plot Is No Flaw in Coens' Latest." *Chicago Sun-Times* 6 March 1998, sec. Weekend Plus: 37. Print.

Houseman, John. "Today's Hero: A Review." *Hollywood Quarterly* 2.2 (1947): 161-163. Print.

Krutnik, Frank. *In a Lonely Street: Film Noir, Genre, Masculinity*. London, New York: Routledge, 1991. Print.

Leyland, Richard. "The Making of *The Big Lebowski*." United States: Polygram Filmed Entertainment Ltd., 1998. 25. Ed. Richard Leyland. Print.

Lowe, Andy. "The Brothers Crim." *Joel & Ethan Coen: Blood Siblings*. Ed. Paul A. Woods. London: Plexus, 2000. 162-166. Print.

McCarthy, Todd. *Review: The Big Lebowski*. 20 January 1998. *Daily Variety*. Available: http://www.variety.com/review/VE1117906660.html?categoryid=31&cs=1. 27 January 2012.

Morreall, John. *The Philosophy of Laughter and Humor*. Albany: State University of New York Press, 1987. Print.

Neale, Steve. *Genre*. London: BFI, 1980. Print.

Nietzsche, Friedrich Wilhelm. *Menschliches, Allzumenschliches: Ein Buch für freie Geister*. Ed. Peter Pütz. München: Goldmann, 1994. Print.

Robson, Eddie. *Coen Brothers*. London: Virgin, 2003. Print.

Rosen, Steven. "A Loser's Escapades the Lure of Lebowski." *The Denver Post* 6 March 1998, sec. WEEKEND: F-03. Print.

Sobchack, Thomas. "Genre Film: A Classical Experience." *Film Genre Reader II*. Ed. Barry Keith Grant. Austin: University of Texas Press, 1995. 102-113. Print.

Stone, Doug. *The Coens Speak (Reluctantly)*. 9 March 1998. *indieWire*. Available: http://www.indiewire.com/article/the_coens_speak_reluctantly. 27 January 2012.

Sweet, Matthew. "Cinema: The Poet Laureates of the Nothing-Much-at-All." *The Independent on Sunday*, sec. FEATURES: 6. Print.

Tatara, Paul. *Review:* Big Lebowski *Is Fun, But Won't Bowl You Over*. 5 March 1998. *CNN Interactive*. Available: http://www.cgi.cnn.com/SHOWBIZ/9803/05/review.big.lebowski/. 27 January 2012.

Verniere, James. "*Big Lebowski*: A High Time with Lowlifes." *The Boston Herald* 6 March 1998, sec. SCE: S03. Print.

Walker, Alexander. "Coppola Makes The Law Pay." *Evening Standard* 23 April 1998: 26. Print.

An earlier version of this chapter/article appeared in Revista Atenea, ISSN 0885-6079, Vol. 28.1, 2008

SPECIAL "COLOR IT YOURSELF PAGE"!

James Grange, *The Dude and His Rug*

Brian Diehl, *Lebowski Flag*

Who's the Nihilist Here?

BY TODD ALCOTT

I have been a fan of the Coen Bros since the first time I saw the trailer for *Blood Simple* back in 1984. I could tell that these guys had a way of looking at cinematic narrative that was different from anything else going. So when *The Big Lebowski* came out, right after *Fargo*, their best movie yet, I rushed out to see it opening weekend.

To my surprise, I didn't like it much. For a comedy it wasn't funny enough, for a mystery it wasn't satisfying. There was too much weirdness, not enough punch, I couldn't figure out what any of it meant. The cowboy, the dream sequences, the dotty peripheral characters, it just didn't gel for me.

But all Coen movies are worth seeing more than once, so when it came out on video I watched it again.

It still didn't work for me as a comedy, although it worked better. It worked better for me as a mystery, but not that much better. It seemed to me that the movie worked best as a study of an unlikely friendship, between two relics from the '60s, the foggy liberal and the hothead Vietnam vet. I still couldn't follow the mystery and of course it doesn't really matter. I shrugged and gave up on it.

But, you know, there's so much going on in it, so many details in it that stick out at weird angles. And a couple of years later I rented it again.

Suddenly, something clicked. And it's not mysterious, I'm not seeing things that aren't there, the movie comes right out and tells you what's on its mind, all you have to do is listen.

What does the cowboy (The Stranger, in a nod to Camus) say at the beginning? "Sometimes there's a man – he's the man for his time and place." And the characters are constantly talking about how things were in the past, and judging current events based on how they feel about the past. Around about the moment where The Dude says to Walter "Man, you're living in the past" and Walter screams "3000 years of tradition, from Moses to Sandy Koufax, you're goddamn right I'm living in the past!" and suddenly my hair stood on end, because a whole other layer of significance snapped into focus.

The Big Lebowski is a movie about how nothing means anything anymore.

The Stranger, a cowboy, the quintessential "American" man, is our narrator. He appears to be a "real" cowboy who has somehow made it out of the mists of history and legend and has kept going west until he has come to Venice Beach in 1991 at the time of the Gulf War. He introduces us to The Dude with profound words of deep meaning, and The Dude answers with actions of deep banality: he shuffles around a 24-hour supermarket and pays for a quart of milk with a check (the date on the check: September 11, 1991).

Then, even in the midst of his well worded, carefully considered, eloquently spoken introduction, the Stranger loses his train of thought. It's like he can't keep up the pretense any more, or the 20th century has suddenly caught up with him. The icon, perhaps the soul, of America is stuck here in the late 20th century and he's looking for something to hold on to. And here comes The Dude.

The Big Lebowski is, of course, not just a mystery, but a noir. And not just a noir, but an LA noir. The title is even a reference to one of the most famous LA noirs, *The Big Sleep*. As we quickly learn, however, the LA of Raymond Chandler, no longer exists. This LA is filled with bowling alleys, burnouts and punks, none of whom ever have the slightest idea of what the hell they're ever talking about.

There's a moment in the second act where The Dude goes over to Jackie Treehorn's house, and Treehorn is talking to The Dude about the money, and he suddenly gets a phone call. Treehorn takes the call and hurriedly jots something down on a notepad. He leaves the room and The Dude darts across the room, takes a pencil and shades the paper. Why does he do that? Because he saw it in a detective movie. The Dude, at that moment, is finally thinking like a detective. A movie detective, but a detective nonetheless. And he shades the paper and what does he find? Treehorn has not written down a phone number, nor a safe combination, nor a cryptic acronym; he has scrawled the image of a man with a big dick.

Because this is a movie about how nothing means anything anymore. LA still exists, but the LA of Raymond Chandler does not. Why does it not exist? Because the noirs of the '40s took place against the backdrop of World War II. The horror and agony and anxiety of that war, which could not be expressed in the actual war films of the day, were instead expressed in noirs, the darkness and duplicity and violence of detective stories. *The Big Lebowski*, by contrast, pointedly takes place against the background of the Gulf War, a war that meant nothing and achieved nothing (and, history has shown, did not have a happy ending).

All detective stories are about things with hidden meanings, but in *Lebowski* none of the detective elements mean anything at all. The Dude is hired to be the courier for a ransom, but it turns out that there is no kidnapping, there is no hostage and there is no ransom. The Dude is cynical enough to suggest that the kidnap victim "kidnapped herself," but he doesn't take it far enough. The fact is, the "kidnap victim" *didn't even know any of this was happening*. And who are the "real" kidnappers? Nihilists, whose cry is "We believe in *nozzing*!"

Why is The Dude the right man for his time? Because The Dude is a man who understands that nothing means anything. And not in some "nihilist" way, either. The Dude simply doesn't care. The Dude abides, The Dude takes it easy. Nothing affects him. The tumbling tumbleweed, at the beginning of the movie? We think it's a talking tumbleweed at first. But it's The Dude. The Dude is the one who is rootless, blowing on the breeze toward the beach.

The Dude understands that nothing means anything, but Walter, on the other hand, clings to everything way too much, searches desperately for *everything* to mean something. No *wonder* he converted to Judaism, it's the only religion that *means* anything to him. And the core of the movie is the scenes between, what's this, "the mismatched buddy detectives," Dude and Walter, one of whom skates along not paying attention and the other whom attaches far too much meaning to every new scrap of clue.

The rich man has no money. The kidnappers have no hostage. The hostage isn't even in town. Donny's death means nothing. No wonder Walter scrambles to find meaning, tries way too hard, there is no meaning in the chaos.

That does not mean, however, that *The Big Lebowski* is meaningless. *Lebowski* is a movie ebulliently overstuffed with meanings, far too many meanings to be gleaned from a single viewing.

The Dude is unique in the Coen universe in being a protagonist who is perfectly happy with his social standing. He does not desire money, social betterment, achievement, a child, a mate, clean clothes or, really, anything besides a state of blissful intoxication. Other people strive, The Dude abides. Anything he does in *Lebowski* he does because someone else forces him to do it. As the Stranger describes him, "he's the laziest man in Los Angeles County, which would place him high in the running for laziest worldwide." He has no real interest in saving the kidnapped girl, recovering the stolen ransom or even defending himself from hoodlums – when the going gets rough, The Dude inevitably goes bowling. Even his desire to reclaim his soiled rug is something that his bellicose friend Walter puts him up to – if it were up to The Dude, his peed-on rug would be worth it just for the story to tell his bowling buddies. (It's also worth noting that, for all the time The Dude spends hanging out in a bowling alley, listening to bowling games of the past and fantasizing about bowling scenarios, we never actually see him bowl.)

The comic premise of *The Big Lebowski* is that ambition-free Dude is pressed into service as a Chandleresque detective, a job to which he is spectacularly ill-suited and at which he repeatedly fails. (When Da Fino, the detective in the blue VW, addresses him as a "brother shamus," Dude recoils in horror.) The Dude takes a staggering 90 minutes to make a single coherent deduction and snap into action as a genuine active protagonist.

And yet *Lebowski's* detective story is quite brilliant in its design. It presents us with a *Big Sleep*-style mystery: What Happened To The Kidnapped Heiress? But the kidnapping plot, we eventually find, is a gigantic red herring. The *real* mystery in *The Big Lebowski* is Where's The Money? This is not an idle plot-point, it is a key subtext to understanding the meaning of the narrative. The kidnapped girl is a worthless idiot of importance to no one, but the money, ah, the money, as Mose in *The Hudsucker Proxy* says, "drives that ol' global economy and keeps big Daddy Earth a-spinnin' on 'roun'." *The Big Lebowski* is a social critique disguised as a mystery disguised as a stoner comedy.

The key to understanding the social dynamics of *The Big Lebowski* is to always follow the money. So where *is* "the money" in *The Big Lebowski*? ("Where's the money, Lebowski?" is, in fact, the movie's first line of dialogue.) The Dude certainly doesn't have it – he lives in a crappy Venice bungalow and is late on his rent. His friend Walter has his own business, but doesn't have any appreciable amount of it. Jeffrey Lebowski, despite appearances, doesn't have it, and his wife Bunny obviously doesn't have it. The Nihilists don't have it and neither does teenage car thief Larry Sellers, even though Walter is *positive* he has it.

Who has *any* money in *The Big Lebowski*? Maude Lebowski, Jeffrey's daughter, the aggressively "feminist" artist, has some money, but even that is not hers, it's her mother's. She hasn't earned it and seems to be frittering it away on ugly art and an inane lifestyle. The only other wealthy personage in *Lebowski* is Jackie Treehorn, the pornographer. So: in the world of *The Big Lebowski*, "Money" is represented by an embezzler, an heir and a pornographer – as harsh a critique of American capitalism as I've ever heard.

Everyone else is barely scraping by or actively losing money hand over fist. The indignities heaped upon The Dude in this narrative are great: his house is repeatedly broken into ("Hey, Man, this is a private residence" he lazily chides a trio of armed thugs), his possessions are smashed until nothing is left of them, his car is shot at, crashed, stolen, crashed again, peed in, bashed and finally set fire to. He is punched unconscious, drugged and hit with a coffee mug. The Rich in *Lebowski* get richer by soaking the Poor, and every transaction between social unequals is a heartbeat away from physical violence. Even Maude, who only wants her rug back, can't resist using force upon The Dude in order to get what she wants.

"Aggression" is a big word in *Lebowski*. The Dude is, of course, the least aggressive person in the story, yet he invites aggression at every turn, from his friends, his bowling rivals, his various contacts in the mystery. The parallel is drawn to the Gulf War, and if there is a coherent critique of the Gulf War to be found in *Lebowski* (and I'm not sure there is) it could be better applied to the war in Iraq: in *Lebowski*, aggression is met with violent retribution – *but it always falls on the wrong person.* Jackie Treehorn wants his money, but his goons beat up the wrong Lebowski. The Dude's rug is peed on, so he demands retribution from a complete stranger. Jeffrey Lebowski sends The Dude to identify the kidnappers as Jackie Treehorn's thugs (he won't take responsibility for The Dude's rug, but insists that The Dude take responsibility for his missing wife), but finds they are completely different people (and gets his car shot up for his trouble). The Nihilists demand a ransom for Bunny, but cut off the toes of one of their own to prove their seriousness. Walter exacts violent retribution on Little Larry Sellers, but ends up bashing the car of a complete stranger.

This, I think, is the meaning of poor Donny's death. In times of war, wealthy, powerful men make up their minds to be aggressive (Saddam against Kuwait, Bush against Saddam), but the people affected are always the poor and powerless, people who die without ever understanding what the true cause of the aggression was. In the case of the Gulf War, it was the Iraqi soldiers and civilians who sided with the US, only to be abandoned, in the case of *Lebowski it's* poor Donny, who's salient quality is that he never knows what the hell is going on and who dies, absurdly, of a heart attack during an attack by the Nihilists.

This is also, I think, why Walter compares Donny's death to the troops lost in Vietnam, although Walter, to be fair, tends to compare *everything* to Vietnam. He compares Bunny's kidnapping to Vietnam, he finds service in diners lacking due to his experiences in Vietnam. The Dude chides Walter for this habit, but Walter, I think, is on to something. Bunny's "kidnapping" *can* be compared to Vietnam, insofar as it's a mysterious act of aggression perpetrated by a wealthy man scheming to steal a ton of money and make a poor man pay for it.

The Big Lebowski rants to The Dude about the rug: "Let me get this straight, every time a rug is urinated upon in this fair city, I have to compensate the owner?" The Dude's rug has been ruined because of the indiscretions of The Big Lebowski's wife, but he feels no responsibility. Instead, The Big Lebowski lectures The Dude about personal responsibility, thrift and hard work.

Then, this leitmotif keeps coming around: "fuck you in the ass." People keep threatening to fuck The Dude and Walter in the ass. This always comes down to people of means using force and violence to make the lives of the poor worse, sending goons into The Dude's house, over and over, to wreck the place. Walter, for one, has had enough, and when it appears that a 15-year-old kid has "fucked him in the ass," he goes out into a street and demolishes what turns out to be an innocent stranger's car while screaming, over and over at the top of his lungs, "This is what happens when you fuck a stranger in the ass!" He's certainly angry at the kid, but in a way he's angry about the ass-fucking that he's getting every day from The Big Lebowskis of the world.

Finally, at Donny's funeral, Walter's had enough. He's not going to pay $182 for an urn. He's not going to get fucked in the ass again. He's going to put his friend's (okay, he wasn't that much of a friend) ashes into a Folger's coffee can and dump his ashes into the Pacific (although, of course, he misses) before he gets fucked in the ass again.

And The Dude and Walter go back to bowling. They are even, miraculously, still in the finals, despite the death of their partner. Yet in the center of this chaotic storm of meaninglessness, there is calm. At the very least, The Dude abides.

This movie, for me, went from being pale and unpersuasive to standing as the Coen's densest, most intricate, most interesting and, in a way, most profound movie.

....

Todd Alcott is a screenwriter living in Los Angeles. He often cycles through the streets of Venice. He enjoys shopping at Ralphs in the middle of the night, sometimes in slippers. He has a blog, What Does the Protagonist Want?, conveniently located at www.toddalcott.com, where he analyzes screenplays.

Eric Streed, *Lebowski Crucifixion*

Takin' It Easy For Us Sinners: The Dude and Jesus Christ

BY DAVID MASCIOTRA

As for man, his days are as grass: as a flower of the field, so he flourisheth. For the wind passeth over it, and it is gone; and the place thereof shall know it no more.
– Psalm 103, 5

Imagine a male figure with long hair and a beard, wearing a robe and sandals. One may immediately think of Jesus Christ, but even though one would be wrong, one would be closer than conventionally thought. Now imagine that male figure in a bath robe and jelly sandals – holding a carton of milk in Ralph's. The image of "the man for his time" – bathed in Christological aesthetic – is how the Coen brothers introduce the audience to The Dude in their seminal work, *The Big Lebowski*.

It has become increasingly common to hear and read comparisons of The Dude's lifestyle to the philosophy of Zen Buddhism. There is certainly ample evidence demonstrating similarities between The Dude and the nirvana-seeking belief system of the Orient, but all of the attention paid to those similarities discourages examination of one of the most obvious comparisons to the beloved character immortalized by Jeff Bridges. The Dude and the Christian Savior have far more in common than mere fashion. Even a cursory look at *The Big Lebowski* and the Gospel reveals that Jesus of Nazareth was an original Dude, and Lebowski of Los Angeles, although not a practicing Christian, is, in his own way and according to his own internal system of ethics, a practitioner of Jesus' way and life.

Because of the movie's strong American context, the consideration of The Dude as a Christ-like figure is particularly important to anyone interested in *The Big Lebowski* and the religion of Dudeism, Not only does the story take place entirely in California, but it also deals with issues of great importance to American history and life – the Vietnam War, California hippie culture, the systemic corruption of conservative oligarchs, and bowling. Viewers can further complicate the dark Americana of the film by casting The Dude as a modernized, symbolic rendering of Jesus. Though many of America's citizens call it a "Christian nation," and its people claim to admire Jesus Christ, Martin Luther King, St. Francis of Assisi, and Mother Theresa, their actions prove otherwise.

The Gospels are radically pacifist documents in which Jesus preaches love and forgiveness of enemies, hospitality for strangers, and compassion for the poor. Conversely, the American government is a war machine that grows more hostile to immigrants each year and shines the boots of the rich before they kick the poor in the face. To make matters worse, the American government carries out all of their atrocities via the mandate, through either apathy or lustful excitement, of its people.

The Big Lebowski is a subversive movie. It is an entertaining, clever and persistently hilarious comic neo-noir. It is also, however, an important film that challenges many of the assumptions taken for granted throughout America – namely that wealth is virtuous by default, the rich are always worthy of trust and respect, progress is always laudable, and the social order fills its thrones with only those who deserve coronation. Someone like The Dude is simply, in his own words, "a loser, a deadbeat, someone the square community won't give a shit about."

The Dude's life undresses all of these principles and shows how morally hollow and intellectually vacuous they are. The principles of Americanism – what social historian Morris Berman calls "the real religion" of America – are the exact principles that Jesus condemned two thousand years ago. Jesus issued his indictment within the belly of beastly Roman Empire, and while doing so, fought the established religious order of his community – the Jewish Pharisees. The Dude, with much less preaching, far fewer miracles, and much less everything, condemns those principles within the belly of the beastly American Empire, and in doing so, presents an alternative to its established religious order – the Christian right.

Jesus was a former carpenter who took long walks and went fishing with his fellow dudes, or disciples as he called them, and had an ambiguous relationship with a strong-willed woman named Mary. Jeffrey Lebowski is a former Metallica roadie who takes long drives, bowls with his friends, and has an ambiguous relationship with his strong-willed "fucking lady friend" Maude. He clarifies the nature of their relationship at one point, explaining that he is "helping her conceive." Dan Brown searched for a similar statement from Jesus in the paintings of

Leonardo Da Vinci, but found only the makings of a middle-brow novel.

Jesus, being a Palestinian Jew with close ties to the Nazarenes – a radical group of Jewish mystics – maintained a close relationship with the Jewish tradition throughout his life, even if he opposed the corrupt and self-serving Pharisees. The Dude's closest friend, Walter Sobchak, is a practicing Jew who, when The Dude discovers the answer to the case of the missing money and missing Bunny that has weighed on his mind throughout the movie, needs reminding that some principles override the law. It is the old distinction between morality and legality that served the Christian activists within the black American civil rights movements so well.

The Dude calls Walter on a Saturday, and exhorts him to pick up the phone, because it is "an emergency." He then explains to Walter that he needs a ride to The Big Lebowski's mansion. Walter claims that it is an impossible favor for The Dude to request, because it is Shabbos – the Jewish Holy Day of Rest – and he cannot drive on Shabbos. He's not even supposed to pick up the phone, unless it is an emergency. The Dude will have none it, and demands that Walter give him a ride. After arguing, Walter agrees.

Jesus Christ was accused of blasphemy and criminality for performing miracles on the Sabbath. He healed the sick, and fed masses of people on the Holy Day of Rest, and after hearing several accusations of sacrilegious behavior, he faced his accusers by saying, "My Father has been working until now, and I have been working."

Jesus was into the whole brevity thing, and the aloof rhetoric he used to deflate the invective and indignant finger-pointing of his enemies bears close resemblance to the ways in which The Dude shows his default distrust and dislike for authority. When Jesus faced the authorities of his time and place, whether they were religious rulers, political leaders, or civil officials, he refused, even when it cost him, to show deference. Earthly hierarchies held no value in the philosophical system or moral practice of Jesus. The Dude, at no point, humbles himself at the feet of millionaires, law enforcement, or known pornographers.

One of the messages of the Gospel is that respect and reverence are qualities afforded a person, regardless of that person's level of income and social status, only after that person has proven herself worthy. Jesus told his followers that what a person puts inside of his mouth does not make him clean or unclean, but only the words that person allows to leave his mouth. He also cherished the gift of one bit from a severely impoverished woman more than a large donation from a boastful tycoon. Jesus asked those around him to look past status and peer into the soul.

The Dude, sitting across the table from The Big Lebowski or the Sheriff of Malibu, knows that these men, despite their wealth or legal authority, are vast reservoirs of emptiness. Their treasure chests are hollow, and their shiny suits of gold exist only to conceal the hideous deformities of their character. The Big Lebowski, surrounded by the accoutrements of wealth and walls that adorn photographic tributes to his own vanity, lectures The Dude about his lifestyle, calls him a bum, and boasts about his achievements. The Dude puts on his sunglasses, and says "fuck it" before walking away. Later in the movie, we find him in another office receiving another cumbersome reprimand. On the opposite side of the desk is the Sheriff of Malibu whose moral compass is so far off that he praises Jackie Treehorn – a known pornographer and extortionist – because "he draws a lot of water in this town" and insults The Dude, because he "doesn't draw shit." After unleashing his tirade, he asks The Dude if he understands that he is not to return to Malibu. The Dude looks him in the eye and says with deadpan delivery, "I'm sorry I wasn't listening."

Jesus stood trial for crimes of blasphemy and sedition before Pontius Pilate –a prefect in the Roman Empire. A prefect was the equivalent of an American governor. He maintained control over a region within the empire, and in doing so, would often act as judge in high profile cases. According to the Gospel of John when Pilate levies accusations against Jesus, asking, "Are you the king of the Jews?" Jesus responds with his own question, "Are you saying this on your own initiative, or have others said it to you about me?" Later when Pilate mockingly says, "So you are a king," Jesus replies, "It is you who say that I am a king."

The sarcasm operates with more subtlety, but Jesus, like The Dude, refused to behave deferentially to authority. Both figures refused to even entertain a genuine conversation with authority. The Dude was one of the authors of the original Port Huron statement, and Jesus remains one of the most influential philosophers in the history of humanity. Certainly, either one could have argued with Lebowski or Pilate. Certainly, either one could have summoned his intellect and imagination to thoroughly defend himself against the words of an accuser, but they chose not to do it, because to engage that conversation is to grant legitimacy to illegitimate authority. Jesus and The Dude would do no such thing. Lebowski, The Sheriff, the Jewish Pharisees, and Pilate were not worth their respective time or energy.

Jesus also had no time for people without strong convictions. He once told a group of fence-sitters, "Since you are like lukewarm water, neither hot nor cold, I will spit you out of my mouth." It is not Nazis who form the third point in the triangle of The Dude's enemies, but nihilists – people who believe in nothing. Walter calls nihilists "cowards," and The Dude dismisses the first nihilist he sees, passed out on a floating device in Lebowski's pool, with a sarcastic description of his life – "Oh, that must be exhausting."

The Dude's history of left-wing activism and agitation, his willingness to help his friend with his dance, and commitment to the quiet rebellion of detachment, demonstrates the existence of strong values within his spirit and strong ideas within his mind. The ideas and values of Jesus were so strong that He faced death to uphold them. Thankfully, The Dude avoided a similar fate, but his values have much in common with the principles of Christ.

One of the most important and most ignored principles of Jesus was an unwavering commitment to non-violence. "Turn the other cheek," "love your enemies," "He who lives by the sword will die by the sword," are all memorable quotes from the Gospels. Early in *The Big Lebowski*, Walter draws a firearm during league play at the bowling alley to threaten an opposing player who stepped over the line on his roll. The Dude immediately disapproves, and when discussing the event, self-identifies as a pacifist. The 40th President of the United States, George Bush, is not a pacifist. He fought in World War II, directed the monstrous CIA as part of his political career, and led a war during his failed Presidency. His warning to the evil tyrant Saddam Hussein, however, resonates with The Dude. Overheard from a supermarket television The Dude later repeats Bush's words during his initial confrontation with Jeffrey Lebowski – "This aggression will not stand." Jesus had a "this aggression will not stand" moment when he threw the moneychangers out of the temple, saying, "My temple should be a house of prayer, but you have made it into a den of thieves." Both The Dude and Jesus, when they decide to take decisive action, target the self-serving and vampiric elite. Even when they move against moneychangers or money managers they uphold their promise of pacifism. Jesus removes the thieves from the temple and then lets them walk away freely. The Dude helps Lebowski back into his wheelchair after Walter physically removes him and throws him to the floor.

The Dude and Jesus have also taken a vow of poverty. Jesus did so publicly and told his followers that they too should give up their possessions. The Dude's vow of poverty remains unspoken and functions only as a quiet alternative to the mindless hustle of consumer capitalism. Whether it is a sermonic religious doctrine or unexpressed form of resistance to the dominant culture, voluntary poverty allows a person distance and detachment from a systemic ideology that limits life to chasing deals, crunching numbers, and evaluating worth and meaning according to a monetary scale. Jesus believed the vow of poverty was a prerequisite to truly serving people with word and deed. The Dude seems to believe it is essential for living in a state of joy.

The vow of poverty is also a crucial component to the "take it easy" philosophy and lifestyle of The Dude. After Jesus witnessed his disciples experiencing great anxiety over material concerns, He gathered them together and said, "Do not worry saying 'what shall I eat?' and 'what shall I wear'? For the pagans run after all these things . . . live righteously and take no thought for tomorrow." "Take no thought for tomorrow" is a more poetic and spiritual rendering of an important phrase that The Dude utters halfway through the movie. The Dude sits in the back of a limousine and tells the driver that he was "down in the dumps" earlier because "he lost a little money." Then, he throws up his hands and says, "Fuck it, man. I can't be worried about that shit. Life goes on, man." The language is different, but the substance is the same.

American culture has reached such a bizarre state of perversion that it has no knowledge or awareness of the religion that its leaders claim to wear on their sleeves and operate in their hearts as an influence over every decision they make. The reality, pesky as always, reveals a different picture. A nonreligious, but deeply spiritual, unemployed movie character who smokes copious amounts of grass, wears a bathrobe to the supermarket, helps a lady friend conceive, and was created by two Jewish brothers, bears closer resemblance to Jesus Christ than most preachers and politicians. The principles that Jesus espoused and practiced, and the lifestyle that The Dude exemplifies, are exactly what can "save" the United States of America, and much of Western culture, from its cannibalistic greed, equally homicidal and suicidal foreign policy, and domestic cruelty.

Even those who do not accept the theological tenets and doctrinal demands of Christianity can respect and regard Jesus Christ as a beautiful hero of love, mercy, and compassion. The atheistic philosopher Slavoj Zizek, for example, has written a book (*The Fragile Absolute: Or, Why Is The Christian Legacy Worth Fighting For?*) on the importance and inspirational power of Jesus. Jesus, in the theological and/or sociopolitical sense, is a mighty projection of sanity and peace in a psychotic and violent culture. The Dude's value, for all the laughs, is similar. As The Stranger puts it at the conclusion of *The Big Lebowski*, "I take comfort in that, knowing that The Dude is out there: Takin' it easy for all us sinners."

....

David Masciotra is the author of *All That We Learned About Livin': The Art and Legacy of John Mellencamp* (forthcoming, University of Kentucky Press). He is also the author of *Against Traffic: Essays on Politics and Identity* (Brown Dog Books, 2013). He has written for *The Atlantic, the Daily Beast,* and *the Indianapolis Star.* For more information visit www.davidmasciotra.com.

Anthony Sims, *Mark It Zero*

Walter Sobchak, Neocon: The Prescient Politics of *The Big Lebowski*

BY DAVID HAGLUND

The Big Lebowski has, in a decade, inspired a following to rival all cinematic cults, complete with annual festivals, monthly podcasts, and teachings to live by. At the heart of this denomination is The Dude, brilliantly incarnated by Jeff Bridges as a Zen slob whose three great loves are weed, white Russians, and bowling. And The Dude is indeed a fantastic character.

Ten years on, though, the movie's most striking role belongs to John Goodman as Walter Sobchak: a hawkish, slightly unhinged Vietnam vet and The Dude's best friend and bowling partner. Watching *The Big Lebowski* in 2008, it becomes clear that appreciating Walter is essential to understanding what the Coen brothers are up to in this movie, which is slyer, more political, and more prescient than many of its fans have recognized. Perhaps that's because Walter, with his bellowing, Old Testament righteousness and his deeply entrenched militarism, is an American type that barely registered on the pop-culture landscape ten years ago. He's a neocon.

If that seems like a stretch, consider the traits Walter exhibits over the course of the film: faith in American military might (the Gulf War, he says, will be "a piece of cake"); nostalgia for the Cold War ("Charlie," he says, referring to the Viet Cong, was a "worthy fuckin' adversary"); strong support for the state of Israel (to judge from his reverent paraphrase of Theodor Herzl: "If you will it, Dude, it is no dream"); and even, perhaps, past affiliation with the left (he refers knowingly to Lenin's given name and admits to having "dabbled in pacifism"). Goodman, who has called the role his all-time favorite, seems also to have sensed Walter's imperialist side. "Dude has a rather, let's say, Eastern approach to bowling," he said in an interview. "Walter is strictly Manifest Destiny."

The Coen brothers present this bellicose figure "in the early '90s" (as an opening voice-over provided by a mysterious cowboy informs us) "just about the time of our conflict with Sad'm and the Eye-rackies." After the cowboy has spoken, the first words we hear come from the elder President Bush: "This aggression will not stand," he declares, responding to the invasion of Kuwait and appearing on a grocery store television while The Dude buys some half-and-half. Bush's threat of force frames all that follows. When Walter hears about the "carpet-pissers," he insists that The Dude draw "a line in the sand."

The Dude has his own politics – or once did, at least: member of the Seattle Seven, co-author of the "original Port Huron Statement" (not the "compromised second draft"). A student activist who's become a SoCal layabout, he contrasts neatly with Walter, a veteran who interprets everything through the lens of Vietnam. In other words, The Dude and Walter are on opposite sides of the American divide that opened during the 1960s. And while The Dude is the movie's hero, more or less, it's Walter who drives the plot. He tells The Dude to seek out the rich Lebowski. He accompanies The Dude during the ransom delivery and insists that they fake the handoff and keep the money. When The Dude's car is stolen, with the money in it, Walter tracks down the apparent culprit and brings The Dude along to interrogate him.

This last scene, if filmed today, would almost certainly be taken as an allegory about the younger Bush's war. The police have recovered the car, and The Dude has found, wedged between the seats, a page of homework belonging to one Larry Sellers. Walter figures out Larry's address and arrives at his house, The Dude in tow, the homework in a plastic bag. He then presents his hypothesis that Larry is hiding the money. Only, as we find out later, there was no money.

But of course, Walter is not to be swayed by facts. Larry says nothing, and Walter proceeds to Plan B: destroying the new Corvette parked outside – purchased, he assumes, using the money left in the car – with a crowbar. Actually, though, the Corvette belongs to a neighbor.

Is this eerie foreshadowing of the second Iraq war coincidental? Not entirely. The Coen brothers created a character with traits that run deep in American culture: unflinching righteousness and a tendency to violence. (He was largely based on John Milius, who wrote and directed *Red Dawn*, the Cold War-paranoia film that later gave its name to the military operation that captured Saddam.)

This character confronts a situation that combines both injustice and the opportunity for material gain. He responds more or less as one would imagine. The Dude's pacifist leanings are no match for Walter's assertiveness: While The Dude's disposition may be admirable, he has little effect on the tide of world events. Refugees from the 1960s can sympathize.

Within the world of the movie, though, the destruction of the bystander's Corvette is a fairly minor incident. Immediately afterward, we see Walter, The Dude, and Donnie – the third and least conspicuous member of the bowling team, played by Steve Buscemi – on their way home in The Dude's car, eating hamburgers and listening to "Oye Como Va." Watching *The Big Lebowski* today, one notices its insight into basic American attitudes but also the lightheartedness with which it's able to treat these attitudes. Donnie does die of a heart attack during a climactic showdown with those German nihilists, and one might call his death a casualty of Walter's aggression and The Dude's inability to reign it in. But his death quickly gives way to Walter and The Dude's reconciliation, at a makeshift funeral they hold for Donnie by the Pacific Ocean.

This gentle, comic conclusion came to mind while I watched the Coen brothers' farce, *Burn After Reading*, which revolves around the misplaced memoirs of an ex-CIA analyst. A similarly sharp satire of American life, there are parallels with the *Lebowski* plot: a greedy attempt at extortion, multiple schemes incompetently botched. The contrast in tone, though, is stark. There's no real friendship in the world of *Burn After Reading*, there's even less heroism, and paranoia abounds. No one mentions 9/11 or the war in Iraq, but these characters, like their audience, are living in a darker world. The cult of Lebowski, I've begun to suspect, has more than a little nostalgia in it – for a decade when one could poke brilliant fun at the national disposition and the stakes didn't feel so high.

....

David Haglund is a writer and editor for Slate (www.slate.com).

Alberto Barina, *Smoking Dude*

Hannah Roberts, *Pin-Up Dudette*

Deception and Detection: The Trickster Archetype in the Film *The Big Lebowski,* and its Cult Following

BY WILLIAM A. ASHTON AND BARBARA A. ASHTON

Themes of the trickster archetype are prevalent throughout *The Big Lebowski* (*TBL*) and these themes are also associated with the film's fan following, the Lebowski cult, which developed four years after the film was released and has grown in popularity over time. While general trickster themes pervade the film, the theme of deception and the detection of deception unite the film with the fan following. Specifically, in the film itself, antagonists attempt to deceive others while the protagonists attempt to detect this deception. As an instance of Jungian synchronicity, the Lebowski cult has grown in popularity as the United States' culture has become more deceptive and Americans have more of a need to detect deception.

What is it about *TBL* which could spark such interest years after the movie was released? In examining the film itself, we see that two thematic elements were intentionally placed in the film: a homage to the Raymond Chandler story, *The Big Sleep*, and the Gulf War.

The Gulf War

> IndieWire: What's the attraction of setting the film specifically in 1991?
>
> Ethan: Well, setting the film during the Gulf War was an opportunity to have Walter gas about something . . .
>
> Joel: That's the main reason. (Stone, 1998).

This may make the Gulf War seem like a very trivial theme in the story. However, this statement must be taken in context; the brothers are being quixotic during this interview. For example, immediately after saying this Joel adds, "because just what is present day?" At another point in the interview, Ethan, a former Princeton philosophy major, when asked for his philosophy on filmmaking answered, "Oooh-I don't have one. I wouldn't even know how to begin. You've stumped me there. None that I've noticed. Drawing a blank on this one." And at other points of the interview, the Coens refuse to answer questions because they consider the questions, "not interesting."

Todd Comer (2005) sees *TBL* as attempting to think through the problem of the violence of the Gulf War, and assimilate this wartime violence into our national myth. However, there is evidence that *TBL* is not just *a working through* of violence as Comer suggests but *a protest to* the violence. While The Dude is unemployed and without a career, his one claim to fame is his protest activities as a college student: The Dude was one of the authors of the Port Huron Statement and a member of the original Seattle Seven. Both references are to actual events and groups from the 1960s and 1970s radical left (Dowd, n.d.; Haden & Flacks, 2002; Smith, 2000; University of Washington Libraries, n.d.). At another point in the film, The Dude states that while in college he spent most of his time occupying various administration buildings and breaking into the ROTC. The Dude is identified as an anti-war radical. We can conclude that *TBL* is, as Comer suggests, about the Gulf War, *and* about protesting war.

Border Wars and Breaking Boundaries

Whether intentionally or not on the part of the Coens, the theme of the Gulf War is one opportunity which allows the trickster archetype to find expression in the film.

The trickster is a boundary dweller and a breaker of boundaries (Doty & Hynes, 1993, p. 19-20) and the Gulf War was a border war begun by a border crossing (F. Lewis, 1990). Thus, the theme of the Gulf War, which was a major theme of the film, is about boundary crossing – the purview of the trickster. While Comer (2005) states that a theme in *TBL* is the Gulf War, it would be more correct to say that this theme is about the beginning of the war (Bush's speech places the action of the film after the invasion of Kuwait but before the war to liberate Kuwait). Thus, the Gulf War theme is more of a theme of Iraq's border crossing.

While the association of the Gulf War theme with border crossing and border crossing with the trickster archetype may be a tenuous set of links, *TBL* contains strong examples of archetypal trickster border crossing.

Specifically, examples of boundaries being broken in trickster ways (e.g. breaking taboos and customs) and examples of people who live on the fringe of our society appear throughout *TBL*.

The protagonist of the film, The Dude, is truly a boundary dweller who lives on the edge of our society. During our introduction to The Dude, he is shopping in a supermarket dressed in a t-shirt, shorts, flip-flops and a bathrobe. His hair and beard are long and unkempt. It is night and he is wearing sunglasses. When Jeffrey Lebowski asks The Dude if he is employed, The Dude responses, "Employed?" as if surprised or confused by the question. The Dude describes his life as driving around, bowling and having acid flashbacks.

The Dude lives in the liminal world of the Trickster. One of the most salient broken boundaries, however, is in the nature of the story itself.

The most immediately apparent broken boundary in the film is that of the narrator. The film begins with a cowboy band playing the song, "Tumbling Tumbleweeds" as we see a tumbleweed blown across a desert setting. The tumbleweed tops a rise and we see modern day Los Angeles. As the music continues and we see the tumbleweed blow through empty Los Angeles streets, the narrator begins to set up the story. The narrator, from his speech and use of words, is identified as a cowboy. Ethan Coen admits that the choice of the cowboy narrator is a boundary crossing: "The Western theme's just another thing that has nothing to do with anything but just seemed right next to the other things (Robertson, 1998, p.44)." As Ethan Coen further explained, "We always like those devices – narration, voice-over. Also it's a Marlowe thing, since all the Chandler novels are told in his first-person narration. But it would be too corny just to have The Dude narrating, you know (Robertson, 1998, p.44)?"

More boundary crossing occurs when the narrator appears in scenes with The Dude. Sam Elliott plays the narrator and is dressed as an old-fashioned western cowboy. The presence of a cowboy in a modern Los Angeles bowling lane is never explained. It is an anachronism treated as normal. This is an example of the trickster narrative (Doueihi, 1993; Rowland, 2006). Doueihi (1993) holds that the features we commonly ascribe to the trickster – contradictoriness, complexity, deceptiveness, trickery – can also be features of the language of the story itself. The purpose of this is to open our minds to spontaneous transformations of reality that may allow us to see the world in an open and creative way.

Similar to the boundary living and crossing described above, but more concrete, is the violation of sexual and excretory taboos. Just as the trickster is impelled to violate all taboos sexual or scatological (Hynes, 1993, p. 42), *TBL* is similarly driven.

TBL is famous for its use of sexual language. Martin & Renegar (2007) report that the word "fuck" and its variants are used 281 times in the film. In a one minute scene, Walter screams, "This is what happens when you fuck a stranger in the ass, Larry," over seven times. At their first meeting, Bunny Lebowski propositions The Dude by saying, "I'll suck your cock for a thousand dollars." Maude's first exchange with The Dude is, "My art has been commended as being strongly vaginal. Which bothers some men. The word itself make some men uncomfortable ... Vagina." In her next line, Maude refers to the male organ as a rod, dick or Johnson. During a one minute scene, The Dude's rug is referred to have been peed, urinated, pissed, or micturated upon seven times.

The penis and the detached penis are common trickster themes (Hynes, 1993, p. 43) and are themes in *TBL*. For instance, when The Dude attempts to detect what Treehorn has written on his notepad, he finds a drawing of a human torso with an enormous penis. A minor role (Green et al., 2007, p. 42) in the film is a bowling rival of the protagonists named Jesus Quintana. The actor wears a "huge codpiece (Green, et al., 2007, p. 42)" and a skintight jumpsuit in the movie. In another scene Quintana suggestively polishes his bowling ball (holding it in front of his crotch) and then erotically licks the ball. This is not the only time bowling equipment represents male sexual anatomy. In The Dude's mickey-induced dream two bowling balls and one bowling pin are positioned to mimic testicles and a penis. Finally, a recurring theme is of The Dude's penis in danger of being cut or bitten off. One scene begins with the kidnappers throwing a marmot into The Dude's bathtub (at groin level) and ends with the kidnappers threatening to cut off The Dude's Johnson (which the German kidnappers pronounce as 'Chohnson'). Later, during The Dude's dream, The Dude is chased by the kidnappers with oversized scissors.

Lastly, regarding breaking taboos, themes of defecation and urination are ever prevalent. The driving force of the film is The Dude seeking redress for his urine-stained rug (Green et al., 2007; Robertson 1998). In addition, a vagrant used The Dude's stolen car as a toilet, and Treehorn's thugs repeatedly shoved The Dude's head into a toilet.

The setting of *TBL* is the Gulf War and by association, the setting is one of boundaries and the breaking of boundaries. The main character is a boundary dweller, the narrative itself plays jokes on us, and dirty talk fills the narrative. This alone would be enough to state confidently that *TBL* embodies the trickster archetype. However, the cast of *TBL* is also packed with tricksters.

Deceivers and Detectives

All of the main characters in *TBL* are tricksters. They are tricksters in the sense that they are deceiving others or they are the two fool-detectives, Walter and The Dude, who are attempting (in spite of themselves) to detect the deceptions.

The antagonists of *TBL* are trickster-deceivers. Jeffrey Lebowski conveys the impression of a self-made millionaire, but he is living on his deceased wife's fortune. It is also unclear what his motives and actions are in attempting to secure the release of his wife, Bunny, from the kidnappers. Did he actually give The Dude one-million dollars or was the case empty of money? Fawn

Knutson (a.k.a. Bunny Lebowski) was hiding in L. A. from her parents in Minnesota and most likely hiding her career as an actress in pornographic movies from her husband. Uli, the "kidnapper," was attempting to extort ransom money from Jeffery Lebowski even though Uli was not holding Bunny prisoner. He went as far as to cut off a female friend's toe to trick Jeffrey Lebowski. Finally, Maude Lebowski tricked The Dude into conceiving a child with her. It is not surprising that many characters in *TBL* are trickster/deceivers. *TBL* is a mystery/detective story and without deceivers, there would be no need to detect.

If a mystery needs deceivers, then it also needs detectives. In *TBL*, the role of detective falls on Walter and The Dude. One of the strongest embodiments of the trickster archetype in the film is the undifferentiated, primal trickster-like qualities of the two main characters, The Dude and Walter. Individually, The Dude and Walter are the undifferentiated fools, while together they make up the archetypical pair of fools.

We first see The Dude when he is shopping (in his bathrobe) for half-and-half for his White Russians. Dress is not the only social convention he ignores in this scene: he casually opens cartons of half-and-half and tastes it. When he finally goes to the check out of the store, he has half-and-half on his mustache. It seems that The Dude does not intend to insult others with his flaunting of social convention but this is due to The Dude's overwhelmingly passive nature (as also noted by Comer, 2005). Thus, The Dude's border crossing is motivated by his laziness (Martin & Renegar, 2007, p. 307) or we could say lack of self-consciousness, a characteristic of the trickster (Jung, 1969, p. 143).

Another trait of the trickster exhibited by The Dude is that of situation-inversion (Hynes, 1993, p. 37). The Dude is able to invert power hierarchies and switch from being powerless to powerful (Martin & Renegar, 2007, pp. 306-307). When meeting Jeffrey Lebowski, The Dude introduces himself as "His Dudeness or El Duderino." Thus, the deadbeat Lebowski is elevating himself with royal titles when with the millionaire Lebowski. The Dude awkwardly uses the phrase, "the royal we." As another form of power equalization, instead of showing respect by use of the term, "Sir," The Dude liberally peppers his speech with the word, "man." He uses this term when speaking to everyone, including police officers, Jeffrey Lebowski and the chief of police. By use of this language, The Dude is constantly deflating power and equalizing status differentials. Finally, in The Dude's second dream, Saddam Hussein gives The Dude a pair of silver and gold bowling shoes. The world leader is now the servant to The Dude who receives shoes made of precious metals.

The other undifferentiated fool, Walter, is also a situation-inverter but in a much different way. Walter is unable to keep his anger under control (Comer, 2005, p. 112) and turns many normal situations into abnormal or dangerous situations. For example, in response to a scoring disagreement in a bowling game, Walter pulls a gun on fellow bowler and in response to a waitress' comment about his cursing Walter brings up the issue of patriotic freedom and that his friends died in the muck in Vietnam. While The Dude lacks self-consciousness due to his passive nature, Walter seems to lack self-consciousness due to his anger issues.

Thus, The Dude (the passive pacifist) and Walter (the Vietnam veteran with anger issues) make an unlikely pair. In fact, The Dude and Walter together are a classic pair of fools (Willeford, 1969, pp.39-40), which illustrates the trickster's oppositional nature (Hynes, 1993, p. 34; Levi-Strauss, 1963, p. 224).

Walter and The Dude's only common interest seem to be bowling, but beyond that, Walter and The Dude are close friends. When something happens The Dude first calls Walter and they know intimate details of each other's lives. A perfect illustration of the oppositional nature of the pair of fools is the ransom drop scene. In this scene, The Dude calls Walter with the intention (we assume) of Walter assisting him with the ransom drop while Walter enters the scene with the intention of manipulating the situation so that they can keep the ransom for themselves. As their car comes closer to the drop point, both are talking past each other because both assume a different plan. It is unclear from the film whether Walter's plan was doomed to fail due to Walter's incompetence or failed because of the lack of coordination between the pair of fools.

The Dude and Walter, the pair of fools, working against and off each other, drive much of the plot of *TBL*. For example, Walter talks The Dude into going to Jeffrey Lebowski to demand a replacement rug, which sets the story and mystery in motion. Walter's involvement with the ransom drop keeps the story open and ongoing. The Dude and Walter, individually, are barely conscious; and, together, are opposites that often cancel each other out. These two characteristics are what lead to their downfall when they attempt to act as detectives.

Through most of *TBL*, The Dude and Walter, the pair of fools, sleepwalk through the mystery. However, there are four instances when these tricksters attempt to take the initiative and act as detectives. These four scenes are very representative of the mystery genre – attempting to outsmart kidnappers, interrogating a suspect, searching for clues, and confronting and exposing a deceiver. However, in each of these cases, the fool's initiative leads to either disaster or nothing. The Dude only solves the mystery with clues obtained as byproducts of his appetites and self-interests.

The first disaster comes when the pair of fools attempt the ransom drop, in this scene, their oppositional motives (or possibly Walter's lack of self-awareness of his own abilities) lead to disaster. One consequence of the botched ransom drop is the second scene when the fools try to act like detectives, during their visit to little Larry's house in which two cars are nearly destroyed but Walter and The Dude leave with no new information on the missing money.

Both of these two scenes could have appeared in traditional detective stories. If Walter would have questioned Larry once, realized that this was a "cold lead," and left, then the scene would have fit perfectly in a traditional mystery. If Walter would have only taken one or two swings at the Corvette, noticed that Larry was unmoved by this method of persuasion and left (perhaps Larry is a hardboiled character), then again this scene would have fit perfectly into a traditional mystery. What makes these scenes comedy and not mystery is the repetition of Walter's lines. The line, "Is this your homework, Larry," appears over eight times in one minute and Walter yells, "This is what happens when you fuck a stranger in the ass!" over seven times in the same time period. A detective should persevere on a case, but Walter's foolish lack of self-awareness (of others' responses and his own abilities) creates the comedy.

The third situation where the fool attempts to act as a detective is when Jackie Treehorn leaves The Dude alone. Left alone, The Dude attempts to trace the notes Treehorn took on a notepad during a phone conversation. This is the one situation where the detective/fool does not cause disaster. A detective is very conscious of what he or she should be doing. However, this is the exception that proves the rule: how will the Trickster respond when the fool acts wise? The Trickster himself directly intervenes and plays a joke on the fool who is trying to be a detective.

Finally, The Dude and Walter go to confront Jeffrey Lebowski with their guesses concerning the ransom money that Jeffrey Lebowski may or may not have given The Dude. This could have been a traditional mystery denouement from Chandler, Hammett, Doyle or Christie. The Dude accuses Jeffrey Lebowski:

> You thought Bunny'd been kidnapped and you could use it as a pretext to make some money disappear. All you needed was a sap to pin it on, and you'd just met me. You thought, hey, a deadbeat, a loser, someone the square community won't give a shit about.

Jeffrey Lebowski then agrees with The Dude by saying, "Well? Aren't you?" Jeffrey Lebowski has been caught in his lies and in mystery-story fashion admits to his crime.

If this were the end of the scene, it could have been a classic denouement from the mystery genre. However, Walter's foolish lack of self-awareness and inability to control his anger again leads to failure and comedy. Walter rages against Jeffrey Lebowski and accuses him of being a phony millionaire and a phony paraplegic. Walter then pulls Jeffrey Lebowski out of his wheelchair, Jeffrey Lebowski then falls to the floor and cries. While The Dude was correct in his accusations and thus gained the initiative, Walter's incorrect assumption embarrassed the pair and squandered the initiative.

Throughout *TBL*, we see the characteristics of the trickster archetype: in the Gulf War/border crossing theme, in the background elements of the story, in the transgression of social taboos and in the characters themselves. This theme also extends to the Lebowski Cult. In order to describe this connection, we must return to the Gulf War.

Synchronicity and the Lebowski Cult: Two Wars with Iraq

One theoretical approach to the trickster is that it is a Jungian archetype (Jung, 1969) and thus may serve as the focus of synchronistic events. According to Jung, synchronicities occur when archetypes in the collective unconscious come into play and provide meaningful connections between acausal events (Jung, 1971). Since archetypes in the collective unconscious exist outside of time, synchronous events may appear in unusual time sequences, as if one event predicts another. While one might describe such an occurrence as precognition it is not, because the term precognition implies a causal chain of events.

TBL was written in the early 1990s during the Clinton administration. This was a prosperous time for the American economy and the United States was in no large scale military conflicts (Comer, 2005). And yet, during this time period the Coen brothers decided to write a film script set during, about and critical of (Martin & Renegar, 2007, p. 301) the Gulf War. *TBL* then spawns a cult following *four years after its release* (the first Lebowski fest was held on October 12, 2002; Green et al., 2007, p. 3). The presence of this cult following four years after the film was released suggests that the film resonated with people at that time. The beginning of the Lebowski cult coincides with the build up to the Iraq War. Is this coincidence or synchronicity?

In order to answer this question, we must describe the Gulf and Iraq wars. These descriptions are general characterizations of the wars and we do not intend to draw definitive conclusions about the wars. In addition, our intention is to be descriptive of how some Americans view the two wars and not to proscriptively espouse a political point of view.

The Gulf War (1990-1991) was undertaken in direct response to Iraq's invasion of its southern neighbor, Kuwait. Thus, the Gulf War was generally seen as justified and was conducted with support from the United Nations (P. Lewis, 1990). The Gulf War was fought with less than 300 American lives lost and at a cost of $61 to $71 billion (CNN, 2001). As of April 2008, costs of the Iraq War tally to (2003- present) 4,058 American dead and in March of 2008 the Pentagon placed the to-date cost at $600 billion (Herszenhorn, 2008).

The rationale for waging the Iraq War has been significantly criticized. The Iraq War Resolution (H. Res. 114, 2002), after being approved by the House of Representatives and Senate, was signed into law on October 16, 2002 (two days after the first Lebowski fest) by President G. W. Bush. This resolution authorized force against Iraq for several reasons, including the threat to the U.S. posed by Iraq's weapons of mass destruction program and that Iraq was harboring known members of al-Qaeda. However, the CIA's Iraq Survey Group concluded that even though Saddam Hussein had intentions to build weapons of mass destruction, he did not have the chance to do so (Borger, 2004; MSNBC, 2005). Regarding the second issue, members of the 9/11 commission (National Commission on Terrorist Attacks enpaneled by President G. W. Bush) found "no credible evidence" that Iraq was involved in the September 11, 2001 terrorist attacks carried out by al-Qaeda hijackers, and they concluded that there was "no collaborative relationship" between Iraq and Osama bin Laden (CNN.com, 2004; Pincus & Milbank, 2004).

The above inconsistencies between fact and White House Policy may have been due to honest mistakes. However, in 2005, the Downing Street Memo was leaked to the press (Pincus & Milbank, 2005). This memo, from British intelligence to Prime Minister Blair, dated July 23, 2002 said that, "Bush wanted to remove Saddam, through military action, justified by the conjunction of terrorism and WMD [weapons of mass destruction]. But the intelligence and facts were being fixed around the policy." If the validity of the Downing Street Memo is to be accepted, then one can conclude that the Bush White House deceived the American people into supporting the Iraq War. Many individuals and organizations have made such conclusions (e.g. Center for Public Integrity, n.d.; Conyers, 2005; Iraq Veterans Against the War, 2008). To summarize this view of the rationale for the Iraq War, the Bush Administration deceived the public with false information in order to obtain the public's compliance.

Which war is symbolized in *TBL*? Jeffrey Lebowski, who bears a resemblance to Dick Cheney (Martin & Renegar, 2007, p. 301), lies to The Dude to gain The Dude's compliance. This deception on Jeffrey Lebowski's part is staged for personal gain. The premise of *TBL* bears more of a resemblance to the Iraq War than the Gulf War. In both *TBL* and the Iraq War, evidence was created and falsehoods told in order to deceive and manipulate people. Since 2002 (the beginning of the deception about the Iraq War and the first Lebowski Fest) America has been, as The Dude is, struggling against and becoming cognizant of deceptions that powerful others have imposed upon us.

We must assume that the Coens had no knowledge of the future and that they were writing a film based upon the Gulf War. However, with the trickster involved with their script (the deceivers in the story, the pair of fools, the other references to trickster qualities) the Coens had opened the door to Trickster. With this archetype in play, synchronicity could have crafted a story more appropriate to a future war than the war the Coens intended.

The Lebowski cult's existence and the reason the cult flourished four years after the movie was released is that *TBL* became meaningful during the build up to and the waging of the Iraq War – *events which are thematically described in TBL*. Jeffery Lebowski, a Dick Cheney look-a-like and conservative Republican, deceives others so they will act for his benefit. The Coens – by the coincidence of combining the elements of a story set during the Gulf War, a Chandler-like mystery story of deceivers and detectives, and the war-protester character of The Dude – produced a film that held more meaning for a future audience than the audience that existed when they wrote and made the film. This future audience would be an audience that would need to detect the deception of a trickster in the context of a war with Iraq.

Conclusions

The two common themes connecting *TBL* and the Lebowski cult are deception and the detection of deception, and a war with Iraq. Connecting these two themes across the film and the fan cult is the trickster-archetype inspired synchronicity. In the center of all of this is The Dude. Recall that The Dude was a war protester in college, an author of the Port Huron Statement and a member of the Seattle Seven (the Seattle Eight; Dowd, n.d.; who were arrested and served sentences for their part in an anti-Vietnam War protest). The Port Huron Statement is the founding manifesto of the Students for a Democratic Society (SDS) from which the "authentic spirit of the Sixties radicalism issued (Haden & Flacks, 2002, p. 18)." In writing a fortieth anniversary retrospective on the document, the main authors of the Port Huron Statement, Tom Haden and Dick Flacks (2002), begin the essay by referring to *TBL* and say:

> We don't remember the "dude" being there, but it's gratifying that the founding manifesto . . . still lives on in the nostalgia and imagination of so many. (p. 18)

About the Statement itself, they write:

> Like today, 1962 was a time when many students were waking up, but the vast majority were smothered in apathy. We couldn't resist . . . war . . . without first piercing this freezing indifference bred by affluence [and] conformity (p. 19).

Thus, *TBL* identifies The Dude with the early stages of the Sixties' protest movement and a document that addressed the nation's apathy towards the war. Due to the Iraq War, the nation is in a similar situation of war and public apathy. And as Hayden and Flacks say, *TBL* has placed (in name, at least) the Port Huron Statement in the minds of our current generation.

Following the trickster archetype in *TBL* has led us on a wide-ranging journey from the Iraq War to *The Big Sleep*. Looking ahead, I would like to address two areas of future interest, the trickster and detective, and the Lebowski cult.

Radin warns us that in viewing the trickster we must be careful:

> The impression one gets in perusing these various trickster cycles is that one must distinguish carefully between his consciously willed creative activities and the benefactions that comes to mankind incidentally and accidentally through the Trickster's activities (Radin, 1972, p. 125).

We feel that applying Radin's remarks to the detective clearly summarizes our view on the trickster and the detective in *TBL*.

One must distinguish carefully between the trickster's consciously willed detection and the clues that come accidentally through the trickster's foolishness.

We have described how The Dude and Walter, our trickster-detectives, were incompetent at finding clues in the mystery and how intentional plans to manipulate the situation led to utter disaster. The Dude was able to solve the mystery only as an accidental outcome of his own desires.

The Lebowski cult has grown in scope, popularity and scale since its beginning in 2002. Why? Our answer is because of the synchronistic connections between *TBL* and the Iraq War, the film resonates with the zeitgeist. There is another answer to this question, *TBL* contains elements of carnival (Martin & Renegar, 2007) and thus lends itself to the carnival-like activities at a Lebowski fest. At Lebowski fests people drink White Russians, dress up in costumes and dance. While not officially part of the 2002 Lebowski fest, the first fest was held at a bowling lane located amid strip clubs (Green et al., 2007, p. 168). However, this theory does not explain why it took four years for the carnival to get going. The Iraq War/Synchronicity theory offered in this paper fits the timing of events much better and is more meaningful.

A second possible approach to the Lebowski cult is empirical. Over the last decade, some researchers have published empirical articles on fan cults. For example, Obst, Zinkiewicz & Smith (2002) examined the psychological sense of community among science fiction fandom at Aussiecon 3. Such an examination of the Lebowski fandom may be interesting. Or, a study related to this paper's interests could empirically examine Lebowski fans' political attitudes. Are Lebowski fans more wary of being deceived by the government and do they hold more negative attitudes about the Iraq War than non-fans? Are they more likely to protest the war? Such an empirical approach may detect whether Lebowski cultists are just there for the party (carnival) or if they are there to seek the fellowship of others who wish to drink White Russians, bowl and wake up to our culture's apathy towards the Iraq War.

....

William Ashton is an Associate Professor of Psychology at York College, CUNY; and his areas of research are in how people assign blame to victims in accidents, social presence in online courses and the psychological aspects of fandom. His webpage is at
http://www.york.cuny.edu/Members/washton/

Barbara Ashton is an Associate Professor of Mathematics at the Boro of Manhattan Community College, CUNY. Her areas of research include a mathematical analysis of cross stitching, labyrinths and sacred mathematics; and the mathematical modeling of the architecture of Frank Lloyd Wright.

The authors wish to thank C. W. Spinks, editor of *Trickster's Way*, for his invaluable assistance.

Works Cited

Borger, J. (October 7, 2004). There were no weapons of mass destruction in Iraq. The Guardian. Retrieved April 30, 2008 from http://www.guardian.co.uk/world/2004/oct/07/usa.iraq1

Center for Public Integrity (n.d.) Iraq – The war card. Retrieved April 30, 2008 from http://www.publicintegrity.org/WarCard/

Chandler, R. (1988). The big sleep. NY, NY: Vintage. (Original published 1939).

Coen, J. (Writer/Director), & Coen, E. (Writer). (1998). *The Big Lebowski* [Motion Picture]. United States: Polygram Filmed Entertainment.

Comer, T. (2005). This aggression will not stand: Myth, war, and ethics in *The Big Lebowski*. Substance: A Review of Theory & Literary Criticism, 34(2), 98-117.

Conyers, J. (June 6, 2005). Did Bush deliberately deceive America about Iraq? Counterpunch. Retrieved April 30, 2008 from http://www.counterpunch.org/conyers06062005.html

CNN (2001). In-depth specials –Gulf War. Retrieved April 30, 2008 from http://www.cnn.com/SPECIALS/2001/gulf.war/facts/gulfwar/

CNN.com (June 18, 2004). Cheney blasts media on al Qaeda-Iraq link. Retrieved April 30, 2008 from http://www.cnn.com/2004/ALLPOLITICS/06/18/cheney.iraq.al.qaeda/

Doty, W. G. & Hynes, W. J. (1993). Historical overview of theoretical issues: The problems of the trickster. In W. J. Hynes & W. G. Doty (Eds.), Mythical trickster figures: Contours, contexts, and criticisms (pp. 13-32). Tuscaloosa, AL: University of Alabama Press.

Doueihi, A. (1993). Inhabiting the space between discourse and story in trickster narratives. In W. J. Hynes & W. G. Doty (Eds.), Mythical trickster figures: Contours, contexts, and criticisms (pp. 193-201). Tuscaloosa, AL: University of Alabama Press.

Dowd, A. (n.d.). Who is the real conspiracy? Vietnam War Era Ephemera Collection. Retrieved on July 8, 2008 from http://content.lib.washington.edu/cdm4/document.php?CISOROOT=/protests&CISOPTR=378&REC=20

Edelstein, D. (August 8, 2004). You're entering a world of Lebowski. The New York Times, p. 21.

Green, B., Peskoe, B., Russell, W., & Shuffitt, S. (2007). I'm a Lebowski, you're a Lebowski: Life, *The Big Lebowski*, and what have you. NY, NY: Bloomsbury USA.

Hayden, T., & Flacks, D. (2002). The Port Huron statement at 40. Nation, 275(5), 18-21.

Hammett, D. (1989). The Maltese falcon. NY, NY: Vintage. (Original published 1930).

Herszenhorn, D. M. (March 19, 2008). Estimates of Iraq War cost were not close to ballpark. Retrieved April 30, 2008 from http://www.nytimes.com/2008/03/19/washington/19cost.html?_r=1&oref=slogin

Hodgkinson, W. (May 11, 2005). Dude, let's go bowling. The Guardian. Retrieved April 28, 2008 from http://film.guardian.co.uk/features/featurepages/0,,1481323,00.html

H. Res. 114, 117 Cong., 148 Cong. Rec. 7739 (2002) (enacted).

Hynes, W. (1993). Mapping the characteristics of mythic tricksters: A heuristic guide. In W. J. Hynes & W. G. Doty (Eds.), Mythical trickster figures: Contours, contexts, and criticisms (pp. 33-45). Tuscaloosa, AL: University of Alabama Press.

Iraq Veterans Against the War (2008). Why we're against the war. Retrieved April 30, 2008 from http://www.ivaw.org/faq

Jung, C. G. (1969). Four archetypes. Princeton, NJ: Princeton University Press.

Jung, C. G. (1971). On synchronicity. In J. Campbell, (Ed.), The portable Jung (pp. 505-518). NY, NY: Penguin Books.

Kesner, J. (August 8, 2004). NYC welcomes his Dudeness convention update: forget the GOP, here comes the Lebowski fest. Daily News (New York), p. 6.

Lebowski Fest. (n.d. A) Retrieved April 28, 2008, from http://lebowskifes http://lebowskifest.com/tpir.asp

Lebowski Fest. (n.d. B) Retrieved April 28, 2008, from http://lebowskifest.com/7thannual.aspt.com

Levi-Strauss, C. (1963). Structural anthropology. (C. Jacobson & B. G. Schoepf, trans.). NY, NY: Basic Books. (Original work published 1958)

Lewis, F. (April 28, 1990). Baghdad rages on. New York Times. Retrieved on July 7, 2008 from http://query.nytimes.com/gst/fullpage.html?res=C0CE1DB103BF93BA15757C0A966958260

Lewis, P. (November 30, 1990). Mideast tensions; U.N. gives Iraq until Jan. 15 to retreat or face force; Hussein says he will fight. New York Times. Retrieved June 21, 2008 from http://query.nytimes.com/gst/fullpage.html?res=C0CE6D6103FF933A05752C1A966958260&sec=&spon=&pagewanted=2

Martin, P. & Renegar, V. (2007). "The man for his time" *The Big Lebowski* as carnivalesque social critique. Communication Studies, 58 (3), 299-313.

Morgenstern, J. (October 7, 2006). Deconstructing The Dude. The Wall Street Journal, p. P13.

MSNBC (April 25, 2005). CIA's final report: No WMD found in Iraq. Retrieved April 30, 2008 from http://www.msnbc.msn.com/id/7634313/

Obst, P., Zinkiewicz, L., & Smith, S. G. (2002). Sense of community in science fiction fandom, part 1: Understanding sense of community in an international community of interested. Journal of Community Psychology, 30 (1), 87-103.

Pincus, W. & Milbank, D. (June 17, 2004). Al Qaeda-Hussein link is dismissed. Washington Post, p. A01.

Pincus, W. (May 13, 2005). British Intelligence warned of Iraq War. The Washington Post, p. A18.

Radin, P. (1972.) The trickster: A study in American Indian mythology. NY, NY: Schocken Books. (Original work published 1956)

Robertson, W. P. (October 13, 2006). *The Big Lebowski* fest: Hey, nice marmot. The Guardian, p. 12.

Rowell, E. (2007). The brothers grim: The films of Ethan and Joel Coen. Lanham, MD: Scarecrow Press.

Rowland, S. (2006). Jung, the trickster writer, or what literary research can do for the clinician. Journal of Analytical Psychology, 51, 285 – 299.

Smith, A. (2000). Present at the creation . . . and other myths: The Port Huron statement and the origins of the new left. Peace & Change, 25(3), 339-363.

Stone, D. (March 9, 1998). The Coens Speak (reluctantly). IndieWire. Retrieved April 28, 2008 from http://www.indiewire.com/people/int_Coen_Joel_Ethan_980309.html.

Stone, J. (October 19, 2005). Careful, man, there's a cult phenomenon here: White Russians, bowling and a Dude join forces at Lebowski Fest. The National Post, p. AL4.

Travers, P. (March 19, 1998). Bowling for laughs with the Coen Boys. Rolling Stone, 782. Retrieved April 28, 2008 from the Academic Search Premier database.

University of Washington Libraries. (n.d.). Vietnam War Era Ephemera Collection. Retrieved July 2, 2008, from http://content.lib.washington.edu/protestsweb/index.html

Viscosity Clothing Company, (2008). Lebowski action figures set – The Dude and Walter. Retrieved April 28, 2008 from http://www.rock-n-roll-action-figures.com/bigleacfiset.html.

Willeford, W. (1969). The fool and his scepter. Chicago, IL: Northwestern University Press.

Yost, M. (July 23, 2003). `All Things Lebowski' as fans of cult film gather to bowl and drink White Russians. The Wall Street Journal, p. D10.

[i] *TBL* is a story about mistaken identity. Thus, writing about *TBL* can be confusing. We will refer to The Dude as The Dude and the millionaire Jeffrey Lebowski as Jeffrey Lebowski.

This article originally appeared in: Ashton, William A. (2009) "Deception and Detection: the Trickster Archetype in the Film, The Big Lebowski, and its Cult Following," Trickster's Way: Vol. 5: Iss. 1, Article 5.

Kate Radomski, *DVD Cover for The Big Lebowski*

Rich Nairn, *Give Me Notes*

"That's just, like, your opinion, man": Irony, Abiding, Achievement, and *Lebowski*

BY BRIAN WALL
Binghamton University

The terms in which the reception of *The Year's Work in Lebowski Studies* played out in the comments to Dave Itzkoff's *New York Times* review in December of 2010 rehearsed a number of the familiar questions that have long plagued academic studies of popular culture: What would it mean to take mass culture seriously? What would be left after refusing the fan's or the cult's uncritical enthusiasm and the elite's dismissal? Or, to put it rather differently, who is the audience for a collection like this? While many fans applauded the editors' and contributors' desire to engage with everything Dude, there were as many or more who substantially resented someone taking their fun seriously (thought apparently being the enemy of pleasure). And on the still more reactionary side, this volume's very existence was cited, variously, as evidence of the decline of the university as an institution, of the death yet again of the canon of seemingly self-evidently great works, and as evidence of the silliness if not sheer irrelevance of the academic study of popular culture. This last seems particularly germane, in so far as the *Times* itself regularly offers its own confidently commonsensical, ideology-free perspective by noting the daft pursuits of the humanities professoriate. The review, while guardedly sympathetic, continues that tendency toward condescension perhaps most egregiously manifested in Jonathan Kandell's shameful obituary of Jacques Derrida in 2004.

These sorts of reception suggest some of the potential pitfalls the editors of any collection about a cult object must navigate: a great deal of fan culture depends upon iterability, repetition and citation, and thus opposes academic analysis; and certain conservative ideas of what constitutes the "proper" object of academic study exclude the mass cultural object by fiat.[1] Commendably, *The Year's Work* stakes out a variety of other possible positions, and, at its best, imagines a necessary rapprochement between academics – who are also always already fans – and a portion of the cult audience who look to deepen their pleasure. For the latter, *The Year's Work* seems to fit neatly alongside the seemingly endless "Philosophy and –" collections that constitute the bulk of the philosophy section at my big box bookstore, collections whose ubiquity suggests to me that someone needs to write a *Philosophy and "Philosophy and"* book. For the former, however, the Coen brothers' film presents a challenge that calls for the most delicate judgment: as both fans and scholars, academics here are forced to countenance the conflicting allegiances of immersion and distance. Some scholars here, seeking to respond to The Dude on his own terms, try to overcome this conflict with the ambivalent aid of irony, while others prefer the detachment of a more traditional academic perspective. Indeed, the volume's own title signals the extent to which irony is here a privileged form of address.

Ultimately, to take *The Big Lebowski* seriously would be to refuse or go beyond the fan's pleasures of citation in favor of elaborating a different context, moreover one that might, very explicitly, threaten to subsume the film itself. In order to deal with this deadlock, the editors have chosen, in an eloquent and spirited introduction, to cast academics as *over*-achievers, which is to say as a special remove from the production and circulation of more traditional Hollywood products:

> Given the aftermarket's vitality, the contemporary Hollywood cult film is not a thing apart. Certain species of cult cinema are not discontinuous from dominant industry or social practices; instead they represent continuity with, even a shining realization of, the dynamics of media circulation today. In this sense, cult is a logical extension of replay culture: it achieves the kind of penetration into viewers' 'hearts and minds' that media convergence and multi-windowed distribution promote; cultish viewing, in turn, represents a particularly dedicated and insistent pursuit of media inspired by replay. (19)

---

[1] As Barbara Klinger has cogently and pointedly argued in the context of *Lebowski*, the participation, quotation, and repetition that largely characterizes the audience's relation to cult film cannot be thought of as uncritically empowering to its fans or at a

case and fraction of the Achievers, the Lebowski cult's preferred self-nomination. Such a term neatly signals both identity and difference, the academic's fannishness and her intellectual "excess."[2] There will be, then, a third term to make a constellation of the binaries of "to achieve" and "to abide": to over-achieve, to reach too far, to try too hard, to do too much. But as the introduction proceeds, it spells out another image of what it might mean to "work" on *Lebowski*, now in terms of the joint:

> The film demands to be seen with bleary eyes, and this *Year's Work* is offered in this vein – laid-back, easy-going, comfortably dead-beat, slack. … Yes, the experience of the film – the experience of our work – focuses not on codes, on the cracking of themes and allusions, but on the process of ideation itself, on an imaginative openness that never ceases to fail to focus into form. (6-7)

To study The Dude, then, one must imitate The Dude; but this mimetic strategy parallels and extends the stance of the cult fan, as academic labor here risks relaxing into stoned riffing, its Promethean overachieving relaxing into the aleatory creation and dissipation of ideas, which dissolve into blue smoke. Such a spirit also implies a dangerous – but very Dude-like – wager, and one, unfortunately, that some are fated to lose: namely, that the loser wins (*pace* The Big Lebowski's claim that "The bums will always lose!" as The Dude leaves with a rug). This wager also implies that a mimesis of the film's logic-which-is-not-one can better serve our encounter than more traditional academic discourse. In a proper and laudably utopian fashion, evocative of Adorno's gloss on mimesis, the wager implies that a toke from The Dude's joint might limber up and break down ossified scholarly postures, the reification of academic subject and cultural object, and the gulf between ivory tower dweller and mass cultural fan.

But to imitate The Dude seems also to risk merely repeating him, quoting him, and citing him – that is, merely reaffirming the logic of postmodern pastiche (inarguably structural to the film), whose worrying political ambivalences and instabilities have been extensively detailed by Jameson, Hutcheon, and many others. An imitation of The Dude might produce new ideas about the film and about mass culture as such, or it might just end up uncritically reaffirming and reifying the commodity culture of which the film is at once an expression, a symptom, and a critique.

The modesty of many of the claims made in this anthology and the explicit and implicit allegiance demonstrated by many of the authors – and by the editors – to the film's fan base and/or cult status authorize us to ask about the implicit – and occasionally, explicit – valuation of intellectual labor and characterization of the intellectual himself. The most successful contributions here thematize this dilemma to a certain degree; but just as many either ignore it as a problem, or more troublingly reject scholarly protocols outright, and proffer instead something much more stoned, ironic, and/or fannish. There is relatively little evidence here of the attitude that characterized postcolonial studies or even cultural studies in their early days, namely the agonizing self-consciousness of the intellectual's position in relation to his object. These fields demonstrated a rigorous and deeply felt sense of conflict between one's various group allegiances and one's subjectivity, a well-nigh Sartrean agon that refused to allow the collapse of tensions constituted by an intellectual distance, on the one hand, and class, ethnic, group, and/or gender allegiances, on the other hand. I would argue that such a tension is evidence of a crucial awareness of history – history of the discipline, of the medium, and also of the mode of production itself. Without this tension, without an explicit awareness of the necessary distance that obtains in the academic's relation to culture, the resulting efforts here risk collapsing into so many gestures of resignation – or worse, of a self-loathing anti-intellectualism. In such a scenario, populism, itself an intellectual and ideological construct, affords academics an opportunity to recite the lines they love – "Nice marmot" or "I can get you a toe!" – and wear jellies while drinking White Russians, but do so *ironically*. The text persists only as culinary and as a commodity, and intellectual labor becomes indistinguishable from consumption.

Against this problematic and pervasive irony, it might be worth considering another rhetorical mode whose very substance is also constituted by oppositions and contradictions of all sorts – that is, dialectics. Adorno writes that "the very opposition between knowledge which penetrates from without and that which bores from within becomes suspect to the dialectical method, which sees in it a symptom of precisely that reification which the dialectic is obliged to accuse" (209). From this perspective, the opposition between fan and scholar itself must be submitted to scrutiny, rather than merely being ironically affirmed and rehearsed. Perhaps the contributions the volume makes to this particular problem are its most valuable, and the ones with the greatest implications for the study of popular culture and the humanities: at its best, *The Year's Work* values the fan's immanent, molecular knowledge of the film and of its attendant culture as well as the academic's more molar perspective, at the same time that it reveals the limits of both the fan's fetishism and the scholar's mandarinism. What resolves itself fitfully here, in glimpses and beyond irony, is a view of culture as a totality – not the alienating totality of global capital and the commodity, but a totality in which the intellectual and the affective, modernism and mass culture, or, if you prefer, achieving and abiding are no longer irredeemably opposed.

To respond to *The Big Lebowski* ironically, then, may in a sense be to be true to it – but it would also leave

---

[2] But maybe we'll have to say "him," because a quick scan of the table of contents — with its overwhelmingly masculine orientation, but not monopoly — invites us to wonder if The Dude's joint is mostly a dude's joint. To register this I have therefore chosen to use the masculine pronoun throughout.

intact and unquestioned the troublesome opposition between fan and scholar, an opposition that the best of these contributions complicate. The most valuable and provocative contributions here are more dialectical than ironic – which is not to say humorless. With more than twenty contributions, the volume cannot be considered in its entirety here, so I single out a number of its exemplary essays.

David Martin-Jones offers one of the most challenging, and, in a very un-Dude-like manner, articulate explorations of the film. His "No Literal Connection: Images of Mass Commodification, U.S. Militarism and the Oil Industry in *The Big Lebowski*" soberingly presents the film as a work of "national cinema," focusing on "the way that U.S. foreign policy is determined by Fordism, the automobile, and the need for oil, as it is represented in the film" (204). The political subtext of the film, Martin-Jones persuasively argues, has been submitted to a kind of dream-work, re-figured under a range of well-documented generic citations and allusions that have too often been dismissed as mere postmodern play. Put another way, there is "no literal connection" between the official narrative of the film and the political subtext Martin-Jones unearths – but rather a figural one that underwrites the comedy, and proves to be its condition of possibility. He begins by examining the confluence, in the opening sequence of the film, of national expansion towards the frontier – an expansion that reaches its terminus in Los Angeles – and American intervention in the Persian Gulf: the latter extends the former, and not just its vector, but its imbrication with a conception of mobile people and capital that is realized in the automobile – which needs oil. Thus the film's striking image of Saddam Hussein standing before a near-infinite tower of bowling shoes becomes a condensation of American foreign policy and the demands of Fordist production, which can tolerate no limits and constantly requires new markets. Even architectural style and bowling itself then come to speak of an economy determined by automobility, mass production, and the commodification of leisure, all of which depend upon and are guaranteed by American foreign policy. But then, keeping the introduction and spirit of The Dude in mind, are we being too serious? Over-achievers? It's a risk I'll take in order to appreciate Martin-Jones's fine essay, even though he betrays slackness, pastiche, repetition and citation – or rather precisely *because* he does: because this essay explicitly recognizes how leisure, play, entertainment, film, fun, fans, and cults absolutely depend upon material and economic structures and upon networks of circulation and exchange; and because this essay implicitly remains faithful to a notion of critical intellectual labor as both taking place at an impossible distance from and absolutely entangled within the culture and the problematics it inherits.

In contrast, the editor Edward Comentale's modestly titled "'I'll Keep Rolling Along': Some Notes on Singing Cowboys and Bowling Alleys in *The Big Lebowski*," ambles along in an appropriately tumbleweed-like fashion, modestly concealing its argument beneath an easy style. Beginning as a meditation on the Western and its generic function in the film, Comentale's essay moves to a fascinating discussion of Gene Autry and the commodification of the cowboy as style. Both moves serve to develop a strong argument regarding the film's deployment of gesture: "for if cinema has proven capable of responding to modernity, and particularly to the loss of coherent experience that accompanied the closing of the frontier, it responds most significantly through its emphatic use of gesture" (229). This is a potent and provocative claim, asserting not simply the ways in which the film points back to the directors' hand, but the extent to which the film and even the Coens' oeuvre presents us with a virtual anthology of gesture. Here, gesture is no longer construed as expressive, but is instead mute, frustrated, excessive, and hermetic. As such, "in *Lebowski*, while many gestures arise out of communicative failure, they also – following Agamben – expose communicability in its purest form" (245). Bowling, therefore, while testifying to the exhaustion and emptiness of the public sphere, also includes, inevitably, this gestural surplus: "Here, gesticulating gracefully on the last frontier, the film loses its voice and makes us feel something more than alienation, something other than violence" (250).

The value of such a claim seems more than a little belied by Comentale's slacker title, which needlessly ironizes his essay's rich content. The title also indicates the extent to which, after careful and rewarding elaboration, the essay demurs from expanding upon what this excess that inhabits or characterizes the gesture actually *is*: does it have a politics? an erotics? Is it a form or a content? The implication here would seem to be that this gestural excess that persists after the impoverishment of various other communicative regimes and after the dissolution of an authentic public sphere might retain some critical or even utopian dimension itself, but the essay's self-description as "some notes" seems to preclude prospective conclusions. It's hard not to feel some frustration here, and to wonder if too strict a fidelity to The Dude's own ethos or to the film's self-ironizing strategies might be responsible.

Surprisingly, at one juncture where the reader might expect the collection to be at its most ironic – that is, in Joshua Kates's "*The Big Lebowski* and Paul de Man: Historicizing Irony and Ironizing Historicism" – irony, even "hyperirony," is everywhere evoked and thematized, but nowhere embodied. This strikes the reader as oddly exceptional, given the film's own ironic tendencies, the directors' much-discussed love of the ironic mode, and the essay's own consideration of irony in de Man's thought and style. But for Kates, this is the effect of history, or rather the way in which irony troubles certain construals of history and announces what we have come to call the postmodern, which is "a pause or gap in the comprehension of history not simply explicable through the workings of history itself" (172). The central ironies, then, that the essay details devolve from de Man's legacy, which emerges and is embraced at a historical point at which the various utopian agents and agendas in the '60s are eclipsed – it lives on past its moment and as a response to its moment, like The Dude. I wonder, though, if the notion of periodization and the linear conception of history, both of which make up part of Kates's target here, are, ironically, also well past their "best before" date – does anyone believe in them anymore? Even or except ironically?

Perhaps the collection's best realization of its untraditional mode and aims is to be found in Judith Roof's "Size Matters," which investigates – and enacts – the film's fluid economies of gender and exchange:

> *The Big Lebowski* is governed by an economy of fluid exchange or the exchange of fluids, which in the end is no exchange at all. This fluid economy moves in all directions simultaneously, producing layerings, erosions, vacuums, dissolutions, and flows that render structure and unidirectional cause/effect irrelevant, or, in contrast with marked efforts at organization (such as genre), at least shows their futility. (412-13)

Genre, exchange, causality, and conception – all exemplary of an unsustainable and phallic regime of "bigness" – are raised as possibilities in the film only to be thwarted, according to Roof's stunning gloss, in favor of a liquid and matrixial femininity that is embodied in Maude (but also in White Russians). And as the film plays, so too does Roof's thought and prose, not in imitation of the film's style, but, pointedly, in imitation of its spirit. Can I say that The Dude would dig her style? Precisely because it is *not* a replica of his own?

The problems of irony, quotation, and play also arise in Thomas Byers's contribution, "Found Document: The Stranger's Commentary, and a Note on His Method," but in contrast to Roof's entry, Byers aims to push the film's logic of pastiche as far as it might go. While the substance of the essay offers some valuable considerations of Jeff Bridges's role, and locates his performance on a continuum with the Cary Grant of screwball comedy (but of Hitchcock too), the opening pages, with their arch disavowal and simultaneous defense of pastiche, both set the stage for and render redundant what is to follow. Byers writes:

> The Other Stranger's discourse may be a form of what I would call "disseminated" parody, in which there is no single target, and the satiric and comic effects arise at any given moment from the juxtaposition of two equally appreciated and equally critiqued discourses. Thus, when the Other Stranger "does" a version of academic cultural studies in his Hollywood Western voice, the reader may smile both at the expense of and in appreciation of both discourses. (190)

Here's an example: "Now, that may seem as obvious as a heifer in a sheep-herd, but here's the thing; we might think we're thinkin' about the sixties, or the forties, or the seventies, but most likely when we do, we're thinkin' about the picture shows at all them times" (200). Byers channels the Stranger channeling Fredric Jameson; and while the point is properly Jamesonian, reminding us of how history always comes to us in a framed and mediated form, it occurs to me that this might not be the unity of theory and practice – or the theory *as* practice – for which Jameson strives. Indeed, "disseminated parody" seems indistinguishable from irony, which would seem to preclude the kinds of appreciation Byers seeks to produce. Or if we agree it is parody, then far from being "disseminating," it risks trivializing Jameson and condescending to the Stranger, who enjoys a privileged relationship to the film's narrative, being both outside and inside of it. It undermines the very Jamesonian ideas that Byers might well want to preserve, by abstracting them from Jameson's rigorous and necessarily dialectical prose and inserting them into this new context, a context that parodies the same style that birthed the ideas to begin with. Byers's parody makes the experience a zero-sum game, one which negates more than it complicates the ideas and discourses it mobilizes, and one that threatens to reaffirm the profound ambiguity that informs many parts of this collection: can the logic and style of irony, parody, and pastiche, a logic and style so prevalent in the film and in its reception, return scholarly dividends?

Perhaps one of the best object-lessons in this regard comes from the collection's other editor, Aaron Jaffe, whose essay "Brunswick = Fluxus" "considers the cultural meaning of 'wood' in *The Big Lebowski*" (427). While the modesty of such a thesis initially suggests "underachiever," Jaffe has some instructive and valuable surprises in store for the reader: far from being a mere catalog of representations, Jaffe's playful contribution works from the outset to estrange rather than ironize the oppositions of nature and culture, self and other, the living and the dead, interior and exterior, concrete and plastic and, finally, Brunswick and Fluxus, which stand for commodity culture and the avant-garde, respectively. Spiritually akin to Roof's fluid contribution, Jaffe's undoes the solidity of wood, revealing it as part of the structural support of a "masculinist, genealogical substrate implicit in the prevailing conceptions of time and space" (439). Wood, whether thought of as bowling surface or result of *Logjammin'*, comes to attest to its own plasticity, which then entails, through Jaffe's careful elaboration, the uprooting of dead wood: debt, exchange, patrimony and patronymics. Jaffe's own thought displays an enviable plasticity, in the best sense of the term.

More essays in this collection deserve attention. But I end with the penultimate contribution, Jonathan Elmer's persuasively Heideggerian "Enduring and Abiding." Elmer argues that the film is essentially underdetermined, offering itself up to a vast and contradictory variety of modes of consumption, interpretation, and enjoyment. The Dude, in his slackness, his paunchiness, and his lack of ambition, embodies this sheer potential, as glossed in Agamben's "Bartleby" essay: Elmer writes, "The Dude embodies *potentia*, he is always employable because he is never employed – merely abiding" (454). "The Dude abides," the Stranger tells us in the film's final moments, adding, "I don't know about you, but I take comfort in that. It's good knowin' he's out there, The Dude, takin' her easy for all us sinners." In this context, perhaps the lesson of not only Elmer's elegant essay but of the collection's varied offerings is that we are the sinners because we cannot simply abide and we cannot let this film abide. For The Dude, abiding *is* an achievement – as it is not for all us sinners who see abiding and achieving as opposed, who must achieve to abide, and who, finally, must achieve to overcome the contradiction between achieving and abiding. Those contributions that work at overcoming the conflict between work and play, rather than ironizing it, are the ones, finally, that most keep faith with The Dude.

....

Brian Wall is Assistant Professor of Film Theory in the Cinema Department at Binghamton University. His "'Jackie Treehorn treats objects like women!': Two Types of Fetishism in The Big Lebowski" appeared in Camera Obscura 69 (2008); an expanded version appears in his recent book Theodor Adorno and Film Theory: The Fingerprint of Spirit (Palgrave 2013).

Works Cited

Adorno, Theodor. "Cultural Criticism and Society." *The Adorno Reader*. Ed. Brian O'Connor. Oxford: Blackwell, 2000. 195-210. Print.

Agamben, Giorgio. "Bartleby, or On Contingency." *Potentialities: Collected Essays in Philosophy*. Trans. Daniel Heller-Roazen. Stanford: Stanford UP, 1999. 243-71. Print.

Iztkoff, Dave. "Lebowski Studies 101: At Least It's an Ethos." Rev. of *The Year's Work in Lebowski Studies*, ed. Edward P. Comentale and Aaron Jaffe. *New York Times* 30 Dec. 2009. Web. 13 Apr. 2010.

Kandell, Jonathan. "Jacques Derrida, Abstruse Theorist, Dies at 74." *New York Times* 10 Oct. 2004. Web. 20 Apr. 2010.

Klinger, Barbara. "Becoming Cult: *The Big Lebowski*, Replay Culture and Male Fans." *Screen* 51.1 (2010): 1-20. Print.

Josua Waghubinger, *Calmer Than You Are*

Dany Rand, *Dude Buddha*

Bowling for Buddha

BY CHRIS "PEPPER" LANDIS

To our Western eyes The Dude of *The Big Lebowski* (Jeff Bridges) looks like a slobbish, lazy, hippie hold-over, decades past his prime. The story even begins with a narration by The Stranger (Sam Elliott), a cowboy, the ultimate icon of a Westerner, noting:

> A way out West there was a fella, fella I want to tell you about, fella by the name of Jeff Lebowski. At least, that was the handle his lovin' parents gave him, but he never had much use for it himself. This Lebowski, he called himself The Dude. Now, Dude – that's a name no one would self-apply where I come from. But then, there was a lot about The Dude that didn't make a whole lot of sense to me.

The Stranger is unable to grasp why someone would call himself a dude – fightin' words to a real cowboy. But appearances are, not infrequently, deceiving. Read that again and replace "Dude" with "Buddha."

The Stranger continues:

> Now this story I'm about to unfold took place back in the early nineties – just about the time of our conflict with Sad'm and the Eye-rackies. I only mention it 'cause sometimes there's a man – I won't say a hero, 'cause what's a hero? But sometimes there's a man. And I'm talkin' about The Dude here – sometimes there's a man who, wal, he's the man for his time and place, he fits right in there – and that's The Dude, in Los Angeles ... and even if he's a lazy man, and The Dude was certainly that – quite possibly the laziest in Los Angeles County, which would place him high in the runnin' for laziest worldwide.

Read that again and try replacing "hero" with "god."

In a Buddhist understanding, The Dude is not lazy: he just doesn't concern himself with unimportant things, or at least important things in the Western sense. Money seems of little value to The Dude. He isn't employed and he doesn't care to be. He even ultimately resists the temptation of the ransom money.

This Is Your Enlightened Brain on Drugs

On The Dude's first meeting with Brandt (Phillip Seymour Hoffman), The Dude reveals something about himself:

> **Brandt**: ... You never went to college?
> **Dude**: Well, yeah, I did, but I spent most of my time occupying various, um, administration buildings –
> **Brandt**: Heh-heh –
> **Dude**: – smoking Thai-stick, breaking into the ROTC.

This passing comment on attending what Westerners would consider an institution of higher learning may seem mundane, but it shows us that The Dude gained his true education by participating in various sit-ins and through other nontraditional means.

Siddhartha Gautama sat under a tree 2600 years ago meditating himself into an altered state of mind until he reached enlightenment, thus becoming the Buddha. Enlightenment likewise came upon Jeffrey Lebowski during one of his college sit-ins, thus transforming him into The Dude. What altered his state of mind? The Dude explains that he smoked Thai stick during the sit-ins; this was the catalyst that freed his mind and allowed enlightenment to sneak in. (That's how it always happens to me – damned sneaky enlightenment.)

The Dude makes a similar comment to Maude (Julianne Moore):

> ... Fortunately I've been adhering to a pretty strict, uh, drug regimen to keep my mind, you know, limber.

We are also privy to other instances of The Dude's visions of enlightenment, brought on by either drugs or punches to the face (enlightenment hurts) and appearing as the transitional vignettes where The Dude experiences dreams or hallucinations. It's clear through all of this that The Dude has become a variety of Buddha.

About a Rug

Gautama the Buddha never claimed to be a god, only a man working toward an ideal existence, and we can only imagine that he had good days and bad. Likewise, Dude the Buddha has obstacles on *his* path to perfection. As Buddhism teaches, "All suffering derives from desire." And to quote Ed Burns from the movie *Confidence*, "Wasn't it Jack Kerouac that said, 'Even if I have a rug I have too much'?" (Ed Burns *does* play a con-man, so this may need to be taken with a grain of salt.)

The Dude's suffering begins when Woo the Chinaman (no coincidence. Free Tibet!) pees on The Dude's rug, after which The Dude seeks out the other Jeffrey Lebowski to get his rug replaced. This other Jeffrey

Lebowski, this Big Lebowski, is the intended target of the rug-peeing. The Dude's troubles continue and his suffering increases as his desire for his rug leads to the temptation for a cut of the million dollar ransom everyone dangles in front of him.

The Big Lebowski is himself a symbol of what The Dude might have become had he followed the road *more* traveled, finished college and fell into the Western idea of success. In other words, The Big Lebowski is the Bizarro-world Dude and stands diametrically opposed to everything The Dude holds dear (with the exception of the use of his legs; I bet he wishes he still had that).

Dude the Buddha Meets Jesus the Pederast

Consider all the stereotypical, symbolic figures in this movie: The Big Lebowski the Capitalist; Maude the Feminist; Smokey the Pacifist; Treehorn the Pornographer; Walter the Bellicose Vietnam Vet; Malibu Chief of Police the Fascist Cop; Karl Hungus the porn star/"Nazi" nihilist – all desire something from The Dude. Originally, The Dude just wanted his rug.

Gautama the Buddha was highly sought after for his wisdom during his life. Had The Dude not placed so much value on his rug and – as an extension of this first misplaced value judgment – not sought to gain a cut of the ransom for helping retrieve the million dollars, Dude the Buddha would have had no reason to meet and be tasked by all of these individuals. They would have had no chance to witness his example and teachings.

The only two who encounter The Dude without benefiting from his Dudeness are Donny, who dies, and Jesus Quintana, the pederast. Neither desires anything from The Dude. Buddhism offers enlightenment to those that seek it. Donny and the Jesus have no use for such things. Donny is a dullard and the Jesus (not Hay-soos, mind you) is the rather blatant symbol and poster boy for the perversions that have befallen other major religions, scandals that – while not unknown – have not so far become prevalent in Buddhism.

> **Dude**: Jesus.
> **Quintana**: You said it, man. Nobody fucks with the Jesus.

So Why Bowling?

Buddha's life was a constant struggle for perfection. Bowling, a seemingly simple game where a big ball is hurled at ten wooden pins – just knock them down twelve times in a row – is a symbol for this same goal. Coen brother films often use circular symbols or themes, so using a perfectly round ball to achieve a perfect 300 game, in rented shoes no less, is actually representative of Buddhist principles. It's more a competition with one's self than with an opponent.

(It's worth noting that many of your better bowlers have the same dimensions as the Buddha. This would have been tough to pull off with a group of bodybuilders; they're too self-involved and superficial. Very un-Dude. But I digress.)

This also explains why The Dude has a picture of Richard Nixon on his wall. Nixon, who had a bowling alley installed in the White House, is pictured in the back swing of his approach. The Dude thus shares a quest with the archetype of his youthful grievances. It is no stretch to speculate that if it weren't for Nixon there would have been no sit-ins by the young Lebowski and consequently no Dude. His placement of this iconic photo on the wall of his home is another example of an enlightened, forgiving mind. Plus, it's damned ironic.

In the end, The Dude is left with no rug, a wrecked car (Creedence tapes intact, thank Buddha!), and a dead friend. As Buddhism explains, the pursuit of material possessions is always an empty venture (there never was any ransom money, in fact).

Appropriately, most of the plot elements are left unresolved – a pretty clear reference to the famous Zen style of questioning (like the sound of one hand clapping) intended to empty your mind. In the final scene the Stranger leaves the viewer to ponder the comment,

> The Dude abides. I don't know about you, but I take comfort in that. It's good knowin' he's out there. The Dude. Takin' 'er easy for all us sinners.

Consider in this context the way The Dude gets his "lady friend" pregnant but doesn't have to be involved with the rearing of the child – akin to the circumstances in the life of Gautama, who left his wife and child to become the Buddha. Apparently, once you get your priorities right and achieve enlightenment, you too can get laid without having to worry about responsibility. Not bad for a chubby unemployed guy in jellies.

....

Chris "Pepper" Landis lives with his wife and four children in Ohio where he enjoys both playing and writing music, writing short stories, and memorizing other movies.

Though not an an academic or philosophical writer, Landis has had another film essay published in the book called *You Do Not Talk About Fight Club*. In that essay, he theorizes that "Jack" (who is Tyler Durden) has an Oedipal complex. That essay is titled "Tyler Durden is a Motherf*cker"

Vincent Carrozza, *Darth Lebowski*

The Big Lebowski:
The Gulf War and Mediated Memory

BY DANIEL KEYES

"We" are all here on this side; "the enemy" is over there. "We" are individuals with names and personal identities; "he" is a mere collective entity. We are visible; he is invisible. We are normal; he is grotesque. Our appurtenances are natural; his bizarre. He is not as good as we are. Indeed, he may be like "the Turk" on Gallipoli Peninsula, characterized by a staff officer before the British landings there as "an enemy who have never shown himself as good a fighter as the white man."[1] Nevertheless, he threatens us and must be destroyed, or, if not destroyed, contained and disarmed.[2]

The Coen Brothers' *The Big Lebowski*[3] (1998) reconstructs the Los Angeles of 1991 with the Gulf War as an allegorical backdrop for a wacky synthesis of cinematic representational modes: the Western, porn, film noir, art house cinema, 1940s dance/musical, the buddy flick, and the white male rampage movie.[4] Moreover, major and some minor characters resonate with a specific nostalgic time and place delimited by these film genres. Thus conflicts between characters reflects a clash of film genres and political world views that propels the film's dizzy narrative. The quote above from Paul Fussell's literary account of the first World War articulates a stable modernist demarcation between the enemy in absolute racist terms in a way that *Lebowski*'s post modern portrayal of "Others" tactically fragments. The film's cinematic pastiche serves as an ironic lament for a "stable" and normative identity for the straight white American male with an implied critique of America's foreign policy. In the opening sequence, George Bush's absolute threat to encourage Saddam Hussein to retreat from Kuwait articulated on a tiny television screen in a grocery store – "[T]his aggression will not stand . . . This will not stand!"[5] – is autisically echoed by characters seemingly trapped in specific genres. Bush's rhetorical attempt to reduce the Gulf conflict to a classic Hollywood Western where "good" challenges and defeats "evil" richotets throughout the various characters and genres demonstrating that such moral abolutes are never absolute and that the classic western's solution of restorative justice via "right" violence seldom provides justice for all. This clash of genres via characters suffering mild echollia provides a critique of their own heavily constructed Hollywood versions of masculinity and the militiaristic bluster of American foreign policy in this post Cold War era.

The blurring of genre in the hybrid space of *Lebowski's* Los Angeles recalls the notion of the chronotope "(literally meaning 'time space')",[6] which the Russian Formalist theorist and literary critic Bakhtin in *The Dialogic Imagination* suggests operates "as the primary means for materializing time in space, [and] emerges as a center for concretizing representation, as a force giving body to the entire novel."[7] For Bakhtin, the chronotope usually operates to unify fractured experience giving the reader of the novel a sense of historical consciousness[8]; Thus the chronotope situates readers in a

---

[1] Robert Rhodes James, *Gallipoli* (New York: Macmillan, 1965), 86.

[2] This epigraph is taken from Paul Fussell's literary history of the First World War, *The Great War and Modern Memory*, 25th Anniversary edition (New York: Oxford University Press, 2000), 75.

[3] The film will be hereafter referred to as *Lebowski*.

[4] Fred Pheil, *White Guys Studies in Postmodern Difference and Domination* (London and New York: Verso 1995). Pheil uses the genre "white male rampage films" to delineate action films in the late eighties and early nineties like serialized film franchises like *Rambo*, *Die Hard*, and *Lethal Weapon*. Typically these films have working class, white male heroes who overcome bureaucratic and feminine forces with brute force. *Lebowski*'s Dude (Jeff Bridges) does not conform to this type.

[5] All quotes from the movie are taken from the script available at Script-o-rama.com, http://www.script-o-rama.com/movie_scripts/b/big-lebowski-script-screenplay.html (March 20, 2008).

[6] Mikhail Bakhtin, "Forms of Time and of the Chronotope in the Novel." *The Dialogic Imagination: Four Essays*, ed. Michael Holquist. trans. Caryl Emerson, and Michael Holquist (Austin: U of Texas P, 1981), 84.

[7] Ibid 250

[8] In applying Bakhtin's term to a film, I recognize the shift in media. Michael V. Montgomery in *Carnivals and Commonplaces: Bakhtin's Chronotope, Cultural Studies, and Film*, (New York: Peter Lang, 1993) lays the groundwork for such applications where he argues film's ability to represent the matrix of time and space

time and a place that is unified rather than fragmentary; however, Lynne Pearce in *Reading Dialogues* suggests Bakhtin's notion of the chronotope should not be restricted to fixing a narrative in a singular time and space, but that chronotopes can exist dialogically overlapping in a narrative in what she dubs "polychronotopes"[9]. Thus in *Lebowski*, there are a number of characters reflecting genres that give disparate forces to the narrative rather than one unifying force typical in Bakhtin's ideal novel dominated by a single chronotope.

The film's use of polychronotopes[10] as embodied by characters' worldviews constructs L.A. with the Gulf War I as a backdrop. From this perspective, this film perfectly reflects the Gulf War I media experience because it ellipses this war as a non-war, which reflects how the war's live media portrayals on CNN render the conflict a clean real time video game. Like *Courage Under Fire* (1996),[11] another early response by Hollywood to the Gulf War I, the violence and destruction of aerial bombardment are displaced to offer the view that the Gulf War I is according to the *Lebowski*'s Vietnam veteran and token while male rampager Walter Sobchak (John Goodman) not a noble "hand to hand" battle but a technocratic victory: "I mean 'Nam was a foot soldier's war whereas, uh, this thing should be a fucking cakewalk. I mean I had an M16, Jacko, not an Abrams fucking tank. Just me and Charlie, man, eyeball to eyeball."[12] This reduction of the Iraqi adversary by means of technologic superiority threatens the very foundations of American masculinity that is refracted through three principal characters in this film.

These characters appear to operate within their own peculiar chronotopes as defined by film, music, and television nostalgia that delineate their identities; consequently, the action of the film arises from a clash of heavily stylized chronotopes that question notions of mediated stable straight white masculinity in relation to a range of cultural "Others." In the film's representation of time and space, nostalgia operates as a strategy for fashioning characters' identities on the tabula rasa of Los Angeles in 1991 with the Gulf War[13] flickering in the mediated backdrop.

Although the film's cowboy narrator's introduction sets the narrative "just about the time of our conflict with Sad'm and the Eye-rackies," *Lebowski*'s three principal characters inhabit a present that is overdetermined by their distinctive pasts: The Dude, born Jeffrey Lebowski, is a product of 1960s student rebellions, the paraplegic Big Lebowski is a self-proclaimed product of the 1950s Korean war and a "can-do" attitude, while the violent and verbose Walter Sobchak, The Dude's bowling teammate, is shaped by the militiary quaqmire of the Vietnam War. All three of these characters define themselves through America's engagement in global real politics in the Cold War era as defined by three distinct chronotopes. The following examines these three characters and associated genres as a way of mapping the film's polychronotopic space as a displacement of a twined anxiety: the Gulf War and masculinity.

Genre-the Western and Its Unlikely Hero: The Dude

Although this film blends a dizzy array of film genres, it is anchored or at least framed by the genre of the classic Hollywood Western that begins, ends, and absentmindedly narrates the action. Typically the Western situates its narrative in a type of nostalgic longing for a simple colonial order where the open frontier demands to be tamed by rugged individualistic white men eager to struggle and triumph over adversity.

The opening sequence, with the actor Sam Elliott's disembodied voiceover serenaded by the Sons of the Pioneers singing, "Drifting along with the Tumbling Tumbleweeds" while the camera tracks a ball of

---

allows "the chronotope [to] reference real life situations rife with everyday associations for audience, helping to create a sense of shared place" (6). Arguably *Lebowski*'s constant shifting of genre frustrates some viewer's identification with a sense of shared space and time.

[9] Lynne Pearce, *Reading Dialogics*, ed. Patricia Waugh, and Lynne Pearce (London: Edward Arnold, 1994), 71.

[10] The film has a cult following with Lebowski Fest being celebrated in various urban centers around America. For these dedicated fans, many of whom judging from the photo gallery on the fan website seem to be white males, this film encourages dressing as characters and symbols from the film, which suggests the film's hyper real nostalgia as play of polychronotopes generates a kind of *Lebowski* chronotope. See the official fan club's website: *Lebowskifest*, www.lebowskifest.com (March 20, 2008).

[11] Edward Zwick, *Courage Under Fire* (Fox, 1996).

[12] *Three Kings* (1999) offers another Gulf War film as displacement of the war genre into the caper genre while *Courage Under Fire* tends to displace the war into a discussion of identity politics within a legal genre. It is Anthony Swofford's autobiographical *Jarhead* (2005) which unflinchingly looks at the Gulf War I and muses on how the conflict marks the end of the American solider as "grunt" while echoing Sobchak's sentiments. *Lebowski* and these three major Hollywood Gulf War films reveal an anxiety about how American heterosexual masculinity in khakis is under threat by technology and gender politics. For a detailed discussion of this theme in *Courage Under Fire*, see Yvonne Tasker "Soldier's Stories: Women and Military Masculinities in *Courage Under Fire*," in *The War Film* (New Brunswick, New Jersey, and London: Rutgers University Press, 2004), 172-192. David O. Russell, *Three Kings* (Warner 1999). Sam Mendes. *Jarhead* (Universal 2005).

---

[13] The choice of the Gulf War as a setting for this notion of identity as chronotopically constructed does not seem accidental. Larry Beinhart's satirical detective novel *American Hero*, (New York: Pantheon, 1993) hypothesizes the Gulf War was essentially created by a Hollywood director to serve President Bush's re-election ambitions. In Beinhart's novel, a director creates a CNN friendly war by taking snippets from all the Great War films including those produced by Nazi Germany. His satirical point is that the Gulf war for American television viewers exists as nostalgic palimpsest divorced from the reality of the Gulf.

Also see Jean Baudrillard, *The Gulf War Did Not Take Place*, trans. Paul Patton. (Bloomington: Indiana University Press, 1995) that articulates the theory that Gulf War I was a complete media war.

tumbleweed rolling across the desert into Los Angeles's barren streets and finally to the ocean, suggests that the Western's colonial enterprise has literally reached the end of its westward expansion. This tumbleweed motif while hinting at the narrative's rambling, spinning nature in its contact with the Pacific Ocean offers the literal end of the mythical Wild West and perhaps the end of a great Hollywood Western tradition or traditions where patriarchal authority, violence as restorative justice, colonial power, and the moral authority to "act" become diffuse.

The choice of the Western as a frame for this movie's pastiche of genres suggests the desire to return to a "historical" genre that continually attempts to remake the mythic and universalizing past in terms of the film's present. Nostalgia in a classic Hollywood Western can operate as a conservative force to indicate an authentic past where the frontier sets the standard for a raw individuality that the present should emulate e.g., John Ford's *Stagecoach* (1939) where the Ringo Kid (John Wayne) guns down murderous villains and is offered escape by the Sherriff Curly Wilcox (George Bancroft) rather than imprisonment for this act of restorative violence.[14] Alternatively, nostalgia can operate as a critique of the past to imply a critique of the present e.g., Clint Eastwood's *Pale Rider* (1985) which in stark terms demonstrates the fallacy of violence as route to restorative justice via the Preacher (Eastwood) original reluctance to use his gun.[15] Nostalgia is essentially a variation of utopic thinking that uses a representation of the past to justify present actions and forecast the potential for an improved future. All nostalgic narratives, including *Lebowski*, use the raw material of the past strategically.[16] *Lebowski* renders nostalgia into a series of distorted chronotopes that all profoundly influence the movie's representation of the present. Within this polychronotopic mediated fun house, characters invoke mediated variations of the past to stabalize their identities; thus, the movie's present of the year 1991 strategically digs into the recent past to demonstrate how the present is assembled by varieties of cinematic and televised chronotopes.

The film's initial jarring segue from the rolling tumbleweed hitting the ocean to the stark fluorescent lighted Ralph's grocery store with the film's protagonist The Dude shopping for milk in his sunglasses and bathrobe and the cowboy narrator's voiceover introducing The Dude as not a hero but as "a man for his time'n place" suggests the Hollywood Western genre has reached a new level of exhaustion or at least downward mobility. This sequence situates the film in a double loop of nostalgia: the Western and the more recent past, the first Gulf war as Hollywood Western where The Dude[17] is not a hero but simply a man who reveals the spirit of his age. That The Dude is dressed in a housecoat, slippers, wearing sunglasses, paying for a quart of milk in the middle of the night with a check for 69 cents and his Ralph's card suggests he is not the standard iconic Hollywood Western hero with cowboy hat, boots, and a confident swagger, but a counter "hero" who reflects a downwardly mobile cashless slacker form of "contemporary" heroism that does not match the expansionist rhetoric of the American empire or the Western's endless expansionist frontier thesis.

This contemporary man of his time and place is not John Wayne or Ronald Reagan ready to do battle with an evil empire, but a character that chooses to call himself The Dude (which as the cowboy narrator notes, no one in a Western "chooses to self apply") and seems to exist to bowl, drink White Russians,[18] smoke dope, and refer to his distant past political activism. The Dude claims to have drafted the Port Huron Agreement and not, as he sanctimoniously claims, the later watered-down version. The film echoes this touchstone document of 1960s leftist politics that rejects the previous generation's materialism:

> Beneath the reassuring tones of the politicians, beneath the common opinion that America will *"muddle through,"* [my emphasis] beneath the stagnation of those who have closed their minds to the future, is the pervading feeling that there simply are no alternatives, that our times have witnessed the exhaustion not only of Utopias, but of any new departures as well. Feeling the press of complexity upon the emptiness of life, people are fearful of the

---

[14] John Ford, *Stagecoach*, (Walter Wanger, 1939).

[15] Clint Eastwood, *Pale Rider*, (Malpaso, 1985).

[16] An example of the tactical nostalgic use of genre as chronotope is in the white male rampage film *Die Hard* (1988) which has its hero police officer John McLane (Bruce Willis) invoke "Roy Rogers" and the tag line "Yippee Ki Yay" to invoke the classic Hollywood Western genre where justice is drolly and violently dispensed by McClane as a luddite working class hero who has lost his wife to her career with a Japanese multinational. McLane's defeat of the silk shirted high tech "terrorists" aligns his character with the masculine trope of the Western but also to more socially conservative reactions to globalization, feminism. etc. For more analysis of this film, see Fred Pheil, *White Guys Studies in Postmodern Difference and Domination* (London and New York: Verso 1995). John McTiernan. *Die Hard*, (Twentieth Century Fox, 1988).

---

[17] The only reference to a character named "Dude" that I can locate within classic Hollywood Westerns is to Howard Hawk's *Rio Bravo* where Dean Martin plays The Dude as an alcoholic deputy of Sherriff Chance's (John Wayne). Martin's Dude sobers up to renew his friendship with his comrades and defeat the forces of evil in this film. There are some parallels between these two Dudes, but it would seem that sobriety is not an issue for the redemption of the *Lebowski*'s Dude. *Rio Bravo*'s Dude's alcoholism is clearly presented as an obstacle for him to achieve true masculinity in the eyes of Sherriff Chance. Howard Hawk, *Rio Bravo*, (Armada, 1959).

[18] His preferred choice of alcohol in the film offers two connotations: one, the sweet combination of vodka, Kahlua and cream is not exactly a "manly" drink by the standards of heroes of Westerns, and two, he is figuratively consuming "whiteness" in this new post-Cold War era. He also orders a Caucasian, which appears to be a variation of the White Russian, and resonates with the notion of the film's hero literally consuming whiteness.

thought that at any moment things might be thrust out of control.[19]

The Port Huron statement attacks political "nihilism" with an agenda The Dude seems to have forgotten. The Dude's reference to this document and his demand when locked up by the Malibu sheriff (Leon Russom) to call the famous civil rights lawyer Bill Kunstler suggests the American left of the 1960s that opposed the war in Vietnam is cast adrift in the person of The Dude who seems content to "*muddle through*" with politics while pursuing the local bowling league championship. Todd A. Comer in "This Aggression Will Not Stand: Myth, War, and Ethics in *The Big Lebowski*," referring to The Dude's inaction in the confrontation scene between his bowling team and the nihilist kidnappers, suggests that "The Dude's pacifism" fails to "hinder violence. Instead, The Dude is *complicit* with the violence that kills Donny."[20] This reading suggests The Dude is incapable of decisive pacifist action. However, in the film's conclusion, the cowboy narrator marvels at The Dude's ability to "abide;" this slacker ability suggests a pacifist approach that precludes the typical expansionist macho rhetoric of the Hollywood Western, and thus suggests that The Dude has an ability to "abide" without relying on violence. Thus The Dude's theft of The Big Lebowski's rug to replace his own rug, after The Big Lebowski has dismissed The Dude's claim for compensation and dismissed The Dude as a "bum," suggests a type of wily passive resistance that viewers and the cowboy narrator can marvel at.

The Righteous Cold War Past as Noir: *The Big Lebowski* and the "Chinaman"

The Dude's alter ego, accidental namesake, and father figure, The Big Lebowski claims to be a self made millionaire who has achieved despite the loss of both his legs in the Korean War to a Chinaman [sic].[21] He sponsors a "young urban achiever" charity to support primarily non-white children from the ghetto. The Dude slyly mis-interprets this "white man's burden" form of charity and assumes The Big Lebowski has many mixed raced children.

While The Big Lebowski appears to be a model for a rugged individualism, American capitalism, and benevolent charity, he is not the selfmade millionaire Reaganite he professes to be, but a man who married into a fortune and has re-married a nymphomaniac trophy wife he cannot afford.[22]

Many have pointed out that the inspiration for The Big Lebowski's character is derived from Raymond Chandler's *The Big Sleep*[23] where the detective Phillip Marlowe becomes a modern day knight errant for his king, the incapacitated wealthy General who has two "wild" daughters: one daughter is an ice goddess and the other a nymphomaniac who is involved in a pornography ring. Beyond the echo of "big" in the film's and novel's title, both narratives focus on a crisis in patriarchal capitalist power that the hero-detective is meant to resolve. The journey of these "heroes" is one that involves sifting through Los Angeles' murky underworld and often being knocked unconscious as they search for the shifting truth.

In *The Big Lebowski*, the nymphomaniac daughter role is relegated to Bunny as The Big Lebowski's second wife, porn star, and "Knutson" runaway from Moorhead, Minnesota, while Maude Lebowski's clipped stiff speech patterns as "vaginal artist" echo the older daughter, ice goddess character of Chandler's *The Big Sleep*. In both the novel and the film, a younger woman threatens the patriarch's precarious *King Lear*-esque existence. Despite these thematic similarities, The Dude is not the metaphorical knight in shiny armor that *The Big Sleep*'s Phillip Marlowe sardonically emulates. Nor is The Big Lebowski as entirely trustworthy as Chandler's noble patriarch the General. This parodic quoting of *The Big Sleep* suggests the 1990s operate as a place where white straight colonial masculinity as embodied by The Big Lebowski and his sycophantic manservant Brandt (Philip Seymour Hoffman) is a mask as opposed to an unquestioned state of noir-esque supremacy and being.

---

[19] Tom Hayden, "Port Huron Statement." *Voices of the Tribe*, http://www.orlok.com/tribe/insiders/huron.html (March 20, 2008).

[20] Todd A. Comer, "This Aggression Will Not Stand: Myth, War, and Ethics in 'The Big Lebowski,'" *SubStance* 34: 2 (2005): 102.

[21] The theft of The Big Lebowski's legs and the micturition on The Dude's carpet create an odd echo revealing a racist distrust of the oriental other. In The Dude and The Big Lebowski's first meeting this othering occurs with Big Lebowski assuming that The Dude is not an American who by his casual dress and manners clearly does not speak the same English as The Big Lebowski.

[22] The Dude and The Big Lebowski share the same name and in many ways mirror each other in their generational divide. When The Dude observes The Big Lebowski's trophy wall, The Dude's face is superimposed on a Time Magazine commemorative mirror that asks "ARE YOU A LEBOWSKI ACHIEVER?" The Dude is the great underachiever. This mirroring occurs on the level of mise-en-scène: while The Dude has a picture of President Nixon bowling in his apartment, The Big Lebowski has a picture of himself with Nancy Reagan (The Big Lebowski's aid Brandt (Philip Seymour Hoffman) solemnly whispers that the President was unavailable for pictures that day).

While The Dude may be cynically celebrating tricky Dick Nixon as a bowler, The Big Lebowski is unable to have his souvenir photo with President Reagan. The Big Lebowski's desire to have his picture taken with Reagan reflects Reagan's presidency that nostalgically invoked the Western as a way of stabilizing a macho version of American foreign policy. Reagan's fuzzy conscious invocation of the chronotope of Hollywood Western sought to reassure voters by simplifying complex foreign policy decisions. The Big Lebowski's attempt to simplify and mythologize his rather complex life is full of dramatic irony that resonates with Reagan's blurring of his filmic acting roles with his real life.

[23] Carolyn Russell notes this connection to Chandler in, *The Films of Joel and Ethan Coen* (Jefferson, NC and London: McFarland, 2001.) 142.

The Diminished Frontier: the Bowling Alley and Walter Sobchak

This shift from Western to a more contemporary and humble reality is signaled within the film's iconography when the rolling westward tumbleweed is replaced in by the bowling ball rolling down a narrow alley towards the pins. The white cowboys of the "wide open" mythic frontier are replaced by images of men of every shape, size, and ethnicity bowling in a neon lit 1960s bowling complex. The Dude's bowling team, comprised of the chronically unemployed Dude, the Vietnam War vet Walter Sobchak, and Donny a "surfer," who conspicuously lacks a surfer's tan or body, suggests the old frontier has been replaced by a more downwardly mobile, dingy, and confining representation of time and space. No longer are real men riding horses, wearing stirrups, and imposing their will on nature, women, and aboriginals; in the bowling alley, lower class leisure is shaped by a type of structured play that tightly regulates behavior with the league's rules of proper conduct where Sobchak's pulling a gun on the pacifist bowler Smokey (Jimmy Dale Gilmore) does not provide restorative justice but violates league rules. Dressed in Desert Storm brown khaki throughout the film, Sobchak represents a pastiche of not often reconciled chronotopes: the frustrated Vietnam veteran attempting to "win" the next war and a Polish Catholic American who has converted to Judaism.

His conversion to Judaism seems at odds with the rest of his standalone macho behaviour since he continues to observer the Sabbath by not bowling on Saturdays despite being divorced for over five years from his Jewish wife. His claim, "I'm as Jewish as Tevye" is ironic because it obliquely refers to the peasant Tevye of *Fiddler on the Roof*, who attempts to preserve his religion and culture in the Czarist Russia of the early 1900s; Walter's preserves a tradition not tied to his own Polish ancestors, but to a Hollywood musical version of Judaism rather than a more authentic or contemporary version of Judaism. *Fiddler on the Roof* provides yet another displaced chronotope for Sobchak to construct his self. Sobchak's identification with militarism and Judaism can be seen as an implied identification with the state of Israel and a cowboy form of Zionism that supports and echoes George Bush's rhetoric about drawing absolute lines in the desert sands.

Sobchak off-handedly references the founder of modern Israel Theodore Hertzel's slogan, "[i]f you will it, it is no dream" thereby suggesting the power of belief to create a concrete reality. This slogan may apply to Israel's creation, but on another level, it points to the American belief in the ability to concretize the "American dream," or in the case of Sobchak to become a devout Jewish, ex-Catholic Polish American Vietnam War Veteran who paradoxically respects the "tenets of National Socialism" because "at least it's an ethos." When confronting the three German nihilist kidnappers, who attempt to collect non-existent ransom money from a kidnapping that never occurred, Sobchak berates them for believing in the "rules" of kidnapping. For Sobchak, the horror of nihilism and those who claim to believe in nothing are more frightening than the Nazi's genocide of six million of "his" people.

Just as normative stable masculinity is undercut in this film, so is the notion of violence as a restorative form of justice that is typically part of the Western and its industrialized late capitalist spawn, the white male rampage genre. The inevitably misguided white male rampager Sobchak challenges the narrative formula of Westerns and specifically white male rampage films like *Die Hard* and *Lethal Weapon* where a decisive corrective violent act combined with droll dialogue resolves the plot. After The Dude has had his rug damaged by two thugs attempting a shakedown on the wrong Lebowski, Sobchak advises The Dude to seek compensation not from the thugs but from The Big Lebowski who was the intended target of the shakedown: "we're talking about unchecked aggression here – . . . I'm talking about drawing a line in the sand, Dude. Across this line you do not [cross]."[24] Sobchak's metaphoric absolute of a line drawn in shifting sand demonstrates a supple moral logic: Sobchak's counsels The Dude to seek compensation from The Big Lebowski rather than the thugs who peed on the rug because The Big Lebowski has money and the thugs clearly do not. Sobchak's call for revenge invokes the language of moral absolutes to invoke a relative moral universe where money and economic interest drive the pursuit of justice. Such logic parallels the decision of the Bush administration to "free" Kuwait from Hussein and return it to the feudal Kuwaiti royal family and ignores how 19th and 20th century Europe and America according to Journalist and Middle Eastern scholar Paul William Roberts drew "somewhat arbitrary border across the sand"[25] that poorly reflected the region's diversity but ensured efficiency in terms of colonial order.

Sobchak's equivocation and attempt to regain The Dude's rug resonates with the shifting ethics and vision of *Operation Desert Storm*'s mission. This linking of the stolen rugs in the movie to Middle Eastern real estate may seem like a tenuous connection if not for this description of The Dude's dream sequence in which the script declares that The Dude "like a sheik" rides "a magic carpet." The camera work in the dream sequences has a peculiar CNN Gulf War perspective with The Dude plunging to earth from great heights with a bowling ball in

---

[24] Sobchak while urging The Dude to ask for compensation from The Big Lebowski chastises The Dude's politically incorrect expression: "Chinaman is not the preferred, uh. . . Asian-American.." Seconds later he contradicts himself when he uses "Chinaman" to refer to The Dude's attacker. Sobchak's quickly forgotten admonishment of The Dude's racism does not mask Sobchak's aggression or intent. Like Bush, Sobchak seeks justice through violence while attempting to maintain a politically correct use of language to mask his intent and the moral ambiguity of lines drawn in the sand.

[25] Paul William Roberts, The Demonic Comedy: Some Detours in the Baghdad of *Saddam Hussein* (New York: Farrar, Straus, and Giroux, 1997). 38.

For an account of this region's fraught colonial history, see pages 38-54.

hand, much like one of the American smart bombs landing on a target in Baghdad.

The repeated claim by The Dude that his Persian "rug really tied the room together" resonates with ambiguous post-Cold War American foreign policy that sees Kuwait as part of the "furniture" on the global map that should not be disturbed by others. Robert's account of the first Gulf War notes that in the days prior to the invasion of Kuwait by Iraq that American senators from the grain-producing Midwest were eager to placate Hussein to keep their states' grain flowing to Iraq;[26] additionally, Roberts asserts the United States ambassador to Iraq, April Glaspie, in a conversation with Hussein on July 25, 1990, just days before the invasion of Kuwait seemingly "hoodwinked Saddam into invading Kuwait"[27] in what Robert's surmises was an attempt by the Bush administration to teach the wealthy Kuwaitis a lesson about manipulating currency markets.[28] Both the first Gulf War and *The Big Lebowski* contain shifting loopy plot lines where the original focus of the restorative justice story lines, respectively freeing Kuwait and seeking compensation for a carpet, are displaced and become diffused. This parallel demonstrates how The Dude as bungling '60s radical penetrates "the fog of war" and, in a film noir detective fashion, distinguishes reality from appearance; unfortunately, his side kick Sobchak fails to restore order because he is fixated on reliving and correcting his Vietnam experience by seeking retribution for the "Persian carpet" or Bunny, who in his words is "a fucking strumpet" who is squandering the legacy of his "buddies [who] die[d] face down in the muck."

Sobchak as the Vietnam veteran represents the memory of a failed colonial mission that will be redeemed by his own "Operation Desert Storm," as he first insists The Dude gain compensation for the rug, and then insinuates himself into The Dude's attempt to exchange ransom money for the apparently kidnapped Bunny. Sobchak's dubious moral outrage shifts throughout the film. His violence is invariably misdirected at a variety of "unworthy adversaries" like Smokey (Jimmie Dale Gilmore), the terrified pacifist bowler; little Larry Sellers (Jesse Flanagan), the 12-year old who stole The Dude's car; The Big Lebowski, whom Sobchak attempts to unmask as a fake "war cripple;" and finally the three ill-fated German nihilists (Flea, Torsten Voges, and Peter Stormare) who crumple under his violence. In all these acts, the violence is uncannily misdirected: Smokey quivers and collapses under the barrel of Sobchak's revolver; little Larry Sellers watches as his neighbor's brand new Corvette is hammered to pieces by Sobchak who believes the child has bought the car with the ransom money; The Big Lebowski is not faking his immobility; and, finally the surfer bowling companion Donny (Steve Buscemi) as aforementioned dies from a heart attack in the showdown over the imaginary ransom money outside the bowling alley. Sobchak's attempt to restore justice or balance alleged debts only leads to comedic pathos; his actions resonate with the Vietnam War euphemism "friendly fire."

Sobchak as picaro seeks to restore, via his Bushian echolated speeches, honor and glory to the colonial enterprise while his actions demonstrate the ridiculous futility of such exercises. Throughout the film, Sobchak's constantly silences Donny by saying "shut the fuck up" whom he accuses of having "no frame of reference." With Donny's death, Sobchak in broad Falstaffian terms attempts to restore nobility by eulogizing Donny's ignominious death in terms of fallen Vietnam War heroes and great surfers while distributing Donny's ashes on the ocean from a coffee can because the two "survivors," The Dude and Sobchak, cannot afford a more dignified internment. Sobchak's linkage of surfing to Vietnam seems arbitrary unless one considers how Coppola's *Apocalypse Now* (1978) links war and surfing with Colonel Kilgore's destruction of a Vietnam fishing village not to achieve a strategic advantage in the war but to locate an ideal place for surfing.[29] Sobchak inhabits a mediated version of the Vietnam that obscures and silences Donny especially in death. The Dude, who is accidentally covered in Donny's ashes by the inept Sobchak, berates Sobchak's chronotopically confused eulogy. For The Dude, the strategic nostalgia that superimposes the "many bright flowering young men, at Khe San and Lan Doc" with Donny's heart attack outside a bowling alley is a "travesty." Sobchak fails in his attempt to redeem and mythologize a petty street brawl as a defining heroic moment where Donny's sacrifice was not in "vain." For the first time in the film, The Dude silences Sobchak and, thereby, suggests a heroism that in the cowboy narrator's argot "abides" rather than seeks to mythologize the folly of restorative justice. This "funeral" scene ends with Sobchak hugging The Dude and suggests at least in this one instance that Sobchak's echolated bluster for war is silenced into a type of masculine bonding that does not depend on violence. The final scene of the movie, focusing on Sobchak and The Dude bowling with black armbands, suggests a return to "a kinder gentler" fraternal order. The buddy genre of the film reasserts itself in this brothers-in-arms moment.

Jesus and Hussein: Bowling with the Others

The one character who refuses to submit to Sobchak's imperialistic masculinity is the erotic pant-suited bowling adversary Jesus Quintana (John Turturro). For Sobchak, Quintana is the quintessential adversary of the bowling alley whose mannerisms – like thrusting on his black bowling glove – deviate from heterosexual masculinity. Quintana periodically appears throughout the film with his own theme music, a Latin version of the Eagles' classic mid-seventies rock song "Hotel California," which

---

[26] Ibid 110-111.
[27] Ibid 119
[28] Ibid 120.

[29] Francis Ford Coppola, *Apocalypse Now* (Zoetrope Studios, 1979).

suggests another version of Los Angeles and otherness. This Spanish translation of this Top 40 radio hit hints at a Spanish version of Los Angeles that does not fit Lebowski's Anglo-western frame. In one episode, Sobchak's voiceovers a sequence where Quintana is apparently forced by the courts to go from house-to-house to explain that he is a pedophile. In this sequence, it is possible that Sobchak's voiceover is a case of an unreliable narrator, who is embellishing the truth about his enemy. This vilification of an adversary parallels the experience of Gulf War television viewers who relied on the type of reportage created by the public relations firm Hill and Knowlton for the Kuwait regime that fabricated Iraqi atrocities like the story about Iraqi soldiers removing "fifteen babies from incubators" and leaving them "to die on the hospital floor."[30] Like the Bush administration's rhetoric that attempted to demonize Saddam Hussein,[31] Sobchak attempts to contain Quintana within a narrative of deviance. Ultimately, Quintana silences Sobchak by threatening to sodomize and kill Sobchak with Sobchak's handgun.[32] Quintana's verbal aggression, to paraphrase Bush's speech from the film, is allowed, "to stand."

Quintana represents a domestic version of otherness that is reflected in the appearance in a dream sequence of Saddam Hussein (Jerry Haleva), who is featured as bowling alley attendant polishing shoes.[33] This dream sequence may simply be used to demean the then Iraqi dictator (in Sobchak's estimation, "not a worthy adversary,") but it also suggests a parallelism between the bowling alley competition and Operation Desert Storm. The final bowling conflict between Sobchak's and Quintana's teams like the United States' showdown with Hussein is one that will not occur in this film. The otherness of Quintana and Hussein stands outside the film's narrative closure: just as viewers will never see Sobchak defeat Quintana, they will never see George Bush Sr.'s administration topple Hussein's regime. Unlike the closure achieved in a typical Western melodrama where good is rewarded and bad punished, in this movie the moral absolutes are suspended in favor of a hero who "abides."

Abiding Chronotopic Hailing

The Dude offers an alternative to The Big Lebowski and Sobchak's hyper-masculine façades as he claims to "abide" various hailings[34] by characters eager to place him in their own mediated chronotope.[35] The types of hailing he encounters, from the moment when the two thugs, seeking to extort money from the millionaire Lebowski, thrust The Dude's head into his toilet bowl and demand, "[w]here's the money Lebowski" are invariably misdirected, but The Dude, coming up for air from the toilet, remains unflappable like the typical hero in a white male rampager film who masochistically responds to torture: "[I]t's uh, it's down there somewhere. Lemme take a look." Unlike the heroes of such tough guy serials like *Lethal Weapon* and *Die Hard*, The Dude does not swear to avenge this case of mistaken identity.

The most pointed example of how The Dude is invested with hyper-masculine qualities by another character operating in a different film genre occurs when he accidentally confronts the private detective Da Fino[36] (Jon Polito) whose phallic over-determined dialogue offers sheer admiration for a brother "shamus" by calling The Dude "a dick, man! And let me tell you something: I dig your work. Playing one side against the other – in bed with everybody – fabulous stuff, man." The Dude does not grasp Da Fino's creaky film noir lexicon and refuses Da Fino's offer to team up to solve the apparent kidnapping of Bunny Lebowski. Da Fino's "master" narrative of the film noir genre that would explain the film's narrative is rejected by The Dude just as The Dude rejects other chronotopic hailings by other characters who seek to box in The Dude's identity.

---

[30] Douglas Kellner, *The Persian Gulf TV War* (Boulder: Westview, 1992), 67.

[31] Ibid 240-242.

[32] The phallic power of the gun in this "Western" is not an absolute for solving problems. Sobchak's first attempt to rescue the supposedly kidnapped Bunny Lebowski results in his Israeli-manufactured Uzi falling out of the car and randomly spraying bullets.

[33] Paul William Roberts notes in a footnote of his account of the early 1990s Iraq conflict that "Saddam (with the stress on the second syllable) translates somewhat literally to 'learned one.' On the other hand, Saddam (with the stress on the first syllable and nasal 'a' as George Bush used) translates to 'shoe shine boy.' Bush was as conscious of this as he was of the way his singular pronunciation sounded to non-Arabic speakers: Sodom Hussein." Perhaps the Coens are playing with this wordplay. Paul William Roberts, The Demonic Comedy: Some Detours in the Baghdad of *Saddam Hussein* (New York: Farrar, Straus, and Giroux, 1997) 125.

[34] The term "hailing" is derived from Stuart Hall's explanation of Louis Althuser's concept of interpellation. Hall describes how individuals are "hailed" or interpellated by various ideological forces and thus accept an identity always already constructed for them.
Stuart Hall, "The Whites of Their Eyes: Racist Ideologies and the Media." *Silver Linings*. ed. George Bridges and Rosalind Brunt. (London: Lawrence and Wishart, 1981) 32.

[35] The Dude is not immune to hailing other characters as if they inhabit a mediated chronotope as is the case when he speaks to a police officer about his returned but badly vandalized car: "can you find these guys? I mean, do you have any promising leads?" To which the policeman laughingly responds, "Leads, yeah. I'll just check with the boys down at the Crime Lab. They've assigned four more detectives to the case, got us working in shifts." This parody of *Dragnet*-speak suggests all the film's characters are lost in the mediated fun house of Los Angeles.

[36] Da Fino shadows The Dude in a '70s style Volkswagen beetle that does not scream heterosexual masculinity or reflect his ultra masculine film noir manner of speech; however, in a strange case of "auto" referentiality the Coens in their first film, the noir styled *Blood Simple* (Foxton, 1984), have the philosophical and murdering detective Loren Visser (M. Emmet Walsh) use a Volkswagen Beetle to shadow characters.

Perhaps the most ironic instance of hailing is when Maude Lebowski (vaginal artist and femme fatale) selects The Dude as her sperm donor. Maude seems to inhabit her own version of a haughty Art house movie. Within The Dude's elaborate dream, Maude Lebowski's chronotope associates her with the goddesses of Norse mythologies: the Valkyries. When The Dude officially meets Maude for the first time, she appears in a flying apparatus shuttling over The Dude's head as she spatters paint onto a canvas on the floor, thus echoing the flight of the Valkyries. In the most explicit reference in The Dude's dream sequence, a parody of a porn movie called "Gutterballs," The Dude dressed as a cable repairman[37] sees Maude in a bowling alley wearing "an armored breastplate and Norse headgear, [she] has braided pigtails, and holds a trident." The scene morphs with The Dude's point of view becoming that of a bowling ball heading down a bowling alley between the legs of a number of a number of women dressed as chorines. This dream sequence cuts to the German nihilists wielding large shears threatening to castrate The Dude.[38] This choice of a female goddess from the ancient violent Norse myth seems particularly apt in a movie that satirizes the pitfalls of white masculinity and the tradition of the contemporary debased hypocritical "warrior code" as exemplified by Walter Sobchak and The Big Lebowski. The Norse Valkyries offer a promethean afterlife to warriors who they pluck from the battlefield and take to Valhalla where the warriors daily enjoy a never ending cycle of eating, drinking, and fighting that result in dismemberment and then the rejoining of their severed body parts.[39] The Dude's dream alludes to both the feminine power to achieve a bountiful feminine peace and the more destructive elements of dismemberment involved in Norse mythology.

The Dude is the willing and, in the beginning, unwitting pawn in Maude's game of insemination. She demonstrates that masculinity and the male gender are redundant. She debunks the myth that her stepfather is a self-made millionaire, and she does not require anything from The Dude other than his sperm and certainly not his surname that would be the same as her stepfather's. Played as an "ice goddess," she suggests a world where men cease to have purpose. In her post Oedipal-Electra world, Western masculinity and strong father figures are not needed. The narrative closure offered by the self-reflexive and forgetful cowboy narrator hangs on the notion of regeneration that perpetuates society no matter how unconventional the method of reproduction: "there's a little Lebowski on the way. I guess that's the way the whole durned *human comedy* [my emphasis] keeps perpetuatin' itself, down through the generations, westward the wagons, across the sands a time until – aw, look at me, I'm ramblin' again. Wal, uh hope you folks enjoyed yourselves." This voiceover's conclusion hints that the Western garb of the larger narrative and Western civilization's "human comedy" continues. I suggest Maude radically disrupts the chronotopic narrative logic of the Western where men subdue women, aboriginals and nature. She suggests the "vaginal artists" are able to engender their own reality and progeny from the raw masculine frontier and the Lebowski name.

Hailing The Last Mediated Cowboy

The genre[40] of the Hollywood Western in this film as represented by the voiceover provides an ironic frame for the film's loose narrative by asserting a kinder, gentler sense of masculinity with less swearing. The Western voiceover as framing device punctuates the action prior to film's resolution when the voice of the cowboy, Sam Elliott playing the role of the "Stranger," appears in full cowboy gear at the bar in The Dude's bowling alley to discuss philosophy after ordering a Sarsaparilla. The Stranger's "cowboy" is not a historical cowboy, but one drawn from Hollywood's Western film tradition. The promotional website for the film (which is no longer available) explicitly credits the inspiration for this intrusive narrator with the "bad Tom Mix movie."[41] As this website asserts in Dude-esque prose of this narrator: "I mean, like who the hell wears a handlebar moustache, and a ten gallon hat in Los Angeles and isn't gay?"[42] In his intrusive, forgetful, and meandering voiceovers and later breaking through the narrative frame with his appearance in the film as a character, the Stranger offers both a campy and a nostalgic way of grasping the narrative that while potentially comforting seems unreliable and vaguely out-of-place with the characters who seem grounded in their own specific chronotope. Whether in the bowling alley or via German nihilism, the film's varied chronotopes of a diverse Los Angeles circa 1990 seem to have little in common with the Stranger's Tom Mix chronotope as narrative frame. His admiration for The Dude's ability to "abide" is weighed against his

---

[37] This scene echoes the early scene where Maude shows The Dude, her step mother Bunny's performance in the pornographic video *Logjammin'*.

[38] This scene echoes an earlier scene where The Dude relaxing in his bath tub is confronted by the three Nihlist kidnappers and a marmot. They threaten to return and cut off The Dude's "chonson" [Johnson]. This film plays with the twined anxieties of The Dude's secure and secured heterosexual masculinity and America's secure phallic military power as foreign policy. Clearly the film's representation of 1991 Los Angeles is one riddled by real and imagined fears for The Dude that evoke anxieties about this post Cold War era where the film's Western and the West fails to coherently "master" the emergent chaotic new world order.

[39] Peter Andreas Munch, *Norse Mythology: Legends of Gods and Heroes*. trans. Sigurd Bernhard Hustvedt (Michigan: Sing Tree, 1968), 32, 48.

[40] I hesitate to call the "Western" a chronotope since typically Hollywood westerns have a very loose historical sense of time and place; the cowboy narrator seems to exploit the lack of historical specificity in the genre.

[41] "Old Shit has Come to Light: The Lost 1998 Big Lebowski Promotional Website." *The Big Lebowski*. http://dudespaper.com/old-shit-has-come-to-light-the-lost-1998-big-lebowski-promotional-website.html/ (December 24, 2012).

[42] Ibid.

moral approbation: "... Dude. Do you have to use so many cuss words?" To which The Dude responds, "[w]hat the fuck are you talking about?" The Dude's inability to hear his own "cuss" words suggests a selective deafness to the other which is rampant in the film and comically indicates how The Dude's chronotope is not an easy match for the Stranger's attempt to idealize The Dude into his Tom Mix western genre.

The self-reflexive *mise en abyme* of the appearance of the disembodied narrator, as embodied character questioning the oblivious Dude, re-iterates the competing and nostalgic versions of masculinity. The Dude refuses the hailing of the Tom Mix version of "good guy" heroics offered by the film's narrator just as he refuses Da Fino's film noir hailing, and Sobchak's attempts to mythologize Donny's death into the fight for freedom, democracy, and surfing.

This mise en abyme is complicated near the middle of the film, where The Dude and Walter pay a visit to the home of Arthur Digby Sellers (Harry Bugin), the creator of over 156 episodes of a television Western serial called *Branded*, who lies unconscious in an iron lung. Sobchak and The Dude seek The Dude's stolen car and the phantom ransom money. Ironically, The Dude tracks down little Larry via a "D" grade paper in history that Larry left crumpled under the seat of The Dude's stolen car. This joke about history resonates within the film where history is not a series of facts but is contingent on characters' chronotopic expressions of the facts in terms of their mediated-constructed identities. While Larry gets a "D" grade on his history paper, his father created a TV western that inspires both The Dude's and Sobchak's identities.

Walter, prior to threatening Arthur's son, the car thief and poor grade school historian, Larry (Jesse Flanagan), speaks in hushed reverential tones of the series and its immobile author. Sellers senior as the source of the Western macho "myth" in the movie is a peculiarly passive agent. If the wheelchair-abled Big Lebowski represents the façade of old style masculinity, it is even more peculiar that the source of Walter and The Dude's myth of manly behavior resides in a coma in an iron lung.

In this scene with the Sellers' family, The Dude appears to accede respect for the show *Branded*, and later after being drugged by the pornographer and heavy Jackie Treehorn (Philip Moon) and left running wild on the highway, The Dude recites the theme song for the show: "He was innocent. Not a charge was true. And they say he ran awaaaaaay." The Dude clearly identifies his own predicament with that of *Branded* and its innocent hero who is hemmed in by hearsay. This television form of the Western exerts a meta-fictional influence on The Dude and Sobchak's sense of honor and masculinity.

The Western *Branded* was first telecast on NBC between January 24, 1965, and September 4, 1966; the show tracks the wanderings of Jason McCord (Chuck Connors), a Civil War officer who is court martialed for cowardice after being the lone white survivor of the Battle of Bitter Creek, a Little Big Horn-like massacre. In most episodes, the outcast McCord teaches heroism to the *faint-hearted*, which explains why both The Dude and Sobchak identify with the show. Perhaps for Sobchak, the show operates as an allegory for the abused and dishonored Vietnam War Veteran; he seems himself like McCord teaching the *faint-hearted* Donny and The Dude that heroism is equated with unflinching and decisive violent act. While for The Dude, McCord represents a post-militaristic form of heroics: the ex-soldier teaching a new code of honor that is clearly disenchanted with the military's solutions.

The show's theme song that The Dude sings presents the narrative arc for the television show where a man fights to reclaim his name. It rhetorically asks "What do you do when you're branded/And you know you're a man?"[43] This question oddly reflects the plot where The Dude is branded as the "Big" Lebowski and must locate his identity elsewhere. Ironically that identity is located in the identity of the "Little" Larry Seller's father. The final stanza of the Branded theme song sums up this sense of a masculinity seeking redemption via quest: "And wherever you go/for the rest of your life/You must prove/You're a man."[44] The Dude, as a 1960s radical and peace activist who in his first meeting with The Big Lebowski is "branded" as a "bum" whose "revolution failed," seems to resonate with this 1960 television show's character. The Dude as the movie's punching bag and oblivious sperm donor offers a different type of heroism than that offered by the apparent masculinity of The Big Lebowski, Sobchak, Da Fino, and American foreign policy. Thus the Western operates as both a framing device for the film and touchstone for characters seeking to connect with an authentic "televised" form of straight masculine behavior.

To paraphrase the Italian modern Absurdist playwright Luigi Pirandello, *Lebowski* offers characters in search of a chronotopic sub genre to construct coherency and stability. Certainly, *Lebowski* subverts genres and comically revels in dramatic and verbal ironies, but there is more than a nightmare in the cinematic vision of *Lebowski* that features a recent past as a way of positing a better future while demonstrating how this "past" hinges on a dialogic integration of a variety of mass cultural imagined pasts from film, television, and music. Against the backdrop of various imagined and real pasts of the Western and other genres, this film posits a type of masculinity and foreign policy that "abides" in stark contrast to current American foreign policy. While it might be easy to consider how to map The Dude's casual approach maps on to varieties of masculinity (accepting alternative definitions of the straight family that empower vaginal artists, encouraging one's shy stout landlord in his pursuit of abstract modern dance, passively resisting the abuse of German nihilists, pornographers, and Malibu sheriffs) while seeking justice, the task of positing what American foreign policy might look like if one "abides" is a difficult one to imagine

---

[43] *Branded TV Show*, http://crazyabouttv.com/branded.html
[44] Ibid.

in an age when America and its allies have troops deployed in "peace keeping" missions that seem more like 19th century colonial occupations. I assume "abiding" means an acceptance of difference rather than an empty or twisted echo of the foreign Other's speech and style, and an agreement in the face of opposition to quietly abide rather than seek justice via violence.

....

Daniel Keyes teaches English literature and Cultural Studies with an emphasis on media studies. He studies the performance of whiteness and masculinity in film, theatre and other invader settler ephemera.

Koen Cassiman, *Bowl and Blow*

Tarot and Tao in *The Big Lebowski*

BY DAVID THORSTEINSSON

THE TAROT AS A FRAME OF REFERENCE

Various characters in *The Big Lebowski* may be associated with the so-called Major Arcana of the tarot. This association seems to us to be so strong as to be almost certainly a conscious choice on behalf of the Coens. It is not clear to us, however, whether the Coens had one particular deck of cards in mind or more. We will refer mostly to the well-known Rider-Waite deck and occasionally to older types, such as the deck of Marseilles.

Occultists believe that the images of the Major Arcana of the tarot have transmitted deep spiritual wisdom since ancient times, and as such they have been likened to the archetypes of Carl Jung. Some of their images, like *Death* and *Justice*, are part of common lore. Their images have probably given the Coens a cue to many details in the film. And if the characters of *TBL* are indeed based on the tarot it may help explain their truly elemental force. We believe we've found 14 convincing correspondences with the tarot cards. But let's get down to cases.

The Dude: the Fool

The image of the *Fool* shows a young man with a white flower in his left hand, a knapsack in his right. His attire in the Waite interpretation is highly decorated but ragged in many earlier decks. In blissful disregard of danger he is about to walk – or perhaps rather to dance – off a cliff. He is followed by a dog which may be playful (Waite) or about to bite at his leg (older styles).

The *Fool* may be marked with the number zero or be unnumbered. According to Wikipedia this can be so interpreted that the *Fool* "moves around always and cannot be pinned down. As such, the *Fool* is everyone and every place." The *Fool* may be considered either as a blundering beginner or an adept. In his oblivion to circumstances he seems miraculously immune to the dangers of the world: He walks off cliffs unharmed and disregards the dog attacking him.

The tarot *Fool* holds a white rose in one hand and a parcel with his belongings in the other as he is walking off a cliff. The Dude carries in one hand a sack containing his bowling ball. Instead of a white flower in the other hand he holds a pint of milk, a joint, or a glass of White Russian – most memorably when he is thrown by force into Big Lebowski's limo.

The *Fool* is considered to have both masculine and feminine elements, as well as childlike characteristics. And so does The Dude. Although eminently masculine, he is often seen occupied in feminine activities like taking bubble baths or tying his hair back with a clip. And he has the infant's habit of grasping and tasting things that lie before him.

Throughout the film The Dude is *falling* over a cliff and into an abyss, so to speak. It begins with his coming home the first night – dancing along and blissfully unaware of the misadventures that await him – and being pushed into his toilet bowl. The falling continues literally or figuratively throughout the film, such as in his vision chasing Maude in the air and then falling to the ground; his falling onto Jackie Treehorn's table; falling backwards in the police office in Malibu; and falling forward over his self-applied door-locking contraption in his home. But he gets over it all relatively unscathed, both physically and mentally. He bears no grudge to anyone, nor does he learn a lesson either, and soon afterwards "it doesn't even hurt any more."

There is indeed a dog around The Dude, and we are talking about the Pomeranian here. The first thing it does when let out of its cage is to go and sniff at The Dude's feet. Perhaps the "marmot" refers to the fierce dog of the older tarot.

Walter: Justice

The tarot image of *Justice* is a seated woman holding a sword in one hand and balance scales in the other. Sometimes she is blindfolded to symbolize the impartiality of justice.

Walter is a man who stays firmly by the Rules – such as they appear to him each time. He metes out his justice gun in hand and at one time with a crowbar. A crowbar may not be a weapon but it *is* a lever and as such it is a close relation of the balance scales of *Justice* - both tools obeying Archimedes' law of leverage.

Walter of course is not the righteous or impartial judge he pretends to be. He is nearsighted (physically as well as mentally) and wears orange glasses, which means that he perceives the world literally in monochrome. He is invariably 100% certain when he utters his sentences, and likewise disastrously mistaken when he executes his penalty. After all, everything about the man is a "fucking travesty." And although he is a bookish man as well as a Vietnam veteran he is wrong about such things such as the number of lives lost on Hill 364 (there were actually no shots fired there[1]) and the breed of Cynthia's dog.

Walter is a Polish Catholic who has converted to the Jewish faith. He runs a firm called Sobchak Security, abbreviated SS in its logo. He respects National Socialism (Nazism) for being "at least . . . an ethos." He's a man of opposites; his language, for example, simultaneously crude and surprisingly rich.

Donny: the Star

Donny is a star player at the Hollywood Star Lanes. The tarot *Star* shows a woman pouring water over both land and sea. The card is thus firmly associated with the elements *Water* and *Earth*. And so is Donny. "Donny who loved bowling and as a surfer explored the beaches of Southern California from La Jolla . . . and up to Pismo."[2] One could say, in a sense, that Donny was amphibious. He is mysterious, trusting and hopeful like the *Star*. Ten stars fade into darkness at his death. Even the Folger's tin can that holds his ashes has a starlike picture on it.

Dude's car: the Chariot

The image shows a chariot driven by a warrior. The Dude may not be a warrior exactly – pacifist is a term he self-applies – but his car undeniably takes part in some real-world skirmishes. True, we see no tank battles here, but let's not forget the following incidents: The car is driven to battle by a stalwart Vietnam veteran. The car is at the receiving end of friendly fire in that same fight. It is involved in several crashes with various obstacles. It is stolen by a dunce and rescued by the police. It is violently attacked and beaten up by Larry's neighbor. Finally, in an apocalyptic spectacle it is burnt to a cinder by German nihilists.

The registration number on The Dude's car is 376 PCE. The letters of course spell *peace*, well befitting the pacifist owner. And if this declaration of peace may seem somewhat incongruous on a vehicle of war it may also serve as a gentle reminder that "pacifism is not something to hide behind"[3].

In the tarot deck the cardinal number of the *Chariot* is 7. Does this have anything to do with the number 376 on The Dude's car? Well, let's take the sum of the digits – a standard procedure in numerology: 3 + 7 + 6 equals 16. Adding those digits again gives the final result 7.

The Stranger: the Magician

The image of the *Magician* shows a man standing behind a table laid out with various objects. In older tarot (such as the Marseilles, shown right) he wears a wide brimmed hat. In Waite's deck the symbol of infinity hovers over his head instead of a hat. The tumbling tumbleweed of the film may allude to that symbol.

The Stranger wears a cowboy hat and we only see him in front of a bar table. He is a mysterious figure as he apparently does not take part in the action of the film but acts purely as an all-seeing, and prescient storyteller. Clearly he has great affinity with The Dude although he seems to understand him and his world rather dimly. Strange things, smacking of the magical, happen when he is around, such as Maude's phone call to The Dude at the nadir of his misery.

Martin 'Marty' Randahl: the World

It is befitting for The Dude's landlord to be a symbol for the world – our blue, hospitable planet. We first meet him - a man of round shape, wearing a blue T-shirt – when he is literally running his circle. He drops by to collect rent but does it without so many words. He asks The Dude to come and see his "Cycle" – his "Dance Quintet" – and to give him notes. The word "cycle" may

---

[1] According to Ray Smith, a soldier of the 1st Battalion 69th Armor in Viet Nam,
cf. http://www.rjsmith.com/info_pages/hill-364-info.html
[2] From Walter's funeral speech.

[3] Walter's words.

mean *the orbit of a celestial body*.⁴ His surname, Randahl, may by its similarity to "around all" suggest a globe or an orbit, and "Martin" (which derives from "Mars") may allude to Mars, the heavenly body. All these words and names harp on the same cosmic theme.

The tarot *World* shows us a scantily clad woman performing a dance. Around her is an elliptically shaped wreath of leaves. In the four corners of the card are the *four living creatures* that draw the throne-chariot of God according to the Book of Ezekiel. The same four beasts have in Christianity come to symbolize the Evangelists. Together the five beings on the card *might* constitute the *Quintet* of the landlord's dance.

In the Landlord's absurd and pathetic *Dance Quintet* we see a plump man dressed in little but leaves who, after a Promethean struggle, seems to break out from a world of shadows and appearances and enter a real world – of pain. He seems to scale a rock in the form of a stool and from there to reach out for the stars, hopelessly – with the abyss, so to say, yawning all around him.

The grotesque dance is set to the music of Mussorgsky's *Dwarf* – appropriate for the creature that Goethe's Mephisto calls *Earth's little god* – which is *Man*. Laughable as is his pathos, not one in the small audience even smiles.

The Big Lebowski: the Emperor

The image shows an elderly man sitting in a formal chair decorated with horned animal heads. He holds a scepter in one hand and a golden ball in the other. According to Wikipedia, the *Emperor* may stand for *Fathering, Stability, Authority, Power, Status quo, Egocentrism, Tradition, Inflexibility,* and *Conservative ways.*

The Big Lebowski is indeed bound to a wheelchair. He holds strong conservative opinions and is both egocentric and inflexible. In his home he is surrounded by bronze statues of dancing women and power figures. There is a mirror on his wall which dares onlookers to compare *their* achievements with his.

**Maude Lebowski: the
High Priestess**

The image shows a young woman sitting between two columns as if residing in a temple. She is reading from the Torah. Maude may represent this archetype. There are indeed columns in her home-atelier-temple. The first time she meets The Dude there she sermonizes him literally *ex cathedra*. Her speech then sounds as if she were reading a sacred text aloud – albeit without 100% conviction. She is strangely innocent about the world, and her surroundings are arty, luxurious, and barren. Even her video artist of a friend looks and sounds like a castrato. For all we know she may have lived chaste for years and she is financially independent of her father: a vestal virgin.

At this point, however, she knows she's getting involved in something akin to a love affair. And from now on we see her changing into a natural woman.

Jackie Treehorn: the Devil

The Devil is the giveaway card in *TBL*: The image of a man with a huge, erect penis automatically drawn by Jackie Treehorn during a telephone call. This is the *Devil* in tarot. (The Waite version, shown right, is politely understated.)

The *Devil* symbolizes amongst other things slavery to lust. In the Waite deck he is shown on a black background of night with a blazing torch in hand, naked humanoids chained to his pedestal. He has goatish features – horns and, sometimes, hooves.

Jackie Treehorn, the pornographer, is clearly associated with lust, darkness and fire. The Dude is forced to meet him at a party where naked people –some looking more like dybbuks than men – are frolicking around a bonfire. Jackie himself seems to materialize out of earth, fire and shadow. His gait is unsteady and goatish. A fire burns in his luxurious sitting room. He laments how standards have fallen in adult entertainment: "Now . . . we can't afford to invest in little extras like story, production value, *feelings*."

Francis Connally: Death

Death is depicted in many tarot decks (such as in the Marseilles, shown at right) and in common lore as a man or a skeleton reaping with a scythe. An undertaker is by vocation firmly associated with death, and doubly so is Francis Connally in *TBL*.

Connally appears first in the film walking up from his

---

⁴ According to http://www.thefreedictionary.com/

underground vault to meet his guests. His voice is hollow and monotonous. On his desk lies a very long paper knife in an awkward position, symbolizing the scythe. There is a long upright Biro pen on his desk which may allude to the handle of the scythe. He explains to the guests that he runs "a mortuary, not a rental house." Our heroes are blissfully ignorant of whom they are talking to. They argue with Death and get the better of him.

The Nihilists: the Tower

The Tower is an image of the downfall of a tower-like building being destroyed by lightning and fire in the darkness of night. This is how we see the German nihilists most of the time. They are creatures of the night leaving destruction in their wake. Their apocalyptic final scene looks like a caricature of the finale of Wagner's *Götterdämmerung*: The Nihilists stand in the car park armed with conventional weapons and – remarkably – a ghetto-blaster. In the background we see The Dude's car ablaze. Instead of the soft music of the Rhine Maidens the Nihilists blast out – ugh, – techno pop. The Nihilists stand squarely for annihilation – *Vernichtung*. No funny stuff here.

Bunny Lebowski: the Sun

The first time we see Bunny she is out sunbathing and varnishing her toenails surrounded by summer and summer's joys. She is a beauty with blond hair and a radiant smile. She beams out *joie de vivre* in a film that is otherwise somewhat *noir*. Her aging husbands affirms that "she is the light of my life."

We also see her at night driving a red sports car moving sexily to joyful music. That drive ended in the water of a fountain. The sun also sets. The last thing we see of her is when she has torn off her red clothes and runs naked a-dancing to celebrate a new day.

Jesus Quintana: the Moon

The tarot image shows the moon, double as it were with a crescent in the shape of a human face within the full moon. The *Moon* may amongst other things symbolize insanity. Jesus and Liam seem to represent this image materialized in two persons. Liam emphatically is of a full round shape while Jesus is tall and thin and does bend and sway into crescent-like forms like the inconstant moon. He and Liam dress variously in violet and blue colors. And let's not forget – let's NOT forget – that Jesus is not only a pervert – he's also a loony.

The Hanged Man

Two commentators on the original version of this essay[5] have pointed out the apparent presence of the Hanged Man in TBL. As one observes the name Karl Hungus literally means hanged man, and in Marcus Bazgrzacki's own interpretation of *The Big Lebowski* and Tarot/Kabbalah[6] we are shown that the pose which Jesus momentarily assumes in his dance at the lane is that of the hanged man inverted.

The Hanged Man may symbolize someone who has come to the end of the road in some sense, and who consequently is forced to make a radical change in his life. We do not feel that this symbol applies to any one character in TBL in particular despite its "obvious" presence. The Hanged Man seems to us to be more like an idea which keeps popping up in the course the film. He is not a person – he is more like a walking shadow.

But of course this is a very complicated case, man.

EASTERN THINGS

They took life as it came, gladly; took death as it came, without care... These are the ones we call true men.[7]

Many achievers accept that The Dude is based on concepts of Far-Eastern origin. He is frequently likened to the Taoist ideal of man – who in turn is sometimes likened to a fool – and this Eastern connection is often taken for granted when discussing things Dude.

There certainly are references to Eastern things in *TBL*. There is for example the posture which The Dude assumes on his new rug – reminiscent of Tai Chi or the *Dance of Shiva*. There is his Japanese cookery book and the box with Chinese inscription in his wardrobe (the

---

[5] http://dudespaper.com/dude-university/unspoken-messages-notes-on-lebowskian-theory/

[6] http://dudespaper.com/tarot-yes-mr-lebowski-the-big-lebowski-kabbalah-and-tarot.html/

[7] From the Chuang Tzu, Thomas Merton's translation.

receptacle of a beaded curtain). It is possible to find passages in the *Lao Tzu* or the *Chuang Tzu* which fit The Dude quite well, and this is probably not coincidental. But actually the film refers to the East mainly as a theater of war and to the people of the East as *adversaries* – albeit worthy ones (in the far East at least). Amongst the few *literal* references to Eastern things in the text are The Dude's own words "what is that, some kind of eastern thing?", Maude's "yoga," and of course the all-encompassing Oriental *rug*.

The foremost of all Chinamen in the film and the only one with a name is Wu – Jackie Treehorn's goon who with fateful consequences pees on The Dude's rug. His name and his spontaneous watery action will ring a bell for someone who has dabbled in Taoism. The term *wu wei* is an important concept in Taoism and has been translated as "without action" or "without effort." In that context it signifies *natural or spontaneous action in harmony with Tao*, which in Tao texts is often likened to the *flow of water*.[8] The whole episode of the rug being micturated upon by a Chinaman called Wu may thus amount to a parody of a central tenet of Taoism – the doctrine of spontaneous action likened to flowing water.

The words *wu wei* may also be translated as "not doing" (*wu* meaning *no*, *not* or *without*, and *wei* can mean *to be*, *to do* or *doing* according to online dictionaries). As such these words are descriptive of The Dude's idle lifestyle. And the first words The Dude says when he realizes what Wu is about to do are "Hey! Don't do –" In the parlance of the East The Dude may, if we understand it correctly, just be saying "wu wei."

Despite its eastern allusions, however, the philosophy of *TBL* seems to us – and this is our point – to be firmly rooted in Judeo-Christian thought. This is clear from its references to the Bible, to the tarot, to existentialism, to Americana of various kinds, and possibly to Kabbalah. We'll allow of course that all allusions to religions and philosophies in *TBL* are whimsical, flippant, and cryptic. The Dude – in the sense of the tarot being the *Fool* – transcends all this, however, and is bound and bounded by no one and nothing.

The wise men of Taoism and Zen tend to be abstract and otherworldly, but not so The Dude. He is entirely of this world, this time and place. The philosophy of The Dude may not be much of an Eastern thing after all. Far from it. But then – as a wiser fella than myself once said – if you go far enough West you'll come to the East.

....

David Thorsteinsson was born in 1948 in Reykjavík, Iceland, where he still lives. He is a teacher of physics at Reykjavík College and has written several textbooks on physics and computer science. David has tried his hand at designing T-shirts, some of them inspired by the social upheaval following the 2008 collapse of the Icelandic economy.

In former years David was an avid amateur photographer and his proudest achievement to date may be the publication in 2011 of his book of black and white photographs, Óður. His book is self-published and printed in Italy to the highest standards of quality. Many of his photographs show individuals in the streets and cafés of central district 101 Reykjavík; among them well known artists and beauties, bums and sages.

David's lady friend Sigga has been his associate during all his Lebowskian studies. Anything of value in this essay would be thanks to her keen intellect and limber mind.

This article is excerpted from Unspoken Messages: Notes on Lebowskian Theory. The full article can be read at: http://dudespaper.com/dude-university/unspoken-messages-notes-on-lebowskian-theory/

---

[8] Cf. Tao Te Ching, ch. 8, http://www.wussu.com/laotzu/laotzu08.html

Brandon Chapman, *It Really Tied the Room Together*

A Brief Cinematic History of Dudeness

BY BEN WALTERS AND J.M. TYREE

Having come of age as filmmakers just after the Reagan years, it is unsurprising that the Coens tend to take up fake masculinity, phony toughness and cowboy acting more than anything else. Like the 'Gipper,' the era harked back to the conceptions of manhood formulated during Hollywood's Golden Age, with a new breed of self-sufficient over-achievers ruthless in their pursuit of capital and status. Yet throughout their work, the Coens have been skeptical of rugged individualism and its flipside, patronizing chivalry.

During old-West themed intro of *The Big Lebowski*, the cowboy narrator's observation that 'Dude' is a proudly worn badge of identity rather than an imposed label of belittlement or shame is one of the earliest signs that we're not in the Wild West after all, but in more-or-less contemporary California. Having come into circulation in the 1870s to denote a man conspicuously concerned with look and dress, in pioneer country 'dude' had pejorative connotations of effeteness, incompetence or unfitness. The 'dude' was the opposite of the manly hero, the outsider, often from back east or the city, incapable of dealing with the rough real-world situation.

Cinematically speaking, this kind of dudeness was one of the earliest forms of clownery: 1898's *Some Dudes Can Fight* and the 1903 Edison silent comedies *The Dude and the Bootblacks* and *The Dude and the Burglars* offered a dandified butt. The tradition continued with the comic short *The Dude Cowboy* (1912) and on to *The Dude Ranger* (1934), about an Easterner who inherits a ranch. The idea of the 'dude ranch' – a resort version of the West catering for city slicker tourists – informed Disney's 1951 short 'Dude Duck,' which cast Donald Duck as a vacationer. Dean Martin's drunk was called The Dude in *Rio Bravo* (1959) and Lee Marvin spits the term at Jimmy Stewart throughout *The Man Who Shot Liberty Valance* (1962). Such regrettable associations reached as far as Yorkshire and Philip Larkin's *The Whitsun Weddings* (1964), in which the speaker of "A Study of Reading Habits" bitterly notes his own resemblance to "The Dude/Who lets the girl down before/The hero arrives." In this context, it is indeed a name few would self-apply.

By the late '60s, however, the term had taken on another meaning, a cordial, even affectionate surfer slang usage. According to Ron Rosenbaum's playful excavation[1] of the term in his essay "Dude, Where's My Dude?", this process of reclamation drew upon the qualities of civility and gentlemanliness implicit in the word prior to its adoption as an ironic insult. When, in *Easy Rider* (1969), George Hanson asks "What's 'dude?' Is that like 'dude ranch?'" Captain America explains that "'Dude' means 'nice guy.' 'Dude' means 'a regular sort of person.'" This could well have been the era when Jeffrey Lebowski formally assumed the title. Over the next few years, movies like *Fast Times at Ridgemont High* (1982), *Ferris Bueller's Day Off* (1986), *Bill and Ted's Excellent Adventure* (1989) and *Wayne's World* (1992), along with animated TV shows such as *Teenage Mutant Ninja Turtles* (1987-1996) and *The Simpsons* (from 1989), enshrined its use as emblematic of affably airheaded, non-conformist youth culture. By the end of the century it was elevated to headline status in *Dude, Where's My Car?* (2000).

The 'dude' type, then, is established in firm counterpoint to that hard-headed, egotistical pursuer of capital and status, Reaganite man. Dudeness is a way of being a man that privileges sociability over industry and civility over self-furtherment. It is a fundamentally good-natured mode. In a 2004 *American Speech* article[2], Scott F. Kiesling identifies it as a signifier of "the small zone of 'safe' solidarity between camaraderie and intimacy" that male friends can occupy without raising eyebrows; a term of endearment, in other words, an expression of a love that need not speak its name. From such a perspective, 'man' is less a mode to strive after than an all-purpose form of address, applicable to anyone and everyone from a 15-year-old boy to a Chief of Police. (The Dude adopts this usage well over 100 times over the course of the film.)

This is not to say that our own Dude has no ego. He has a tendency to refer to himself in the third person, and shows a hint of nonchalant pride when telling Maude and Brandt about his '60s activism. Nor does it mean that he is altogether lacking in the attributes becoming a conventional man's man: he angrily confronts Da Fino when he feels Maude's safety is in question. When it

---

[1] observer.com/2003/07/dude-wheres-my-dude-dudelicious-dissection-from-sontag-to-spicoli/
[2] *American Speech* 9:3, 2004, pp.281-305

comes down to it, he sticks his neck out for justice. Rather, it's that he has rejected conventional codes of masculinity in favor of his own terms, except for a camp appreciation of their surfaces. "I dig your style too," he tells the Stranger, good-naturedly deflecting what could have been seen as a pass, "got a whole cowboy thing goin' on." As the film's signature track by Bob Dylan has it, "The man in me will hide sometimes to keep from being seen/But that's just because he doesn't want to turn into some machine." In The Big Lebowski's mind, this non-conformism makes The Dude a bum, but there's little doubt which of them is better equipped to deal with outrageous fortune, the "strikes and gutters, ups and downs" that constitute life as it's lived. Even in the old West context, a dude's outsider status could be a boon. The Allied Artists comedy *The Dude Goes West* (1948) concerns an intellectual Easterner who, in between pratfalls, offers some salient probing at the normative conceptions of women, Indians and bad guys. The Dude might be 'the wrong man' in more ways than one, but he isn't a phony, and that makes him nigh-on unique in his world. Excused from the tiring, vain, arbitrary business of being a man, he can concentrate instead on being human.

....

J.M. Tyree and **Ben Walters** wrote the BFI Film Classic on *The Big Lebowski* (2007), from which this article is excerpted.

Ben has also written books about Orson Welles and *The Office*, programmed seasons for the National Film Theatre in London (including one on the Coens), and co-directed the documentaries *This Is Not a Dream* and "Vinegar to Jam". He edits *Time Out London*'s cabaret section and programs BURN, a platform for moving images by cabaret artists.

J.M. studied Buddhism in grad school and publishes frequently on topics related to cinema and other what-have-yous.

Bryan Thornsberry, *Dude, Here*

"It's a Complicated Case": On the Modest Menippeanism of *The Big Lebowski*

BY PETE PORTER

Introduction

Upon its 1998 release, *The Big Lebowski* (Joel and Ethan Coen) met with an indifferent box office and polarized reviews. By 2013, however, *Lebowski* has attained cult film status, buoyed by followers who quote dialogue, sport Little Lebowski Urban Achiever t-shirts, and gather for an annual *Lebowski* conference, among other miscellaneous manifestations of fan ardor, including Dudeism, a quasi-religion inspired in part by the film. Now it is probably not a matter of if but when *Lebowski* will surpass *Rocky Horror Picture Show* (1977) as most beloved misfit film.

Possible reasons for this exalted status are many: exceptional performances and characters, very funny dialogue, a surge in stoner cinema, a deep and penetrating critique of mainstream culture, heretofore repressed cultural desires for bowling and White Russians, and what have you. What remains unfamiliar is another, undoubtedly more obscure explanation, one that both overlaps and complements these; *The Big Lebowski* draws on an amazingly fertile form from antiquity whose shape is familiar but whose name is strange: Menippean satire, or menippeanism (Porter, 2003).

Being menippean is no guarantee of becoming a beloved film, but many such cult (and some more-than-cult) films fit the form: the aforementioned *Rocky Horror Picture Show*, *Duck Soup* (McCarey, 1933), *Help!* (Lester, 1965), *Bedazzled* (Donen, 1967), *Head: The Monkees* (Rafelson, 1968), *Taking Off* (Milos Forman, 1971), *The Life and Times of Judge Roy Bean* (Huston 1972), *Annie Hall* (Allen, 1977), *Monty Python's Life of Brian* (Jones, 1979), *Monty Python's The Meaning of Life* (Jones and Gilliam, 1983), *South Park* (Parker, 1999), *Human Nature* (Gondry, 2001), and *Borat: Cultural Learnings of America for Make Benefit Glorious Nation of Kazakhstan* (Charles, 2006), to name a handful of well-known titles, and in English too. The list of menippean literature is expansive, but the big three are *Gulliver's Travels*, *Candide*, and *Alice in Wonderland*. Given such an apparently diverse group of works, one might reasonably ask, what justifies their attribution to a single form?

The answer is simple: Menippean works set out spectacular banquets of incongruous elements that suggest, at least at first glance, the incompetence or folly of the author as their dominant constructive principle. Further scrutiny, however, reveals a commodious form (with excremental meanings intended) that supports such atrocities: an aesthetic of parody and violating decorum, storytellers who are ridiculous, burlesques of language and learning, meandering plots that contain abrupt shifts in setting, and the theme of the wisdom of common sense (Porter 2007, Relihan 1995). Of course, these elements appear singly in an enormous number of works but a preponderance of the syndrome indicates fidelity to Menippean satire, which has also been called the menippea (Bakhtin 1984), the anatomy (Frye 1957), or simply menippeanism (Porter 2003). Northrop Frye's observation regarding menippean literature applies equally to menippean film: it has "baffled critics" and few under the influence of the form have escaped being "accused of disorderly conduct" (313). Such disapproval is *de rigueur* to those who read criticism of the Coens, as are descriptions of their work, including *Lebowski*, as postmodern.

Although postmodernism (a notoriously plastic concept) might share some elements with menippeanism, such as a taste for irony and contrast, the postmodern may be viewed as a descendant of menippeanism that favors pastiche over burlesque, has less interest in poking fun at learning, and typically abandons the play of language. Menippeanism also identifies specific motifs of plot and narration where postmodernism typically does not. Perhaps most centrally, the menippean preference for the common life contrasts with the postmodern tendency to champion nihilism. Labeling *Lebowski* as postmodern, and therefore nihilist, seems especially perverse given the film's obvious disdain for self-described nihilist Uli and his cohorts. Theodore Kharpertian (1990) argues that postmodernism essentially updates menippeanism, but others are less charitable toward the newcomer. Robert Stam (2004) finds "that the very fact that we can see Cervantes as postmodern suggests that the term itself is somewhat inflated and ahistorical; what postmodern discourse presents as 'new and exciting' is in fact not new at all" (54), i.e., it is Menippean. Postmodernism, however, is not merely a duplication of menippeanism and shifting our view of *Lebowski* from "postmodern pointlessness" (Palmer 2004) to what I will call "menippean modesty" is a significant change that alters our understanding of the work and its artistic context.

The Coen discovery of menippeanism seems to have been a matter of intuitive understanding, a consequence of exposure to works, such as those above, that employ the form. As Ethan explains the construction of *Lebowski*:

> It's that it's kind of wrong in a way, but also kind of right in a way. I mean, even the things that don't go together should seem to clash in an interesting way – like, you know, a Cheech and Chong movie, but with bowling … You kind of do it by feel and not with reasons. (Qtd. in Robertson, 1998, 45)

Despite this apparently haphazard approach to creation, or perhaps because of it, the Coens have thus far produced three films in keeping with the standards of Menippean satire: *Raising Arizona* (1987), *Lebowski*, and *O Brother, Where Art Thou* (2001). Whether the contours of the final film sprang from imitation or intuition little changes the conscious effort that ultimately shaped it. In the case of *Lebowski*, we would do well to consider menippeanism, even if the Coens didn't.

Years of beautiful tradition: defining menippeanism

Since the introduction of the term "Menippean satire" to describe a literary form rather than a particular work in 1581 (Relihan, 12), scholars have struggled to define it precisely. Most fundamentally, "Menippean" means simply in the style of Menippus the Ancient Cynic (third century BCE) and "satire" means what the ancients often meant by satire: a form of medley or miscellany. Unhappily, medley in the style of Menippus is problematic as his works now exist only as fragments and were not consistent to begin with (Kirk; Relihan). In broad terms, Frye proposes "the impression of shapelessness" (313) and Blanchard suggests the "form of formlessness" (18). For his part, Bakhtin insists on "the deep internal integrity of this genre" (119) while adding that each subsequent age has tended to favor its own variations. In response to such challenges, Relihan returns to the extant works of antiquity frequently counted as Menippean in order to specify the essence of the form:

> … a continuous narrative, subsuming a number of parodies of other literary forms along the way, of a fantastic voyage to a source of truth that is itself highly questionable, a voyage that mocks both the traveler who desires the truth and the world that is the traveler's goal, related by an unreliable narrator in a form that abuses all the proprieties of literature and authorship. (10)

All of these admit of specific motifs and broader purposes, such as the mixture of prose and verse, which functions as part of menippeanism's "indecorous mixture of disparate elements, of forms, styles, and themes that exist uneasily side by side" (Relihan, 34). Menippean indecorousness also stems from a tendency, present from the beginning of the form, to assimilate elements from other works. Broadly speaking, Menippean satire began as a burlesque of Old Comedy, Plato's dialogues, and Homer's *Odyssey* (Relihan, 33) and residue of all of these remain. Reading *Lebowski* as Menippean acknowledges its debt to this ancient form and recognizes how, like many of its characters, it too is living in the past.

***The Big Lebowski* in a Menippean Frame**

Although critics commonly fault *The Big Lebowski* for its lack of unity, grotesque mixture dominates any menippean work. Relihan notes that

> Menippean satires are often constructed in their broadest outlines as parodies of other genres of literature or types of discourse … Within (which) are parodies in passing of other distinguished authors, authoritative works, and sober modes of discourse. (25)

In the case of *Lebowski*, the broad outline is a mock noir into which are stuffed a multitude of parodies: the work of Alfred Hitchcock, Howard Hawks, and Busby Berkeley, Looney Tunes, the Western, the sports film, the war film, the kidnapping film, the porn film, techno-pop, and high art. The "Multiple Paradosis" (Kroll) decried by many critics is analyzed in glorious detail by Robertson, Mottram, Porter (2003), Tyree and Walters, among others (including many in the current volume), so I will only mention it here. Indeed, one of the chief pleasures of *Lebowski* is decoding the sideways glances of the Coens as they weave allusions into a patchwork plot that nonetheless qualifies as the continuous narrative that Relihan requires.

Seeing *Lebowski* as menippean brings into relief how these allusions accompany the mixture of prose and verse, a motif that Relihan takes as essential to ancient Menippean satire but that has diminished in significance over the centuries. In *Lebowski*, a soundtrack of popular music, a variation of verse, plays a pivotal role in establishing theme. Bob Dylan's "The Man in Me" plays over the opening credits and reprises in the first vision of The Dude (Jeff Bridges). Other insertions of music burlesque other forms. When a flamenco-style Spanish-language version of The Eagles' "The Hotel California" by The Gipsy Kings introduces Jesus Quintana (John Turturro), the scene is mock showdown, lifted directly from the Western, complete with slow motion. After Jackie Treehorn (Ben Gazzara) drugs The Dude, The Fifth Edition's "Just Dropped In (To see what condition my condition was in)" accompanies a grotesque Busby Berkeley-style dance number, complete with Maude Lebowski (Julianne Moore) in Valkyrie costume and bowling ball breastplate. The Dude wears the cable rcpairman outfit from *Logjammin'*, a porn film starring Bunny Lebowski (Tara Reid) and Karl Hungus (Peter Stormare). The hallucination degenerates into bad trip as the three nihilists (Stormare, Flea, Torsten Vorges), wearing red bodysuits and wielding giant scissors, chase The Dude, presumably to make good their earlier threat of castration. The songs in *The Big Lebowski* add an absurd levity to the noir proceedings, mixing the comic and serious, and filling its episodes to overflowing with "parodies in passing" (Relihan).

The Stranger

Collecting this tangle of parodies is The Stranger (Sam Elliott), an earnest but baffled storyteller who fails to shoehorn his tale of bizarre people and places into a proper and respectable form. To The Stranger, all of Los Angeles is an exotic and fantastic land, populated by a variety of characters who are one-sided abstractions, complete only in their eccentric behavior and strange language patterns. And talk they do, often in philosophical terms, asking "What makes a man?" as *The Big Lebowski* does or claiming that "We believe in nussing!" as the Nihilists do. As The Stranger might say, each character has chosen a horse and they are going to ride it full tilt until they reach that great corral somewhere further on down the trail. The same might be said of The Stranger, who has "that whole cowboy thing goin' on" and who doggedly pursues his tale despite its many attempts to buck him. If Los Angeles were not fantastic enough, The Stranger follows The Dude into the more peculiar world of dreams (and perhaps the occasional acid flashback). Even these adventures fail to liberate; The Dude returns to life much as it was. The Stranger wonders "what's a hero?" at the outset of *The Big Lebowski* and this question prompts some quite unheroic adventures, which find sympathy with the menippean tendency to champion common sense and to view as naïve any pretentions to transcending ordinary human experience. In the end, The Stranger acquiesces to reality, admitting his own limitations as well as the limitations of his less-than-heroic hero, The Dude.

Seeing *The Big Lebowski* as Menippean helps us to appreciate how it structures itself around the narration of The Stranger, an astonished traveler in an alien land, a parody of the omniscient and omnipotent explorer of adventure tales in the tradition of the *Odyssey* (Relihan). (It is probably worth noting that The Coens would more explicitly parody the *Odyssey* and its hero Ulysses in the subsequent *O Brother, Where Art Thou?*) The mock travelogue is a common type of Menippean satire, one stretching through Lucian's "Icaromenippus" to Swift's *Gulliver's Travels* and Samuel Butler's *Erewhon* (Williams). In most cases of Menippean mock travelogue, the efforts of a narrator to understand and exercise some control over the universe fail. Affinities with Menippean satire's burlesque of travel literature are evident from The Stranger's introduction:

> ... They call Los Angeles the City of Angels. I didn't find it to be that exactly, but I'll allow as there are some nice folks there. 'Course, I can't say I seen London, and I never been to France, and I ain't never seen no queen in her damn undies, as the fella says. But I'll tell you what, after seeing Los Angeles and thisahere story I'm about to unfold – wal, I guess I seen somethin' ever' bit as stupefyin' as ya'd see in any a those other places, and in English too...

By embracing his limited understanding and admitting his lack of cosmopolitan expertise, The Stranger declares himself an unreliable narrator as menippeanism requires. His inability to shape or intervene in the story is evident in the scene where he fails to persuade The Dude to use fewer curse words.

Tracing the narration of The Stranger to film noir is a partial explanation, but we might go back even further to see how both owe something to menippeanism, as Kaplan suggests. In addition, the narration of *The Big Lebowski* inverts noir tradition in that The Stranger is neither detective nor is he central to the case. His story is more a tall tale about a fabulous adventure beyond comprehension than it is a noir caution tale about how reality disappoints human aspirations. The Stranger parodies the pessimism of film noir by investing it with the wonderment of the fable and tall tale; he seems neither disillusioned nor defeated as film noir would require. Instead, his experience humbles him. In this sense, menippeanism offers an alternative point of view on the grim tales of survival that make up noir. Rejecting the noir quest, which inevitably comes too late or fails altogether, The Stranger instead accepts the menippean offer of relief through humility. He appreciates that as the world is bountiful in its variety, it exceeds him. Ultimately, The Stranger also abides.

The Dude, Walter, and Who Have You

The Big Lebowski opens by introducing The Dude, tracing the windswept journey of a tumbleweed to the tune "Tumblin' Tumbleweeds" and the voice-over of The Stranger. As the tumbleweed travels over desert, beach, and cityscape, The Stranger sets the stage for The Dude – Los Angeles in the early nineties. He describes The Dude as

> a man – I won't say a hee-ro, 'cause what's a hee-ro? – but sometimes there's a man... and I'm talkin' about The Dude here – sometimes there's a man who, wal, he's the man for his time'n place, he fits right in there – and that's The Dude, in Los Angeles... and even if he's a lazy man, and The Dude was certainly that – quite possibly the laziest in Los Angeles County... which would place him high in the runnin' for laziest worldwide – but sometimes there's a man... Sometimes there's a man... wal, I lost m'train of thought here... but – aw hell, I dun innerduced him enough.

The accompanying visual shows The Dude shopping in a bathrobe, Bermuda shorts, v-neck T-shirt, sandals, and sunglasses. He searches for the freshest half & half, furtively opens it, and smells it. At the register, half & half on his shaggy mustache, The Dude pays with a check for sixty-nine cents. The thesaurus suggests many synonyms for dude, including novice, fop, city slicker, greenhorn, and asphalt cowboy. We might also add amateur, an expletive that Walter hurls with particular relish. Of course, the name also evokes the stoned California surfer made famous by Sean Penn's Jeff Spicoli in *Fast Times at Ridgemont High* (Heckerling, 1982). The Dude retains facets of all of these.

The Dude has a know-it-all counterpart in Walter Sobchak (John Goodman), a Vietnam vet who has an answer for everything. Such a duo is common in menippean works, with characters who represent "two differing clear-cut levels of perception," such as a "know-it-all" divorced from everyday reality and another who "has a view of man's struggle" (Payne, 9-11). To this mix *Lebowski* adds the defiantly plain Donny (Steve Buscemi), who counteracts The Dude and Walter by being a know-nothing whose comments inevitably digress from the topic at hand. Walter's apparent knowledge seems to impress The Dude, as when his suggestion to seek compensation for the soiled rug from "the other Jeffrey Lebowski" sets the plot in motion. Unfortunately, Walter's schemes tend to contain momentous errors. For example, before they are to deliver ransom money to the nihilists, Walter confidently pitches the following plan to The Dude: "When we make the hand-off, I grab the guy and beat it out of him … the beauty of this is its simplicity. If the plan gets too complex something always goes wrong." When The Dude explains the demand that they throw the money from a moving car, Walter's responds, "We can't do that, Dude. That fucks up our plan." An-Chi Wang observes that such "dialogue is the most often adapted form in Menippean satire to present a conflict between the glorious philosopher and the pragmatic realist. Certain philosophical systems become ridiculous when pitted against changeable realities" (23).

To someone anticipating a classical Hollywood plot, where the central characters articulate a goal and finally achieve it, the incompetent characters in *The Big Lebowski* must seem a travesty. Menippean stories, however, imagine a universe where human control is an illusion and human aspirations meet with brute reality rather than wish fulfillment. The Ancient Cynic virtue of self-sufficiency, which they preached would preclude the suffering that comes from the folly of failing to live within human limits, seems a key gift to the form that bears the name of Menippus. This modest value also bears a resemblance to the virtues taught by Buddhism, references to which occur throughout *Lebowski*. Menippeanism revels in annihilating human schemes and has little sympathy for those who deny the complexity of the universe. As Walter angrily mutters, without a trace of irony, "the world does not start and stop at your convenience, you miserable …" Of course, lessons in the indifference of the universe often populate themselves with characters that adopt a philosophy that promises to insulate them.

The Big Lebowski collects a motley encyclopedia of characters that caricature ideas, ruling passions, occupations, and embody attitudes toward the world. Donny is an innocent child, or, as Walter describes him, "like a child who wanders into the middle of a movie and wants to know … " what he missed. *The Big Lebowski*, the other Jeffrey Lebowski, (David Huddleston) paints himself as the picture of the American Dream, a self-made man (though this proves a false front). His assistant Brandt (Philip Seymour Hoffman) exudes lackey in every gesture. Bunny Lebowski, young trophy wife of The Big Lebowski, has a past in pornography. The Dude later learns from private detective Da Fino (Jon Polito) that Bunny is her screen name, altered from the Fawn Knutson that her Moorhead, Minnesota parents gave her. Jackie Treehorn, whose relentless pursuit of Bunny Lebowski's debt to him incites the story, is drug pusher, "a known pornographer," and Devil. His thugs are classic examples of inept Devil's henchmen. Maude Lebowski, a parody of the heiress daughter of classic noir, describes herself as a feminist. The Nihilists claim to believe in nothing (although this proves false). *Lebowski* even evokes Saddam Hussein (Jerry Haleva) as the man who rents bowling shoes to The Dude in a dream. Some characters evoke nationalities, such as the Mexican Jesus Quintana and his Irish bowling partner Liam O'Brien (James G. Hoosier) and colorful ethnic slurs are common. The laziness of The Dude, Walter's Vietnam prism, Maude's feminism, the vacuity of the Nihilists, the duplicity of The Big Lebowski, the fascism of the Sheriff of Malibu, all suggest how these characters have been reduced to caricature.

The menippean fondness for collecting faux philosophers that we would do well to ignore traces back at least to Lucian, whose dialogue "Philosophies for Sale," auctions Classical philosophers into slavery. This mock symposium becomes an opportunity for copious talk that ridicules grand philosophies by pointing out their irrelevance to common life. Such mock symposia where characters play with language and defend their particular worldview are a persistent menippean motif and some menippean plots consist of little else. *The Big Lebowski*, however, injects a healthy dose of mock adventure into its fantastic journey.

The Fantastic Journey of Air

The Menippean plot is a fantastic adventure that collects ideas and the characters who champion them; it is an "intellectual odyssey" (Elliott). In its course, *The Big Lebowski* compiles an inventory of ideas and their representatives, taking "the pulse of the times," much as the Stranger describes The Dude as "a man for his time and place." The author's "magpie instinct to collect facts" (Frye, 311) manifests most explicitly as the tendency of Menippean satire to digress from the central plot, as in *Lebowski* when Walter describes Jesus Quintana as a sex offender and the film inserts shots of Jesus notifying his new neighbors of his criminal conviction for exposing himself to a minor. Ethan explains,

> Inserting the flashback of Quintana going door-to-door in the middle of the scene we did because, stylistically, it's just kind of a wild leap. It's not part of the rest of the

movie. It's an accent in the same sense that the metal-flake blue is an accent in the bowling alley, against all that orange and cream. (Qtd. in Robertson, 143)

Such narrative leaps license the plot to accumulate multiple shifts in perspective, a Menippean motif perhaps best known from *Gulliver's Travels* and *Alice in Wonderland*. When Maude Lebowski's thug (Carlos Leon) socks The Dude, he enters a dream where he flies over Los Angeles, much like Menippus flies over Greece in Lucian's *Icaromenippus*. The Dude observes the city at night with all of its lights and activity. He watches helplessly as Maude, on the stolen rug now a magic carpet, recedes before him in the distance. He looks into his hand to find a bowling ball, gapes like Wil E. Coyote, and plummets toward the earth. Now he finds himself reduced to the size of a bug, threatened by an approaching bowling ball, as Maude towers over him, the apparent source of the ball. This first dream thus accumulates the Menippean commonplaces of catascopia (view from high above), bug's eye view, and dream-like states. *The Big Lebowski* also contains altered states of mind when The Dude drinks the Mickey Finn from Jackie Treehorn. This precipitates a second dream-like episode. Both of these digressions are odd in that they are part dream and part vision; important elements of both episodes later come to pass. *Raising Arizona* contains similar mixtures of dream and visions. The collection of altered states amounts to invitations to see the world anew and to question ossified patterns of perception. The Dude's claim to be keeping his mind "limber" initially plays as a joke, but it enables him to solve the case by seeing past the idea that The Big Lebowski has wealth.

When Menippean protagonists find themselves as giants, bugs, and hostages to utopian schemes, this variety of perspectives broadens their experience of the world but makes them long for the certainty of a home that they foolishly left behind. Gulliver, before his fourth voyage, remarks that he was "in a very happy condition, if I could have learned the lesson of when I was well" (213). Relihan calls these "journeys of air" to indicate their futility. In *Lebowski*, The Dude realizes that he could be "sittin' here with pee stains on my rug," an insight that enables him to realize how giving into the temptation of Walter's advice has made things worse.

The Dude is especially prone to appropriating the perspectives of others, often as a mechanism for managing an unfamiliar and complex situation. Upset by the ruining of his rug, The Dude takes Walter's advice to petition "the *other* Jeff Lebowski." When The Big Lebowski deflects his inquiry, The Dude adopts Walter's adoption of George Bush's posturing, saying "this will not stand, ya know, this will not stand, man." In encounters with more assertive characters, The Dude absorbs their mannerisms as a means of gaining favor or understanding, much as he tries to match Maude Lebowski's wit by adopting her speech patterns. Most centrally for Menippean satire, imitation indicates The Dude's lack of confidence and satisfaction with self. It is only when "The Dude abides" and returns to being himself that he recovers his serenity. This final diminution, which comes from The Dude himself, equates him with the children who abide at the end of *The Night of the Hunter* (1955) (which the Coens also quote in *Raising Arizona* when H.I. utters the phrase "it's a hard world for little things"). As with Gulliver, Candide, and Alice before him, accepting the limitations of being human liberates The Dude from foolish pursuits.

Conclusion

Acknowledging how the shape of *The Big Lebowski* matches the Menippean form enables us to appreciate that its apparent messiness is all part of a plan, a plan to forge a work that preserves the vagaries of human experience. *The Big Lebowski* is a mock travelogue in the Menippean tradition of Lucian, Swift, Butler, and others. Its teller is The Stranger, an alien to the world of his story, who follows a circuitous investigation through various settings and digressions to observe characters who caricature worldviews and occupational outlooks. Nihilism, pacifism, feminism, and a host of other isms are readily apparent among its many animated conversations, conversations that seem to revel in language as much as they do anything else.

The lunacy of the Los Angeles that The Dude and Walter inhabit finds them seeking asylum in the bowling alley, as close to a Utopia as our imperfect world might admit. It provides refuge after The Dude's rug is ruined, after the failed ransom hand off, after The Big Lebowski shoos them out of his mansion, and after Donny's memorial. Finally, it is where they recognize that, as the bowling alley is as perfect a place as any might be in this world, they are as perfect as they might be. It is here that The Dude acquiesces to a humble and common existence. As "a man for his time and place," The Dude embodies his cultural ethos; he neither transcends nor impoverishes his epoch. The rather equivocal triumph of The Dude in *The Big Lebowski* is that he "abides," which is as clear a statement of modest menippeanism as might be found in any work. Menippus would approve.

....

Pete Porter is Associate Professor of Theatre and Film at Eastern Washington University, where he has actually taught Lebowski 101 (except it was called Seminar in Film Criticism). He wishes to thank Lesley Brill of Wayne State University for suggesting *The Big Lebowski* as a case study for *Menippus at the Movies* (2003).

References

Bakhtin, M M, and Caryl Emerson. *Problems of Dostoevsky's Poetics*. Minneapolis: University of Minnesota Press, 1984. Print.

Blanchard, W S. *Scholars' Bedlam: Menippean Satire in the Renaissance*. Lewisburg Pa.: Bucknell University Press, 1995. Print

Brill, Les. The Western, The Westerner, The Westernest William Wyler, Menippean Satire, and *Huston's Roy Bean*. In *John Huston: Essays on a Restless Director*. Eds Tony Tracy and Roddy Flynn Jefferson. NC: McFarland, 2010. Print.

Elliot, Robert C. *The Power of Satire: Magic, Ritual, Art*. Princeton: Princeton UP, 1960. Print.

Frye, Northrop. *Anatomy of Criticism: Four Essays*. Princeton: Princeton University Press, 1957. Print.

Kaplan, Carter. *Critical Synoptics: Menippean Satire and the Analysis of Intellectual Mythology*. Madison [N.J.: Fairleigh Dickinson University Press, 2000. Print.

Kharpertian, Theodore D. *A Hand to Turn the Time: The Menippean Satires of Thomas Pynchon*. Rutherford [N.J.: Fairleigh Dickinson University Press, 1990. Print.

Kirk, Eugene P. Menippean Satire: An Annotated Catalogue of Texts and Criticism. New York: Garland Pub, 1980. Print.

Kroll, Jack. "All-Purpose Parody." Rev. of *The Big Lebowski*, dir. Joel Coen. *Newsweek* 16 March 1998: 72.

Martin, Paul P, and Valerie R. Renegar. ""The Man for His Time:" *The Big Lebowski* as Carnivalesque Social Critique." *Communication Studies*. 58.3 (2007): 299-313. Print

Mottram, James. *The Coen Brothers: The Life of the Mind*. Dulles, VA: Brassey's Inc, 2000. Print.

Palmer, R B. *Joel and Ethan Coen*. Urbana and Chicago: University of Illinois Press, 2004. Print.

Payne, F A. *Chaucer and Menippean Satire*. Madison: University of Wisconsin Press, 1981. Print.

Porter, Peter S. *Menippus at the Movies*. Diss. Wayne State U., 2003.

_____. "The Case for Menippeanism: *The Meaning of Life*." In *The Journal of Moving Image Studies*, Vol. 6, No. 1 (Fall 2007): 9-19.

Relihan, Joel C. *Ancient Menippean Satire*. Baltimore: Johns Hopkins UP, 1995. Print.

Robertson, William Preston. *The Big Lebowski: The Making of a Coen Brothers Film*. New York: Norton, 1998. Print.

Stam, Robert. *Literature Through Film: Realism, Magic, and the Art of Adaptation*. Malden, MA: Blackwell Pub, 2004. Print.

Stevick, Philip. "Novel and Anatomy: Notes toward an Amplification of Frye." *Criticism* 10 (1968): 153-165. Print.

Tyree, J. M., and Ben Walters. *The Big Lebowski*. BFI film classics. London: British Film Institute, 2007. Print.

Wang, An-Chi. *Gulliver's Travels and Ching-hua yuan revisited: A Menippean Approach*. New York: Peter Lang Publishing Inc., 1995. Print.

Williams, Juanita. *Towards a Definition of Menippean Satire*. Diss. Vanderbilt U, 1966.

Jeffrey Peterson, *The Achievers*

Joe Ward, *The Thor Abides*

We Need *Another* Hero: Masculinity, Rebellion, Heroism, and the Big Prometheus

BY JEREMY DAVIES

... sometimes there's a man – I won't say a hee-ro, 'cause what's a hee-ro? – but sometimes there's a man. And I'm talking about The Dude here – sometimes there's a man who, wal [sic], he's the man for his time and place, he fits right in there – and that's The Dude, in Los Angeles.[1]

Heroism, and in particular male heroism, is a state regarded in our postmodern times with some suspicion; "we don't need another hero" is a familiar cry. Very few men would want to be considered a "hee-ro" – there is a certain baggage attached to the title. Men, and the construction that is known as masculinity, are looked upon poorly enough without considering that there might be anything heroic or admirable[2] that can be considered socially positive.[3] And yet, fascinating male characters in fiction and myth continue to defy such neo-conservative values, the kind of heroes that are complex, human and distinctly admirable. The Promethean gift of fire still burns, the gift which gives rise to rebellion coupled with endurance, and ensures that the rock of society the hero is chained to, and the vultures sent by the postmodern gods of ideology that circle him, cannot win. "In the thunder and the lightning of the gods, the chained hero keeps his quiet faith in man. This is how he is harder than his rock and more patient than his vulture"[4], is how Camus once put it.

To the ancient Greeks, the titan Prometheus was the first hero of mankind. His gift of fire, transgressing the rule of Zeus, was the gift of those things that make up the elevated status of mankind above all other creatures. His heroic status began with his love of humanity, and his rebellion in putting the welfare and betterment of mankind before his own wellbeing. "Wrong?" Aeschylus has him say, "I accept the word. I willed, willed to be wrong."[5] If the hero is told what is "right" by a dominant force, and believes that something other than this "rightness" is what should be, then there is little concern over such moral intricacies. The rightness or wrongness is for the audience to decide, and upon that will hinge his title of hero or villain. The hero can call it wrong, but shall will his vision into being all the same. And he will do this despite the odds against him, and even the inevitability of failure and/or the most vicious punishment. Prometheus understood Zeus's omnipotence, but he stole the fire anyway; he took on the role of trickster in a context that could never allow his tricks to go un-noticed. Although he knew he would succeed insofar as humanity would be blessed with the means to fashion such things as artistry and mechanics, he could not avoid the terrible consequences.

Once these consequences fall upon him, another feature of Prometheus's heroic status is revealed: his endurance. "I must endure as best I can"[6] Aeschylus speaks for him, and Shelley writes: "No change, no pause, no hope! Yet I endure."[7] But what is the point of his endurance? The fact that he has stood up to the gods, knowing of his fate, and now he endures his punishment, and the benefits to man live on through his endurance. He endures not without complaint; he is still in touch with his own subjective idea that he has transgressed for the greater good and therefore does not deserve such hideous punishment, but he endures it just the same. He

---

[1] *The Big Lebowski*, Universal, Los Angeles, producer E. Coen, 1997 (motion picture). Also the script of *The Big Lebowski* as obtained from www.

[2] Hero: 1. Man of great courage, admired for his noble deeds. 2. Man who is greatly admired for any quality. David Blair, ed., The Pocket Macquarie Dictionary, Jacaranda Press, Milton, 1982, ,p. 424.

[3] Paul Nathanson & Katherine K. Young, *Spreading Misandry: The Teaching of Contempt for Men In Popular Culture*, McGill-Queen's University Press. Montreal, 2001, p. 8.

[4] Albert Camus, *Lyrical and Critical Essays*, trans. Ellen Conroy Kennedy, Alfred A. Knopf, New York, 1969, p. 142.

[5] Aeschylus, *Prometheus Bound and Other Plays*, trans. Philip Vellacott, Penguin, London, 1961, p. 29.

[6] Aeschylus, *Prometheus Bound and Other Plays*, trans. Philip Vellacott, Penguin, London, 1961, p. 24.

[7] Percy Bysshe Shelley, *The Complete Poetical Works of Percy Bysshe Shellley*, Thomas Hutchinson Ed., Oxford University Press, London, 1952, p. 208.

would quit if he could. He would quit if he had the opportunity to quit, if he was not compelled to keep going on as the circumstances present themselves. He is not beyond human need.

In *The Big Lebowski*, Ethan and Joel Coen have created a contemporary character that embodies a new type of Promethean male hero, that is at once more interesting and more relevant than the action hero types that we are being instructed to accept and then reject as heroic[8]. His name is Jeffrey Lebowski, but he is called The Dude. He lives for nothing more than ten pin bowling, his two bowling team mates, beer and smoking. But yet, he is happy, content, at one with the world around him. He is at peace with his condition. Then, he is mistaken for another Jeffrey Lebowski – a millionaire with a wife who owes money to a celebrated pornographer, Jackie Treehorn. Two of Jackie's thugs come around to collect the money and before they discover they have the wrong man, one of them urinates on The Dude's rug during the process of intimidation.

What follows is The Dude's reluctant engagement with the god-like powers of the world around him: Jeffrey "the Big" Lebowski (money), Jackie Treehorn (power), the Police/Jackie Treehorn's thugs (Strength and Violence[9]), Maude Lebowski (ideological feminism), Bunny Lebowski (promiscuous feminism), the nihilists (ideological violence). Walter, a Vietnam veteran and one of The Dude's bowling buddies, convinces The Dude he must get some sort of recompense for his soiled rug. Walter tells him emphatically: "I'm talking about drawing a line in the sand, Dude. Across this line you do not, uh – …"[10] The line in the sand is the classic call of male heroism, coming from a character who represents a classic heroic type of the modern action hero model – the returned Vietnam veteran. The Dude's reluctance to rebel against all the gods around him is allayed by his apparent rightness. "Am I wrong? Am I wrong?" Walter constantly asks his buddy. The call to heroism is too difficult for The Dude to avoid, and he reluctantly rebels – a reluctant Prometheus is modern man. He steals a replacement rug from The Big Lebowski and the wrath of the gods follow him.

It is against the wrath of the various modern gods that The Dude exhibits heroic endurance. 'This aggression will not stand, man,' he echoes George Bush (the film is set during the first Iraq war) while waving a beverage in the air. He realizes he is chained to the rock, that he really cannot move from there or avoid the vultures that stand ready to tear him apart, stronger than him, quicker than him, smarter than him, but yet he endures their wrath and he continues to be The Dude. He doesn't change to fit their pattern, their design for what is to be *him*, even when he is threatened with castration. Instead, The Dude takes it in, works out what is going on through a combination of street-level intellect and serendipity, and endures. He endures the ending of the story, the death of Donny (his other bowling buddy), and the fact that – despite having worked out how the whole mess went down – he is powerless to do anything about it. Instead, he endures, and he abides. "Awww, fuck it Dude. Let's go bowling"[11] Walter offers at the end of the film, and perhaps that is all he and The Dude have, but they will do it and enjoy this pointless beer-swilling and joint-smoking past-time and let the gods do what they will. The hero does not say: I am a god. The hero says: the gods are wrong.[12]

Every society has its god or gods that represent the dominant social ethos of the day. In ancient Greece, these were the Olympians, with Zeus supreme amongst them, the grand patriarch who held power through the strength of his lightning bolts. In our modern, secular world, the gods are those people that have power sustained through wealth or ideological purity. Both represent conservatisms insofar as they contain vested interests in avoiding rapid change and extremes to retain their hold on power. But, equally, both came about *through* transgressive processes. Every conservatism is preceded by a process of transgression, and every transgression holds within it the seed of a projected conservatism. Zeus gained power only through transgressing the power of Kronos. Human beings gained power only through Prometheus transgressing the power of Zeus. Treehorn/Bunny/Maude/the nihilists only gained power through transgressing the Promethean achievement-orientated ethos of the likes of The Big Lebowski, and the modern conservatism is born. The Dude transgresses this neo-conservatism in his complete and fatuous unwillingness to become engulfed in it.

Considering this process, the rebel hero becomes an almost oxymoronic term. To be a rebel is to transgress, but to be considered a hero is to be admired within a conservatism that was made possible through the act of transgression. And so, the rebel hero conveys messages that are both fundamentally transgressive *and* conservative. They transgress and in the act of transgression allow for a future conservatism. Implicit in the definition of a hero is the recognition and admiration of certain qualities. Therefore, the nature of heroism is one of value-judgments. A rebellious man in the past who exhibits qualities that are particularly valued *now* is a male rebel hero[13] – a hero must be a man for his time and place: he must fit right in there. Just as Prometheus once did, now The Dude follows.

Tensions also exist between the poles of conservatism and transgression which lie at the heart of rebellious heroism. These heroes must be capable of resisting

---

[8] John Lash, *The Hero: Manhood and Power*, Thames and Hudson, London, 1995, pp. 27-30.

[9] Aeschylus, *Prometheus Bound and Other Plays*, trans. Philip Vellacott, Penguin, London, 1961, p. 20.

[10] *The Big Lebowski*, Universal, Los Angeles, producer E. Coen, 1997 (motion picture).

[11] *The Big Lebowski*, Universal, Los Angeles, producer E. Coen, 1997 (motion picture).

[12] Albert Camus, *The Rebel*, Anthony Bower trans., Penguin, Harmondsworth, 1977, pp. 30-31.

[13] Lash, John, *The Hero: Manhood and Power*, Thames and Hudson, London, 1995, p. 31.

change through endurance, and, at the same time, exhibit the qualities of change. Prometheus brought rapid change to humanity in his gifts, but also he refused to change himself and bow down before Zeus in repentance. The Dude offers a laid back, personal and free-ranging model for humanity that heralds change, but must remain unchanged to herald these very gifts. Similarly, a moral and lawful code operates within these men while at the same time they refuse to operate within the limits of morals and laws offered to them by others. The rebel hero must face these ambivalences and succeed despite them.

"I am not suggesting that male heroes don't exist among us, but they are often publicly unknown and bear little, if any resemblance to those larger-than-life Greek heroes"[14] Ryce Menuhin writes, echoing the differences in gender-related social values from one time to the other; it is the change in what is seen as admirable, and therefore, the change in what is seen as heroic. Some modern feminist interpretations of the Prometheus myth place his rebellion against patriarchy[15], then makes him representative of all men and women who rebel against such authority[16]. Emphasizing Zeus's masculinity while androgenizing Prometheus reflects quite adequately the current brand of neo-conservative values that require myth to be feminized – Strength and Violence have changed their clothes, but the nail and hammer remain poised. The Promethean hero would have nothing to do with this ideological feminist approach that wishes to nail him up as a champion of dualism – negating the collective other (men) – and essentialism – affirming the collective self (women)[17]. It is freedom that is in his words – too much freedom in fact[18]. In our modern world, it is The Dude that stands for that freedom, without pausing to adopt the mores that the gods have constructed for him. When Maude tells him that men feel uncomfortable with the word "vagina." but are happy to refer to their penis by a number of names, he quite comfortably says nothing, but when Maude later refers to a pornographic film as a "beaver picture" he asks her: "Beaver? You mean vagina?"[19]

"Indeed, if Prometheus were to reappear, modern man would treat him as the gods did long ago: they would nail him to a rock, in the name of the very humanism he was the first to symbolize."[20] And of course, as The Dude understands, they do. The sheer width and inclusiveness of a word like "humanism" can make people uncomfortable (even more so than "vagina"). The rebel hero changes through time, and the Promethean man adapts and abides[21]. But the gift of fire to humankind remains within us – rebellion meshed with endurance, freedom engulfing imagination. This is the cocktail of transgression, that puts society through its rumbling cycles despite the efforts of the gods. And while we might blame the giver of this gift, and those that follow him, for the troubles that come from it, the very act of assessing such blame is to put the gift into action. When The Dude is at his lowest, the narrator of *The Big Lebowski* enters the film and advises him – advice that could have been given to Prometheus himself, nailed to his rock: "... sometimes you eat the bar and sometimes the bar, wal [sic], he eats you." Hang in there transgressor – your time will come. Of course we need *another* hero. And another, and another, down through the generations.

....

Jeremy Davies works as an editor and plays as a writer in Melbourne, Australia; he has been a major long-term lover of all things Dude. While he rarely bowls, and doesn't really own a rug to speak of: he Abides, and enjoys a beverage.

---

[14] Joel Ryce-Menuhin, *Naked and Erect: Male Sexuality and Feeling*, Chiron Publications, Wilmette, 1996, p. 64.

[15] *Myth and Ideology Part B: Quests and Heroes*, Study Guide, Deakin University, Geelong, 2001, p. 129

[16] *Myth and Ideology Part B: Quests and Heroes*, Study Guide, Deakin University, Geelong, 2001, p. 134.

[17] Paul Nathanson & Katherine K. Young, *Spreading Misandry: The Teaching of Contempt for Men In Popular Culture*, McGill-Queen's University Press. Montreal, 2001, pp. 201-202.

[18] You are defiant, Prometheus, and your spirit
In spite of all your pain, yields not an inch.
But there is too much freedom in your words.
Aeschylus, *Prometheus Bound and Other Plays*, trans. Philip Vellacott, Penguin, London, 1961, p. 22.

[19] *The Big Lebowski*, Universal, Los Angeles, producer E. Coen, 1997 (motion picture).

[20] Albert Camus, *Lyrical and Critical Essays*, trans. Ellen Conroy Kennedy, Alfred A. Knopf, New York, 1969, p. 139.

[21] *The Dude abides. The Big Lebowski*, Universal, Los Angeles, producer E. Coen, 1997 (motion picture).

Bibliography

Aeschylus, *Prometheus Bound and Other Plays*, trans. Philip Vellacott, Penguin, London, 1961.

The Big Lebowski, Universal, Los Angeles, producer E. Coen, 1997 (motion picture).

Blair, David, ed., *The Pocket Macquarie Dictionary*, Jacaranda Press, Milton, 1982.

Camus, Albert, *Lyrical and Critical Essays*, trans. Ellen Conroy Kennedy, Alfred A. Knopf, New York, 1969.

Camus, Albert, *The Rebel*, trans. Anthony Bower, Penguin, Harmondsworth, 1977.

Coen, Ethan & Coen, Joel, *The Big Lebowski*, screenplay obtained from www.

Lash, John, *The Hero: Manhood and Power*, Thames and Hudson, London, 1995.

Myth and Ideology Part B: Quests and Heroes, Study Guide, Deakin University, Geelong, 2001.

Myth and Ideology Part B: Quests and Heroes, Reader, Deakin University, Geelong, 2001.

Nathanson, Paul & Young, Katherine K., *Spreading Misandry: The Teaching of Contempt for Men In Popular Culture*, McGill-Queen's University Press. Montreal, 2001.

Raglan, Lord, The Hero: A Study in Tradition, Myth and Drama, Watts & Co, London, 1949.

Ruthven, K. K., *Myth*, Metheun & Co, London, 1976.

Ryce-Menuhin, Joel, *Naked and Erect: Male Sexuality and Feeling*, Chiron Publications, Wilmette, 1996.

Shelley, Percy Bysshe, *The Complete Poetical Works of Percy Bysshe Shelley*, Thomas Hutchinson Ed., Oxford University Press, London, 1952.

Kyle Hellkamp, *Lonelybowski*

The *Zanni* of Our Time and Place: Socio-Political Protest through Modern Commedia dell'Arte in *The Big Lebowski*

BY JESSICA BELLOMO

Introduction

As the level of oppression waxes and wanes within a given society, carnivalesque forms of protests have increased and decreased accordingly. According to M. Lane Bruner, protests utilizing carnivalesque styles and methods "are particularly prevalent when those benefiting from rampant political corruption lose their sense of humor [and] become ridiculous in their seriousness" (136). Centuries ago, actors of La Commedia dell'Arte improvised political satire in Italian and French plazas; today, the carnivalesque has stayed alive via film. As seen in Ethan and Joel Coen's *The Big Lebowski*, the carnivalesque continues to serve its purpose: to address corruption, expose the flexibility of paradigms, and provide a sense of catharsis to the frustrated and silenced majority through the use of comedy.

The goal of using a carnivalesque style is to force audience members out of their paradigmatic bubbles, allowing them "to recognize the constructed and thus changeable nature of society" (Martin & Renegar, 300). The key to the success of the carnivalesque is the use of humor as the medium for protest. I propose that *The Big Lebowski* acutely reflects this need for protest according to the political problems of the culture they represent. *The Big Lebowski*'s initial unpopularity in the prosperous late 1990s followed by its huge cult following in the new millennium demonstrates the carnivalesque quality of the film in that it utilizes the techniques of the Commedia to make a statement of social and political protest that is more poignant amongst audience members in today's turbulent political age than upon the film's release. The carnivalesque qualities of the film allow for a biting social commentary through the use of what Millicent Marcus terms "serious humor." Just as the poor and oppressed people of Italian villages used the Commedia dell'Arte as a cathartic release for their political strife, *The Big Lebowski* offers the same sort of philosophical pressure valve for today's audiences.

Exploring the Carnivalesque in *The Big Lebowski*

The Big Lebowski is reflective of the Commedia in that it utilizes a particular genre, what Mikhail Bakhtin originally called the *carnivalesque*, to express protest. Bakhtin argues that the "Carnival sense of the world" seeps through all "serio-comic genres from top to bottom." This permeating of all genres eventually leads to "a weakening of [reality's] one-sided rhetorical seriousness, its rationality, its singular meaning, its dogmatism" (qtd in Hyman, p. 14). In other words, the paradigms that are delegated to all genres begin to shift and break down through the use of serious humor. The result is that an entirely new genre, that of the carnivalesque, is created. As Hyman illuminates, "the carnivalesque invokes a laughter linked to the overturning of authority" which inevitably leads to the overturning of the ideas and ideals that that authority proclaims. This style of socio-political protest is manifested through three particular methods: grotesque realism, the inversion of hierarchies, and structural and grammatical experimentation (Martin and Renegar, p. 304).

Through the use of stock characters centered around a protagonist based upon Arlecchino (*Harlequin* in English), as well as through the use of the three aspects of the carnivalesque, the Coen brothers successfully reflect the feelings of animosity and frustration that many still feel toward the government, toward big business, or toward "the man" in general. During the economically prosperous times of the late 1990s, *The Big Lebowski*'s carnivalesque style of poking fun at hegemonic paradigms was not necessarily needed; however, in a post-9/11 world of political head-butting and economic hardship, the American people began to find themselves relating more to the Dude and enjoying his carnivalesque qualities.

Stock Characters

Arlecchino was one of the most well-known and often used stock characters in the Commedia, playing the role of one of the servants or "valet-buffoons," known as *zanni*, from which the English word "zany" derives (Duchartre, p. 20). The character of Arlecchino has been arguably in existence as long as humankind has been able to tell stories (Defries, p. 292). When the Commedia dell'Arte reached its heyday in Italy and France in the 16th century, Arlecchino became a key figure in carnivalesque plays and street performances (Wynne, 19). As Defries states, "Harlequin is, as mediaeval jester, the character who performs the combined functions of critic and caricaturist. If so, then is he not *indeed* himself a forerunner of the sociologist, criticizing not only society, but every type of human being in his jests and philosophisings?" (289). Oreglia acutely describes the contradictory nature of Arlecchino, explaining that "at first this Mask personified the stupid and ever-hungry servant, but it later assumed a more complex form; credulous and diffident, a lazy-bones but also a busybody, a mixture of cunning and ingenuousness, of awkwardness and grace" (pp. 56-57). The only stock character from the days of the Commedia that is still a household name is Harlequin, the sociologist, the joker, who reminds us of the absurdity of seriousness. The Dude (Jeff Bridges) is today's Arlecchino.

In addition to Arlecchino, the Coen brothers also revive other stock characters from the Commedia to aid in the telling of the story through a carnivalesque lens. The "big" Lebowski is quite similar to the *vecchi* (old man) known as Pantalone, or Pantaloon. He is a character full of contradictions, a theme that runs through many of the profiles of stock characters. Oreglia describes him as being "avaricious yet a lover of pomp and splendor, wily yet rash; slanderous and quarrelsome, subject to sudden explosions of fury and vehement outbursts of curses and invective" (p. 78). His character is meant to be antagonistic to the zanni, representing the clash not only between classes but between generations (Oreglia, p. 80). In addition, he is often married to a young a pretty woman who "unaware of the honour of being the wife of a reputable merchant, she deceives him at every turn" (Ducharte, p. 182). The big Lebowski personifies Pantalone in many ways. He is financially supported by his daughter and has no real wealth of his own, yet he is obsessed with keeping up appearances and maintaining his high society status. He is a hypocrite who offers ranting lectures to "bums" like the Dude, yet he has no real talent and is always losing money. His wife, Bunny Lebowski (Tara Reid), is a blond, ditzy teenager and porn star who has no concern for her aging husband other than the allowance he provides her. From the introduction of his character through the end, the Big Lebowski is a very antagonistic character whose every trait and attribute is diametrically opposed to those of the Dude's.

Walter, the infamously loud, obnoxious, opinionated friend and sidekick to the Dude is the progeny of the even more notorious stock character called Pulcinella. Like Arlecchino, Pulcinella is a zanni and another ancient character whose origins are still disputed. He is a decidedly different character, though, whom Ducharte describes as such:

> Pulcinella was never one to be bowed down by the cares and responsibilities of a profession….As a general rule he appeared as an old bachelor, an eccentric and selfish old curmudgeon strongly inclined to sensual and epicurean gluttony…Being self-centered and bestial, Pulcinella had no scruples whatever, and because the moral suffering from his physical deformity reacted upon his brain at the expense of his heart, he was exceedingly cruel (pp. 214-215).

Walter's character, though not a hunchback like Pulcinella, is "deformed" in the sense that he is a Vietnam veteran who seems to be suffering from post-traumatic stress disorder. He cannot seem to let go of his experiences in the war, and he never ceases to compare every situation to Vietnam. It is his experiences in Vietnam that cause him to feel entitled to be loud and obnoxious, often to the point of being cruel. He also seems to care little for his job, if he has one. He is a divorcé with no children, the archetype of the "eccentric old bachelor" who spends his time eating, drinking, smoking, and bowling. His system of ethics is full of a sense of entitlement, reminding anyone within earshot that his friends "didn't die face-down in the muck" just so his rights could be trampled upon, making him very self-centered and self righteous.

Maude Lebowski (Julianne Moore) is similar to the Commedia's most recognizable female Mask, Colombina, considered Arlecchino's female counterpart. Known for her craftiness and her ability to fool everyone, Roberto Delpiano describes her as "free, insolent, not slave of love bonds, sometimes brilliant, vane always, chatterer, gossiper, always prone to intrigue at somebody else's expenses." Also, Green and Swan explain that female characters in the Commedia were a "prominent presence, but with a single significance of sexual identity" (p.15).

Self-sufficient and full of wit, Maude's character echoes many of Colombina's characteristics while roundly rejecting the Commedia's gender standards. Certain from the beginning that Bunny has not been kidnapped and constantly updating the Dude on recent events, Maude is always ahead of the other characters. Much of the new information that she imparts on the Dude seems to be gleaned from gossip and chatter. She is free from societal restraints on what a woman's role ought to be, creating art that is "highly vaginal" for a living and choosing the Dude to impregnate her so that she can raise her child free from a man's constraints, or "love bonds" (Coen and Coen). In fact, the Coen brothers seem to have constructed Maude's character to be the ultimate archetype of the liberal feminist to juxtapose how much women in the Commedia and the carnivalesque have historically been sidelined as sexual objects. Yet even while expounding modern views toward gender, the fact that Maude is constantly referring to sex makes her a character centered around sexual identity, keeping with the theme of Colombina and female Masks in general.

He Peed on Your Fucking Rug: Grotesque Realism

I will examine two scenes that demonstrate the way in which *The Big Lebowski* utilizes the carnivalesque to deliver its message, namely "The Rug" and "The Other Lebowski." "The Rug" opens with the Dude returning home from buying half and half, includes the encounter with "the carpet pissers" and concludes with the Dude's conversation with Walter and Donnie at the bowling alley about how the rug "really tied the room together" and that the Dude is entitled to retribution from the other Lebowski. "The Other Lebowski" opens with Brandt's (Philip Seymour Hoffman) exposition on Mr. Lebowski's achievements and awards, includes the Dude's dialogue with the big Lebowski requesting compensation for his rug, and ends with the Dude telling Brandt that he could have any rug in the house.

The first indicator of the carnivalesque is the use of grotesque realism. Martin and Renegar explain that each grotesque detail "encourages viewers to remember the fact that all of them are earth bound animals, linked to it and one another by those very vibrant, if 'dirty,' biological processes that this truth entails" (304). The grotesque details originally outlined by Bakhtin include "copulation, pregnancy, birth, growth, old age, disintegration, [and] dismemberment" as well as "defecation, the use of billingsgate, or abusive language, and profanity" (Martin and Renegar, 304; Bakhtin, 19-20).

The first instance of grotesque realism is the simple visual focus on the plumpness of the Dude and of Walter. Their fat bellies are highlighted by shirts that do not cover them entirely and an informal straddling position. The focus on the characters' less-than-ideal bodies speaks to the "preoccupation with the 'lower stratum of the body, the life of the belly'" (Martin and Renegar, 305; Bakhtin, 20).

Profanity is another favorite avenue for expression of rebellion that the Coen brothers use. In the scene "The Rug," the word "fuck" is uttered 17 times in the course of a few minutes. The subject matter is also concerning a man urinating on the Dude's rug, which brings the subject of bodily functions to the forefront of the conversation. These two examples show how being crude and base brings the subject matter, which is actually a discussion of ethics, into the realm of the familiar and ridiculous.

In "The Other Lebowski," the audience discovers that Mr. Lebowski is an amputee victim in a sense; furthermore, the topic of his paralyzed legs comes up repeatedly in the course of the film. When Brandt is showing the Dude pictures of Mr. Lebowski, the Dude comments that Mr. Lebowski is "a cripple, I mean, uh, uh, a handicapped guy…" and Brandt corrects the Dude by remarking, "Mr. Lebowski is *disabled*, yes." During the conversation between the Lebowskis, Mr. Lebowski explains that "some Chinaman" took his legs. The use of amputation to force the focus of the audience to be on the physical, the bodily, is a common technique used in carnivalesque theatre.

The Bums Will Always Lose: Inversion of Hierarchies

The disruption of the current world order is one of the most important duties of the carnivalesque. The act of turning paradigms upside down is depicted through the dethroning of rulers and the rise of the lowly. Martin and Renegar explain that the "thronings and dethronings of fools and kings is a common trope of carnivalized rhetoric" (307). Part of questioning the current order in the real world, then, is to continually restructure the sense of order throughout the course of the story.

The title of the scene "The Other Lebowski" is itself questioning hierarchy, as does the title *The Big Lebowski*. After all, who is the other Lebowski? Who is the big man and who is not? To the audience, it is the wealthy, materially successful Lebowski who is actually the "other" Lebowski since the audience was introduced to the Dude first and sympathizes with him and his situation much more than the old, self-interested man with no sense of humor who symbolizes the ruling class. While society would like to distance the Dude as the "other," the Coen brothers turn the tables on the situation. Furthermore, it is Mr. Lebowski's supposed wealth that makes him so powerful among the "square community," but the audience discovers that his neo-feminist, liberal, artist daughter, Maude has actually provided an allowance for him. Sitting on his fake throne, Mr. Lebowski's rants against the anti-conformist "bums" become ridiculous and hypocritical.

The Dude takes advantage of a line he had heard George Bush, Sr. say, "this will not stand, this aggression, against Kuwait." When Mr. Lebowski accuses the Dude of being another bum wanting a hand-out, the Dude defends himself by retorting, "this will not stand, you know, this aggression will not stand, man." By using a quote from a very powerful, conservative, wealthy man, the Dude has turned Mr. Lebowski's own class against him.

Finally, the Dude, whose crown is symbolized by his large, dark sunglasses (which fell in the toilet when the thugs came to visit him, thereby dethroning him from his peaceful, undisturbed existence), effectively dethrones Mr. Lebowski by putting on his sunglasses while Mr. Lebowski is still mid-rant, declares, "fuck it," and leaves calmly, fooling Brandt into helping the Dude get the rug he feels he deserves. This act has emasculated Mr. Lebowski by challenging his power and circumventing the rules of the upper class in order to vindicate the situation (Martin and Renegar, 307). The Dude actually mentions his crowning when explaining to Mr. Lebowski that "I'm the Dude, so that's what you call me. You know, that or his *Dudeness* or Duder or El Duderino if you're not into the whole brevity thing" (Martin and Renegar, 307). The Dude has rejected the name that society has tried to force upon him, and instead chooses a name which "seems to indicate no outstanding individuality other than presence," offering him anonymity and freedom from the capitalistic world (Swanson, 124). This act qualifies him to be "his Dudeness," the king of the slackers.

Walter, What's Your Point?: Structural and Grammatical Experimentation

In general, the entire plot is rambling and confused on purpose. As Roger Ebert noted in his critique of the film, "'The Big Lebowski' rushes in all directions and never ends up anywhere. That isn't the film's flaw, but its style" (RogerEbert.com). "The Rug" scene is the perfect example of structural and grammatical experimentation, exemplified through Donnie's character, who is always a few steps behind in the conversation, forever doomed to be outside the loop. For instance:

> Walter: This was a valued rug. This was a...
> Dude: Yeah, man it really tied the room together.
> W: This was a valued...eh...
> Dude: Yeah
> Donny: What tied the room together?
> Dude: My rug.
> W: Were you listening to the Dude's story?
> Due: Walter!
> W: Were you listening to the Dude's story?
> Donny: I was bowling.
> W: So you have no frame of reference here, Donny. You're like a child who wanders   into...
> Dude: Walter!
> W: ...the middle of a movie and wants to know what...

Both the Dude and Walter are trying to carry on their conversation without having to bother explaining the situation to Donnie, leaving him to continually wonder, like the audience, "What is the point?" (Swanson, 120).

When the Dude is explaining the violation of his rug, the dialogue is very stammered, adding to the confusion of the scene:

> Dude: Wha...Walter, what's the point?
> Walter: There's no reason, here's my point, Dude, there're no fucking no reason why these two...
> Donny: Yeah, Walter, what's your point?
> W: Huh?
> Dude: Walter, what is the point? Look, we all know who is at fault here. What the fuck are you talking about?
> W: Huh, now what the fuck are you!...I'm not!...We're talking about unchecked aggression, here, Dude.
> Donny: What the fuck is he talking about?

As Swanson argues, "This scene outlines the confusing and difficult nature of both the personal and political layers of contemporary ethics" (119). In other words, the confusing, twisting, winding nature of the dialogue experiments with language itself, thereby challenging the status quo in general.

In "The Other Lebowski," the use of semantics also is one of the ways that the Dude usurps power from Mr. Lebowski. His playing with Bush's line about aggression in Kuwait to rebut Mr. Lebowski's accusation is one example. Also, the Dude's casual way of speaking is unaltered in the formal setting of Mr. Lebowski's office, e.g. use of the words "pee," "fuck," and reference to Mr. Lebowski as "man."

The Man for His Time and Place: Conclusions

The Dude is a man for his time and place because Arlecchino is timeless. He will continue to adapt and remold himself around the culture of the day, yet he will never need to truly change who he is or what he represents. As the social critic who illuminates audiences through exaggeration and a flair for the ridiculous, this seemingly simple clown has brought the effective and cathartic form of protest to the masses. As the state loses its sense of humor, the carnivalesque steps in to provide a safe outlet of protest. The directors' use of serious humor through the utilization of grotesque realism, the inversion of hierarchies, and structural and grammatical experimentation, as well as their adaptation of classic stock characters, has created a film that is both a work of art and a sharp socio-political critique. Their works demonstrates the effectiveness and timelessness of the Commedia and the carnivalesque, which will continue to exist as long as authoritative figures keep making ridiculous decisions.

....

A St. Louis native, **Jessica Bellomo** serves as the Director of the International Visitor Leadership Program, a State Department program that hosts international visitors for 3-week professional programs, for the World Affairs Council of St. Louis. Jessica holds a double undergraduate degree from St. Louis University in Sociology and International Studies, with a minor in Political Science, a certificate in Italian Studies and a certificate in Women's Studies. She also has her Master's in Public Relations with an emphasis in media literacy from Webster University. She is on the board of the Gateway Media Literacy Partners and the United Nations Association of St. Louis. Jessica speaks conversational Italian, enjoys gardening, running, studying film and media literacy, playing flute, and listening to local blues, soul, and jazz musicians.

Works Cited

"Arlecchino." January 13, 2009. *I Verdi Confusi/The Confused Greenies*. December 15, 2009.
<http://filer.case.edu/org/commedia/masks/arlecchino.html>.

Bakhtin, M. M. *Rabelais and His World*. Trans. H. Iswolsky. Bloomington: Indiana University Press, 1984.

Bastian, Jon. "The Big Lebowski (1998)." 2008. *Film Monthly*. November 1, 2008.
<http://www.filmmonthly.com/video_and_dvd/the_big_lebowski.html.>

The Big Lebowski. Dir. Joel Coen and Ethan Coen. Working Title Films, 1998.

Bruner, M. Lane. "Carnivalesque Protest and the Humorless State.*" Text and Performance Quarterly*. April 2005, Vol. 25, No.2: 136-155.

Defries, Amelia. "The Origins and Social Significance of Harlequin and of the Commedia dell'Arte." *The Sociological Society.* May 7, 1927, Vol. 19: 289-296.

Delpiano, Roberto. "Columbina." *Delpiano.com*. n.d. Web. January 23, 2011.

Duchartre, Pierre Louis. *The Italian Comedy*. Trans. Randolph T. Weaver. New York: Dover Publications, 1966.

Ebert, Roger. "The Big Lebowski." March 6, 1998. *RogerEbert.com*. November 1, 2008.
<http://rogerebert.suntimes.com>.

Geoffroy-Menoux, Sophie. Spring 2007. " Taste, Entitlement and Power in Vernon Lee's Comedy of Masks Cum Puppet Show: *The Prince of The Hundred Soups* (1880)." *The Sybil.* December 21, 2009.
<http://www.oscholars.com/Sibyl/one/Article_on_The_Prince.htm>.

"History: The Commedia dell'Arte." *Histrionics*. December 21, 2009. <http://www.histrionicstheplay.co.uk/page12.htm>.

Hyman, Timothy. "A Carnival Sense of the World." *Carnivalesque*. Berkeley: University of
California Press, 2000: 8-73.

Marcus, Millicent. "Me lo Dici Babbo Che Gioco É?: The Serious Humor of *La Vita É Bella.*" *Italics*. Summer 2000, Vol. 77, No. 2: 153-170).

Martin, Paul and Renegar, Valerie. "'The Man for His Time' *The Big Lebowski* as Carnivalesque Social Critique." *Communication Studies*. September 2007, Vol. 58, No. 3: 299-313.

Oreglia, Giacomo. *The Commedia dell'Arte*. Trans. Lovett F. Edwards. New York: Methuen and Co., Ltd., 1968.

"Pedrolino." January 13, 2009. *I Verdi Confusi/The Confused Greenies*. December 15, 2009.
<http://filer.case.edu/org/commedia/masks/pedrolino.html>.

Swanson, Peter. "The Stranger in the Dark: The Ethics of Levinasian-Derridean Hospitality in Noir." Diss. Graduate College of Bowling Green State University, 2007.

Wynne, Peter. "Zanies, Lovers, Scoundrels, Fools." *Opera News*. December 5, 1992: 18-20.

Brandon Yarwood, *Cheers, Jackie…*

A Way Out West

BY MATTHEW J. BARSALOU

A way out west there was a fella, fella I want to tell you about ... I only mention it 'cause some- times there's a man--I won't say a hee-ro, 'cause what's a hee-ro?--but sometimes there's a man ... sometimes there's a man who, wal, he's the man for his time'n place, he fits right in there--and that's The Dude, in Los Angeles.

If one was to seek understanding of the American myth one need look no further than the West. The West, more than any other time and place in history, is the shape of that myth. But the roots of the Western myth are more than figurative; Columbus literally sailed west, America expanded westward. The myth takes on the shape of history. The myth fits right in to its own place and time. Is the "cowboy" the American hero? This remains to be seen, but a way out west there was a country, and that's America, *the* West.

The Big Lebowski, with its absurd plot of urination on a rug, a toe with nail polish, nihilists and a marmot, and more than moderate doses of white Russians and marijuana cigarettes aside, is much more than your typical slapstick comedy. In fact, the movie could very well be one the greatest commentaries on the West ever made. The opening lines of the movie quoted above serve to frame the story in its western context. The words are spoken by a man known only as the Stranger. This man wears the clothes of the American West; he is, at least through the lens of the Western myth, a cowboy.

In his introductory words the Stranger gives us insight into the American myth here. First, and most obviously we are given the setting of Los Angeles, almost as west as west gets. Los Angeles is today of course an iconic image of the West from Hollywood to memories of the gold rush. But on a subtler note, Los Angeles was not immediately the city it is today during expansion. It was not until the 1880s that the Santa Fe railway was built, a line that was significant in the opening up of that land. Second, we must accept, and history shows us, that it is man, not woman that the myth is based on. This can be seen historically in the violence committed toward women and their portrayal, or lack thereof, in the Western myth. Third, and on a deeper level we must question the hero, "'cause what's a hee-ro?" The myth may very well have a superficial answer to that question, but history certainly does not. That, depends on which side of the story we are listening to, or telling.

The East and the West as separate, as different is mentioned in the film as well. First, we see a debate between The Dude and his neoconservative friend Walter Sobchak in regards to who should be held accountable for the rug. Walter says "The Chinaman is not the issue! ... uh--and also, Dude, Chinaman is not the preferred nomenclature ... Asian-American. Please." The Dude says "Walter, this isn't a guy who built the railroads here." This dialogue gives the audience yet another reference to the West, the significance of Chinese workers building the railroads. This East and West dichotomy is also mentioned when the Stanger tells The Dude that "sometimes you eat the bar ... and well, sometimes he eats you." The Dude asks if this is an "eastern thing" and the Stanger replies "far from it." On a philosophical level the phrase gives us an insight into the bipolar nature of life. On a literal level this duality is part of the character of the Western myth. In addition, it may or may not be coincidence that Preacher Roe, a baseball player, on the then Brooklyn Dodgers, used the phrase once after being removed from a game. The coincidence lies in the fact that the Dodgers eventually moved west to Los Angeles.

Now, at this point it should be mentioned that there are countless references to the West in the film, further evidence that this is, in fact, what the movie is about. At any rate, only two more will be mentioned. First, when The Dude recovers his stolen car he finds the homework of Larry Sellers, son of Arthur Digby Sellers, writer of a television series called *Branded*. Larry's homework is a paper for his history class, and the thesis of his paper further brings to light the thesis of this very essay. He wrote: "The most important point in United States was the Louisiana Purchase when Jefferson doubled the size of the nation by purchasing the Louisiana Territory from France in 1805." (Even though Little Larry got a 'D' on his paper, we award him extra credit for accidental insight.)

Secondly, is not a coincidence that this show was selected out of the many Westerns released in the same time period (the 1960s). The protagonist of *Branded*, Jason McCord, is similar to The Dude in many ways. In the show McCord must face accusations of cowardice; in the film The Dude faces his own accusations of being a bum. But both are charged with the task called for in the closing lines of the lyrics to the *Branded* theme song.

> And wherever you go
> for the rest of your life
> You must prove . . .
> You're a man!

This verse alone says more about the American Western Myth than any analysis here. We look at one more reference in the film.

> I guess that's the way the whole durned human comedy keeps perpetuatin' it-self, down through the generations, westward the wagons, across the sands a time until –

Here the Stanger reflects on the story that he has told us. This is the ultimate commentary the film has to offer. The myth of the West is the story of man(kind). The West sees itself as the epitome of history, as a cowboy, as a hero. The Stanger would of course say that he "didn't find it to be that exactly." But the myth is not finished being written. "Until" what?

....

Matthew J. Barsalou has a Bachelor's degree in American Studies from Western Connecticut State University, the time and place where he first discovered Dudelosophy.

Bas De Voogt, *This Will Stand, Man!*

Josua Waghubinger, *Fuck it, Let's Go Bowling*

The New Left and Laziness: Why The Dude is "The Man for His Time"

BY REUBEN J. COHEN

The word and concept of "laziness" often carry negative connotations. Traditionally, laziness has not been accepted, and it is considered one of seven deadly sins in the Catholic church. However, more recently, laziness has come to be accepted and even idealized (Russell). The word "lazy" is defined as "disinclined to activity or exertion" (Merriam-Webster). The word "disinclined" suggests a conscious choice to avoid activity. There are reasons one would do so. "Only in laziness," wrote John Steinbeck, "Can one achieve a state of contemplation which is a balancing of values, a weighing of oneself against the world, and the world against itself" (Steinbeck 151).

Jeffrey "The Dude" Lebowski, the main character in Joel and Ethan Coen's classic film *The Big Lebowski* (1998), was "quite possibly the laziest [man] in Los Angeles County". His laziness, though, was highly conscious and politically-motivated, inspired by a movement that had all but died out by the time *The Big Lebowski* was set. The Dude was one of a kind during his time period and the identifiable displacement that is apparent when seeing him inspired the character's enduring popularity.

The New Left was a political movement that developed in the 1960s as a response to bigotry and the Vietnam War. It developed from the "Old Left" (i.e., communism), but differed in that it did not have the same focus on manual labor as communism – rather, it emphasized contributing to society in a way that each person finds interesting and stimulating to themselves, thereby accepting laziness (S. Thompson). Its key document – its manifesto, so to speak – is the Port Huron Statement, written in 1962 by the radical group Students for a Democratic Society (SDS). The Statement says, "Work should involve incentives worthier than money or survival. It should be educative, not stultifying; creative, not mechanical; self-directed, not manipulated, encouraging independence, a respect for others, a sense of dignity, and a willingness to accept social responsibility" (*Port Huron Statement*). The movement, known for its development into radicalism, saw the capitalist labor system as a machine that removed the beauty from the world by forcing people into unnatural roles for themselves, thus the need for more fulfilling work. As Bill Milliken, an evangelical missionary-turned-SDS supporter, said, "The silhouettes of gray buildings lost their beauty. Outwardly, the buildings had an aura of beauty – majestic, a picture of strength… But their beauty was only steel-and-concrete deep. Inside those buildings, a death-producing machine had been created. The middle masses … had been shaped into robots, pushing their assigned buttons so that the monarchs could grab the kingdom and the power and the glory" (Milliken, Swartz). This depiction of manual labor shows a clear difference from traditional Communism, which would have glorified the laborer. Both models of leftism would have valued the working man over the "monarchs," as Milliken says, but Milliken's model suggests that the lower class, in all their valiant labor, were only supporting the upper class.

By the early 1990s, ideas like this were far from vogue. The New Leftist movement, at one time so prominent, had faded away. Journalist and novelist Hunter S. Thompson compared the movement's life cycle to a wave, cresting and then receding. "So now, less than five years later, you can go up on a steep hill in Las Vegas and look West," Thomspson wrote, "and with the right kind of eyes you can almost see the high-water mark – that place where the wave finally broke and rolled back" (H. Thompson 68). In the meantime, conservatism similar to that which SDS was rebelling against had taken a stronger hold on the United States. President George H.W. Bush was in power. Vietnam was over, but another war had begun, the Persian Gulf War. The Gulf War did not have as much of an impact on American history as Vietnam did, but it was provoked by similar American principles in response to Iraq's violence against Kuwait. "This will not stand," Bush said, "This aggression against Kuwait" (Bush). This was an example, as was Vietnam, of American interventionism – attempting to spread American morals and government around the world in the belief that it works better regardless of other circumstances.

There was at least one man, albeit a fictional character, who clung tightly to the New Left's values in 1990 – The Dude. It was at this time, the beginning of the Gulf War, that *The Big Lebowski* was set. *The Big Lebowski* is unique because of the kind of reception it's received. When the film first came out, it was largely ignored and considered a disappointment as a follow-up to the Coen Brothers' Academy Award-winning *Fargo* (1996) (McCarthy). However, several years later, the film made a miraculous comeback. The film not only achieved popularity, it attracted a unique and unprecedented cult following of extremely devoted fans. The movie's fans' infatuation with the movie revolves around anything from the iconic persona of its main character to minor lines which fans can quote in the blink of an eye. This following has spawned, among other things, numerous books, an entire *Lebowski*-devoted store in New York City and a popular series of festivals known as Lebowski Fest.

The main characters of the movie, The Dude and his friend Walter Sobchak, are ultimate foils – The Dude pacifistic and lazy, Walter an overbearing veteran. They each represent and, at times, consciously stand for opposing political viewpoints – Walter the dominant conservative policy of the time of Reagan and Bush, The Dude the New Left movement (at its base, not all of the counterculture that developed from it) of the 1960s.

Walter's embodiment is, on the surface, more apparent. He is a caricature of the conservative regime that was in power almost constantly from 1969-93. Walter clearly dwells on war, mentioning his experience in Vietnam as often as he can. He resorts to violence to solve even small problems, like Smokey's toe slipping over the line while bowling. Walter even represents American conservatives' devotion to the state of Israel – he is an observant Jew, he quotes Herzl and he even brings an Uzi, an Israeli gun, to the ransom exchange. But The Dude sees Walter's Jewish identity as a manifestation of a senseless fixation on his ex-wife, Cynthia, a relationship that many would say is similar to the United States' with Israel.

The Dude's laziness is conscious and not careless, a fully fleshed-out demonstration of life as described in the Port Huron Statement. The Dude even claims to have helped write the Statement – "The *original* Port Huron Statement," he says, "Not the compromised second draft." The Statement says that one should only do work that they find interesting and stimulating. The Dude, despite his laziness, later shows his ability to do serious work, or at least commit himself to attempt serious work, when he is offered the detective job, something that actually does stimulate him for once, by The Big Lebowski. So The Dude is lazy, but not apathetic, as he shows by readily embracing work that he wants to do. The Dude's maintenance of this lifestyle is philosophical, though, not outright political. The Dude proves that he cares more about the ideals of leisure more than any political movement by placing a picture of Richard Nixon bowling on his wall. This seems odd considering The Dude's background and the New Left's extreme distaste for Nixon, but it shows that The Dude cares more about the bowling – which is, for him, the ultimate form of leisure activity – than who is doing the bowling and what his politics are.

The Dude is alone within his world. He lives during a time of unrest, a time where there was not much need for the fashionably lazy. Throughout the movie, The Dude is constantly shouted at by numerous people – The Big Lebowski, Maude, Jackie Treehorn, Jesus, etc. – who try to use him for their own gain. In fact, the only character who truly understands how The Dude lives is a minor one, the landlord, Marty, with whom The Dude participates in a bizarre economic system of bartering in which The Dude pays his rent through support of Marty's artistic endeavors (S. Thompson). Despite The Dude's loneliness, the Stranger calls him the "man for his time and place". Why would he do that? The filmmakers are not saying that The Dude is typical of a man of his time period, they are saying that he is needed in his time period to provide an alternative to conservatism and all of the personality traits associated with it, as typified in Walter.

The film does make the statement that The Dude's lifestyle is more fulfilling than Walter's, because Walter is missing contentment in his life and gravitates towards those completely unlike himself, such as The Dude. The one character in the movie whom Walter shows complete reverence for is Arthur Digby Sellers, the former TV writer attached to the iron lung, father of Little Larry. Walter loves Sellers's show, *Branded*, but that is in his past. Vietnam is similarly in Walter's past – he feels extraordinarily sentimental about it, but he does start to have a change in heart about war. It is not clear that he supports the Gulf War that is going on during the movie, that he criticizes sometimes in his own offbeat way, such as by comparing the quality of his foes – the Vietnamese were "worthy adversaries" while Saddam Hussein is a "camel-fucker." Since directly after the bowling alley incident, when Walter tries to be calmer than The Dude in The Dude's car, Walter does not find satisfaction through his own lifestyle, but rather by living vicariously through The Dude. Even in The Dude's detective case, which The Dude actually does get excited about, Walter is the one who really looks for a conspiracy, and finds excitement where there should be none to be found, presumably because he will feel more satisfied, perhaps more like he did in Vietnam. Walter is the one who truly believes that Bunny kidnapped herself, even though it was The Dude who first suggested the idea – "That poor woman … kidnapped herself, Dude. You said so yourself." Walter also believes, in this case entirely baselessly, that The Big Lebowski is feigning his disability.

It is important to note that the film came out about seven years after it was set: in 1998. From a liberal point of view such as The Dude's, things were generally considered better in 1998 than in 1991, at least. Bill Clinton was in the White House, the U.S. was not involved in any war at the time, the economy was good – generally, things were peaceful and prosperous for most. At this time, The Dude was not quite as unusual as he would have been in 1990, since the American populace was comfortable and unthreatened, and not particularly obsessed with politics, economics or lifestyle. This meant that, to the film's first audiences, The Dude's was not as much of an alternative lifestyle as the Coens had intended, and the character was not so romanticized in the eyes of the viewer.

There are many clues about the movie's message that can be found in the Stranger's various monologues. The Stranger functions as a stand-in for the audience of the movie, at least the Coen Brothers' vision of the ideal audience member. He certainly seems like a middle American conservative type, but he shows an innate understanding of and sympathy to The Dude and his lifestyle. He points out The Dude's laziness awfully early in the movie, and refers back to it at the end of the film. The key revealing line is when he says that he is glad that The Dude is "out there taking it easy for all us sinners." Often, laziness is considered a sin itself, but here, the Stranger deliberately sets The Dude apart from sinners. When the stranger says "way out west in Los Angeles" and then the camera continues to the sea, it refers to American expansionism, such as westward expansion in the 19th century, but also implies that the wars in Vietnam and Iraq and their interventionist policies are natural successors to expansionism. As Walter said, there was "no *literal* connection" between The Dude's relating a story of economic unfairness and the war in Vietnam, but there he contended that there was a connection (Martin-Jones).

The film was very deliberately set when it was. As the Coen brothers have said, "We've written the story from a modern point of view and set it very precisely in 1991, during the Persian Gulf War … which also has a direct effect on The Dude and his friends" (Martin-Jones). This message was not immediately received because of the different climate at the time of the film's release. But the movie's audience changed as times changed once again. When Clinton left office, circumstances remarkably similar to those of 1991 developed. There was a conservative in the White House again – another Bush, even. There was more unrest, especially after 9/11. The United States was getting involved in another foreign war based on preemptive intervention. The economy was sliding back into deficit. And, in these times, the American people needed a contrarian hero. And in this period of need, it was The Dude who became the "man for his time."

....

Reuben J. Cohen is a devoted student and Achiever. Born in Philadelphia, he grew up in the Washington, DC area but is a Canadian citizen. Reuben is an avid media consumer – he especially enjoys the Muppets, the films of the Coen Brothers and Wes Anderson, and cult classic TV shows. Obviously, he is a golfer. In the fall of 2013, Reuben will begin studies at Sarah Lawrence College in Bronxville, NY.

Works Cited

Russell, Bertrand. "In Praise of Idleness." *Harper's Magazine* 165 (October 1932): 552-559. Web.

Steinbeck, John. *The Log from the Sea of Cortez*. 1951. London: Penguin, 2001. Web.

Coen, Ethan and Joel. *The Big Lebowski*. London: Faber and Faber, 1998. Print.

Thompson, Stacy. "The Dude and the New Left." *The Year's Work In Lebowski Studies*. Ed. Edward P. Comentale and Aaron Jaffe. Bloomingon & Indianapolis, IN: Indiana University Press, 2009. 124-148. Print.

Milliken, Bill. *So Long, Sweet Jesus*. Buffalo, NY: Prometheus Press, 1973. Web.

Swartz, David R. "The New Left and Evangelical Radicalism." *Journal for the Study of Radicalism* 3.2 (2010): 51-79. Web.

Thompson, Hunter S. *Fear and Loathing in Las Vegas*. 1971. New York: Vintage, 1998. Web.

McCarthy, Todd. "The Big Lebowski." *Variety* 19 January 1998. Web.

The Big Lebowski. Dir. Joel Coen. Universal, 1998. DVD.

Martin-Jones, David. "No Literal Connection: Images of Mass Commodification, U.S. Militarism and the Oil Industry in *The Big Lebowski*." *The Year's Work In Lebowski Studies*. Ed. Edward P. Comentale and Aaron Jaffe. Bloomington & Indianapolis, IN: Indiana University Press, 2009. 203-227. Print.

Allen, Dennis. "*Logjammin'* and *Gutterballs*: Masculinities in *The Big Lebowski*." *The Year's Work In Lebowski Studies*. Ed. Edward P. Comentale and Aaron Jaffe. Bloomington & Indianapolis, IN: Indiana University Press, 2009. 386-409. Print.

The Big Lebowski. Dir. Joel Coen. Universal, 1998. DVD.

Birkerts, Sven. "The Mother of Possibility." *Lapham's Quarterly* Spring 2011. Web.

Bush, George H.W. 6 August 1990. Speech.

Byers, Thomas B. "Found Document: The Stranger's Commentary and a Note on His Method." *The Year's Work In Lebowski Studies*. Ed. Edward P. Comentale and Aaron Jaffe. Bloomington & Indianapolis, IN: Indiana University Press, 2009. 189-202. Print.

Desch, Michael C. "America's Liberal Illiberalism: The Ideological Origins of Overrecation in U.S. Foreign Policy." *International Security* 32.3 (2008): 7-43. Web.

Falsani, Cathleen. *The Dude Abides: The Gospel According to the Coen Brothers*. Grand Rapids, MI: Zondervan, 2009. Print.

Green, Bill; Peskoe, Ben; Russell, Will and Shuffitt, Scott. *I'm a Lebowski, You're a Lebowski: Life, The Big Lebowski, and What Have You*. Bloomsbury USA, 2007. Print.

Hall, Dennis and Susan Grove. "LebowskIcons: the Rug, the Iron Lung, the Tiki Bar, and Busby Berkeley." *The Year's Work In Lebowski Studies*. Ed. Edward P. Comentale and Aaron Jaffe. Bloomington & Indianapolis, IN: Indiana University Press, 2009. 321-340. Print.

Honore, Carl. *In Praise of Slowness: Challenging the Cult of Speed*. San Francisco: HarperSanFrancisco, 2005. Print.

Lebowki Fest. Lebowski Fest. Web. 12 November 2011.

Martin, Paul "Pablo" and Renegar, Valerie. "The Man For His Time: *The Big Lebowski* as Carnivalesque Social Critique." *Communication Studies* 58.3 (2007): 299-. Web.

Merriam-Webster Free Online Dictionary. Merriam-Webster. Web. 12 November 2011.

Port Huron Statement.

Quester, George H. "The Bush Foreign Policy and the Good Society." *The Good Society* 14.3 (2005): 15-21. Web.

Russell, Bertrand. "In Praise of Idleness." *Harper's Magazine* 165 (October 1932): 552-559. Web.

Tyree, J.M. and Walters, Ben. *Film Classics: The Big Lebowski*. London: British Film Institute, 2010. Print.

Winkler, Carol. "Parallels in Preemptive War Rhetoric: Reagan on Libya; Bush 43 on Iraq." *Rhetoric and Public Affairs* 10.2 (2007): 303-334. Web.

Matthew Killorin, *Dude and Walter*

Riccardo Rosanna, *The Big Lebowski Tribute*

Who's the Fucking Nihilist Here?: Structural and Cosmic Lawlessness in *The Big Lebowski*

BY ALEX BUFFER

The Coen Brother's cult classic film, *The Big Lebowski*, presents itself in a comic light, but that tone is an absurdly nihilistic facade for the movie's real social commentary. "When art becomes so abstract," says film critic Erica Rowell, "that it becomes ridiculous, indescribable, or unrecognizable, it can border on meaningless and nothingness. But it can also point to weighty issues underneath the surface" (Rowell 229). And the Coen Brothers' film does just that, making an art form out of degeneracy for the sake of degeneracy.

Adequate analysis of the topic necessitates a certain understanding of nihilism, which is by more accounts a more esoteric and unorthodox school of thought than most others. Most closely associated with 19th Century German thinker Friedrich Nietzsche, nihilism by definition is "the belief that all values are baseless and that nothing can be known or communicated" (Pratt). A strict nihilistic thinker would bear no attachments or loyalties to any person, place, or thing and resoundingly reject the concept of existence. Nihilists see all values held by those in the mainstream as flawed, and part of a "defective Western mythos" (Pratt). The realization that existence is a lie, to believers in this creed, means nothing short of absolute freedom. Nihilists are free to endeavor as they wish because it ultimately means nothing, but this also means that their endeavors are, themselves, entirely pointless. Nietzsche himself saw nihilism as a result of the natural progression of history (White). Those who attributed value to the world and worldly endeavors are inevitably disappointed, he says, and nihilism comes about as a radical rejection of the notion of value when individuals have been thoroughly disenchanted (White). However, not every nihilist is strictly such, and nihilism occurs at different levels with different individuals. By the late 20th Century, the philosophy had evolved in part to characterize the "postmodern man ... dehumanized, alienated, indifferent, and baffled ... directing psychological energy into hedonistic narcissism" (Pratt) – a description quite apt to characterize the protagonist of *The Big Lebowski*.

As the camera pans in over the Los Angeles skyline, and the voice of Sam Elliott gruffly discloses the details of what is about to come, *The Big Lebowski* ripe with nihilistic noir (Hibbs 31). Thomas Hibbs argues in his essay that the use of nihilism and noir helps to perpetuate comedy, and that the Coen Brothers use these motifs in *The Big Lebowski*. Voice-over narration is in itself somewhat nihilistic, emerging from nothingness, a disembodied entity that doesn't really generally even exist within the context of the actual plot. Elliott introduces the film's protagonist, Jeffrey Lebowski, pointing out that the name he has chosen to give himself is a name that no other man would "self-apply" where he comes from: "The Dude." The mere fact that Lebowski would opt for a lowbrow nickname over his legal name immediately separates him from mainstream society, making him a less real entity than other characters in the film who embrace their given names.

As he strides briskly through a convenience store, wearing aviator sunglasses, flip-flops, checkered-shorts, a v-neck t-shirt, and an old bathrobe, The Dude grabs a carton of milk from the refrigerated section. He makes it to the register and, realizing that he doesn't carry cash (probably because he doesn't have any), writes a check for 69 cents. His actions in this scene set the tone for the film well, they epitomize what it means to not care about yourself, your actions, and what others think of them. The Dude, in a sense, actively tries not to fit in with the rest of the world (other than the fact that he carries a check book).

Upon meeting his namesake, Jeffrey Lebowski, the contrast between the two men could not be more evident: The perpetually stoned, perpetually uncaring Dude versus the elderly, retired businessman turned philanthropist, who served in the army and lost function in his legs because of it. It is a classic case of anti-establishment versus establishment. If the younger Jeffrey Lebowski is "The Dude," then the elder is what counter-culture activists may have referred to as "The Man" back in the day. The latter is the perfect model of societal aspiration and success – a man of the community – while the other resides on the polar opposite end of this spectrum; The Dude is a man who cares about nothing, who does nothing, and ultimately who amounts to nothing cosmically. While not a self-proclaimed nihilist (as he'd never refer to himself as anything but "The Dude," or colorful variations of the moniker), he lives a life that is, in many ways, decidedly nihilistic.

The individuals that The Dude surrounds himself with add to this mystique. The Dude's fiercely loyal and fiercely neurotic pseudo-sidekick, Walter, is a Vietnam war veteran who cannot stop living in the mentality of the past in an effort to install the order and stability that he and his comrades failed to install in the jungles of Vietnam. Whether spouting off about the inherent flaws of pacifism and communism or claiming to be a devoted Jew (he converted for his ex-wife, and still practices), Walter's inability to let go renders him a man trapped in the amber of time. His personality is destructive, and he brings with him a trail of violence and (comical) ineptitude. Yet there is an ironic twist to his conservative, order-valuing character; not only is Walter best friends with the hippie-stoner, The Dude, but Walter's actions consistently result in disorder and chaos. In one scene, Walter pulls a gun on an opponent during a league bowling match over a relatively insignificant dispute, one that The Dude (his bowling partner) doesn't seem to really care about in the slightest. In doing so, Walter gets himself, The Dude, and their third, Donnie, tossed from the bowling alley and threatened with legal action. Another venture finds Walter interrogating a teenage boy that he and The Dude suspect of having stolen a briefcase containing a considerable sum of money from The Dude's car, which itself had been stolen. Seeing that the interrogation is going nowhere, Walter removes a crowbar from his trunk and begins to desecrate the sports car parked out front of the boy's house, only to find that it belonged to the boy's neighbor. His reckless predisposition to violence makes The Dude's universe all the more unhinged (this time, without the aid of drugs) and all the more of an uncertain place to live in. Walter, despite his intentions, prevents the achievement of balance. Walter's addiction to his own beliefs, from anti-communism to his pseudo-Judaism, makes him anything but a nihilist. Yet his behavior produces the opposite of the order and meaning he craves because he fails to consider their potential consequences, selfish motivations, and destructive results of his ill-founded idealism.

The Big Lebowski's storyline itself is structurally meaningless. The film revolves around Jeffrey Lebowski recruiting The Dude and his companions to deliver a ransom for the kidnapping of his trophy wife, Bunny. A series of eclectic plot twists ensue as The Dude's friend, Walter, looking to rescue Bunny and keep the million dollar ransom to himself, botches the trade-off, which results in a limited amount of gunfire. Afterwards, The Dude's car is stolen, and with it the briefcase that still contains the million dollar ransom. Reasoning that he will face the wrath of Jeffrey Lebowski, a violent porn executive, or both in one unpleasant combination or another, The Dude embarks on what turns out to be a wild goose chase for a suitcase that never contained any money. Lebowski's daughter, Maude, reveals to The Dude that her father has no money of his own and that her deceased mother was the true breadwinner of the family. Fearing his financial irresponsibility, she had entrusted her fortune to a charity where Jeffrey Lebowski wouldn't be able to touch it.

Putting two and two (or perhaps one and one and one and one and so on, considering the complex nature of the plot) together, The Dude reasons that there must have never a kidnapping, and that Lebowski had simply manipulated a few coincidental circumstances in an attempt to extort one million dollars from his late wife's foundation. Up until that point, the entire storyline had leads the audience on by implying the existence of some great mystery only for the entirety of the plot to have been a farce. As hilarious as it is, and as much as *The Big Lebowski* drives home certain social criticisms, the plot itself is utterly pointless, as it achieves literally nothing, except to accentuate nihilistic noir. "*The Big Lebowski* pushes us to wondering whether we can't comprehend the subject because we're right and there is no subject . . . or that the fact that we can't command its subject and are wondering is precisely what the film's subject has led us to" (Natoli 245). Just as Rowell stated, this meaninglessness in and of itself points to something more. Retrospection following the discernment of the true nature of the film's structure allows audiences to analyze individual scenes for deeper meaning rather than focus upon a mere string of events. Instead of trying to search for some incredibly deep meaning to *The Big Lebowski*, the audience is able to grasp more evident criticisms of persons, actions, and of society at large based on various incidents from the film. While the movie does string itself together with regards to its overarching meaning, the Coen Brothers utilize a sort of "divide and conquer" approach in terms of how they use bits of the movie to advance certain ideas.

The whole twisting and turning plot line also serves to provide a subtle social criticism of mainstream society. Jeffrey Lebowski, more than any character featured in the film, is a symbol of the status quo – and yet he proves to be as crooked and corrupt and lazy as he accuses The Dude of being. The hypocrisy evident here devalues the meaning that has been prescribed to society by folks that would otherwise have admired a man like Lebowski. Society has come to define success as Lebowski has over time. Adorning the man's walls are pictures of himself with Ronald and Nancy Reagan, children his (but really his daughter's) philanthropic organization benefited, and a key to the city of Pasadena. By all means, Lebowski seems to have done it all – become wealthy of his own accord, and given back to his community in a meaningful way that has been recognized be influential members of society. But if Lebowski is a fake, than can a society that embraces men like him with open arms be considered fake, too? It reflects rather poorly on any society that would admire a man like that – and raises the question about whether or not any of society's chosen heroes are worth looking up to, as they too might secretly be liars and cheaters. He is nothing short of a fraud, and his deception gives The Dude the moral high ground in their dynamic (Natoli 249). Coen noir typically incorporates the theme of "the common man," and *The Big Lebowski* is no exception (Green). While The Dude isn't exactly common per se, he definitely possesses an air of commonality that other characters lack – in short, he can be sympathized with. If there's any meaning behind all the nothingness in the film, it's that The Dude is worth your consideration as much as somebody like Jeffrey Lebowski, perhaps even more.

In fact, The Dude has the moral high ground over a lot of people featured in the film that subscribe to society's status quo. Walter values order and stability as much as Lebowski does (even though he does not criticize The Dude, and seems to secretly worship his image) but his logic is rooted in his experiences in Vietnam and belief in the dog-eat-dog nature of the world. Walter is very much a proponent of the belief that the ends always justifies the means, often pursuing unorthodox methods (like trying to trick kidnappers while delivering a ransom to save the kidnapped party and keep the money or trashing a sports car with a crowbar in order to prove a point) to achieve the order and stability that he values so much. Though The Dude does commit countless minor legal infractions (including but not limited to being stoned for the entirety of the film) he is ultimately a morally sound individual, mostly only caring about himself and his own interests but doing his best not to rile up or disturb anyone else because that would infringe upon his own ability to be as laid back of an individual as he is. While The Dude by no means contributes to society in any meaningful way, he doesn't really take anything away from it. This also makes The Dude's existence itself a more nihilistic one than those around him, who contribute to the degradation of society with violence, deceit, and greed among other things.

One of the film's penultimate scenes then highlights the hypocrisy of the German so-called Nihilists. When they confront The Dude, Walter, and Donny (their quiet friend who is comparatively less relevant to the progression of the story) demanding the million dollars, they are informed of the fact that the money never existed and that Lebowski had been playing them all along. "It's not fair!" cries on of them, to which Walter angrily interjects, "Fair? Who's the fucking nihilist here? What are you, a bunch of fucking crybabies?" (Hibbs 34). Here, Walter sheds light on an inherent flaw in nihilistic thought: pure nihilism is not something that can be achieved (Hibbs 34). "An utterly amorphous and completely pointless life would deprive an individual not just of any inspiring sense of purpose but even of the basis for deliberating and pursuing anything whatsoever." (Hibbs 34) What makes the Nihilists anything but is their want of something – in this case, money. The Nihilists of *The Big Lebowski* are only purported to be such as it suits their image. Just as The Dude is nihilistic without effort or attempt to be so or even possess an intellectual fondness for the epistemology, the Nihilists are not nihilistic because they believe themselves to be so adamantly so. Believing yourself to be a nihilist goes against nihilism's basest tenant: possessing no beliefs (Kates 153). Granted, there are no pure nihilists in The *Big Lebowski*, but pure nihilism is more of an idea than a reality to anyone that subscribes to any sort of nihilistic philosophy. For those making a conscious effort to be nihilists, the Germans do a spectacularly terrible job. They will do and say nihilistic things, but the moment that they perceive themselves as being wronged or as not getting something that they want, they instantly shed all philosophical inhibitions and give themselves over to their greediness and material desires (Treanor 224). Ultimately, so many of the film's major players are motivated by a want of money – Lebowski, Bunny, the Nihilists, even Walter – The Dude's only real motivation all throughout was to be right back where he started (prior to his assault at the hands of the Nihilists). He wants the entire situation resolved so he can get back to his quiet existence of few wants and needs.

The Dude, being carefree as he is, couldn't care less about most of the things that those who surround him are concerned with as long as they don't impede upon his freedom to indulge himself in a far more private, spiritual, and (of course) drug addled manner than anyone else. The way of The Dude, as unorthodox as it may seem, juxtaposed with all the other alternatives presented throughout the film, can come across as a dark horse candidate to be considered the middle ground between the Nihilists that have become so wrapped up in their conceptual vision of their philosophy that they've ceased to become nihilists and characters like Walter and Jeffrey Lebowski who are so consumed by their conceptual vision of order, stability, justice that they've become destructive forces in society and walking caricatures of their former selves. Walter is a war veteran who fought to protect his country, now wreaking violence upon the (mostly) innocent, and Lebowski's entrepreneurial productivity has been transformed into an unproductive cancer.

Though many throughout *The Big Lebowski* reject The Dude and refuse to take him seriously because of his appearance, demeanor, and general lack of sobriety, he is often the most reasonable party in any interaction. This is also where the starkest and most apparent social commentary comes into play in the movie. Nothing against The Dude (I'd want to be his friend if I knew him), but it's a sad reflection on society when the unemployed stoner is the sole voice of reason. Especially when that unemployed stoner is one dim enough to believe, at one point, that a pubescent boy stole one million dollars in ransom money from him and possesses the emotional fortitude to withstand Walter's interrogation (when in fact he was probably just either confused, had knowledge of the fact that he was indeed innocent, or like so many other characters in this film, stoned). So many figures that should be responsible individuals and upstanding members of society – from war veterans to wealthy philanthropists – are anything but. And to top that off, the remaining cast of characters is comprised of a lot of people far more unsavory than The Dude, including but not limited to a vengeful porn baron, the German faux-Nihilists, and a Latino pedophile turned effeminate and übersexual bowling champion. While the juxtaposition of characters and events together may make *The Big*

Lebowski seem like an outlandish film, individually a lot of the characters come across as totally plausible. Joe and Ethan Coen, as directors, have even admitted that a lot of the characters featured in the film are based on real life people, who all just happen to be ridiculous and do ridiculous things (Green). This helps in making *The Big Lebowski* a true convergence of as many of society's ills as the Coen Brothers could feasibly imagine, and a wickedly hilarious display of (somewhat realistic) decadence.

The fact that The Dude does not attempt this brand of nihilism is precisely what makes him a different sort of nihilist –less "pure" but probably more plausible. As much as The Dude applies to certain tenants, he is ultimately too skeptical of the world around him by nature to adopt any particular ethos, choosing instead to flow along as the world happens around him (Hibbs 35). Rather than perceive existence as nothing, The Dude just views a lot of what's going on to be insignificant to his own ends. "His way of life affirms the equal significance or insignificance of all human endeavors" (Hibbs 35). The Dude is a more of an objective egoistic nihilist – one might presume he has a dash of Ayn Rand in his outlook. If everything is equally significant or insignificant, he's free to endeavor as he wishes, conscious of the fact that it's all going to prove itself cosmically pointless in the end.

....

Alex Buffer wrote this essay between 2AM and 7AM for one of those introductory film courses during his freshman year, following a hard drive malfunction that resulted in the loss of the original paper. He likes to think that that's how The Dude would have done it, if he'd gone to college. Alex attends The George Washington University, where he studies History. His work for Lebowski 101 is dedicated with much love and admiration for Professor Sandie Friedman, who abides spectacularly.

Works Cited:

Ben Peskoe, Bill Green, Scott Shuffitt and Will Russell. I'm a Lebowski, You're a Lebowski : Life, *The Big Lebowski*, and What-Have-You. New York: Bloomsbury, 2007. Print.

Hibbs, Thomas S. "The Human Comedy Perpetuates Itself: Nihilism and Comedy in Coen Neo-Noir." *The Philosophy of the Coen Brothers*. Lexington, Kentucky: American UP, 2009. 27-40. Print.

Kates, Joshua. "*The Big Lebowski* and Paul De Man." *The Year's Work in Lebowski Studies*. Ed. Edward P. Comentale and Aaron Jaffe. Bloomington: Indiana UP, 2009. Print.

Natoli, Joseph P. *Postmodern Journeys: Film and Culture, 1996-1998*. Albany, NY: State University of New York, 2001. Print.

Ed. Pratt, Alan. "Nihilism [Internet Encyclopedia of Philosophy]." *Internet Encyclopedia of Philosophy*. 3 May 2005. Web. http://www.iep.utm.edu/nihilism/#H2.

Rowell, Erica. *The Brothers Grim: The Films of Ethan and Joel Coen*. Lanham, MD: Scarecrow, 2007. Print.
The Big Lebowski. Dir. Joel Coen and Ethan Coen. 1998.

Treanor, Brian. A Passion for the Possible: Thiwnking with Paul Ricoeur. New York: Fordham UP, 2010. Print.

White, Alan. "Transformations of Nihilism." *Williams College: Alan White, Professor of Philosophy*. Web. http://www.williams.edu/philosophy/faculty/awhite/WNL web/Transformations frames.htm.

Jane Labovich, *This Etch A Sketch Really Ties The Room Together...*

Gregg Firestone, *Where's the Fucking Money, Lebowski?*

Strikes and Gutters: How *The Big Lebowski* Has Ruined Movies for Me

BY JIM DEFILLIPI

"Ups and downs, strikes and gutters," The Dude tells the Stranger, offering a succinct and universal description of life in all of its aspects. We tend to forget that watching the movie caused viewers some gutters along with its many strikes.

First, for me it ruined all future movies in which The Dude appeared. In 2003, while the rest of the world was praising the inspirational story and marveling at the emotional impact of "Seabiscuit," I just sat there exclaiming, "Look! The Dude bought a horse!"

It was a good horse for sure, but where did The Dude get the money? And will he have to bring it bowling, like Walter brings his ex's Pomeranian?

And what the heck was The Dude thinking by imitating Kris Kristofferson in "Crazy Heart"? Kristofferson is the original drunken, broken-down, gravelly-voiced cowboy singer. The Dude is the diametric opposite – he's a drunken, broken-down, gravelly-voiced singer who sometimes talks to cowboys in bowling alleys.

"And now, accepting the Oscar for Mr. Bridges, is Kris Kristofferson," as the orchestra plays "Me and Bobbi McGee."

"True Grit" – same thing, more ersatz Kristofferson, or you could call it "The Dude with a touch of the Duke."

But let's face it, I don't watch movies just to see The Dude trying to be something he's not. Like most other men, I watch movies for one main purpose – to see girls in their underwear. Or better yet, in nothing at all.

Watching porn doesn't do it, it presents no challenge; seeing porn stars naked is like hunting tigers in a game preserve, or shooting caged rhinos at the Bronx Zoo.

On the other hand, few things beat the lascivious thrill of watching the female lead in a movie undress. And of course, the two typical times in the plot when this is likely to happen are: 1) When she takes a stranger home; and 2) When she takes a bath.

Julia Roberts in "Sleeping with the Enemy," with the tub water slightly above nipple-level, sees her towels hanging straight and knows that her lunatic husband is in the house. Her face mirrors terror, her eyes are filled with dread, as I'm thinking, "Stand up! Stand up!"

JayLo cuddling with a tub-soaking George Clooney in "Out of Sight": It's merely a dream sequence, but who cares, I'm thinking, "Roll over! Roll over!"

By now you might be asking yourself: But what does this have to do with The Dude? How do The Dude's experiences put a damper on a bit of red-blooded cinematic voyeurism?

The simple answer: marmots.

Ever since I watched the adventures of The Dude, all I can think of when I see *anyone* in a bathtub is: "Uh-oh, I hope a nihilist doesn't come in with a marmot on a leash." There is no longer even a hint of a carnal thrill; it's been replaced by repulsion and SPCA concern.

I shower daily, but I haven't taken a sit-down bath since 1998 and I don't intend to.

So, dear reader, you can see: for each of life's strikes, there is also a gutter ball. The best we can do is to endure, to yearn, to struggle, to abide, and to hope that some crazy fuck doesn't pull a gun next time we foot-fault.

I should mention that as a result of that scene where Walter pulls a gun on Smokey, I have become a terribly nervous bowler. It seems *The Big Lebowski* has ruined bowling for me as well.

....

Jim DeFillipi is a novelist (*Blood Sugar, Duck Alley,* etc.) who grew up in Duck Alley, NY, lived most of his life in northern Vermont, and now lives in Salem MA.

Will Staub, *Walter and The Dude*

Nomenclature is Not The Preferred Nomenclature

BY ANDREA KANNES

The Dude, our protagonist in *The Big Lebowski* played by Jeff Bridges, is a mellow, lazy guy who, in the parlance of our times, does his own proverbial "thing," and gets mixed up in a confusingly hilarious plot of greed and clashing ideologies. He responds to the chaos around him by "abiding" through doing what he is told by various authoritative characters, eventually proclaiming, "Ah, fuck it," when he realizes that all the falderal isn't worth whatever compensation he might receive. The Dude rolls through life like his bowling ball down his alley, strikingly similar to the tumbling tumbleweed shown navigating the streets of Los Angeles in the very beginning of the film. He just *is*, very much like the Tao of Taoism. In fact, one of the rare times that he gets flustered, his friend Walter notices: "C'mon, you're being very un-Dude," – one might suggest "un-Tao" instead.

As Zhuangzi, an ancient leader of Taoism, wrote: "The Tao cannot be seen: if you see it, it is not that. The Tao cannot be spoken, if you speak it, it is not that" ("Zhuangzi"). The Dude is effortless in his manner. No matter what happens he somehow always becomes "privy to the new shit" and things seem to work out for the best. As long as he keeps his mind limber and open – usually with the aid of a "strict drug regimen" – he is able to figure out all of the crazy happenings that unfold before him.

Another man who flowed in the same fashion is the Buddha himself. The Four Noble Truths and The Eightfold Path of Buddhism are eerily present within The Dude in *The Big Lebowski*.

For those who aren't familiar with the whole Buddhist "Eastern thing," the Four Noble Truths are:

1) Life is suffering,
2) Suffering is due to attachment,
3) Attachment can be overcome, and
4) There is a path for accomplishing this
(From "The Basics of Buddhist Wisdom")

Who's more unattached than The Dude? He has no wife, no family, no kids, no job, no money, and he seems perfectly content. Tai-chi, bowling, driving around, the occasional acid flashback, drinking White Russians, and smoking marijuana just may be The Dude's own abbreviated version of The Eightfold Path. After every time something significant happens to him, he's either at the bowling alley, rolling a joint, or having a drink. One potent example of this is when the millionaire Lebowski calls upon The Dude to act as courier. Brandt, The Big Lebowski's assistant, ushers The Dude in to discuss the situation. It is awkward for the viewer to see The Dude in a dramatically dark room lit only by the serious fireplace, which The Big Lebowski is sitting in front of in his wheelchair with a blanket on his lap. Brandt stands solemnly in his tailored suit between the two men with his head down, arms stiff at his side, fingers spread apart robotically. The Dude, however, is dressed in a dingy baseball t-shirt and leans back in his chair listening to The Big Lebowski blubber about his manhood and the alleged kidnapping. The Dude interrupts: "Mind if I do a jay?" This juxtaposition is visually intoxicating. In this Western World, The Dude keeps his Eastern composure and stays on track in the face of trouble which turns out to be a scam, anyway. The viewer learns a Buddhist lesson from *The Big Lebowski*. Once The Dude experiences attachment through desire – or in Sanskrit, "trishna" – of compensation for his rug, life isn't so pleasant. Suddenly he's responsible for the removal of a woman's toe, the destruction of a Corvette, and the death of his friend.

When The Dude eventually gives up on the promise of monetary gain, he finally gets his "Dudeness" back and in the end shares his motto with The Stranger, "The Dude abides." "Abiding" is essentially what Buddhists refer to as nirvana: "the letting go of clinging, hatred, and ignorance; the full acceptance of imperfection, impermanence, and interconnectedness of life" ("The Basics of Buddhist Wisdom"). One could argue that The Dude "abides" everything because he's too lazy to do anything else, but with this one should remember that the real Buddha did spend several years sitting under a tree until he was Enlightened. Perhaps this was The Dude in college, "occupying various administration buildings" and "smoking Thai stick." When The Dude and The Stranger are sitting at the bowling alley bar for the first time together, much is revealed. The Stranger offers The Dude a helpful aphorism: "Sometimes you eat the bar, and sometimes the bar, wal, he eats you." The Dude replies,

"Is that some kind of Eastern thing?" to which The Stranger answers with twinkling eyes full of wisdom, "Far from it."

The film accomplishes its wide appeal and taps into pop-cultural knowledge not only through various characters' hilarious ravings about everything from Vietnam to hating the band The Eagles, but through the hodge-podge of different traditional genres. Robert Scholes, author of "On Reading a Video Text," is concerned with this idea of American universal "cultural knowledge" that allows the Coen brothers to make such an intriguing film (205). The different genres present serve as a form of "cultural reinforcement" for the viewer (206). We notice the different elements fused together, which is refreshing because it serves as "a defense against the ever-present threat of boredom" (206). There is a little bit of everything in *The Big Lebowski*: a cowboy, part of a romance, comedy, a crime drama… there's even a musical number resulting from a drug-induced stupor. All of these components would be considered very "Western" in essence, revealing American values such of entertainment, escape, and intrigue. The use of a Western archetype, the cowboy, to narrate an Eastern message is also striking. To display the Eastern values of The Dude in such a Western way is to poke fun at both sides of the ideological spectrum, as few aspects of life ever neatly and completely fit into one category or the other. Is sitting under a tree for several years actually fruitful meditation or just an excuse to leave your wife (as the Buddha did) and take a load off? As Brandt would say, "Well, Dude, we just don't know."

There are a few times during the film that the viewer feels like he or she should be taking notes, especially when trying to figure out the significance of the very surreal scene that takes place at pornographer Jackie Treehorn's so-called "garden party." Topless women are tossed in into the nighttime sky near a bonfire by the blanket held by a circle of men gazing up at them with mouths agape in ecstasy. All of this occurs in slow motion. Even the viewers who are also on a "strict drug regimen" will want to ask the Coens, in the parlance of our Dude, "What the fuck are you talking about!?" at least once during the movie. An episodic, seemingly unrelated plot is a vital allusion to the most important genre that *The Big Lebowski* toys with: the Neo-Noir.

Lee Horsley, in an essay titled "An Introduction to Neo-Noir," writes that Neo-Noirs, "draw on films and novels of earlier decades," and this proves to be true. A sister Neo-Noir, *L.A. Confidential*, was inspired by James Ellroy's *L.A. Quartet* series of noir novels, and the Coen brothers were influenced by writer Raymond Chandler and 1946 private-eye flick, *The Big Sleep* ("An Interview with The Coen Brothers"). *L.A. Confidential* can be considered the other side of *The Big Lebowski*. It gives us insight into The Dude's "worthy adversaries," the rich, the powerful. One of The Dude's enemies is the fascist Malibu Chief of Police, and *L.A. Confidential* is a story about policemen like the Chief, who are caught up in a mixture of lies, corruption, sex, and murder. There are essentially the same elements in each film: political corruption, drugs, pornography, prostitution, and California. *L.A. Confidential* is set in 1953 and its events can be considered responsible for molding the corrupt world in which The Dude of the early 1990s lives. When compared to *The Big Lebowski*, *L.A. Confidential* is more of a classic noir as it deals more directly and literally with what Neo-Noir usually tackles: consumerism. *The Big Lebowski* deals with our American emphasis on material possessions and consumption, but with a more frivolous intricacy and an Eastern protagonist twist. Lee Horsley mentions Frederick Jameson and his essay titled "Postmodernism and Consumer Society" because Jameson poses this interesting question: "Are self-consciously 'noir' contemporary narratives to be seen as escaping from or engaging with contemporary issues?" (Horsley). For *The Big Lebowski*, the answer is both. Although the Coen brothers do leave little trinkets of repeated dialogue and images throughout the movie for devoted eagle-eye viewers to spot and wring out extensive meaning, they also provide the more passive viewer with more obvious jokes.

At the end of a classic Neo-Noir such as *L.A. Confidential*, loose ends are tightly tied like the shoelaces of an accomplished adult, similar to the works of Raymond Chandler consisting of tiny little interactions that perpetuate the plot. The "ins and outs" of the incongruous events are curtly explained, leaving the viewer thinking, "Ahh, now I get it." This is not the case in *The Big Lebowski*, whose end resembles the loose double-knots and bunny ears of the too-long shoelaces of your average toddler. Not everything ends up making sense, and the viewers are on their own if they want some kind of definite answer. The Coens aren't concerned with – or, perhaps, are above – providing analyses of their films. It's up to the viewer to provide meaning for themselves. But that's how, according to The Stranger, "The whole durned human comedy keeps perpetuatin' itself:" our lives' distinctive events may not always be overwhelmingly meaningful upon first glance. To bring back some Eastern perspective, The Western Stranger is promoting the Buddhist principle of "anatman," or the notion that all things are interconnected and interdependent; nothing has a separate existence ("The Basics of Buddhist Wisdom").

One of the most brilliant characters actually appears in the film only twice. The arch-nemesis of The Dude is portrayed in a dramatic, slow-motion shot, complete with his own theme song (The Gypsy Kings' rendition of The Eagles' classic "Hotel California") and lavender jumpsuit. The music builds and swells as Jesus Quintana rolls an emphatic strike and poses in a flamingo-like fashion after his success. The Coens let the characters spend a significant amount of time revealing the background of the character, even employing a rapid flashback to show us his mandatory door-to-door punishment of announcing to his pederasty to his neighbors.

The character Jesus Quintana is a favorite of many fans but really has nothing to do with the rest of the plot … or does he? Perhaps if the movie was given a little more time we might have seen the second coming of

Jesus as a distant relative of Bunny's or a former member of the German Nihilists' techno-pop group, "Autobahn." Even if this didn't turn out to be the case, sometimes the most significant events in our lives are the moments that last just a few seconds. Neo-Noir and Eastern philosophy are serious in their critiques of the human existence; the Coens are not. Life's peculiarity is beyond labeling or classifying, as the message of *The Big Lebowski* isn't in The Dude himself, but in the process of getting it from him. Although it is often detrimental to their enjoyment to dissect and inspect films, *The Big Lebowski* is one of the few whose value increases exponentially with each viewing. If we think hard enough or let a sufficient amount of time pass, we can provide some kind of explanation and label for anything if we really want to – except maybe the floating topless women. Anybody got any leads?

....

Andrea Kannes is currently an employee and student at The New School pursuing a graduate degree in Media Studies while exploring every single creative outlet that exists. This most recently includes producing, "We Lived Alone: The Connie Converse Documentary," dabbling in found footage of the 16mm variety, and the occasional stand-up comedy. Her Twitter handle is @ZBogart, if you're into that whole brevity thing.

Works cited

"An Interview with The Coen Brothers, Joel and Ethan about 'The Big Lebowski.'" IndieWire. 02 Mar 2007. Coen Brothers. 29 Mar 2007
<http://www.coenbrothers.net/interviewlebow.html>.

Boeree, C. George . "The Basics of Buddhist Wisdom." Shippensburg University. 29 Mar 2007
<http://webspace.ship.edu/cgboer/buddhawise.html>.

Horsley, Lee. "An Introduction to Neo-Noir." Neo-Noir. 02 Mar 2007. Crime Culture. 29 Mar 2007
<http://www.crimeculture.com/Contents/NeoNoir.html>.

Pregadio, Fabrizio. "Zhangzi." Taoism and the Taoist Canon. 02 Mar 2007. Stanford University Department of Religious Studies. 29 Mar 2007
<www.stanford.edu/~pregadio/taoism/texts_zhuangzi.html>.

Scholes, Robert. "On Reading a Video Text." The Advanced College Essay: Education and the Professions. Ed. William M. Morgan and Pat C. Hoy II. Boston: Pearson Custom Publishing, 2007. 205-206.

Dave Johnson, *Who Wants Some Big Lebowski?*

The Dude: A Retrospective

BY JAMES MADEIROS

To say that a foray into Dudeism is a highly personal journey may seem at first blush to be a matter of stating the obvious, especially to, ah, veteran students of The Dude (who may or may not have dabbled in pacifism at one time or another).

After all, any serious investigation of a particular way of life must necessarily come with the cost of at least some individual introspection and reflection. And this despite the fact that The Dude's teachings are most often delivered through a communal medium.

But, is this really the way of The Dude? Is The Dude really an island unto himself? Is The Dude's line in the sand actually a circle?

Perhaps it is better to see the The Dude's journey within the framework of any ordinary laid-back dude, especially when considering that our resonance with dudeness comes from shared experience and a sense of kindred spirits. Let's explore.

The Dude: Misanthrope

We're introduced to The Dude at his most comfortable, and most assuredly in his element: ensconced in a bathrobe, clad in jellies and in search of a fresh carton of half-and-half. As he writes his check for $0.69, you might conclude that this is a man easily dismissed.

Some may even take it a step further, assuming The Dude is a self-serving, hapless bum with no concern for the larger body politic. Look at him! He lives alone. The toilet seat is up, *man*. He unabashedly shops in sleepwear. He carries no cash or credit.

To the *bourgeoisie*, he is barely human.

Of course, students of Dudeism know better. The Dude fits right in there. It's not that he doesn't care – he's a modern-day ascetic. The Dude has renounced the trappings of consumerism, not people. As we see later, The Dude is very much into community (quite clearly articulated in his uncompromised original draft of the Port Huron Statement, circa 1962).

The Dude: Responsible Tenant, Art Appreciator and Valued Ralphs Member

The Dude's commitment to prompt rent payment, support of Marty's theatrical endeavors and loyal patronage to Ralphs is only a prelude to a greater contribution to L.A. society and the world at large. People more prone to karmic interpretations of Dudeism might say that the beauty of The Dude's life stems from his seemingly selfless and effortless engagement with those around him.

It's obvious that The Dude lives a humble life and is happy to do so. When he is set upon by thugs in his modest dwelling his only concern is for his rug, which obviously holds more aesthetic value for him than anything else. As students are fond of recounting, he felt that "... it really tied the room together."

But, to assume that The Dude is just a Samaritan with an eye for art (although lacking the necessary means, ah, necessary means to purchase it) would be an oversimplification. Dudeists are later confronted with the flawed humanity of The Dude when he nonchalantly asks Jackie Treehorn: "What's in it for The Dude?"

The Dude: Capitalist

There are an abundance of instances where students take note of Dude's enjoyment of all the things money can buy, from "oat sodas" to fine rugs. He revels in being given a beeper, and is obviously upset when the nihilists finally kill his car.

That said, The Dude is also acutely aware of his financial limitations and is, for the most part, unconcerned about them – a refreshing aspect of Dudeism. When it's suggested he pay $1,000 for a blowjob, his amusement at the absurdity of paying for something he knows he can get for free if he tries (*à la* George Costanza) is a true reference to the karmic nature of Dudeism.

His humility, however, does not stand in the way of his attempts to make a better life for himself. The Dude's entanglement in the entire affair with The Big Lebowski is prompted by a desire to get his rug back, which in turn leads to the temptation of a bigger score, which ultimately leads students back to the beginning of the story, which is to say a snapshot of the perpetuation of "the whole durned human comedy."

(*A note on philosophical doctrine*: There are numerous moments in which The Dude demonstrates the importance of exploring other social theories, specifically socialism, nihilism and fascism. These are not just words bandied about between The Dude, his friends, and the Chief of Police of Malibu – these are culturally significant modes of thought that Dudeists are encouraged to investigate.)

The Dude: Friend, Bowling Partner and Diplomat

Over and above this examination of the many faces of The Dude is the fact that he espouses a personal philosophy of "live and let live" that resonates with laypeople, students and dedicated Dudeists alike. At the end of the day, he's "takin' 'er easy for all us sinners," but in turn we are charged with taking it easy for him and one another as well.

As a representation of a critical element of any friendship (or bowling team), The Dude is the calm center in an otherwise untenable relationship between the naïve and put-upon Donny and Walter's militant intensity. Walter obviously loves Donny, despite his desperate wishes that he shut the fuck up, but without The Dude he would very likely be unable to show it.

The Dude's ability to act as an unassuming catalyst between people is drawn as much from his own self-interest as it is from his willingness to be forthright in his dealings with other humans. As he emphatically exclaims to The Big Lebowski, "I'm not trying to scam anybody here!"

The Dude: Symbol of Simple Success

In our heart of hearts, we love The Dude because he represents reliable and honest acceptance in a world that sits in constant judgment. He has opinions and ambitions, but they do not come at the expense of others. He is happy with the little things in life, but is not too proud or ashamed to take what is offered to him, whether it's a night of unrobed passion with an eccentric heiress, a Caucasian or two, or a chance to roll his way into the semis.

Dudeism may be a reflection of Taosim and several other more circumspect -isms, but The Dude himself would likely excuse such esteemed comparisons and remind students and Dudeists that the search for meaning in life is a personal journey unique to each of us and best traveled in our own way.

In so saying . . . mind if I do a jay?

....

James Madeiros, Seattle scribe and average bowler, has been a somewhat not non-practicing Dudeist since 1998, when he was introduced to The Dude's message while earning an achievement badge at Miami University of Ohio (a mere 300 miles from Port Huron). In 2010, James attended the Seattle Lebowskifest Movie Party on his 30ish birthday dressed as Walter Sobchak, which greatly invigorated his faith. Today – ah, whatever day this is – you can usually find him just fuckin' relaxing, or ruefully compromising someone's first draft.

Steven Cote, *Waltercolor*

The Big Lebowski: Serious Philosophical Underpinnings to a Hilarious Movie

BY MATTHEW CIARDIELLO

Let's wander into the middle of the movie.

It's the climax of the film. The Dude realizes he's been played by the other Lebowski. He and Walter race to Pasadena to confront the millionaire. And then...

The audience waits in suspense for some hilarious release, but to no avail. At that moment, Walter decides the old man is faking his disability. He grabs the defenseless "spinal" from his wheelchair and hurls him to the floor. The man lays sprawled out and weeping.

It's quite a pathetic scene, and the viewer is left feeling ill at ease. The comedic flow of the movie is mortally injured, and at the point when Donny dies from a random heart attack a few minutes later, the comedic flow expires alongside him.

This un-humorous ending is seriously *out of its element* in a slapstick comedy. If we concede that the film is otherwise well written, it's hard to see poor authorship as the culprit for a disjointed story line. So what other motivation could there be lurking behind the jokes? What is *The Big Lebowski* really about?

It's a simple question, but the answer is more profound than you might expect (or accept) from a major motion picture comedy.

First, a *frame of reference*. Nihilists are unusual characters in any genre. When they do surface, you can be sure something philosophical is in question. Now consider that Ethan Coen, one of two fraternal producers, was a Princeton philosophy major. *That's interesting, man.*

Now, an observation. Many of the film's more bizarre elements fit coherently into one of three themes: unchecked aggression, travesty, and aimlessness. Sounds a little existential. *Am I wrong?*

Yeah, Walter. What's your point? Well, the introductory narration informs us that "Sometimes there's a man for his time and place," and that's The Dude. The movie is a philosophical exposition about The Dude surviving, nay abiding, in a world gone crazy. Maybe that sounds like a joke, but "I'm telling you, I got definitive evidence." Let's take a look.

A travesty of the sacred

"Everything's a fucking travesty with you, man."
– The Dude to Walter

In *The Big Lebowski*, travesty is all around. The plot and its characters systematically mock those aspects of the human experience that society holds most sacred:

Birth: Conception becomes a mechanical, loveless (if *zesty*) affair when Maude scouts out The Dude to sire her a child only because he's healthy and uninterested in being a father.

Religion: Walter is a paragon of religious devotion, what with his insistence on being *shomer shabbos* and all. But it turns out he's actually a Catholic masquerading as a zealous Jew only to maintain a connection with his ex-wife. Oh, and the man named Jesus – *he's a pederast.*

Success: Jeff Lebowski, the millionaire, leads a "life of achievement," one of "challenges met, competitors bested, obstacles overcome," and he has the wall of plaques and the smarmy butler to prove it. Yet he's a complete phony. He married into his wealth, and he's trying to steal money from his own charitable foundation. Meanwhile, the only man of true success and achievement in the film, the screenwriter Arthur Digby Sellers, is a comatose vegetable who resides in an unassuming community with a thieving dunce for a son.

Death: Donny dies of a heart attack while a gang of nihilists attack his friends – not very glorious or solemn, and it only gets worse. Walter and The Dude won't splurge on a *moderately priced* urn, so they use a coffee can. Walter then orates a completely irrelevant eulogy which he ties back to 'Nam. And to top it off, when he scatters the ashes, they blow all over The Dude's face.

Unchecked aggression

"This aggression will not stand."
– George Bush

Unchecked aggression is a dominant theme in this film. Much of the time, the examples of it are laugh-out-loud:

Walter taking a crowbar to the Corvette; Walter pulling a piece out on Smokey over a league game; Woo peeing on the wrong Lebowski's carpet. But in a few cases, humor gives way to puzzlement and discomfort, for example when Walter throws the crippled man upon the floor to see if he's really crippled. The feeling is heightened when the aggressor is a natural force, like the one that gave Donny a heart attack or put Arthur Digby Sellers in a coma.

And unfortunately for the characters of *The Big Lebowski*, all too often the aggression does stand. No one gets full, or even partial, recompense for the wrongs done them, at least not from the aggressors. The Dude never gets his carpet back. Arthur Digby Sellers's son goes unpunished for stealing a car. Jackie Treehorn and his goons disappear from the plot. And the Malibu sheriff can throw a heavy coffee mug square at The Dude's forehead with complete impunity.

The Los Angeles of Lebowski is indeed a bleak world where indifferent and meaningless aggression can befall anyone, good or bad, deserving or innocent, at any time.

The tumbling tumbleweed

"I guess that's the way the whole durned human comedy keeps perpetuatin' itself, down through the generations, westward the wagons, across the sands a time until – aw, look at me, I'm ramblin' again."
– The Stranger

The viewer stumbles into Lebowski's world with the random tumbling of a tumbleweed. And he is escorted out by the rambling words of The Stranger. Within those bookends, Walter accuses Donny of having no frame of reference, but the same can be said of him, The Dude, and everyone else.

The whole story is a maelstrom of wandering characters who are trying to figure out the goings on around them. Their wanderings and occasional bumpings into one another are a key driver of the plot (and the humor).

Where does all the wandering lead? Nowhere in particular. No one wins or loses. Nothing important is learned or gained. The characters just move on with their lives. And according to our cowboy narrator, humanity's path is perhaps similarly aimless. He speaks of it perpetuating itself across space and time but stops short of saying where it's all headed.

Tying the room together

"The Dude abides."
– The Stranger

The synthesis of these persistent themes is that the world of *The Big Lebowski* is not an inviting one. It's devoid of things sacred. It's aimless. The forces at work in this environment are raw and indifferent to its victims. In sum, the setting of *The Big Lebowski* is purely an existential one.

However, the point of *The Big Lebowski* is how to survive such a setting. Its characters are challenged to endure a world that lacks meaning greater than themselves. They don't all manage well.

There are the nihilists. They assert that nothing matters, so they devote their life to worldly pleasures alone. But this has perverse consequences. Uli, a.k.a., Karl Hungus, for example, is at different times a drunk sybarite, a porn actor, and a violent money-grubbing con artist.

Then there is Walter. He can't accept that nothing matters. He saw his friends "die face down in the muck" in Vietnam, and he spends the rest of his life trying to justify it. He tries too hard though, and his attempts to connect 'Nam to a trophy wife's antics, a cup of coffee, or Donny's funeral become ridiculous.

Finally, there is The Dude. He's the man the movie celebrates. He's the hero. He's the shining example to follow. The Dude abides his existential surroundings the best. How does he do it? By doing . . . well, by doing not much at all. Bowling, music, white Russians, recreational drugs – these are his modest expectations from life. The pleasures they bring are the only meaning he needs in life. The rest is just – *aw, look at me, I'm ramblin' again*.

....

Matthew Ciardiello is a corporate finance professional currently based in Denver, Colorado. He first developed a love for *The Big Lebowski* while studying abroad in Rome in 2002, when, after seeing it for the first time, he had a lengthy discussion about the film with his Latin professor. Since college, Matthew has lived and worked all over the world, including in New York, England, the United Arab Emirates, and Portland, Maine. Matthew has a bachelors degree in Classics and Medieval Latin from Harvard University.

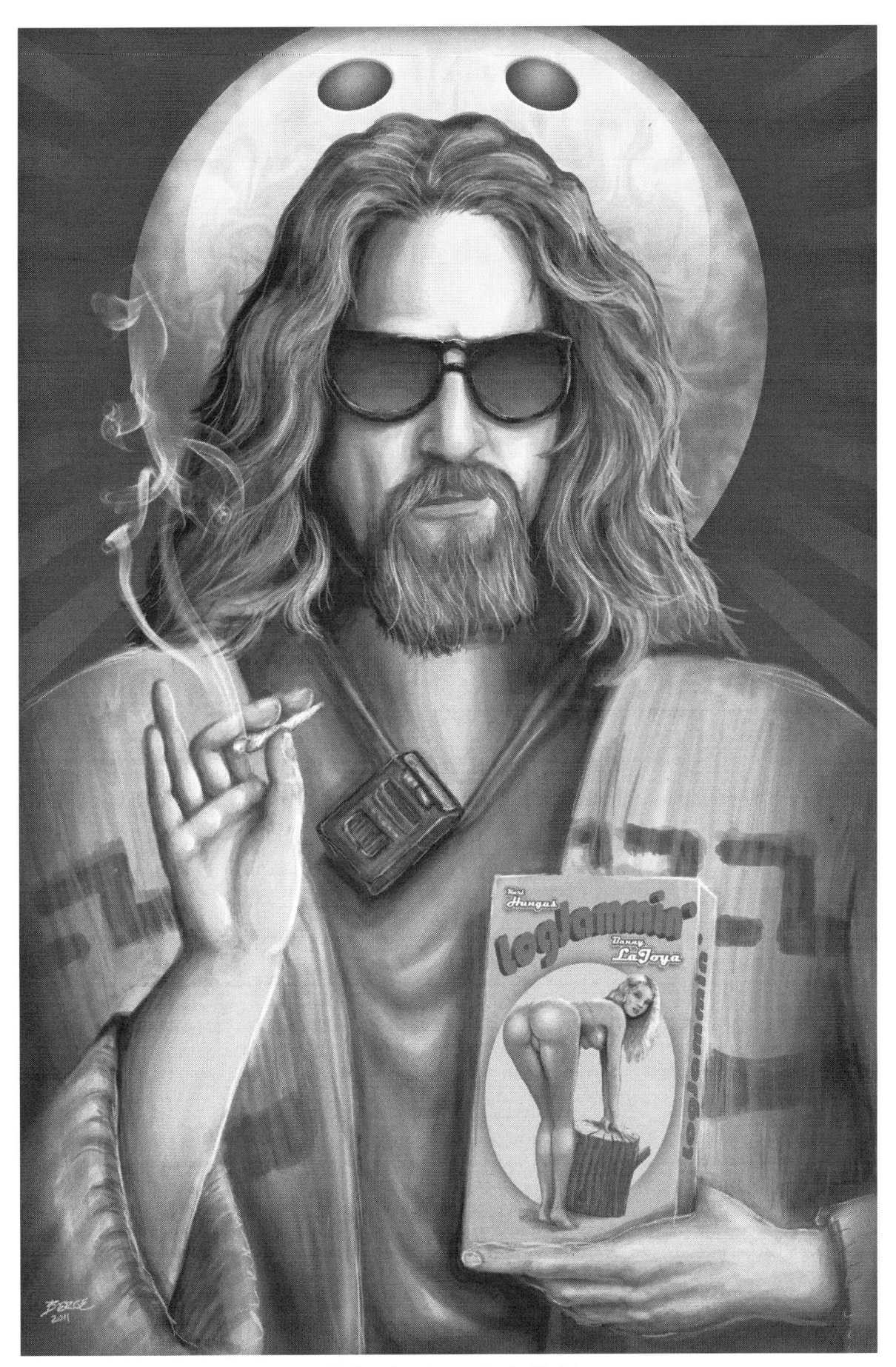

Christopher Berge, *Dude Christ*

The Bible Lebowski: Biblical Themes and Tropes in *The Big Lebowski*

BY TREVOR MILLER

THE CHARACTERS

Jeff "The Dude" Lebowski

The Dude is the Christ-figure of the film, but not in a conventional manner. Visually, he resembles the popular image of Jesus, long-haired, bearded, in long, flowing robes, wearing sandals and generally hippie-like, but The Dude is a Christ-figure in a world where he failed in his attempt to save humanity, had not been crucified, and went on to drift through life without direction or purpose. He is a jumbled, confused version of the biblical Jesus, shuffling through a mostly aimless life without purpose. To borrow the term from his nemesis, The Big Lebowski, he is the Jesus of the Bums. His revolution failed, the bums lost, and now he's just floating through without purpose or direction. The only motivation we see from him is the restoration of his valued rug, because it really tied the room together. He has given up on the project of saving the world, now all he wants is to restore the integrity of his own home space.

John's Gospel begins with the statement, "In the beginning was the Word, and the Word was with God, and the Word was God," (NIV) and in line with this identity of Jesus as the Word, and The Dude as a skewed Christ figure, we get the result that nearly every scene in the movie contains an exchange where one character completely misunderstands what's been said by another. When The Dude quotes Lenin, Donny responds by saying "I am the Walrus," referring to John Lennon; when Brandt shows off all of Big's various awards and photos with the famous and powerful, as he gets to the picture of the Little Achievers, The Dude gets confused over the phrase "These are Mr. Lebowski's children, so to speak," assuming that Brandt means that the children are his own illegitimate children by various mothers of various ethnic backgrounds.

The phrase "What the fuck" occurs at total of 23 times throughout the movie, usually in the form of "What the fuck are you talking about?" or some variation on this theme. People in this film do not understand each other, they talk past one another; misunderstandings and confusion abound throughout. This is a world where ambiguities are never understood in the way they're intended, it is almost as if Los Angeles is suffering a new confusing of language in the manner of Babel in Genesis 11:5-8.

In addition to the confused dialogue between characters, The Dude echoes back lines throughout the movie, but rarely correctly. The opening scene of Bush Sr. talking about Iraq's invasion of Kuwait features the famous line, "This aggression will not stand . . . This will not stand!" comes back in his first meeting with Big as, "No, look. I do mind. The Dude minds. This will not stand, ya know, this will not stand, man. I mean, your wife owes –" Maude's phrase "she has been 'banging' Jackie Treehorn, to use the parlance of our times," turns into the misapplied "Young trophy wife, I mean, in the parlance of our times," when he tries to use a term he doesn't quite understand fully.

In addition to the merely ambiguous use of words, the Nihilists speak German without translation, Maude speaks Italian, the Stranger speaks through a moustache-obscured mouth with a drawl that turns "bear" into "bar" (causing The Dude to completely misunderstand what's been said), and heavy accents are common among supporting characters. Words are confused, meanings are misunderstood, people trail off and jump from one topic to another without any connection. It's a world where language has come detached from meaning, where the film's incarnation of the Word is out of connection with his purpose.

Isaiah 9:6 reads: "For to us a child is born, to us a son is given, and the government will be on his shoulders. And he will be called Wonderful Counselor, Mighty God, Everlasting Father, Prince of Peace." (NIV).

The term "Prince of Peace" is a popular term of reference for Jesus, but while The Dude self-identifies as a pacifist, he is not a very peaceful person much of the time. There are spots through the film where The Dude is at peace (usually when he's in contact with his valued rug or soaking in his tub while finishing off a joint) but in nearly every conversation with Walter, The Dude gets to a point where he's yelling and swearing, and in the final confrontation with the Nihilists, he makes an attempt at physical violence before Walter steps in and finishes the fight. As a self-proclaimed pacifist, he's often not very peaceful, a further misalignment in The Dude's role as Christ-figure.

While lying in bed with Maude, The Dude claims to be one of the authors of the *original* Port Huron Statement (not the compromised second draft) and a member of the Seattle Seven (there were six other guys), pointing to his role as a failed savior figure. He was once an idealist, a radical hippie who tried to change the world and save it from itself, but now he does, "Oh, you know, the usual. Bowl. Drive around. The occasional acid flashback." Rather than the Savior of Mankind, The Dude is a drug-addled burn-out who can't keep the thread of what's going on around him in spite of being witness to everything that occurs in the film except Bunny passing behind him and Jesus Quintana walking around his neighborhood to inform people of his status as a sex offender.

The Dude was once a passionate crusader, fighting to right the wrongs he saw in the world, attempting to enlighten people about the dangers attached to our modern lifestyle, but his peers sold out, fell out and generally tuned out of the movement, leaving The Dude aimless and alone. This is the Jesus of an alternate universe, a world where millionaires are broke, kidnapping victims are driving sporty red convertibles around Palm Springs and a visit to the doctor about a sore jaw is really screening for a potential father.

Matthew 13:55 identifies Jesus as the son of a carpenter, and at 1:13:40 of the film we see The Dude rather inept at working with wood. He pounds several bent double head nails into a piece of 2x4 as a brace for a chair intended to block his front door. However, the door opens to the outside, so his work is for nothing and Jackie Treehorn's thugs walk in through the unlocked entrance to fetch him for their boss. Two scenes later, he trips over the board he nailed to the floor as he returns home and falls at Maude's feet. This is in keeping with the theme of viewing him as a cockeyed Christ figure, a carpenter who can't manage to nail a board to the floor, or notice that the door he's blocking from the inside opens the other way.

In contrast to Christ, when The Dude is faced with temptation, he gives in almost immediately. When Walter hatches his plan to steal the ransom money, The Dude offers only token resistance as his friend runs away with the job of delivering the million dollars to the kidnappers. Earlier, when he meets Bunny, it is only his lack of money that keeps him from acting on her offer of a sexual exchange, even though he had just moments before met the girl's husband. When Maude presents herself to him and asks him to love her, he is distracted by the fact she had been wearing his robe, but as the scene fades back in, we find them in bed together. Drugs, alcohol, women and bowling represent irresistible temptations for him, in rather sharp contrast to the way Jesus is described in Hebrews 4:15, "For we do not have a high priest who cannot sympathize with our weaknesses, but one who has been tempted in all things as we are, yet without sin." (NASB) While The Dude resembles Jesus in that he is frequently tempted, he consistently fails the test and goes along with whatever plan is presented to him. He genuinely does want to do the right thing, but he completely lacks the strength of character to resist anyone's influence.

The scene where The Dude comes to Jackie Treehorn's home is a nice parallel with Jesus' temptation by the devil in the synoptic Gospels, but true to form it runs backwards in The Dude's case. Rather than ending on a high place, Jackie takes The Dude into his house, high above the hedonistic beach party he emerged from. At the first offer of money, The Dude gives up everything he knows without hesitation. There is no need to press him further, no need for two more temptations; he caves in immediately and completely.

The end of the movie has The Dude talking with the film's narrator, and his closing words, "Yeah man. Well, you know, The Dude abides," come out as a profound statement, that despite all that has happened, The Dude remains himself, unchanged and "takin' it easy for all us sinners." It has the feel of a passage like Psalm 25:13, "His soul will abide in prosperity, And his descendants will inherit the land," (NASB) describing someone living in the will of God. The Dude is nothing if not humble, and this is in the end what ties his character to the traditional notion of a Christ-figure. He never had any personal ambition past the restoration of his rug; it's the only thing that The Dude holds on to from beginning to end. His home is his sanctuary, his Garden of Eden, and when it is violated nothing else matters to him but restoring it to its original state.

In this, The Dude again exhibits a genuine resemblance to Christ; his desire to restore his home leads him through difficult, dangerous times, through persecution and violence. In his negotiations with Big, with Maude and with Jackie Treehorn, this is the one constant of his character; he is driven by his desire to tie his home back together. It is a parallel to God's desire to restore humanity after the Fall and the lengths He went to in order to make that happen. When humanity fell in the Garden, it was not entirely unlike Woo urinating on The Dude's rug; the world was thrown out of order, in much the same way that the harmony of The Dude's living room was broken by that act of unchecked aggression. In the end, The Dude is at peace, abiding; he has brought his life and his home back into alignment, and a new life has been brought about in the process of restoration, a new creation.

Walter Sobchak

Serving as a foil to The Dude is his best friend Walter. He is a Vietnam vet, and ties nearly everything in his life back to that experience. The other defining aspect of his character is his relationship to his ex-wife, Cynthia. Before marrying her, Walter converted to Judaism; in particular, he became shomer shabbos, which means that he follows an orthodox interpretation of Jewish religious law. He does not work, drive, ride in a car handle money, turn on the oven or bowl on the Sabbath, the Jewish day of rest. This is rooted in a strict interpretation of Exodus 31:13-17, which establishes Saturday as a day of rest in honor and remembrance of God's creative work, from which He rested on the 7th day.

Throughout the movie, Walter presents himself as a strict adherent to the Law and to the letter. When Smokey's toe goes over the line, Walter is so insistent that it be marked as a zero that he pulls out a loaded gun and threatens to shoot his opponent if he marks it an eight. When he is confronted by the waitress in the café about how loudly he is talking, he cites legal precedent from the Supreme Court and even more loudly insists upon his right to be obnoxious in public, throwing in the fact he served in Vietnam for good measure. He represents the Law and the gospel's teachers of the law, the strict legal tradition that strains at gnats but swallows camels. He is willing to threaten deadly force in order to regulate a league game, but in doing so violates the higher law against pulling a gun in public and sticking it in someone's face over a bowling match.

His personal identity is tied to "Three thousand years of beautiful tradition, from Moses to Sandy Koufax," in spite of the fact that he is divorced from the woman who was his original reason for converting. He identifies with it the same way that the Pharisees and Sadducees did, claiming Abraham for his father in Matthew 3:7-9; not in the sense that they and Walter share Abraham's relationship to God, but in that they are merely his blood descendants, or in Walter's case his descendent by marriage. His faith is about following rules and seeing to it that others do as well. There is no grace or forgiveness in him, just a blind devotion to his idea of the Law, with a capital L.

In keeping with a Christian view of legalism, Walter is wrong nearly every time he makes a truth claim, and the surer he claims to be of something, the more certainly he is wrong about it. This hits its peak when Walter and The Dude confront Big, and Walter insists that Big is faking his disability, then lifts him out of his chair, only to find upon releasing Big that he is indeed crippled. In the gospels, the teachers of the Law are consistently portrayed as wrong about everything; they fail to understand what God is like, the very God who wrote the Law they claim to revere. Walter is the personification of Romans 4:14-16; he is all law and wrath, without a trace of real understanding or faith to temper his bluster with mercy or grace. He is a violent man, incapacitating all three of the Nihilists in spite of two of them being armed, and his amputation of Uli's ear is reminiscent of a poorly and brutally applied "eye for an eye" (Exodus 21:23-25) ethical framework. The other amputation in the film is the toe taken from Uli's girlfriend, so the system of retribution is out of line with what's really going on.

In the end, Walter is chastised by The Dude for the mess he makes of Donny's eulogy by rambling on about Vietnam when he's supposed to be focusing on remembering their friend. This is the only point in the film where we see Walter genuinely remorseful, and it is the point where Walter asks The Dude for forgiveness. He realizes that he's missed the point of what's going on, and appeals to The Dude's forgiving nature in response. There is a complete change in demeanor on display, his shoulders slump and he takes on the posture of a child being scolded. Unable to stay mad at his friend, The Dude relents and embraces Walter, and their benediction is pronounced, "Aw, fuck it, Dude. Let's go bowling." As Big pointed out at the end of his first meeting with The Dude, that really is his answer for everything, to just let it go and return to the alley. Walter has adopted The Dude's way of being, he's a changed person in the end while The Dude simply abides.

Theodore Donald 'Donny' Kerabatsos

Donny is, simply put, an innocent. He is to The Dude what Christians are to Christ, though to a small extent he is himself a type of Christ-figure in the background. He is seen bowling a perfect game through the movie until a single pin fails to fall, foreshadowing his own imminent death. He is a loyal friend to The Dude, and serves as the canary in the mine in relation to The Dude's dedication to peacefulness. As the last of The Dude's principles falls and he actively (if ineffectively) enters into a fight with the Nihilists, Donny falls victim to a fatal heart attack.

At his core, Donny represents the 1 Corinthians 13:4-6 sense of love, he is patient, kind, he doesn't envy anyone, he never gets angry at Walter's constant refrains of "Shut the fuck up, Donny" and similar abuse. In keeping with the skewed tone of the other characters, he does indulge in boasting about how well he's bowling on two occasions, but in a world where the main Christ-figure is rarely without either a joint or a drink in his hand, Donny is as close to a pure soul as can be found among the main characters.

Jeffery "The Big" Lebowski

Big is a scheming, bombastic, judgmental man whose insecurities drive him to steal a million dollars from the family charity he co-directs with his daughter. He presents himself as an "Achiever," but in reality he has achieved nothing for himself except a fortunate marriage to his deceased wife. He is a total hypocrite when we first meet him and he berates The Dude for being a layabout and a bum. The irony of his position is that while he is in the position of the rich man who is less likely to get into heaven than a camel is to pass through the eye of a needle (Matthew 19:24), he is in fact personally broke. He has no money of his own beyond the allowance his daughter provides him with. In the end, his judgmental nature comes back home, as he is confronted with the truth by Walter and The Dude. They know he is broke, that he stole a million dollars from underprivileged children and his late wife's family fortune, and that his wife is in fact a runaway high school cheerleader and sometime underage porn star from Moorhead, Minnesota, but he still clings to his illusion of position and power in the face of it all.

Like the powerful men of the Gospels, Big attempts to place The Dude in legal trouble, but in keeping with the overall theme of broken parallels, he fails utterly in his scheming. He is as broken as any of the other characters, but with the further flaw that he fails to find any catharsis in his character arc. It's assumed that he has the cash in the end, but he also has his daughter to deal with, and the money will not be his for long.

Maude Lebowski

Maude is the least tragically flawed of all the film's characters; she is a source of enlightenment and wisdom for The Dude, revealing information he would never otherwise have discovered himself. In biblical terms, she embodies Wisdom, guiding The Dude in his way through his journey. Walter also makes passing reference in his comment, "Aitz chaim he," or "It's the tree of life," possibly a reference to Proverbs 3:18, "She is a tree of life to those who take hold of her; those who hold her fast will be blessed." (NIV) In as much as The Dude takes hold of her and follows her advice, he is blessed; by the same token, by rejecting his daughter, Big falls from his lofty position.

In keeping with the tree of life metaphor, she becomes a literal vessel of life as she conceives a child with The Dude. She is an artist, a creator, source of life and wisdom for those who avail themselves of what she offers. She rejects The Dude's half-baked ideas about what is going on in the case, she prudently has him screened by her very thorough doctor before selecting him to father her child, and she is the source of restoration for his valued rug. Without Maude's contributions, there is no way The Dude would have made his way through the case without winding up in jail or worse.

Bunny Lebowski/Fawn Knutson/Bunny LaJoya

In contrast to Maude, Bunny is the woman of Folly from Proverbs 9:13-18. She tempts men to their ruin in succession; Jackie Treehorn loses money to her, Uli loses his ear and a million dollars, and Big loses everything. Just as in verse 13, "she is simple and knows nothing," (NIV) Bunny is completely oblivious of the chaos her spur of the moment trip to Palm Springs sets in motion. She is not who she presents herself to be, and is known by three different names by various people in the course of the movie.

Jackie Treehorn

Jackie is, simply put, the devil. He emerges from the shadows as a throbbing, hedonistic party carries on behind him. He deceives The Dude, drugs him, tempts him with money, and gets everything he wants from the protagonist. His is also the name that evokes the most biblical and traditional imagery, a combination of the Tree that the snake talked Adam and Eve into eating from and the popular idea of Satan being a red, goat-legged being with horns. He is a pornographer, a hedonist and has corrupted the local police sheriff to his side; it is difficult to tack on much more that would make it any clearer who the bad guy is when he enters the scene. His thug Woo is the one who urinates on The Dude's rug, despoiling his personal paradise and putting him on his path of action.

The Germans/Nihilists

The Nihilists are an example of Psalm 53:1, "The fool says in his heart, 'There is no God.' They are corrupt, and their ways are vile; there is no one who does good." (NIV) They have rejected the idea of God and any notion of meaning in the world. They believe in "nossing," and they are indeed vile, cutting off a girlfriend's toe in order to extort money from someone and threatening castration against The Dude. In keeping with biblical story lines regarding what happens to the wicked (particularly in the Old Testament), their only payment for the evil they've done is pain and disfigurement. They only lose from their efforts.

The Stranger

The narrator of the film is an unnamed cowboy, who has no internal frame of reference to the events he's talking about to provide him with his story; he has no particular role in the proceedings, except for an encounter with The Dude at the mid-point of the film and in the final scene. He has intimate knowledge of The Dude, his personal habits, his character and the existence of his unborn child, and no obvious source for this information. It seems clear that if The Dude is a flawed Christ-figure, the Stranger serves as the film's stand-in for God.

In line with the other off-center archetypes, the Stranger is a rambling, absent-minded God-figure who steps into the world for a sarsaparilla at a bowling alley bar and to chat with his wayward Son, chiding him for the number of cuss words he uses. The two speak warmly, but there is no recognition, no relationship, and a fair deal of mis-communication.

SUMMARY

At its bottom, *The Big Lebowski* is the story of The Dude bringing his world back into harmony, if only in the limited scope of his living room. He is a Messiah who has messed up, compromised and all but completely surrendered his redemptive role. However, in keeping with the political rhetoric of the day, he has drawn a line in the sand; his compromise with the world goes just this far, no further. This aggression will not stand, and it is The Dude's desire to restore his home's integrity. It is a kaleidoscoped view of salvation history, but if you tilt your head at just the right angle and squint a little, you can see the whole durn Judeo-Christian comedy perpetuatin' itself, down through the generations. There may be a literal connection indeed.

....

Trevor Miller is a former pastor and a former bouncer, holds Bachelor's degrees in Theology and Philosophy, and is currently a university tutor in Creighton, Saskatchewan. When he's not slacking off on the internet or playing with his son, he blogs at http://onefellswooper.wordpress.com, but don't hold your breath between posts, as he does an awful lot of slacking.

Camille Custard, *Dude*

The Dude Accepts:
Walt Whitman & *The Big Lebowski*

BY KERRY GIBBS

abide v. tolerate, endure, remain, continue [OED]
accept v. consent to receive, treat as welcome, tolerate [OED]

"The Dude abides." It's almost a throwaway line, Jeff Bridges delivers it at the end of the movie as he recedes into the darkness. You could easily miss it if the Stranger didn't repeat it and yet it really ties the movie together. In fact that simple phrase transforms the Coen brothers' film *The Big Lebowski* from a classic stoner flick into a religious experience for thousands of Dudeists around the world. And say what you like about the tenets of Dudeism, Dude, at least it's an ethos. As any Dudeist will tell you, however, the core beliefs of the faith do not stop and start with The Dude or with the film. There have been many other, I won't call them hee-ros, but men and women for their time and place who have espoused similar ideas. Whether you are talking about Epicurus or Jesus or Buddha or any of the thousands of unnamed dudes who have come and gone perpetuatin' the whole durned human comedy, there have always been individuals who choose to take 'er easy and not let their thinking get too uptight.

In particular Dudeism draws a strong link between Lao Tzu, the founder of Taoism, and the ethos of The Dude. Now, while Lao Tzu is certainly one of the Great Dudes in History and a wiser fella than myself, I would like to suggest that the central tenet of Dudeism, the concept of abiding, is not just some kind of eastern thing. The Chinaman is not the issue here. Abiding, as practiced by The Dude, is also a western thing. Moreover, it is a particularly American thing.

It may seem as if America has no frame of reference. Philosophically speaking, America seems like a child that has wandered into the middle of a movie. However, despite its relative youth as a country, America has furnished us with plenty of examples of abiders. Two hundred years of beautiful tradition, from Thomas Paine to Tom Waits . . . you're goddamn right I'm living in the (recent) past. If there is a specifically American tradition of Dudeism predating *The Big Lebowski* then where is the American equivalent of the Gospels or the *Tao Te Ching*?

I would suggest Walt Whitman's poem *Song of Myself* – specifically the original 1855 version – as the primary sacred text of American Dudeism.

Now Whitman lived most of his life in and around Manhattan just about the time of the Northern States conflict with the secessionists. I only mention it 'cause sometimes there's a man – I won't say hee-ro, 'cause what's a hee-ro? – but sometimes there's a man. And I'm talking about Walt here – sometimes there's a man who, wal, he's the man for his his time and place, he fits right in there – and that's Walt in 19th century America. And even if he's a lazy man, and Walt was certainly that – sometimes there's a man.

How lazy was Whitman? Well, before publishing *Leaves of Grass* in 1855 he held various jobs as a schoolteacher or in printing and journalism, but none for very long. He was invariably dismissed – sometimes for his political opinions (like The Dude, the young Whitman dabbled in politics) – but more usually for laziness. The *Eagle*, one of the papers he was fired from, described him as "slow, indolent, heavy, discourteous and without steady principles . . . [and] a clog on our success." When it was suggested that Whitman had kicked a prominent politician down the stairs the same paper's editorial responded: "Whoever knows him will laugh at the idea of his *kicking any body*, much less a prominent politician. He is too indolent to kick a musketo"[1]. Whitman could have described his typical day as "Oh you know, the usual. Taking the Brooklyn ferry to Manhattan, riding the omnibuses along Broadway. Taking a dip at the Fulton Ferry Salt Baths." All of this while he was supposed to be at work. He even wrote an editorial titled "A Plea for Bathing" (March 23, 1846) advising that "a good bath" was the best thing for "slight attacks of illness, and quite all fits of hypochondria, and such nervous diseases."[2]

Now, "Dude" is not a name Whitman would have self-applied. As Popik, Shulman, and Cohen show in *Material*

---

[1] Loving, J. *Walt Whitman; The Song of Himself*, University of California Press, 1999, p.146
[2] Loving p.104

for the Study of DUDE, Part 1[3] the term "dude" was introduced to the US during Whitman's lifetime but originally denoted "a man affecting an exaggerated fastidiousness in dress, speech, and deportment, and very particular about what is aesthetically 'good form'." Whereas Whitman wrote: "Washes and razors for foofoos … for me freckles and a bristling beard."[4] In fact Whitman describes himself in *Leaves of Grass* as "Walt Whitman, an American, one of the roughs" (499). A rough being the opposite of a dude in the parlance of Whitman's time. Bronson Alcott (Louisa May's Dad) described Whitman as "Broad-shouldered, rouge-fleshed, Bacchus-browed, bearded like a satyr and rank … he wears his man-Bloomer [baggy trousers] in defiance of everybody … [and] a slouched hat, for house and street alike." [quoted in Loving, p.224] Let's put it this way: you wouldn't go out looking for a job dressed like that, on a weekday.

Just as Jeff Lebowski never had much use for the handle that his loving parents gave him:

> Look, let me explain something. I'm not Mr. Lebowski, you're Mr. Lebowski. I'm The Dude. So that's what you call me. That, or Duder. His Dudeness. Or El Duderino, if you know, you're not into the whole brevity thing–

In *Leaves of Grass*, Walter Whitman journalist, printer and sometime schoolteacher becomes:

> Walt Whitman, an American, one of the roughs, a kosmos, Disorderly fleshy and sensual … eating drinking and breeding, No sentimentalist … no stander above men and women or apart from them … no more more modest than immodest. (499-501)

Both "The Dude" and "Walt Whitman" have turned their backs on the roles assigned to them by society or their background because new shit has come to light. In Whitman's case there was an experience that occurred on a June day in either 1853 or 1854:

> I believe in you my soul … . the other I am must not abase itself to you, / And you must not be abased to the other. […] / I mind how we lay in June, such a transparent summer morning; / You settled your head athwart my hips and gently turned over / upon me, / And parted the shirt from my bosom-bone, and plunged your tongue / to my barestript heart, / And reached till you felt my beard, and reached till you held my feet. / Swiftly arose and spread around me the peace and joy and knowledge / that pass all the art and argument of the earth; / And I know that the hand of God is the elderhand of my own, / And I know that the spirit of God is the eldest brother of my own, / And that all men ever born are also my brothers … and the / women my sisters and lovers, / And that a kelson of the creation is love; (73-86)

Nobody knows exactly what Whitman experienced that day (maybe an acid flashback?) but it profoundly changed the way he felt about himself and the way he saw the world. His attempt to put words to these new feelings, this new shit that had come to light, was a 1336 line poem which he published with eleven other poems in a slim volume entitled *Leaves of Grass* in 1855. He would later give the poem the title *Song of Myself*. The message of *Song of Myself* has most often been characterized as one of accepting.

Accepting that the world is as it is, accepting that this moment is literally as good as it gets:

> There was never any more inception than there is now, / Nor any more youth or age than there is now; / And will never be any more perfection than there is now, / Nor any more heaven or hell than there is now (32-35)

Accepting, like abiding, is not a product of ignorance or of apathy. It is about keeping one's mind limber, looking the world square in the face but with a sense of humor and compassion. Despite everything that happens to The Dude, he remains The Dude, he abides. As Whitman put it:

> Apart from the pulling and hauling stands what I am, / Stands amused, complacent, compassionating, idle, unitary, / Looks down, is erect, bends an arm on an impalpable certain rest, / Looks with its sidecurved head curious what will come next, / Both in and out of the game, and watching and wondering at it (66-70)

It seems to me that accepting and abiding are essentially the same thing.

Abiding is knowing that life is, "you know, strikes and gutters, ups and downs, but you know, man, The Dude abides." Whitman says:

> I exist as I am, that is enough, / If no other in the world be aware I sit content / And if each and all be aware I sit content (413-415)

Abiding means accepting other people, the good and the bad. It means treating all others the same. You don't get more respect if you are The Big Lebowski or less respect if you are his nymphomaniacal trophy wife. You sit through your landlord's cycle and you give Smokey the benefit of the doubt because he is your friend and has some problems but you don't eat shit in front of the Sheriff of Malibu. Everyone gets the same laid-back, if slightly sarcastic, treatment. As a wiser fella than myself once said: "Everybody's just trying to get by. And fuck 'em if they can't take a joke" (My wife, Lia O'Brien, the wisest fella I know). Or as Whitman said:

> In all people I see myself, none more and not one a barleycorn less, / And the good or bad I say of myself I say of them (401-402)

---

[3] http://dudespaper.com/dude-university/material-for-the-study-of-dude-part-1/

[4] All Whitman quotations are from the original 1855 *Leaves of Grass* the number in parentheses denotes the line number so that it can be referenced in any Publisher's edition. In this case, the line number is 468

Abiding also means acknowledging that there have been, and always will be fucking fascists and that sometimes it is necessary to say "I do mind man, The Dude minds, this will not stand, you know, this aggression will not stand, man." Nobody is trying to scam anybody here but sometimes you just want your rug back. We are all in this together and the greed and dishonesty of The Big Lebowskis and Jackie Treehorns of the world just bring us all down. Whitman wrote:

> Whoever degrades another degrades me . . . and whatever is done or / said returns at last to me, / And whatever I do or say I also return. [. . .] / I speak the password primeval . . . I give the sign of democracy; / By God! I will accept nothing which all cannot have their counterpart / of on the same terms (504-508)

Occasionally, however, the case gets complicated, a lot of ins, a lot out of outs, a lot of what-have-yous. You might find yourself saying: "You're not wrong Walter, you're just an asshole" or "I love you, but sooner or later you're going to have to accept the fact that you're a fucking moron" or even, "There is an unspoken message here, it's leave me the fuck alone . . . Yes, I'll be at practice." Even The Dude can sometimes be very undude. But as Whitman said:

> "Do I contradict myself? / Very well then . . . I contradict myself; / I am large . . . I contain multitudes." (1314-1316)

Whitman's proto-Dudeism doesn't deny or require a Deity:

> And I call to mankind, Be not curious about God, / For I who am curious about each am not curious about God, / No array of terms can say how much I am at peace about God / and about death. / I hear and behold God in every object, yet I understand God not / in the least, / Nor do I understand who there can be more wonderful than myself. (1271-1275)

Neither does it require special esoteric knowledge or religious training. It isn't an Eastern thing or a Western thing. It is a human thing. As Whitman said:

> Only what proves itself to every man and woman is so, / Only what nobody denies is so. (654-655)

In *Song of Myself* Whitman was simply saying: we are all dudes, we can all abide:

> "I have said that the soul is not more than the body, / And I have said that the body is not more than the soul, / And nothing, not God, is greater than one's-self is, / And whoever walks a furlong without sympathy walks to his own / funeral, dressed in his shroud, / And I or you pocketless of a dime may purchase the pick of the earth, / And to glance with an eye or show a bean in its pod confounds the / learning of all times, / And there is no trade or employment but the young man following / it may become a hero, / And there is no object so soft but it makes a hub for the wheeled universe, / And any man or woman shall stand cool and supercilious before a / million universes" (1262-1270)

Whitman was a good poet, and a good man. He was . . . He was one of us. He knew that in the face of life's complications, it's ins and outs, gutters and strikes, all the sensitive person can do is try to Abide. Walt was a Dude, man. I don't know about you, but I take comfort in that.

....

Kerry Gibbs is originally from Australia and has been, among other things, an English teacher in Japan, a bookstore clerk in England and, most recently a bartender in Philadelphia. His career has slowed down a bit lately. Currently he lives in North Carolina with his wife and son. A full-time Dad and a part-time writer, Gibbs is working on a nonfiction book that he hopes to finish someday. Other work by Kerry regarding Whitman, Thoreau and others can be found at www.facebook.com/TheAccidentalTranscendentalist

Rich Nairn, *The Dopeman Empire*

Dudes and Dudeism in the Ancient World

BY GRAHAM MCILROY

This essay is about ancient Romans, and how your modern-day Dude can relate to them. More specifically, it's about the ancient Roman philosophy of Stoicism, which was an early form of Dudeism. The Stoics used to be chilled-out Dudes who discussed their ideas whilst hanging out in porches in the marketplace (Stoa means "porch" in ancient Greek: a Stoic was a Dude that hung out under a porch while everybody else was rushing around). I am going to show you that in many ways Stoicism is a mirror of Dudeism. Any mistakes are my own, and all quotations are taken from Meditations, by Marcus Aurelius (Oxford, 1998 Edition), which was initially written down over 1800 years ago.

The Stoics felt very strongly that the universe around them was rational, and they tried to observe how everything fit together. Subsequently, given the nature of the new information that came to light as a result of this, they began to appreciate that each of us sees with our own unique perceptions. A good metaphor for this phenomenon would be the way in which the two Lebowskis argue over exactly who is responsible for The Dude's ruined rug. Indeed, as far as the Stoics were concerned, when certain things did come to light, they promoted the belief that things could be complex and that one's perception of events were dependent on their context, which can be kind of reassuring. After all, as the Stranger says, sometimes you eat the bear, and well, sometimes the bear, he eats you. This isn't some kind of Eastern thing. Far from it. it's simply a recognition that even though life has it's little ups and downs, we can still make sense of it. I think this is what Marcus Aurelius meant when he said:

> Nothing is so able to create greatness of mind as the power methodically and truthfully to test each thing that meets one in life, and always to look upon it so as to attend at the same time to the use which this particular thing contributes to a Universe. – *Meditations*, 3.11

Stoicism encourages us to be cool. To accept the fact that occasionally metaphorical bears will be dining out on us. You win some, and you lose some. But the thing is, if we accept that shit happens, we can use this to navigate life's stresses and tensions. We can also use this knowledge to promote harmony in the little part of the universe with which we come into contact. And harmony begins with little things. Like a rug that really ties a room together. To this end, Aurelius said:

> Let not the future trouble you, for you will come to it, if come you must, bearing with you the same reason which you are using now to meet the present. – *Meditations*, 7.8

So, let's say we have a rug that ties the room together, and it gets ruined through the actions of another. Now, exactly who the "other" is not the issue here: the issue, so Stoicism teaches us, is that the act of a rational man in harmony with nature will be to replace that rug, and thus restoring the natural cosmic balance, because aggression will not stand, man. Thus, in Stoicism, the virtuous thing to do would be to confront the man whose responsibility it is to replace the rug, not for revenge, but in order to return balance to our little part of the universe by tying the room back together. This is similar to Aurelius' statement:

> Let men see, let them study a true man, a man who lives in accord with Nature. – *Meditations*, 10.15

In the same way that The Dude and Walter discussed the merits of action and inaction over the rug incident while they were in the everyday environment of the bowling alley, the Stoics, in the humdrum environment of their porches, discussed how a person would know for sure whether or not they were doing the right thing. Their answer was that in order to have Dude-like virtues like magnanimity, freedom, simplicity and consideration for others, you have to consciously put the virtue of wisdom first. You get wisdom through using the power of reason (i.e. talking a problem over with a friend in the bowling alley), so that when you get certain information, and certain things come to light, you can try to do the right thing:

> To obey reason is no great matter, but rather you will find rest in it ... see whether magnanimity, freedom, simplicity, consideration for others ... are ... sweeter than wisdom itself. – *Meditations*, 5.9

Calmness about the things that go on around us is pretty important in both Dudeism and Stoicism. that's because when people get excited about stuff they can wind up pointing firearms in peoples' faces during league games. The way to achieve calmness, then is to remember that a Dude can get in between people who give a shit about the rules and people who don't give a shit about the rules because he recognizes that your opinion is just, like, your opinion, man. There are countless points of view, whether they're the points of view of vaginal artists, dancing landlords, or porn magnates that draw a lot of water in Malibu. Remember that, and everything will be calm and rational. As Aurelius says:

> The Universe is change, life is opinion. – *Meditations*, 4.3

> Get rid of the judgement; you are rid of the 'I am hurt'; get rid of the 'I am hurt', you are rid of the hurt itself. – *Meditations*, 4.7

Following on from calmness, another aspect of Stoicism was that like a Dude, a Stoic could find pleasure in the simple things in life. You know, the usual. Like bowl, drive around, and having the occasional acid flashback. Doing tai chi with a white Russian in one hand. Listening on head phones to a recording of pins being knocked down. Because the most peaceful place to abide is in your own head, man. The Stoics would have agreed that in the same way that it's un-Dudelike to live to austere extremes like nihilists or fascists, it's also un-Dudelike to go to hedonistic extremes like the Jackie Treehorns of this world:

> For nowhere does a man retreat into more quiet or more privacy than in his own mind. – *Meditations*, 4.3

Since both Stoics and Dudeists are such a moderate and open-minded bunch, it's sometimes pretty tough to pin down what they're against. Nihilists, however, that believe in nothing at all (or at least claim to believe in nothing), and fascist cops that throw mugs at peoples' heads are the natural enemies of all that is Dudeist. But they're not the enemy simply by virtue of being called fascists or nihilists: they're the enemy because of the way they act, and the way they act is a result of their little pea brains and their limited thinking: the problem is that their thinking is just too small-minded, and there's frankly little evidence of imagination with those guys (with the possible exception of the nice marmot). I mean, say what you like about dancing landlords, vaginal artists and porn magnates, but at least they're making an effort to break free from their social programming. The Stoics, putting it slightly differently, would say that the only thing to really be afraid of is being so vacuous that you never begin to live. To be so full of life that you live in harmony with the world around you – that is the complete antithesis of nihilism. The poverty of nihilism is therefore far worse than death, because at least as long as you're alive you know you've got the chance to do something positive with your time.

> If what you dread is not that some day you will cease to live, but rather never to begin at all to live with Nature, you will be a man worthy of the Universe that gave you birth. – *Meditations*, 12.1

The idea of ethical living is therefore deeply important to both Dudeists and Stoics. This is because a Dudeist, like a Stoic, is attempting to live as a real person, who tries to promote harmony in his or her little part of the universe. Dudeists and Stoics don't only do this when it's easy: it isn't simply the pursuit of fun that underlies their principles, but a fearless sense of duty – think about it: the easy thing for The Dude to do would be to *not* confront Lebowski about the rug. Or *not* tell a brutal cop he's a fascist. Or *not* question the price of a funeral urn. But a Dude is, on occasion, required to shout "bullshit" when they've got certain information and certain things come to light. A Dude abides because he or she believes that abiding is the right thing to do. But oddly, the consequence of this is that abiding isn't a chore. Far from it. The consequence is that abiding is one of the most deeply satisfying things that a Dude can do:

> Each hour be minded, valiantly, as becomes a Roman ... do each act as though it were your last, freed from every random aim. –*Meditations*, 2.5

To conclude, then, it is clear to see that the Stoics were early Dudeists. Both philosophies are clear that life has it's little ups and downs, that harmony is essential, that ethics are important to maintain harmony in one's own little part of the universe, and that rational thought is the cornerstone of good ethics. Both philosophies evidently value calmness and life's simpler pleasures, as well as using your imagination to do something positive with your time here on this earth. And all of this can be rolled up into that big burrito that we call abiding, which is sometimes difficult to do, but always deeply satisfying. The Stoics were certainly a little bit more pragmatic than Dudeists, but even so, it still goes a long way to show the way the whole durned human comedy keeps perpetuatin' itself. Compeers, you know?

....

Graham McIlroy is a professional freelance writer and features journalist. He is a genuine Classical scholar and holds an MA(hons) in the subject from the prestigious University of Glasgow, Scotland. They also saw fit to give him a Postgrad Diploma in Teaching Adults, but that was probably just to get rid of him. And you guys had better have learned something, or he wants his money back from the university loans people. In his spare time he is a Marathon Runner, and recently ran the Loch Ness Marathon in the Highlands of Scotland, as well as the super-tough Heartbreaker Marathon in the trails of The New Forest, Hampshire, England (he likes the wilderness). He makes a mean meatball fusilli too, and everyone knows how important it is to know a good fusillist. If any of you would like to hire him as a writer with a high standard of excellence, contact him via his professional profile at LinkedIn. This essay is dedicated to his Dudeist Mentor, Cheryl Lawford.

Rich Nairn, *Private Dicks*

El Duderino, P.I.

BY AXEL HOWERTON

That Joel and Ethan Coen's cult classic *The Big Lebowski* is a modern take on the outdated "Detective Story" is an accepted fact. Sure, the film echoes aspects of old Hollywood screwball comedies, late 60's psychedelia "freak-out" flicks and the classic Western, but it goes without saying that the primary influence in the creation of the story, if not The Dude himself, was the great detective novels of past and not-quite-present. Joel and Ethan themselves have admitted to loosely basing it on Raymond Chandler's seminal Detective novel, *The Big Sleep*.

The Detective Story, as die-hard fans of Edgar Allan Poe (and few else) can tell you, had its genesis with the original Man In Black, ol' Eddie himself. Poe's 1841 story *The Murders In The Rue Morgue*, is roundly accepted as the very first true Detective fiction. His C. Auguste Dupin is the template for every sleuth from Sherlock Holmes to C.S.I.'s Gus Grissom. The genre puttered along from there, with a fairly standard cozy mystery feel until the dark years after the first World War, when cynicism, violence and, yes, even nihilism, turned the stereotypes on their head and the spinster sleuths, plucky consultants and scholarly gentlemen of means gave way to a new animal – the Private Dick.

The "hard-boiled" detectives began a trope that still stands as a model for most of our fictional heroes today. Typically, these were stories of a good man awash in a sea of organized crime, corruption and a careless legal system. These were men who were whip smart, resourceful and humorously cynical. They began their careers in the cheap pulp magazines of the time – *Black Mask, Detective Story Magazine, Dime Detective, Thrilling Detective*, etc. – and soon began to creep out into the wider world as stars of their own books and series, and here is where Our Beloved Dude begins to take shape.

The Coens have admitted to creating *The Big Lebowski* in their attempt to "do a Chandler story," namely one that features "characters unraveling a mystery," as well as "having a hopelessly complex plot that's ultimately unimportant." *The Big Lebowski*, like most of the works of Raymond Chandler, accomplishes this in spades, denying the traditional ideal of plot-driven fiction, preferring instead to wallow in the shady motivations of weird and colorful characters whose double-dealing and self-serving ways never end well. The only one who walks away unchanged (though usually after several beatings, druggings and threats upon his life) is the rumpled anti-hero, shambling about his business, disregarding the evils of the world around him while he looks for a hot cup of coffee, or something stronger. You mind if I do a J?

Let's start with Phillip Marlowe, Chandler's steadfast anti-hero. Marlowe falls somewhere between book smart and street savvy. He's quiet and contemplative. He's uncompromising in his values and a willing slave to his vices – smoking and drinking and chess. The Dude may eschew tobacco for the Maui Wowie, and substitute ten-pin for knights and rooks, but the comparison stands. As Marlowe says of himself in various sections of The Big Sleep: "There's very little to tell ... went to college once and can still speak English if there's any call for it." He describes himself as "not a collector of antiques, except unpaid bills." Sounds very Dude to me, man. They also both tend to have a weakness for getting mickeyed by the bad guys and getting their asses handed to them by the henchmen of human paraquats and fuckin' fascists. They also share an ability to stave off the advances of lesser femme fatales, in favor of the more refined dilettante lady friends. Phillip Marlowe has no trouble spurning the advances of hot young thing Carmen Sternwood, but finds himself stammering and questioning his manhood in the presence of the statuesque older sister, Vivienne Regan. Likewise, The Dude chuckles off Bunny Lebowski's offer of a thousand-dollar BJ ($100 for Brandt to watch), but he finds himself crumpled and stymied by the forceful femininity of Maude Lebowski and her "vaginal" art.

Other famous fictional dicks seem to have been just as crucial in the creation of His Dudeness. Dashiel Hammett's Continental Op, who frequently manipulates bad situations and nefarious characters in order to extract proper justice, usually worked outside of the law. Likewise, Hammett's more lighthearted amateur sleuth, Nick Charles, seems to have some input. Charles stumbles around, cheerfully stoned (in the parlance of his times) unraveling mysteries with his debutante wife and their dog, Asta (who most likely will not be taking your turn). Hammett's most famous protagonist, Sam Spade of *The Maltese Falcon*, seems to have thrown his detached air and ability to mix with unsavory criminals into The Dude-mix. James M. Cain and Jim Thompson contribute the sometimes uncharacteristic, and usually brutal, violence and depravity displayed by Walter, the nihilists and lesser characters like Jackie Treehorn. These two seem to inform a lot of Coen brothers action, from the savagery of their first film, backwoods Detective-noir *Blood Simple*, through the gangland film *Miller's Crossing* and the slow-boil tension of *The Man Who Wasn't There* all the way up to *Lebowski* and newer fare like *Burn After Reading*, which was much-maligned for its sudden acts of explosive violence.

The list goes on, at length, to include Bill Pronzini's "nameless detective," Max Allan Collins' grumpy operator Nate Heller, and Lew Archer, Ross MacDonald's popular sleuth, whose stories were known for focusing on the quirks and foibles of every character but Archer, who had almost no backstory and very little emotional input in the goings-on. Very Dude-like. Gregory McDonald's *Fletch* books featured a smartass non-detective who frequently found himself abused by the local Chief-Of-Police and other representatives of authority. Carrol John Daly's Race Williams, Walter Moseley's Easy Rawlins and Kinky Friedman's self-modeled easy going "dude" persona all add something to the mix.

Most like The Dude, perhaps, is John D. MacDonald's (notice a trend with these names here?) Travis McGee, the laid-back "salvage consultant," who frequently takes on cases where the missing item is a person, and the motivations of all involved become highly suspect. McGee is most often seen as an itinerant beach bum, lazy, shambling and frequently tipsy, all of which is used to disguise his true skill as a detective and his abilities at recovering lost "items." In the end, however, McGee truly just wants to be left alone, to lounge on the shore and enjoy his boat drinks. As McGee puts it in *The Deep Blue Goodbye,* "The proper folk-hero crinkle at the corners of the eyes, and the bashful appealing smile, when needed." "I am tall, and I gangle. I look like a loose-jointed, clumsy hundred-and-eighty." His banter may be slightly more verbose than His Dudeness usually employs, but I'd wager Travis McGee enjoys a Caucasian here and there, maybe a roach in the tub and some Creedence on the headphones.

The ever-reluctant Coen brothers might not be prone to openly admit it, but the evidence points to their obvious love for Detective Fiction, not only in the creation of Jeff Lebowski, but most characters from Maude (Chandlerian dames like Vivian Regan in *The Big Sleep*) to The Big Lebowski himself (General Sternwood, Caspar Gutman and other portly Achievers). Walter Sobchak seems born of Mike Hammer's violent misanthropic tendencies. Jackie Treehorn represents every skeezy pornographer and pimp that ever treated an object like a woman, man. Which puts him in the company of thousands of questionable gentlemen in this genre. Donny Kerabatsos can be seen in any number of sidekicks and mild-mannered chums; and wild-eyed maniac Jesus Quintana carries shades of Raymond "Mouse" Alexander from the Easy Rawlins books. DaFino, he of the Brotherhood Shamus, actually *is* an old school P.I. and even the nihilists (as well as Treehorn and Maude's thugs) seem to be a reflection of every dimwitted gang of thugs we've come to expect in everything from Chandler's *Guns at Cyrano's* to Bugs Bunny cartoons. Even Knox Harrington, he of the "cleft asshole" has a mirror in Detective Fiction – S.S. Van Dine's Philo Vance, the obnoxious effete with the cleft chin.

Even the dialogue of *The Big Lebowski*, and its cadence, owes a paternal debt to the Detective fiction of yesteryear. Think of The Stranger, pontificating on Jeff Lebowski and his place in the world: "Sometimes there's a man, well, he's the man for his time and place. He fits right in there, and that's The Dude, in Los Angeles . . ." a maybe-not-so-strong, but certainly ringing endorsement of our hero. Compare it with this line from Chandler's *The Big Sleep*: "As honest as you can expect a man to be, in a world where it's going out of style." You could almost hear those words falling out of Sam Elliott's double-wide lip-warmer the same as the actual script. In fact, I'd wager someone out there could mash-up the two and create an amazing piece of literary planetoid just as entertaining as Adam Bertocci's *Two Gentlemen of Lebowski* or Robert B. Parker's *Perchance To Dream*. Consider the exchange between The Dude and Maude Lebowski regarding "the physical act of love." Here I've added in a few lines from Chandler, just so you have a frame of reference:

> "Do you like sex, Mr. Lebowski?"
> "Excuse me?"
> "Sex, the physical act of love. Coitus. Do you like it?"
> It's so hard for women – even nice women – to realize that their bodies are not irresistible.
> "I was talking about my rug . . ."
> She lowered her lashes until they almost cuddled her cheeks and slowly raised them again, like a theatre curtain . . . That was supposed to make me roll over on my back with all four paws in the air.
> "You're not interested in sex?"
> She bent over me again. Blood began to move around in me, like a prospective tenant looking over a house.
> "You mean coitus?"

For the millions of us Dudeists, Achievers and Lebowskiites out there, this may offend our innate knowledge of the films sacred dialogue, but I defy even the most Dudeliest of Duders to deny the syncopation of the Master of Detectives and El Duderino (if you're not into that whole brevity thing).

Without delving into the even more substantive area of Detective fiction in films and TV, I would like to make one small detour to mention what is likely the number one correlation between His Dudeness and Raymond Chandler's steel-jawed hero. Almost half-way between the last Marlowe book (*Playback*, published in 1958) and the release of *The Big Lebowski*, auteur filmmaker Robert Altman gave Marlowe a post-modern makeover, shoveling a rumpled, bedraggled and frequently confused Elliott Gould into the wrinkled suit. Gould played Marlowe very much in the '70s Dudeist style. Laid-back, unambitious to the core, chain-smoking, hard-boozing and completely unfazed whether he wakes up on the beach, or a concrete floor. Exceptionally violent, beautifully filmed, filled with dark humor, Altman's "western" sensibilities (he had made his name directing TV war and western series like *Combat!*, *Maverick* and *Bonanza*, though by no means the bulk of the series) and an endless cavalcade of weird criminal characters, *The Long Goodbye* is a film of equal cult status to our beloved Dude, and one of the finest examples of neo-noir from the era. Many consider it a better film than *Chinatown* or the Jack Nicholson version of *The Postman Always Rings Twice*.

That these numerous similarities could merely be common tropes, or simple coincidence on the part of the Coens is debatable but – considering the influence such works have had on almost every one of their films, especially *Blood Simple*, *Miller's Crossing*, *Barton Fink* and *Fargo* – highly unlikely. I like to think that it really boils down to two very big fans of an oft-maligned, frequently overlooked section of our literary history, pouring their love for hardboiled noir storytelling, saturating my favorite film with the flavor and flair of all that's come before it. The truth is, Joel and Ethan Coen are *crime* filmmakers, just as much as an Elmore Leonard or James Ellroy, or Raymond Chandler, is labeled a *crime* writer. They can make westerns, screwball comedies, musical adaptations of ancient Greek epic poems . . . each film also features just as much of a nod to the crime, noir and detective fiction they obviously love so well.

Me, I like to think The Dude found his new calling in the aftermath of the rug incident, and that, out there in some amazing universe just beyond Cassiopeia and a nice Thai stick, Dude & DaFino Investigations is doing a brisk business to this day.

....

Axel Howerton is the author of the quirky neo-noir "detective" novel *Hot Sinatra*, the mini-anthology *Living Dead at Zigfreidt & Roy*, and a bevy of short stories and hidden gems. His work has recently appeared in *Big Pulp*, *Fires on the Plain*, *Steampunk Originals*, *A Career Guide To Your Job In Hell* and the holiday anthology *Let It Snow: Season's Readings For A Super-Cool Yule*. Axel is is a member of the Crime Writers of Canada and the co-creator of the annual Coffin Hop author extravaganza. He lives in the untamed prairies with his two brilliant young sons and a wife who is way out of his league. You can visit Axel online at www.axelhowerton.com

Giuseppe Christiano, *The Limo Scene*

Epicurus' Place in the Yin-Yang of Dudeism

BY MARCUS CUBBEDGE

A lot of folks who admire The Dude seem to be privy on all the eastern influences, what with *The Dude De Ching* rambling about Taoism and such. Although I'm a fan of Lao Tzu, I think he's been given plenty of Dudeist kudos by others already. I'm writing this to answer a question some people have: Is Dudeism exclusively an eastern thing? Far from it! In fact, the symbol for Dudeism (the Yin-Yang bowling ball) makes it clear that there are two sides to the story man.

So what makes a dude? Is it a pair of worldviews? I think so. Just like our brains have two hemispheres, Dudeism has two main influences. I think the case for the ultimate eastern dude has been made, but sometimes there's a man … sometimes there's a man … aw hell, I think you know who I'm talking about it's in the fucking title. He abides in the western hemisphere of Dudeist thought, and he went by the handle *Epicurus* (born 341 BCE).

Now, "epicurean" is not a title many Dudeists would self-apply these days, and here's why: When Christianity became the official religion of the Roman empire, most folks at that time were followers of Epicurus. Some real reactionary human paraquats at that time decided that in order to spread Christianity they had to shit all over epicureanism by burning their books and writing new ones which twisted the ideals of epicureanism into something it was not. As luck would have it, these people could not extinguish all the true teachings of Epicurus. Some of his writings did in fact survive and fuck … old shit had come back to light, man!

Before getting into what Epicurus taught let's get rid of all the misinformation those dipshits spread all over town. They claimed that Epicurus was nothing but a hedonist glutton who had parties and orgies all the time. Many people thought that kind of nihilism and excess could only come from someone "evil." Even today, someone with refined taste in luxury and foods is commonly referred to as Epicurean. While some of that don't sound too bad, it just ain't the truth man … far from it.

Our main ancient source for the real Epicurus comes from a series of books called "Lives and opinions of eminent philosophers" by Diogenes Laetrius (225 CE). The last book in the series is dedicated to Epicurus and he is noted by Diogenes by saying "Let us, however, now add the finishing stroke, as one may say, to this whole treatise, and to the life of the philosopher; giving some of his fundamental maxims, and closing the whole work with them, taking that for our end which is the beginning of happiness." Now that's a fucking interesting man. Epicurus' main concern was how to be happy, in fact, he is quoted as saying "Vain is the word of a philosopher which does not heal any suffering of man. For just as there is no profit in medicine if it does not expel the diseases of the body, so there is no profit in philosophy either, if it does not expel the suffering of the mind." Many philosophers at that time were up their own asses about things that didn't matter much to the happiness of the individual.

Focusing on happiness, Epicurus came up with what was called the "Tetrapharmokos" (meaning "four-fold cure") which was preserved as the first four of his "Principal Doctrines." They are:

> 1. That which is happy and imperishable, neither has trouble itself, nor does it cause it to anything; so that it is not subject to feelings of either anger or gratitude; for these feelings exist only in what is weak. (i.e. Don't fear supernatural beings)
>
> 2. Death is nothing to us; for that which is dissolved is devoid of sensation, and that which is devoid of sensation is nothing to us. (i.e. Don't fear death)
>
> 3. The limit of great pleasures is the removal of everything which can give pain. And where pleasure is, as long as it lasts, that which gives pain, or that which feels pain, or both of them, are absent. (i.e. Happiness is easy to obtain)
>
> 4. Pain does not abide continuously in the flesh, but in its extremity it is present only a very short time. That pain which only just exceeds the pleasure in the flesh, does not last many days. But long diseases have in them more that is pleasant than painful to the flesh. (i.e. Misery is easy to endure)

In essence, Epicurus was saying that if you have irrational fears about the supernatural, death, pleasure and misery then you can't take it easy man. Epicurus even had a word for takin' it easy: "Ataraxia" which meant that true happiness didn't come from searching for it, but rather experiencing it by letting go of things that cause pain. He taught that we measure everything by pain and pleasure. As children we only know pain is bad and pleasure is good. In fact, Epicurus was so certain that pain and pleasure, rather than virtues, are the good and evil in life that he said:

> Doctrine 10. If those things which debauched men consider pleasurable in fact put an end to the fears of the mind, and of the heavens, and of death, and of pain; and if those same pleasures taught us the natural limits of our desires, we would have no reason to blame those who devote themselves to such pursuits.

> Doctrine 8. No pleasure is intrinsically bad; but that which is necessary to achieve some pleasures brings with it disturbances many times greater than those same pleasures.

In other words, Epicurus suggested as long as we don't overdo it, whatever we do (even things society has labeled bad) which leads to true happiness and not over-excess, well, go for it. This is where Lebowski comes in, and I'm taking about The Dude here. The Dude may smoke pot, drink, use cuss words etc. but does he not also take it easy? Has The Dude attained ataraxia? I think so, but that's just like my opinion man. Although The Dude partakes in earthly pleasures, it is because he doesn't over do it and cuts out the irrational bullshit from his life that he emanates that pure happiness that we all find inspiring. So The Dude unknowingly follows this:

> Doctrine 15. The Natural desires are easily obtained and satisfied, but the unnatural desires can never be satisfied.

Unnatural desires like over-achievement, being addicted to the "money," pretending to be someone you're not, trying to control every detail of your damn life, being too attached to things, treating objects like women, striving to be the most pious hypocrite, worrying about death constantly, living in the past, et cetera. These are the some of the bullshit things that The Dude doesn't care about, and in turn with all these things banished from The Dude's mind he's able to enjoy the real important stuff in life like Friendship, simplicity, relaxation, and son on. You know, taking it easy.

In order to tie up this rumination in a way you understand what I'm blathering about, here's the gist: In my humble view, all of Dudeism boils down to two basic tenants:

1. Take it easy (with Epicurus being the ultimate ancient example).

2. Abide (with Lao Tzu being the ultimate ancient example).

It's all about balance man, so complement the eastern and western parts of your brain and you'll be well on your way from admiring The Dude to BEING The Dude for your own place and time. Isn't that the point?

Fuckin A-man!

Further reading material can be found at Newepicurean.com and Epicurus.info

....

Mark Cubbedge is a high school teacher's aid who works with special education students. His main goal is to teach his students how to just take it easy and enjoy life, trying always to lighten their mood and teach them the way of The Dude. His favorite quote is from his favorite philosopher, Epicurus: "Vain is the word of a philosopher which does not heal any suffering of man. For just as there is no profit in medicine if it does not expel the diseases of the body, so there is no profit in philosophy either, if it does not expel the suffering of the mind."

Brian Diehl, *Mrs. Jamtoss*

Rich Nairn, *Maude Lebraski*

What Makes a Feminist, Mr. Lebowski?

BY CATE GOOCH

In a movie filled with so many male characters, it is easy to dismiss Maude as the stereotypical "Radical Feminist." Some argue that Maude's character is simply a parody of feminism, but perhaps they're just misled by her exaggerated mannerisms. As we see Maude continuously distinguish herself throughout the movie, it becomes apparent that the exaggeration serves a purpose. Maude's overweening confidence and haughty mastery of her environment serves to disprove and undermine the notion that women are inferior to men. Moreover, Maude's character essentially depicts a middle ground between Third Wave Feminism and Post-Feminism, providing an alternative feminist way for those who do not identify with either group.

Feminism itself is a word that makes most men – and people in general – uncomfortable. The mere mention of the word immediately brings to mind a variety of stereotypes that tend to generalize feminists as a group of man-hating, angry women. Part of the reason behind this may be because they are unaware of the full history and scope of feminism, the changes it has gone through, and what beliefs it currently entails. All too often, people simply associate feminism with the protests of the Women's Liberation movement of the 1960s and '70s without any concern or awareness for the different types of feminism that have developed over the years.

Many critics agree that we are no longer in the era of Second Wave Feminism; their progress was achieved through various milestones, such as Roe v. Wade, legal contraceptives, an abandoning of the traditional housewife role, and Title IX, amongst others. However, beginning in the 1990s, the "Third Wave" arose, in which different concerns about feminism were voiced. The movement began focusing its attention on a different generation and the concerns of younger women, resulting in a generational gap and differing beliefs between the Second and Third Waves (Showden 179).

Though Second Wave Feminism essentially provided the foundation for Third Wave Feminism, the Third Wave tends to have different concerns. While the concerns and goals are different for every individual, they are generally centered on broader issues, such as anti-racism, freedom from gender roles, or social class. This movement is commonly associated with the punk rock "Riot grrrls" or the "Grrrl Power" groups of the 1990s, and thus the angry-teen feminist stereotype was born. Many feminists in the '90s felt pressured to abandon their Second Wave beliefs to join the Third Wave movement, so as not to risk being called outdated or a bad feminist (Showden). However, Maude's character is not tied to such a clearly defined type of feminism; these pressures and strict beliefs do not seem to apply to Maude throughout the film. She seems to be the sole determiner of her actions, and her independence seeps through every scene in which she appears.

While Maude does not seem to be confined to the Third Wave feminist group, she doesn't quite fit in with any other groups either. Many critics argue that we are either in a transitional phase between Third Wave feminism and Postfeminism, or we are just in an entirely Postfeminist world. Postfeminism subscribes to the belief that we no longer need feminism and that the previous "waves" achieved everything that needed to be accomplished for women as a whole. It implies that equality has been achieved and feminism is no longer necessary (McRobbie 255). However, Maude stands in stark contrast to Postfeminists, simply by virtue of calling out societal double standards. She is fully aware of gender inequalities and presents herself as one who deeply cares about women's issues, defying Postfeminism and providing us with another option: not generalized Third Wave feminism or contented Postfeminism, but instead an independent, strong-voiced approach to gender issues.

One of the most common stereotypes women deal with is that they find it hard to get any message across or be taken seriously by their male counterparts. However, the Coen Brothers' exaggerated portrayal of Maude capitalizes on these stereotypes to depict her character as equal – or even superior, in many cases – to her male counterparts in the film.

Almost immediately after meeting The Dude, Maude asserts herself as a dominating verbal presence. She bluntly tells The Dude that her work is considered "vaginal," and, since it makes some men uncomfortable, she tests him to gage his reaction to her feminist beliefs: "The word itself makes some men uncomfortable . . . Vagina." The Dude remains perplexed, indicating that he is confused by what Maude is saying, not that he is offended by it. Maude continues to call out the double standards women face in regards to discussing genitalia. She explains, "Yes, [men] don't like hearing it and find it difficult to say, whereas without batting an eyelash a man will refer to his dick, or his rod, or his . . . Johnson." Naturally, The Dude reacts in a laid back manner, remaining very dude-like, but still confused. However, this exchange is important because it establishes Maude's independence and sets the stage for her strength as a woman and character. Furthermore, we see Maude accept The Dude with her confirmation of, "Okay, Mr. Lebowski," indicating that he has indeed passed her test. Maude knows that she has to work harder to overcome the idea that her gender makes her weak or inferior, thus her exaggerated and rather extreme approach ensures her the artillery to do so. It is also quite apparent that Maude does not subscribe to Postfeminist beliefs here; instead, she blatantly calls out the inequalities that Postfeminism denies.

While the initial exchange between Maude and The Dude is enough for many people to discount or dismiss her character as a caricature, further analysis reveals that Maude is indeed much more than just a stereotypical, radical feminist. As we are exposed to Maude more and more throughout the film, her intelligence becomes quite apparent. She is clearly an eccentric artist, and though that's not a name many would self-apply, it can still be highly commended. Her erratic telephone conversation with Sandro reveals that she is bilingual, a surprise that serves as another indicator of her intelligence. Maude clearly had the necessary means for a necessary means for a higher education. In addition, she consistently uses big words and jargon that seem to make The Dude uncomfortable. This portrays a way in which Maude is superior to the males in the film; we see no male character explicitly match her intelligence. This is perhaps why so many women – and men, too – can relate to Maude. Her confidence and sharp wit not only earn her respected status in the film, but also draw the audience to her as a character.

Despite Maude's exaggerated, radical views, we see no rejection or condescension on behalf of The Dude. Instead, he accepts Maude for who she is and even gradually picks up some of her characteristics. The Dude's embrace of Maude's ideals is apparent when Maude mentions the "beaver picture." He responds in a state of confusion, "Beaver? Uhhh, you mean vagina?" The Dude's response portrays how he sincerely believes Maude is his equal and agrees with, or at least is willing to embrace, her opinions. If Maude's character was less exaggerated or more passive – as many female characters are – she likely would have been dismissed as weak or unimportant. Had Maude been a representative of Postfeminism, her agency would have been severely diminished and the entire dynamic of the film would have changed. Her strong voice results in a strong impact on The Dude and a larger overall statement. A sense of equality between Maude and The Dude is apparent, which essentially provides a bit of social commentary that can be applied on a larger scale to society as a whole.

Much like The Dude, Maude can be thought of as the woman for her time and place. As women continuously feel pressured to either join the Postfeminism camp – ignoring inequality and feminist beliefs all together – or try to fit in with the Third Wavers, the need for another option seems necessary. Maude provides this option, and her powerful character exerts a strong sense of voice and independence without being bound to the particular confines of specific ideologies.

Further indication of Maude as an alternate option for Feminism is present – albeit somewhat conspicuously – in The Dude's dream sequence. Maude appears in The Dude's dream fully dressed in a Norse Viking costume, almost identical to the descriptions and even paintings of the mythological Valkyries, or women warriors. Snorri Sturlson's *Prose Edda* is considered a comprehensive source of the Medieval mythology that still inspires contemporary art and literature today; the works of authors such as J.R.R. Tolkien, Richard Wagner, and Henry Wadsworth Longfellow have all drawn from the Edda, and it continues to influence various art forms. In the *Prose Edda*, Valkyries are described as women warriors who are sent by Odin – the highest and oldest God – to select which soldiers live and die in battle. The soldiers they select to live follow the Valkyries to Valhalla, where they spend their days as a part of Odin's army and nights drinking or participating in festivities. However, the crucial aspect of the story is the role the women warriors play in the mythology. The Valkyries are said to have not only entered the battlefield – dressed in the full armor, which is known today as the popularized image of a Viking – but are also trusted with the task of selecting soldiers based on who they deem worthy. This establishes a clear connection with the portrayal of Maude in The Dude's dream sequence. Maude not only appears in the full Valkyrie costume, but also maintains a strong presence throughout the entire scene. The first time we see Maude, she is surrounded by women who dance around her and even appear to be worshipping her or at least recognizing her superiority; she indeed stands out amongst them and even has a more elaborate costume.

The most striking part of the dream sequence, however, is the interaction between The Dude and Maude. Initially, Maude walks away from The Dude, almost as if to reassert her power. But shortly after, they embrace and roll the bowling ball together. Though this may seem trivial, it still shows and acceptance and equality between the two. Moreover, the interaction parallels same power and process of selection held by the Valkyries in Medieval mythology. If we think of Maude as one of the prominent Valkyries in Mythology, such as Freya or Brynhild, it is easy to see the connection with the female warriors. Both not only maintain a level of power and independence, but also have the ability to decide which males are worthy of their own goals. Just as the Valkyries selected soldiers on the battle field, Maude is selecting The Dude as worthy and as her complete equal, as indicated by the collective bowling ball roll. This is why The Dude's ability to pass Maude's test in the earlier scene was so important. The dream sequence, then, depicts Maude essentially selecting The Dude to help carry on this new ideology of acceptance and equality between genders that is not focused on ideological labels or societal constraints, as the different waves of feminism can be.

The final indication of total acceptance is apparent towards the end of the movie, when Maude and The Dude "bang," to use the parlance of our times. Maude's initial plea of "Love me" makes her seem a bit more vulnerable, but she simultaneously maintains her independence by willfully choosing The Dude as her partner. In doing so, she also depicts the same sense of acceptance The Dude previously displayed towards her. This is yet another illustration of equality amongst both genders and the importance of such equality in society. However, if Maude's character had not been exaggerated initially, this acceptance would not have been apparent. The hilarious boldness of Maude's character resulted in an even playing field between herself and a world run (and sometimes run into the ground) by men who might not otherwise afford her the proper respect.

Maude illustrates that feminism is not a word to be afraid of; rather, it can be a natural, zesty enterprise. Perhaps more importantly, she can serve as a signpost for contemporary feminists looking for somewhere to hang their ideological robe.

....

Cate Gooch has a BA in Political Science, a Graduate certificate in Sociology and Social Justice, and is working on her PhD in English Literature. In an effort to keep a limber mind, she spends most of her time reading, writing, and playing guitar or piano. She is a dedicated Dudeist, who loves vinyl records and White Russians.

Lanny Tunks, *Some Burgers, Some Beers, a Few Laughs…*

Chris Hoffman, *Lebowski Sketch Card*

"Like Tumbleweeds Blowing Across a Vacant Lot": The Mythic Landscape of Los Angeles in Chandler's *The Big Sleep* and the Coen Brothers' *The Big Lebowski*

BY ANTHONY DYER HOEFER

The accessibility of formula fiction arises in part from the audience's familiarity with a cast of characters and the recognizable, if not convoluted, circumstances of plot. However, these stock characters and stock settings – the white hats and black hats, the hardboiled detectives and femmes fatales who move through the shadows of the modern metropolis – are more than reproducible components included in some sort of hardboiled do-it-yourself kit, and their formulaic nature offers a certain critical utility.

As variations on easily identifiable types, these characters readily yield insights into the fragmented subject positions they occupy, as well as the fragmented modern and postmodern landscapes they inhabit. These generic conventions have been put to both radical and reactionary ends: as they map out the dystopian possibilities of the modern city, hardboiled writers lament the excesses of modernity, work to expose systemic inequality, and assault the authority of the wealthy. While these progressive, if pessimistic, tendencies have been thoughtfully considered by scholars and critics, the nostalgia of the genre is often neglected: detective fiction often frequently mourns an expiring moral order. These impulses – the first, a willingness (perhaps a compulsion) to confront the excesses of bourgeois life by writing about popular culture in popular form, and the second, to nostalgically idealize an earlier moral and social order – seem to be contradictory, simultaneously progressive and conservative. But like any popular literature, these novels were produced by and contain the ideological tensions of their respective moments; these tensions have provided material for both literary critics and for postmodern, neo-noir imitators, including novelists Walter Mosely, James Ellroy, and the filmmakers Joel and Ethan Coen.

The Coen Brothers' 1998 film *The Big Lebowski* in particular invites the audience to revisit and reconsider Raymond Chandler's seminal hardboiled novel, *The Big Sleep*, The Coens' film, perhaps more so than Howard Hawks' classic adaptation, invokes the powerful influence of a mythic landscape in Chandler's novel and reveals the function of space and place in the production of its detective protagonist, Philip Marlowe. By reminding their audience of Los Angeles's genealogy as a expansionary outpost-cum-modern metropolis, the Coens rightly recognize the implicit influence of a frontier mythos in the construction of race and gender in the hardboiled genre, generally, and in Chandler's L.A. specifically. The Coens' Los Angeles is an utterly postmodern urban environment, stretching from the desert, across the suburban sprawl of the valley, through the city proper, to the beaches of Malibu. Considered alongside *The Big Lebowski*, *The Big Sleep* suddenly seems less a tale of a corrupt, modern city than one of the *emergence* of a corrupt, modern city and the resulting disappearance of an overwhelmed, mythic frontier.

"[T]he best adaptations of books for film," writes Neil Sinyard, "can often best be approached as an activity of literary criticism, not pictorialization of the complete novel, but a critical essay which stresses what it sees as the main theme" (117). Such is the case with the dialogue that exists between *The Big Sleep* and the film *The Big Lebowski*; I say "dialogue" because *The Big Lebowski* is not an adaptation of the novel, a remake of Howard Hawks' classic film noir, nor a translation of either. While the plot of the Coens' film is perhaps less familiar than that of Chandler's novel, the basic elements and befuddling convolutions are reproduced

In a review for another Coen Brothers film, *The Ladykillers*, David Edelstein offered perhaps an intriguing take on the Coens' unique engagement with source material: he suggests that the Coens' films emerge from an interest in movie "fodder" – the "found objects" of ideas and images that they consider to have a uniquely cinematic utility – rather than a conventional concern with topics or themes ("Thieves Like Us"). "It's about movie storytelling in the abstract – i.e., fooling around with fodder," he writes. By the Coens' own admission, Chandler's book is the "found object" at the center of *The Big Lebowksi* ("Making of *The Big Lebowski*"), and the Coens' emphasis of certain particular "fodder" from Chandler's novel invite a new critical perspective on *The Big Sleep*. Specifically, the opening scene of *The Big Lebowski* is worth no small amount of consideration. Scholars have most frequently approached Chandler's detective, Philip Marlowe, as a chivalric figure: his name recalls the Elizabethan playwright; in the first chapter, he offers a detailed description of a stained glass window that features a knight and damsel in distress at the Sternwood mansion, and he soon embarks on his own quest to protect a young woman (Carmen Sternwood); in his moment of greatest frustration, he notices the unfinished game of chess set out in his apartment and reports that, "knights [have] no meaning" (154).

While the chivalric model offers purchase into an interrogation of the text, it is by no means the only archetype we might employ in our reading. Indeed, the use of several western images in the Coens' film suggests that the cowboy might be the more appropriate model for Marlowe. The film opens on a single tumbleweed blowing across the Southern California landscape, accompanied by the song "Tumbling Tumbleweeds" by the Singing Cowboy, Gene Autry. The camera follows the tumbleweed across the desert at sunrise and over a ridge that overlooks the city: the juxtaposition between the barren desert and the metropolis below is sudden and emphasized by an unknown mechanical hum. The tumbleweed blows through the city and into the Pacific Ocean. The Coens seem to have found the inspirational "fodder" for this sequence in a short comment from Marlowe: "There was a gusty wind blowing in at the windows and the soot from the oil burners of the hotel next door was down-drafted into the room and rolling across the top of the desk like tumbleweed drifting across a vacant lot" (*BS* 126). Tumbleweeds still roll in the few open spaces left in the city, providing a bizarre and unexpected contrast that illuminates a crucial aspect of Los Angeles: it is "a big city layered on a Wild West frontier town" (Fine 118). Similar juxtapositions of the city and the frontier are evident throughout *The Big Sleep*: a "hundred odd lonely canyons" (*BS* 63) mark the landscape of the city; the Sternwood oil wells are off a dirt road in La Brea, but the sound of city traffic remains "curiously" audible (217).

Marlowe's descriptions of Realito are even more telling:

> A mile or so east of Realito a road turns toward the foothills. That's orange country to the south but to the north it's bare as hell's back yard and smack up against the hills there's a cyanide plant where they make stuff for fumigation.
>
> [...] Frame houses were spaced far back from a wide main street, then a sudden knot of stores, the lights of a drugstore behind fogged glass, the fly-cluster of cars in front of the movie theater, a dark bank on a corner with a clock sticking out over the sidewalk and a group of people standing in the rain looking at its windows, as if they were some kind of a show. I went on. Empty fields closed in again. (182)

Marlowe's narration imparts consequences to the "closing of the frontier" far beyond those foretold by Frederick Jackson Turner. Modernity and urbanity take on the characteristics of plagues or perhaps fungi, consuming the rural spaces of Southern California and emitting toxic byproducts. Cyanide is hardly the only poison released here, however; indeed, images of corruption, pollution, and decay recur throughout the novel, most notably in the twinned notions of the Sternwoods' "dried" (71) and "rotten" blood (148) and the dried-up oil wells, from which they have drawn their wealth. However, the physical decay of the landscape is not simply a metaphor for the moral decay that infects those who occupy it. Rather, the unfettered, ill-conceived development of Southern California is an element of the same swirl of economic forces that have overwhelmed any semblance of social order. The promise of paradise in these eternally-sunny climes has given way to an emerging dystopian metropolis, which threatens to overwhelm every residual element of the region's frontier past.

Chandler's description of Orange County belongs to a long tradition in which Los Angeles is emblematic of modernity's dystopic possibilities, according to Mike Davis. Davis contends that the city contains, in obvious and exaggerated ways, the contradictions of (post)modernity in their fullness, and, thus, "has come to play the double role of utopia *and* dystopia for advanced capitalism" (18). In the account offered by his book, *City of Quartz*, Los Angeles appeared almost out of nothing – or at least, in the absence of the factors that typically determine a city's growth: it lacked "comparative advantages [such] as crossroads, capitals, seaports, or manufacturing centers," he writes (25). According to Davis, the city's remarkable growth between 1885-1925 was a product of "real-estate capitalism" (25): this period of explosive development was fueled by the claims of boosters who exhorted others to come and take advantage of the curative properties of the sun and the endless possibilities to make one's fortune. The transformation from a small frontier outpost to the largest city in the West "required the continuous myth-making and literary invention with the crude promotion of land values and health cures" (26).

We are at no pains to find works that seek to debunk either the metropolitan mythos constructed by these original boosters (or the subsequent sunny suburban idylls of the post-World War II period). In particular, writers working in the hardboiled genre and filmmakers in their *noir* adaptations "repainted the image of Los Angeles as a deracinated urban hell," Davis writes (37). In their works, the California dreamscape imagined by real estate speculators, oil barons, and movie moguls is an empty façade – little more than the false scenery of a soundstage. In the void behind it is a nightmare world, in which the rich indulge decadent desires and corrupt the middle- and working-classes, over whom they have absolute dominion. The glamorous façade conceals the illicit activities of the wealthy and the famous, and it draws attention away from a criminal underworld thriving in the seediest spaces in the Los Angeles geography. In his essay "The Simple Art of Murder," Chandler describes this place (not Los Angeles specifically, but the abstract *mean streets* of detective fiction) as

> a world in which gangsters can rule nations and almost rule cities, in which hotels and apartment houses and celebrated restaurants are owned by men who made their money out of brothels, in which a screen star can be the fingerman for a mob, and the nice man down the hall is a boss of the numbers racket; a world where a judge with a cellar full of bootleg liquor can send a man to jail for having a pint in his pocket, where the mayor of your town may have condoned murder as an instrument of money-making, where no man can walk down a dark street safely because law and order are things we talk about but refrain from practicing . . . (59)

But, he writes, "down these streets a man must go" – the detective, not because he is going to bring order (though he might try), but because he – and we – are compelled to *know* the world obscured by the myth.

And what the detective – in this case, Marlowe – finds is a fairly simplistic structural and material understanding of corruption: the ruling oligarchy of Los Angelinos all but owns the poor, and – more importantly in the novels – spreads its corruption to the middle class, tempting them with the possibility that they too might own a piece of paradise. The solution, however, is anything but simple: corruption is endemic, and it is spreading. The detective survives only by ruthlessly maintaining a cynical, detached position and, typically, closing off the possibility of a relationship with a woman. Thus, while Chandler's fiction may lay bare the material and economic forces that produce the city, it offers no solutions: the cyanide plant in Realito is all but inevitable.

The cynicism of the genre emerges from the inability of both the writer and the detective to resolve the fundamental tensions of modernity, several of which are made evident in Chandler's descriptions of the Southern California geography. Rather than chart alternative modernities or new possibilities for the city, Marlowe clings to an idealized, pre-modern, pre-urban past – namely, that of the frontier. The juxtapositions between city and frontier lament the loss of something that never existed, then; and this contrast likewise configures Marlowe's – and the novel's – fraught understanding of masculinity and sexual morality. From the mythos of the West, Marlowe derives a vocabulary that he uses to classify other characters, particularly men. For most of the minor characters, a simple change of clothes would allow them to slip from the pages of Chandler's novel and into a saloon in a John Ford film. The more significant the characters, the less subtle the Western allusions. The stained glass window might be the most frequently discussed aspect of the Sternwood mansion's décor, but it is hardly the only piece of art worth note: a large oil portrait of a "stiffly posed . . . officer in full regimentals of about the time of the Mexican war" hangs just below "two bullet-torn or moth-eaten cavalry pennants crossed in a glass frame." When Marlowe meets General Sternwood, he sees his client and the officer share the "the same coal black eyes." In light of the painting, their conversation is revealing. Marlowe tells Sternwood that he has always tested "very high on insubordination" (10); Sternwood responds approvingly. Such predilections do not necessarily fit the profile of a general, but, coupled with his late "indulgence in fatherhood," the manner in which he was crippled (competing in a steeplechase, despite his age), and the cavalry pennants on the wall, they begin to paint a familiar picture. Insubordination is hardly a chivalric virtue. It is, rather, a virtue of the American West, a trait ascribed to the frontier heroes and the cowboys of pulp novels and, later, Hollywood.

David Fine suggests that fictive Los Angeles was created largely by migrants who came from the east into "an expansive landscape that appeared to them to have no discernable center, no reigning architectural style, and no sense of regional past that . . . [could] convince them that they had, in fact, arrived in a place" (18). Perhaps this was true with regard to the concrete artifices and roadways of the urban landscape, but writers like Chandler clearly had an alternative source of geographic identity – a particular discourse of place that, even amidst radical changes in the built environment, carried enormous rhetorical power. Indeed, frontier rhetoric is critical to the novel – and to Marlowe's – representations of criminality. Crime exists in two spheres in this novel, though they are not wholly separate. Marlowe seems quite comfortable with old-fashioned bootlegging, thievery, and gambling, as well as their small-time practitioners – the activities of a suitable outlaw.

True corruption, however, is manifest in crimes of decadence and indulgence such as pornography and drug abuse. These too are described in terms of the region's history, namely the inherent threat to the (white) frontier ideal posed by the "Oriental." The initial corrupt act that sparks the events of the novel is localized in the figure of the pornographer A.G. Geiger, who is murdered after drugging and photographing Carmen Sternwood. Though ostensibly white, Geiger is coded as "Oriental," and fits the role of sexual deviant – one of six archetypal images of "Orientals" enumerated by Robert G. Lee in his study, *Orientals: Asian Americans in Popular Culture* (83-106): Marlowe describes him as "a husband to women and a wife to men" (*BS* 100); his initial view into Geiger's store is obscured by "Chinese screens" and "a lot of oriental junk in the windows" (22). Geiger himself has a "[f]at face" and a "Charlie Chan moustache" (29); his corpse is clad in Chinese slippers, black satin pajama pants, and a Chinese embroidered coat (36). The conflation of Asian-ness with deviance emerges, at least in part, out of the particular history of Chinese immigrants in late-nineteenth century California, according to Lee. The 1870s marked a moment of transition in the American West, and California in particular: women arrived, en masse, in which the "male-dominated homosocial world of gold rush California" gave way to a "settled domestic Victorian discipline" (88). In this space, male Chinese laborers "represented a third sex" unto itself, at once connoting the threat of sexual deviance and reduced to the role of desexualized servant. This was exacerbated by both the (often forcible) importation of 10,000 Chinese women to the western U.S. as prostitutes and the Asian origins of opium. In many ways, then, the figure of the Oriental as either a de-sexed servant or a deviant and potentially subversive figure recalls similarly objectionable representations of African Americans.

Of course, Marlowe looks back to a West that exists only in popular imagination; while he might approach the booster view of L.A. with great skepticism, he nonetheless has accepted an idealization of frontier violence into cowboy heroism and capitulated to the obfuscation of abuses by a prior generation of Angelinos. Wesley A. Kort contends that places should be investigated as "as repositories of meaning" and "sites of social relationships" (177); there is a danger, however, that an uncritical discourse of place might image a location as a "constructed whole" or "surrogate reality," which "particular and economic interests can employ in order to validate themselves" (177). In Mike Davis's account, Los Angeles real estate boosters, since the late nineteenth century, have imagined and reimagined their city in this very way. Marlowe, however, is no less guilty of perpetuating Los Angeles as a "constructed whole." He rightly recognizes the artifice of the real estate boosters' vision of the city, and indeed, he is compelled to confront the corruption that this artifice obscures. However, his rejection of this narrative of place – of sunshiney Southern California – does not lead him to interrogate its production; instead, he dismisses it and, inevitably, turns *backward* to an older narrative. Marlowe thus remains invested in the "surrogate reality" of an organic lost frontier; it, he believes, is the reality that has been displaced by the artificial society of the metropolis. However, this West is just as ephemeral. As Davis notes, the booster myth suppressed any "intimation of the brutality inherent in the forced labor system of the missions and haciendas, not to speak of the racial terrorism and lynchings that made Anglo-ruled Los Angeles the most violent town in the West during the 1860s and 1870s" (26).

Just as the novel's nostalgia whitewashes the frontier past, its understanding of gender fails to accommodate anything beyond several narrow, frontier-inspired categories. As Jon Thompson notes, "the sexual politics of much of the hard-boiled genre in general undermine the genre's political radicalism by affirming the hierarchies and relations between the sexes sanctioned by bourgeois society" (143-44). The misogyny of the genre – in particular, that evident in the formulation of the *femme fatale* – has been widely discussed, but Chandler's gender trouble extends beyond that: as a protagonist and a narrator, Marlowe reaffirms a static formulation of masculinity and ascribes the status of deviance to anything outside its boundaries. Troubled as the novel is by the material changes to physical spaces wrought by modernity, it is equally concerned with the changes in gendered social spaces: the proper performance of gendered role and the appropriate obligations of one sex to another. Again, rather than reaching for a new, emancipatory formulation of gender, Marlowe can only turn to the past and mourn older narratives of gender and place; once upon time, he believes, these systems were self-evident, and they offered the individual all he needed to understand the world he inhabited.

The conflict between these two competing discourses comes to a head in Marlowe's apartment. When he finds Carmen naked in his house, the detective reacts with startling anger, violently tearing his sheets from the bed. The frontier myth, however, provides a context by which we might understand his response. He tells the reader: "I didn't mind what she called me, what anybody called me. But this was the room I had to live in. It was all I had in the way of a home. In it was everything that was mine, that had any association for me, any past, anything that took the place of family" (158). Implied in this articulation of frustration is the influence of the frontier myth: Marlowe almost sounds like a homesteader, driven from his land by a robber baron. The modern, urban environment provides precious little opportunity for the crucial, frontier-tinged expression of individuality – the ownership of private space. For Marlowe, the invasion of his small apartment is no different from the forcible appropriation of land that drives the plot of so many Westerns. Regardless of size, the apartment offers Marlowe the only space that he considers undeniably his, the only space through which he can define himself. Those boundaries – between private and public, between the individual subject and the physical and cultural spaces in which s/he lives – are far more fluid than Marlowe would like to admit, and Carmen's intrusion makes this reality painfully obvious. Her presence seems to introduce the chaos – the gender trouble and the threat of corruption and deviance – to the personal space he has rigorously maintained as a safehouse from the swirl of modernity. In reality, however, this chaos is and has always been present in this space; Marlowe, despite his protestations otherwise, is a modern subject, struggling with the contradictions of modernity. In both his narration and his interactions with other characters, he insists that he is an autonomous subject. These insistencies, offered with frequency and force, serve to suppress the reality that this self is a product of its context.

The contradictions that characterize the modern subject are reflected in the jarring contrasts of landscape; again, we turn to the scene on the road to Realito and the stark and suggestive juxtapositions between agrarian possibility and modern decay. The tension between these possibilities haunts Marlowe; indeed, it is indicative of the turmoil and confusion he confronts regularly. Or, at least, it is representative of how he understands that turmoil – that is, as antinomies. Marlowe seeks to preserve himself from the monstrous present by aligning himself with an idealized past. The reality is that this stark contrast is not accurate; the demarcations between *then* and *now* are never particularly clear in any modernist text, and *The Big Sleep* is no exception. However, this middle space between then and now – where perhaps some answer to the questions of modernity might lie – is never resolved. Instead, Marlowe comes to the belief that one absolute – the present – will necessarily overcome the past. Realito will give way to suburban expansion; the hermetic seal on his apartment has been broken, and so his homestead will give way to the city. The only escape, he finally contends, comes in the titular *big sleep* – in the death that finally removes the subject from the influence of its moment.

***

Earlier, I suggested that *The Big Lebowski* offers a new critical perspective on *The Big Sleep*; the interaction between the two is not simply one of comment, however. Rather, these works engage each other in dialogue, and when we consider them together, we gain new insight into the production of modern and postmodern urban spaces, particularly as we consider how the two protagonists move through these spaces. Both men project – or perhaps, perform – a cool detachment; they imbibe with frequency. These commonalities aside, the two men are dramatically different. When Marlowe rips the sheets from his bed, the reader is offered a glimpse of what lies beneath the hardboiled shell – a frustration that contradicts the very cool, calm sarcastic wit, which otherwise makes him and his shamus brethren so appealing. Here, we get a hint of why a bottle of rye rests in his hip pocket. Simply put, Marlowe is struggling to understand how to live in this modern moment, and he actively seeks out confrontations with the darkest elements of his dystopian city in order to gain that knowledge.

The Dude suffers a similar invasion of his personal space: two men, seeking to shake down the other Lebowski for money owed by Bunny, break in and urinate on it. The rug "really tied the room together," he later tells Walter and Donny; its soiling disturbs the harmony which the tai chi-practicing Dude has sought to establish. The Dude is motivated to seek remuneration, however, not to uncover *why* this has happened; neither this event nor the several subsequent break-ins constitute the sort of violation that Carmen's presence does for Marlowe. Likewise, the mystery plot does not seem to pose any existential problem for The Dude.

The difference between the ways in which these two men respond to invasions of their respective homes is suggestive. Marlowe has struggled mightily to maintain some distance between the private space of his home and the public space of the world; The Dude is well-behind in his rent and has made no efforts to forestall eviction. Thus, while Marlowe actively works to resist the world around him, The Dude, in his own words, simply "abides": he moves through the world, comfortable that his indifference distinguishes him from the "square community" and protects him from its influence. However, this does not constitute any real resistance, as the Stranger tells us. In his introduction, the Stranger offers a useful, if not elliptical, description of The Dude: "Sometimes there's a man – I won't say a hero, because what's a hero? But, sometimes there's a man – and I'm talkin' 'bout The Dude here – but sometimes there's a man . . . ah well, he's the man for his time and place." The statement seems curious, especially if The Dude is understood as an anachronistic character. However, such contradictions are not problematic in the context of postmodern subjection: The Dude is at once both an anachronism and a product of his moment, for the moment is all encompassing. Unlike Marlowe, The Dude is not seeking resolution, but compensation for a befouled rug; he has neither the interest nor the ability to pursue resolution in the way that Marlowe does – because his time and his city easily incorporate contradiction.

Thus, in typically postmodern fashion, the Coens' translation revels in the differences and contrasts that Southern California landscape. Like Chandler's Los Angeles, the Coens' L.A. remains an environment of geographic incongruity, but without the dissonance posed by the cyanide plant in Chandler's Realito. Indeed, Marlowe's tumbleweed metaphor brings together disparate images: gusts from oil burners in the adjacent building are so thickly laden with soot that Marlowe endows them with the semi-tangibility of tumbleweed. The Coens' tumbleweed, however, is no metaphor, but a physical presence that rolls easily and unobstructed from the desert, through suburbia, into the city, and out into the ocean. Crucially, the metropolis offers no resistance: it seems that the postmodern urban environment easily incorporates all of these elements into a seamless cityscape. Any tension between neighborhoods, between the people who occupy them, beneath the artifice of the built environment, has been repressed; it is as if the desert, the stripmalls, the skyscrapers, the bowling alleys exist *sui generis*.

Similarly, the forms of mass culture that both produce and are produced within this space represented myriad ideologies and subjectivities of the contemporary urban landscape. As a result, the postmodern subject is malleable in a way that modern subject might not be: though ideologies might be classified as "mainstream" or "alternative," none are truly transgressive or revolutionary. Marlowe rejects the ideology of modernity and urbanity, but must turn to the only viable alternative available, that of the Old West. No such rejection is possible for The Dude, because his L.A. can happily accommodate and, ultimately, subsume an exponential number of ideologies and subjectivities. Thus, The Dude and his friend Walter Sobchak live out the narratives of their youth. The former, a former student radical who claims to be one of the original authors of the Port Huron Statement, continues to fashion himself a drop-out; Walter can't help but see everything through the lens of his experiences in Vietnam, no matter if the situation bares no relation. Like Marlowe, Walter and The Dude are anachronistic figures; but unlike Marlowe, they belong to a community of anachronistic characters. The postmodern city, it seems, has negated any insurgent effort to question its production by simply enveloping and creating a space to contain any possible insurgent ideology. For instance, The Dude's antagonists, a group of self-proclaimed nihilists, squabble of over their orders of pancakes and "pigs-in-blanket" at a chain diner (perhaps an IHOP). Though these characters purport to "believe in nothing" and frequently announce their rejection of all forms of ideology, they do not exist outside the banality of contemporary consumer culture.

And so, while Marlowe struggles tirelessly to distance himself from his context, The Dude's resistance is nearly effortless. Like Marlowe, The Dude rejects the dominant ideological tropes of society, preferring to live out an anachronistic narrative. He is the archetypal "drop-out": he claims to be a former student radical and roadie for the heavy metal band, Metallica; he rejects the ideology of the "work ethic," preferring to bowl, get stoned, and listen to old tapes of a California band from the late 1960s and early '70s, Creedence Clearwater Revival. The Dude carries only one form of identification: a discount card for Ralph's, a chain of grocery stores. He can elude the influence of governmental bureaucracy – he does not have driver's license or a Social Security card – but not that of corporate empire. Likewise, The Dude's bowling league is a haven for alternative subjectivities: stoners, Vietnam vets, and even convicted pedophiles are permitted membership. They may be marginalized, but the postmodern city affords them both the physical and the ideological space to construct their own community. Deviance, it seems, is not only acceptable: it has been given its own space in this fragmented city. Indeed, Malibu is the only space in which The Dude's movements and access is formally restricted, but that is only because the local constabulary have been so ordered by one of their wealthy residents – the pornographer Jackie Treehorn.

None of this is to say that *The Big Lebowksi* offers an optimist portrait of the postmodern city or that it suggests that postmodernity resolves the contradictions of modernity confronted by Marlowe. Rather, the Coens' postmodern metropolis seems to have dulled any impulse to resolve these contradictions, and even in their attempt to claim an insurgent subject position, Walter and The Dude remain products of their cultural contexts. The Stranger tells the audience that his story takes place "in the early '90s, sometime around our conflict with Saddam and the Iraqis." Consequently, The Dude mimics the rhetoric of George H.W. Bush. Early in the film, The Dude watches as Bush 41 tells a television audience, "This will not stand, this aggression against Kuwait, this will not stand." The Dude later repeats these words almost verbatim in his argument with the other Jeffrey Lebowski, a rich, old man whom he identifies as a member of "the square community." Similarly, when thrust in the role of detective, he takes on the crime-solving methods of popular culture: after watching the pornographer Jackie Treehorn scribble a note onto a pad, The Dude takes the pad and shades it in, hoping to reveal the imprint of some crucial information recorded on the previous page. All that he finds, however, is a doodle a man with an enormous penis. His sidekick Walter, likewise, adopts the clichés and methods of countless action films. The experiences of neither prepare them to deal with their circumstances. However, popular culture provides them with models. In this sense, The Dude is indeed "the man for his time and place" – but only because he is a man *of* his time and place – a place that has subsumed any possibility of a resistant subjectivity.

....

Anthony Dyer Hoefer, PhD, is the Director of the University Scholars Program in the Honors College at George Mason University, where he also teaches literature and writing courses. His recent book, Apocalypse South: Judgment, Cataclysm, and Resistance in the Regional Imaginary (The Ohio State University Press, 2012), takes on very un-Dude-like topics.

Works Cited

The Big Lebowski. Dir. Joel Coen. Perf. Jeff Bridges, John Goodman, Julianne Moore, Steve Buscemi, John Turturro. DVD. Universal Home Video, 2003.

"Making of *The Big Lebowski.*" *The Big Lebowski.* DVD. Universal Home Video, 2003.

Cawelti, John G. *Adventure, Mystery, and Romance.* Chicago: University of Chicago Press, 1976.

Chandler, Raymond. *The Big Sleep.* New York: Vintage Crime/Black Lizard, 1992.

Davis, Mike. *City of Quartz: Excavating the Future of Los Angeles.* London: Verso, 1991.

Emerick, Laura. "All the Young Dudes Abide." Chicago *Sun-Times.* 7 March 2008. B3.

Edelstein, David. "You're Entering a World of Lebowski." New York *Times.* 8 Aug. 2006. ARTS & LEISURE 21.

"Thieves Like Us." *Slate.com.* 26 March 2004. 28 April 2008. http://slate.msn.com/id/2097804/.

Fine, David. *Imaging Los Angeles: A City in Fiction.* Alburquerque, NM: University of New Mexico Press, 2000.

Lee, Robert G. *Orientals: Asian Americans in Popular Culture.* Philadelphia: Temple UP, 1999.

Slotkin, Richard. *Gunfighter Nation.* New York: Antheneum, 1992.

Routledge, Christopher. "A Matter of Disguise: Locating the Self in Raymond Chandler's *The Big Sleep* and *The Long Good-Bye.*" *Studies in the Novel.* 29:1 (1997): 94-107.

Thompson, Jon. *Fiction, Crime, and Empire: Clues to Modernity and Postmodernism.* Urbana and Chicago: University of Illinois Press, 1993.

Originally published in Clues: A Journal of Detection, Vol. 26, No. 3 © 2008. Executive Editor Margaret Kinsman. Managing Editor Elizabeth Foxwell by permission of McFarland & Company, Inc., Box 611, Jefferson NC 28640. www.mcfarlandpub.com.

James Duncan, *Walter and Dude's Roadtrip*

Everything I Know, I Learned from *The Big Lebowski*

BY WILL RUSSELL
Founding Dude, Lebowskifest

Well maybe not everything, but this weird little film has taught me quite a bit and changed my life in ways I could have never imagined when I first sat in that Kentucky movie theater alone in 1998. I walked out and shrugged, completely unaware that I had just seen my favorite movie of all time and having no inkling that I would one day create a festival in its honor that would bring untold thousands of fellow fans together to fawn over the dialogue and celebrate the irresistible brilliance of the Brothers Coen.

I've picked up some new terms, such as *pederast*, broadened my understanding of certain religions and now grasp the meaning of Shomer Shabbos or at least Walter's definition and now know what the V.I. in Lenin's name stands for. These fun facts are trivial and are in fact perfect fodder for Round 1 Trivia at Lebowski Fest but they can't really change my world.

The biggest lessons come from our hero, The Dude, the man for his time and place which seems to be anytime and not just the time of our conflict with Saddam and the Iraqis. The Dude is a nice guy. He will come give you notes on your dance cycle, he will tolerate Walter's incessant rantings about Vietnam, he will help Maude conceive, however The Dude is not a rug to be micturated upon. The Dude minds, man and when people are being jerks he stands up for himself.

The Dude knew that he should be compensated for the rug and after the other Jeffrey Lebowski insulted him he took any rug in the house. A victimless crime, like playing Robin Hood for himself, The Dude made himself whole and thought his fucking troubles were over. Of course it was his desire for this rug that is the root of all his suffering which instructs me that worldly things can be had but there is a price to be paid for putting too much value on them and that price has nothing to do with finding a cash machine.

Ol' Duder seems pretty content in his life and yet has nothing that most Americans work themselves into emergency rooms to get. No job, a shitty car, no wife and kids, just a tiki bar, some whale sounds, Mr. Bubble bubble bath, bowling with his buddies, and a little weed are all The Dude wants and he can die with a smile on his face without feeling like the good lord gypped him.

The Dude Abides and it's good knowing he's out there taking er easy for all us sinners. I don't know about you but I take comfort in that.

....

Will Russell is the founder of Lebowski Fest, co-author of *I'm a Lebowski, You're a Lebowski* and proprietor of the WHY Louisville store. More on Lebowski Fest at http://lebowskifest.com or follow him on Instagram @KentuckYeti.

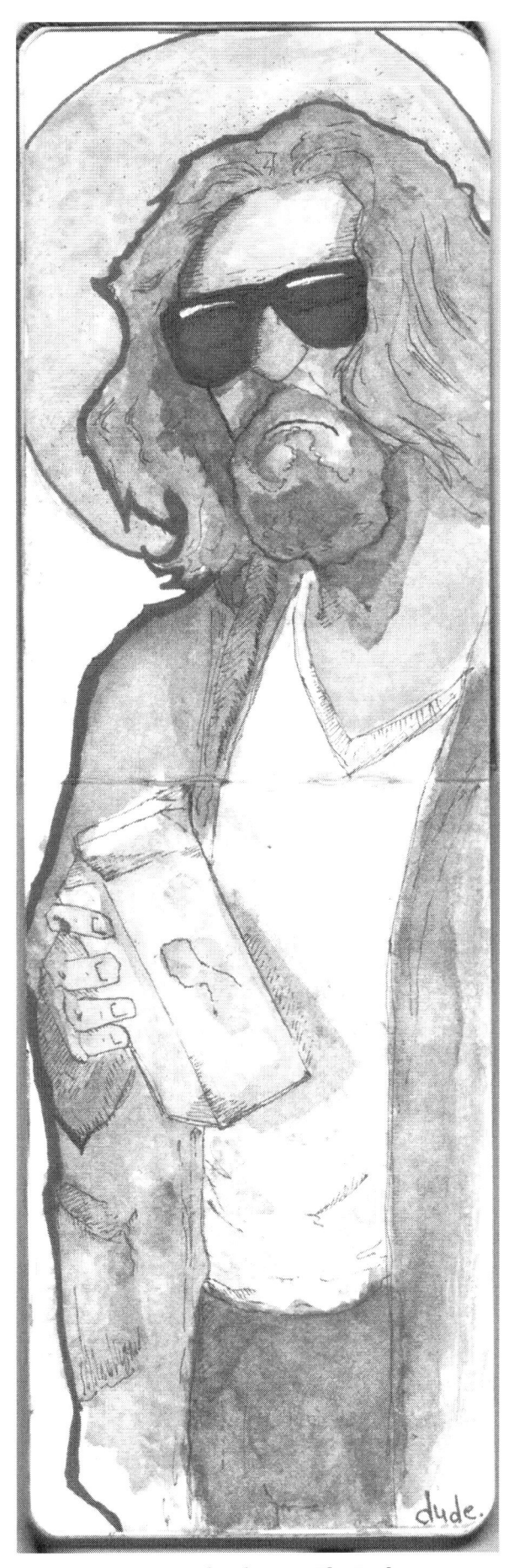

Lama Under the Hat, *The Dude*

Abide or Die: Affective Escape from Radical *Noir* Doom

BY KATE CARSELLA

Film Noir would suffer greatly without its inherent temperament of futility, resultant isolation and the grasp for the past. The Coen Brothers' contribution to the genre, *The Big Lebowski*, upholds these tropes, granted, with a healthy dose of wacky hijinks.

Their protagonist, The Dude, is segregated from the troupe of Los Angelenos who represent "an institution with cracks of corruption eroding its foundation." (Olivier 1) As a result, El Duderino – if you're not into the whole brevity thing, seeks to elude the post-Reagan, Gulf War-era "today" of the film with which his sensibilities cannot be reconciled. One of his methods, much like classical *noir* protagonist Sam Spade, is to rely on habit: where Spade is ever rolling cigarettes and drinking whiskey, Dude is endlessly sparking joints and topping off White Russians, frequently meditating and cranking his C.C.R. tapes. Another is his staunch nostalgia for and adherence to 1960s countercultural ideals, i.e. pacifist (albeit languid) protest of the aggressive status quo and blatant non-conformism. This non-conformity leads Dude to dwell in his low-lit apartment and often chill at the bowling alley, his own private affective community. Peopled with other outlaws from rational community, Dude is able to integrate his demeanor, habits and desires with ease into the social sphere. He does not have to face harsh judgment and further, has no need to dole it out. Abiding in the bowling alley is easy, but out *there*, in the "rational" (Wolff) community, is the radical evil. (Olivier) Once Duder enters that world, and of course he must, his choice to abide will be tested. Will the mantle of The Dude remain, or like the many *noir* heroes before him, will his resolve be twisted by greed, deceit and doubt? This is the backbone of what *noir* is: the battle for the integrity of his psyche and the power of choice. This paper argues that bearing all this in mind, *The Big Lebowski* is *neo-noir* in one of its finest illustrations: retaining *and* experimenting with the conventions.

Los Angeles, early 1990s. *The Big Lebowski* opens with a slow pan of a desert floor with time-lapse video from day to night. The Sons of the Pioneers' "Tumbling Tumbleweeds" plays over the scene. A lone tumbleweed emerges rolling from the desert to the cityscape, down the road, and finally to the beach. The open water. "Lonely but free, I'll be found," croons the soundtrack.

At the checkout counter The Dude writes his check for 69¢, watching the televised George Herbert Walker Bush asserting "this aggression will not stand," thereby characterizing the sociopolitical location of the film as trying to erase the past and depict a polished present. Disillusionment hit the national consciousness during the Vietnam/Watergate/Nixon era, and the effects remained up through the Gulf War over which H.W. presided. Marc Singer articulates the latter war was presented in such a way as to erase the collective memory of the mucked-up early '70s, and consequently negate the need for public outcry against the system, which was enlivened by the Vietnam War. (Singer 1) Those are the times. As for the place: "heartless" L.A. (Anderson, ENG 363 Film Noir). A sprawling city representing the "rational community," peopled with the indifferent and inexorable. Compassion and alternative opinions fell out of vogue.

Paul Wolff defines the "rational community as 'that reciprocity of consciousness which is achieved and sustained by equals who discourse together publicly for the specific purpose of social decision and action' (192) . . . such a community could be 'an element of a possible general good' but by no means requires it (187)." (Raczkowski 119-120) The film provides a sampling of wealthy elite to demonstrate the rational community: The Lebowski clan, and their associates Jackie Treehorn (complete with flunkies), and the nihilists. Sean McCann argues that these characters embody the vampirical quality of the rational community, "[surviving] by leeching the vitality of the forthright and honest (166)." (Singer 4) They subsist on the material, their sole focus on the ransom money. Theft, pissing on an innocent rug and mutilated feet are deemed suitable methods in their chase. On top of that, each of the seekers of the money: Jackie, Bunny, Maude & The Big Jeffrey Lebowski himself, are tied together in many variations of intimacy, yet have no qualms sabotaging each other for the ill-gotten gains. Material reward over personal – a common thread throughout the noir universe. Ultimately, these "rationals" come up empty-handed and without the power they seek.

Enter, Dude: A man, "not into the L.A. health, fitness and beauty [scene]," unlike much of the populace. The Stranger, the somewhat-numinous timekeeper of the film fills in the picture of the world The Dude is surrounded by and estranged from with image, rather than physical facts of the place. Like all cities that colonize the noir-verse, the oppressive feeling that emanates from the nightly, crowded, decaying environment is what sticks. The physical characteristics could be the same in L.A., New York, Chicago, but what each noir-ized town has in common is the congested desolation. The oozing futility. When faced with such mainstream, widespread ugliness, where can the noir hero turn? To the bowling alley, away!

Finally, peace. The bowling alley is The Dude's sanctuary in the midst of the labyrinthine city. As he enjoyed subculture in the '60s, he has cultivated it in the '90s. The bowling alley, Dude's favorite haunt, serves as the home of his affective community. He and the other rational outlaws can rendezvous here and escape daunting "reality." His disillusionment with the corruption of the times and the erasure of the qualities he held dearest from his past (activism, liberal drug usage, Bill Kunstler) sends him to the loving arms of the lanes and the leagues. His pals Donny Kerabatsos and Walter Sobchak accept his dress, his proclivities for creamy alcoholic beverages and green smokables, and his attitude without judgment or hesitation. Even The Jesus and Smokey, while not teammates, are comrades in their outsider status. The Jesus, a "pederast" (as Walter articulates), and Smokey, a Vietnam veteran, are unwanted and are no longer of use to the mainstream. Smokey in particular helps The Dude keep ties to the past alive. This runs contrary to other noir men who must rely on themselves to take refuge in memory or further down the line, delusion. As Joel & Ethan Coen pan the lanes, showcasing the members of this community, the audience sees obesity, unfortunate fashion choices, gross hairdos, et cetera. Each trait misdemeanors that leave them stranded out there. But in here, they are accepted and can gain a measure of success and better, relief.

The past as a noir concept is the referent for the feeling of relief. The noir hero feels potential and power from the past – a time where the future was further away and the system didn't seem so encompassing. The Dude subverts this with affective community, where he can remain in his Dudest of states. He isolates from the rational community, as opposed to simply being isolated by them. His choice here is central to the fate of his integrity.

But what is "affective community"? Paul Wolff characterizes this group as "the reciprocity of awareness between oneself and the others" as the unifying trait. (Singer 119) "It is this mutuality of awareness, and not merely familiarity or habit, which makes participation in one's own traditions, however meager they may be, more satisfying than observation of the rituals of others, no matter how elaborate or aesthetically excellent." (186)

In an update of the isolation trope in classical noir, the Coens reveal an entire subculture of isolation "flying scandalously beneath the radar." (119) It is not only The Dude that resists, it is a group of men seeking and achieving "mutual enthusiasm and enjoyment, [without] politics or notions of social change ... [in] the quasi-utopian social space [of the bowling alley] within postmodern Los Angeles. It is where The Dude abides and takes it easy for all us sinners outside." (Raczkowski 119-120, 122) He engages in a shared alternative with others who, also rejecting the outside community or rejected by it, abide by a specific system of rules where language is unnecessary, and understanding of the code and the members thrives. "The reciprocity of awareness [there] is largely non-verbal. In fact, nothing jeopardizes the ties that form that community more than talk between the players." (122) In this space, image loses value, as signifying becomes a hindrance, rather than a requirement as in the rational community. As that object/subject inversion renders the rational community perverse, the affective community is equally rendered unspoiled, uncorrupt.

It is in this small alley of the world that The Stranger first chooses to appear. It is the only place he appears throughout the film. For the audience, this is a signal of the underlying currents of mystery only the affective community can house. It is not dangerous mystery, it's an appealing mystique. Is there something greater keeping an eye on The Dude? What is the nature of this affective community that makes the potentially supernatural feel safe in appearing? It may simply be the aura of Dude Lebowski, the Other Lebowski, that entices the specter Stranger, rather than the wealthy, gaudy Lebowskis just across town. It is The Stranger, after all, who decides the story of The Dude should be told: "Sometimes, there's a man..."

Not too terribly long after this vague and halting introduction does the outside world come a-callin'. Or a-throttlin', as the case may be. Upon returning home with the half & half for the all-important White Russian, The Dude is attacked by Jackie Treehorn's flunkies who have already invaded his private sanctum, and don't stop there. His head is debased in the toilet bowl, his rug is stained with urine, and his 69¢ is wasted as the half & half sprays the bathroom walls. It should be noted here that that rug really tied the room together. With the invasion of his home by Jackie Treehorn (phallic symbol, anyone?), Duder's inevitable clash with the outside community is hastened. Though as the audience finds out, it's the result of a careless misnomer, the underlying currents of the film bespeak greater reasoning. It's unavoidable that The Dude's integrity must be tested in order for his resolve to be measured. For such a laid-back guy, the question is valid: is The Dude flexibly stalwart, or floppy? This aggression will not stand. In fact it will sit in a wheelchair, awaiting him.

The Dude's first *entré* into the dark city is his meeting with his doppelganger, "Big" Jeffrey Lebowski. The latter owns a sprawling mansion, the inside glittering with plaques and awards detailing contributions to society and success. Trotting around the halls is a sniveling manservant Brandt, and deep in the study is the abrasive, miserly, fatted Big Man himself. As noted by Marc Singer, Big Lebowski is a take on The Big Sleep's General Sternwood. (Singer 2) Both impotent figures – confined to wheelchairs, at the mercy of the women in their respective families, and yet "predatory … [parasites]" who revel in "decadence." (Singer 4) As it turns out, Big Jeffrey "is far more predatory than General Sternwood, his wealth more illusory." (Singer 4) Both men, as rational community requires, are subject to reciprocity in order to maintain their façade. General Sternwood relies on "Rusty Regan for 'the breath of life', (Chandler, Big Sleep 11) and seeks to replenish that breath with Philip Marlowe." (Singer 4) Big Jeff relies on many images to keep the perception of his lifestyle in check. From the placards on his wall that signify his political connections to the Reagan family, to his supposed care for the future and humanity with the Little Lebowski Urban Achievers. Even the submissiveness of Brandt empowers him, supplying him a commanding dynamism that overshadows the impotence of his crippled state. The size of his home and his achievements are ultimately overcompensation for a virility he secretly does not feel. His empty marriage to Bunny is the cherry on the sundae – a signifier for a great big phallus, a.k.a. grand masculine power. Maude, his daughter, informs The Dude that one of her father's great vices is his vanity. This is the Big man boiled down to his essence – the signifiers, like the quality of vanity, are what sustain him and form his rationale, as opposed to any actualities.

As Christopher Raczkowski explains, the "social institutions" of the rational community "are governed by quasi-legal business interests, human lives are measured in exchange values, and possessions are valued in human terms. In the classic Marxist formulation … *The Big Lebowski* reveals a world where subjects are transformed into objects, and objects are transformed into subjects; or as The Dude explains of the film's ethereal underworld kingpin and adult movie mogul: 'Mr. Treehorn, treats objects like women, man.'" (Raczkowski 103)

These "aesthetics," Raczkowski argues, "[are wagered] on the possibility of resistance or escape from the reified modern social world that is the *sine qua non* of almost all forms of *noir* narrative." (Raczkowski 102-103) The perverse corruption of LA is not uncommon in *noir*, much less in the Los Angeles brand of "heartless" (Anderson, 3.4.11) *noir*. With no heartbeat, signifying no human rhythm to the city, the rational community is completely able to persist without regard for humanity, but for only desirable objects (money) and perpetuating image.

The Big Lebowski's nostalgic bent for the 1980s Reagan era of economy and hierarchy informs the audience further as to his truth, and to the ideologies that remain potent. Jeffrey Lebowski clings to Reagan ideals because again, the value is on image – the concept of the free market especially: individuals are expected to pick themselves up by their bootstraps to gain affluence and agency, meanwhile the "impassable gulf" (Singer 1) is created. Gaining more and more impassability by the hour between those already in power and those who seek to gain some, the rich get richer and the poor keep struggling. Reagan himself was an actor, a professional image-maker. He was largely deified for his ability to speak and carry out a persona, a la "Mr. Gorbachev tear down this wall," more so than his controversial actions of "believing in the magic of the marketplace," (*Enron: The Smartest Guys in the Room*, 2005) and tearing down regulations in business. Let's not even mention Star Wars or Iran-Contra.

The Big Lebowski does not adhere to the 80s Reaganomic ethic of individual success, much the same way the actual ethic didn't either. His primary goal is immense wealth, but his method of attainment certainly isn't to work for it. Opportunism is easier, and Bunny's impromptu vacay provides him exactly what he needs. Moolah. The big man's complex web of deceit takes little time or effort from him–the nihilists, Jackie Treehorn and The Dude do all the running about town with threats of castration (toes and johnsons), the occasional drugging and spilled drinks. Fool's errands, he can sit back from and grasp to reap the benefits.

Similarly, the past is very much alive for the *other* Jeffrey Lebowski, though at the opposite end of the cultural spectrum. The mind-altering '60s, where image and objectification were fodder due for a teardown. This marks a philosophical difference between the Jeffreys: one needs the image to keep the world appearing as he desires, which belies passivity. The other needs get to the heart of the matter and discards the image as false, intrusive. This belies activity. This is why Duder's touch with the past remains valid where Big's does not: the past keeps The Dude in touch with choice, with his own integrity. His openness to spirituality as embodied by his easy rapport the Stranger, his meditation techniques aided by whale song and bowling pins crashing. Taking a look at his pad, loaded as it is with candles, neutral tones and much open space – the man is not a tense type and works for it. Dude invokes the name Bill Kunstler and has a Nixon picture on his wall – the only image Dude keeps around.

The image of Nixon bowling hangs over The Dude's White Russian station. This positioning of The Dude's tools for keeping his mind from being "uptight" like a Nixon-type, seems pointed. He counteracts the image of Nixon with the power of his choices. Duder must not become this man, even when the wolf is packaged in bowler's clothing. (122) Dude keeps this image as a reminder of the power of that image, and of its consequences. From the rationals, Dude is "constitutionally disabled and disinterested." (122) Should he ever feel weak and backslide into it, he has Nixon to prophesy what could befall him.

Each of these examples speaks to a perversion of value within the rational community. As is common with its members, Jeffrey Lebowski places most importance on image or object, rather than subject. For example, what Bunny displays – youth, sex, a symbol of much male desire (and in being able to enlarge the phallus) in being a porn star, is what is vital to The Big Lebowski. Her actual self is of no consequence here. As for Maude Lebowski, Big's daughter and Dude's next stop in the complex city, language is the image she wants to portray.

Maude is largely complicit in the perversion of the rational community, despite her best "enlightened" intentions. Her transgressive use of language is meant to signify power. She insists on littering language, often composed of masculine-inspired signifiers, with feminine signifiers, "vagina," "beaver picture." Her speaking voice, a fluty, Katharine Hepburn-esque inflection represents in her mind enlightenment, aristocratic intelligence and therefore power. Her ability to speak many different languages – English and "tittering" Italian, reveals what a priority signifying is to her (Singer 5) This "excludes and mystifies" the affective community's Lebowski, who is at home in a sphere where language is unnecessary for coherence and understanding. (Singer 5) Furthermore, Singer references James Mottram's suggestion, that this "'indicates [Maude's] work is not as radical as she may think.'" (Mottram 145) Again the power of image and of objects is used to show her enlightenment. Maude utilizes language, wealth, her avant-garde art and supposed sexually liberated feminism to keep power and manipulate others into working for her, treating The Dude as a "befuddled servant." (Singer 5) While these images together are meant to cohere as a vision of Maude The Transcendent, her means make that image just that. A flat image. Her alternative to financial corruption is no alternative at all, only, as Ringo Starr put it, "a smokescreen of bourgeois clichés," meant to corrupt language and what passes for smarts. (Help!, 1965) A true *femme fatale* and member of the *noir* rational community, Maude's greatest mental acumen is with wo-manipulation of the male.

Throughout the film, The Dude is threatened with castration too many times. He dreams of the nihilists in red spandex wielding enormous pairs of scissors, giving lackluster chase to his johnson. Then of course is that horrible scene in the tub with the 'marmot'. But the dream of the spandex is loosely tied to Maude, as the color scheme relates back to her vivid painting in her studio. As if an omen, Maude suddenly turns up at his ransacked apartment, asking him to "love [her]." Again, Maude conflates image with meaning to get her results, as she invokes "love" to say "fuck."

Post-coitus, The Dude has a confrontation with Da Fino, a bumbling PI who confuses The Dude for a "dick," at which point The Dude loses some of his cool. This reverts The Dude's meaning down to only his johnson, which Maude can "remove" into her body, and manipulate with ease. However. Yes, The Dude is manipulated by Maude to help her conceive a child. Yes, she gets what she wants. Except, she's getting more than she bargained for. Effortlessly, The Dude may subvert her plans *and* her image: the Lebowski name and her feigned image as mother. She seeks to have a child without any input from the father so that, perhaps, she may condition it to be in her image. Genetically, this is impossible. Duder may be physically absent from the child's life, but in the genes it'd be a good bet to say he's a strong influence. True to form, as The Dude is inserted, literally, into the rational community, he provides an alternative to it. The Dude, already an affective citizen, affects *again*, into the rational community, to create even more alternatives. This johnson aggression will not stand, Man. Duder will not just be castrated and sucked into the swamp. He'll undermine it without even realizing it

It seems that The Dude, not even consciously, is a radical subversive to the overpowering corruption and false nature of his surroundings. He is often threatened with castration that never materializes. He is assumed as a "loser," a perfect patsy bagman for Big L and Bunny; yet he deduces what's really happening and quickly. In contrast to his *noir* forefather Philip Marlowe who "leaves his opponents speechless by virtuoso verbal performance," (Raczkowski 113) The Dude slips into "bewildered silence" (115) in the face of opposition. This is not due to stupidity or weakness; it is more as a result of his "constitutional disability or disinterest in the rational community; such a community could never coordinate The Dude's pacifism with Walter's angry nationalism and Donny's obtuse silence." (122) In serving the stereotype of the male *noir* protagonist, The Dude does become embroiled in the crime of the evil as a bagman. Yet, the entire endeavor he suspects something more is going on and does not completely resign himself to the "facts."

As El Duderino dodges and moseys through L.A., his name is a constant issue. Is he or isn't he one of *those* Lebowskis? Is he *the* Jeffrey Lebowski? Well, he's *a* Jeffrey Lebowski, but he's *The* Dude. Unlike the doppelganger Lebowskis of L.A. who cling desperately to their name for all it means to the world and can provide them, Dude has fashioned his own identity. A recurring theme again creeps up – choice. Where the image of "Lebowski" is quite valuable materially to Maude, Jeffrey, even Bunny; the actual name is hollow for The Dude. When the name "Jeffrey" or "Mr. Lebowski" is put back on Duder, he reflexes instantly and corrects. When they try to put the name Lebowski back on The Dude, "Jeffrey" – Maude, "Mr. Lebowski" – The Big Lebowski, The Dude bristles each time and corrects it immediately in one of his most articulate moments with a member of the rational community:

> Let me explain something to you. Um. I am not Mr. Lebowski, you're Mr. Lebowski! I'm The Dude, so, uh, that's what you call me, ya know? Uh, that or, uh, his Dudeness, or uh, Duder, or uh, El Duderino if you're not into the whole brevity thing.

The Dude makes clear this authenticity whenever it is called into question. Should that not suffice, he provides choice via nicknames. Throughout the film, Dude crafts options out of the situations given to him, rather than settle on inevitability. This proves useful in his battle against radical evil.

On that note, let's foray into radical evil territory. Bert Olivier argues that evil in film noir can be radical, not only diabolical. The radical facet allows The Dude choice. It is not guaranteed that he will make the right choice in resisting, but it gives that alternative. (Olivier 128) Radical evil: "one that acknowledges the 'reality' of evil, while simultaneously contending that it is through human agency, through actual decisions and consequent actions that could have turned out otherwise, that evil enters the world … the claim that there is indeed an innate tendency towards evil in humans which, while ineradicable – because it is radical evil … is resistible. It is the outcome of specific choices and decisions." (126) This brand of evil rings more true as noir over its diabolical cousin, because it makes for a more critical film. (Olivier 129) Olivier continues that the Coen's evil in LA's rational community is radical, not diabolical, so The Dude is allowed the option to escape if he can. It provides a "… ray of hope … for being able to speak meaningfully about human morality … allowing for the possibility that humans can retain their capacity for choice." (Olivier 131) This quality of the film accounts for *The Big Lebowski's* capacity to be noir, and simultaneously a parody of the genre. In plot points typically tangential and meandering, the Coens can infuse the ridiculousness with humor while retaining convention. Clever, these brothers.

One may question then, the validity of *The Big Lebowski* being included as a *film noir* at all. Even the Coen Brothers argue that The Dude is 'trapped,' or a 'prisoner'; not free to transcend the noir themes encompassing modern society. (Singer 1) The bowling alley is not as utopian as it may seem – what with The Jesus being a pederast, Walter being able to freely wave a gun around. I beg to differ: The Dude is not trapped, he picks his battles. He carries out this protesting of rational community in a social space where he feels safe, he contributes, and his awareness is reciprocated by others. (Raczkowski 119) As a subculture member, he can continue to abide, continue to have integrity, and avoid the ugliness of the rational community he cannot stomach.

While The Dude is able to trump the downward spiral of noir, which places the film more in comedy than drama, it is nonetheless, as Olivier suggests, a "critical film … *films noirs* are critical films, because of their implicit (and sometimes explicit) questioning of the coherence and Cartesian transparency of the self, of the conventional view of society (as represented by its various institutions), and of our coherent and continuous sense of time and space." (Olivier, 123)

The character that stands for this point, even more than The Dude himself, is The Stranger. Similarly, he has a unique name for himself. Similarly, his doctrines fall without the norm of rational community. He provides the aspect of the mythical – blowing in and out of scene at will, having a diegetically unexplained, yet utterly natural rapport with The Dude, and with his cowboy image, representing an authenticity from the past, unique and out of place in LA. That he is the teller of The Dude's story bestows upon it a divine nod, placing The Dude and his "style" above the material, and thusly base, style of the rational community.

The *noir* trait of the voiceover is utilized well in *The Big Lebowski*, if not slightly askew. In that The Stranger provides voiceover, rather than The Dude "cornily" providing his own, he advances the theme of choice inherent in The Dude. (Singer 3) If *The Big Lebowski* followed *Sunset Blvd.'s* example, a pall would be cast over the film, trapping the narrative, creating claustrophobia in which escape would be less possible. However, The Stranger delivers the tale of The Dude, which transforms it from confession or warning, into something more like a parable. Along with the tie to nature at the opening credits of the film, following the tumbleweed through the town, and later when Donny's ashes are scattered into a mask upon The Dude's face, there is a signal to the viewer to associate with the authentic over the material.

Speaking of Donny … following his death, The Dude may finally quit his excursion into the rational community and as follows in *noir*, commit a return of a kind. Happily, The Dude is allowed to return to his space of comfort and logic – the bowling alley. This is a departure from Jack Gittes in *Chinatown*, or to Phyllis for Walter Neff in *Double Indemnity*. Once he does so, The Stranger reappears for a final check-in with Duder and the state of the film itself. While he "did not like seeing Donny go," he counters his own disappointment with hope, that of a Little Lebowski potentially in the wings. This is the final corruption of typical *noir* corruption, perpetrated by the Coen Brothers. The Dude is not only able to transcend the inevitability of death and futility of life, he disseminates life.

By the end of the film The Dude appears to be very much in the same space, but is not in the same place. Despite his sojourn to the *noir* city, The Dude is associated with natural elements unhindered by regulation or decorum, on a path that seems aimless to outsiders, but for himself has purpose. As Marc Singer notes, the Coens' version of Philip Marlowe's "knightly manhood" in The Dude is "a mockery." He doesn't follow the common *noir* protagonist's/detective's code of ethics, but does have an ethic, and is therefore right for the place and time in which he finds himself. (Singer 3)

> Sometimes there's a man, I won't say a hero, cuz what's a hero… but sometimes there's a man, and I'm talking about The Dude here, sometimes there's a man, well, he's the man for his time and place. He fits right in there. and that's The Dude, in Los Angeles. And even if he's a lazy man, and The Dude was most certainly that, quite possibly the laziest in L.A. County, which would place him high in the running for laziest worldwide. But sometimes there's a man… Sometimes, there's a man. Aw, lost my train of thought here. But, aw hell. I done introduced him enough.

....

Kate Carsella:
Last Known Location: Glen Ellyn, IL
Education: Knox College graduate
Employer: Helen M Plum Memorial Library, Lombard, IL
Known Aliases: Katie, Kitten, The Kitten, Kit Kat, Kit Kat Katie Car, Betty
A Favorite Book: Geek Love by Katherine Dunn
Last Words: Vagina.

Works Cited

Spicer, Andrew. "Neo-Noir 2: Postmodern Film Noir." *Film Noir*. Harlow, England: Longman, 2002. 149-51. Print.

Raczkowski, Christopher. "Metonymic Hats and Metaphoric Tumbleweeds: Noir Literary Aesthetics in Miller's Crossing and *The Big Lebowski*." *The Year's Work in Lebowski Studies* (2009): 98-123. Indiana University Press. Web.

Singer, Marc. "'Trapped by Their Pasts': Noir and Nostalgia in *The Big Lebowski*." *PostScript: Essays in Film and the Humanities* 27.2 (2008): 1-16.

Olivier, Bert. "The Logic of Noir and the Question of Radical Evil." *Film and Philosophy* 8. (2004): 122-137

The Big Lebowski. Dir. Joel Coen. Perf. Jeff Bridges, Julianne Moore, John Goodman and Steve Buscemi. Polygram Filmed Entertainment, 1998.

Help! Dir. Richard Lester. Perf. George Harrison, Ringo Starr, John Lennon and Paul McCartney. Walter Shenson Films, 1965.

Sunset Blvd. Dir. Billy Wilder. Perf. William Holden and Gloria Swanson. Paramount Pictures, 1950.

Double Indemnity. Dir. Billy Wilder. Perf. Barbara Stanwyck and Fred MacMurray. Paramount Pictures, 1944.

The Big Sleep. Dir. Howard Hawks. Perf. Lauren Bacall and Humphrey Bogart. Warner Bros., 1946.

The Maltese Falcon. Dir. John Huston. Perf. Humphrey Bogart and Mary Astor. Warner Bros., 1941.

Enron: The Smartest Guys in the Room. Dir. Alex Gibney. Perf. Bethany McLean and Peter Elkind. Magnolia Pictures, 2005.

Hyndira Borba, *Your Dudeness*

A Dude's Guide to Emergency Management: Incorporating *The Big Lebowski* Into Community Resilience

BY DANIEL NEELY

"Abide," such an important word to fans of *The Big Lebowski*, affords several different meanings. One is: "To endure, sustain, or withstand without yielding or submitting." In the world of emergency management, the preferred nomenclature for this notion is *resilience*. The aim is to develop resilient infrastructure, resilient economies and importantly, resilient communities that prepare for, respond to and recover well from an emergency event.

The dictionary defines resilience as "an ability to recover from or adjust easily to misfortune or change." Like many complex sociological matters, difficult to digest for the average fella, *The Big Lebowski* serves as an elegant metaphor for resilience and how we might engage and empower communities to be better prepared for a natural or man-made disaster. The story's subtle highlighting of adaptability in the face of uncertainty and the importance of personal relationships are in line with the most up-to-date academic thinking in this field. From the emergency management point of view, community resilience really ties the movie together.

Strong men also cry. However, strong networks facilitate positive outcomes for communities before, during and after a tearjerking event. *The Big Lebowski* provides numerous examples of almost impossibly aligned individuals linked together in some incongruous way. Yet despite the superficially ill-matched friendships and partnerships, challenges are met, competitors are bested, and obstacles are overcome.

There is a stupefyin' expression for this concept that some academics from fancy schools came up with awhile back – *social capital*. Many protracted and meandering definitions exist to describe this term like, "the sum of the actual and potential resources embedded within, available through, and derived from the network of relationships possessed by an individual or social unit. Social capital thus comprises both the network and the assets that may be mobilized through that network" or "features of social organization such as networks, norms, and social trust that facilitate coordination and cooperation for mutual benefit." There are plenty more long-winded explanations, and one can easily lose their train of thought trying to determine what in God's holy name they're blathering about.

For us amateurs, it simply means being able to count on your friends in hard times. It might be as simple as having your ex watch your Pomeranian while you vacation in Hawaii. Or, it could be as important as bearing the responsibility of committing your friend's mortal remains to the bosom of the Pacific Ocean in some meaningful way. In short, sometimes you eat the bar, and sometimes the bar eats you. When confronted with the latter, it's crucial to have your friends nearby.

This is what we know, ya know ... A high level of social capital is one of the best pre-determinants for how well a community will respond to and recover from a natural or man-made disaster. Imagine your pal is in a bind and for some inexplicable reason, needs to obtain a human toe by 3 o'clock that afternoon. Among those that can effectively pool resources and trade information, this seemingly improbable task requires less effort that one might think, at least according to those with the necessary means for a necessary means. With the right person at your side it may even be possible to obtain a toe with a specific shade of nail polish. Basically, when the metaphorical plane crashes into the mountain, social capital held between compeers, lady friends, people with disabilities and urban achievers, among others, improves adaptive capacity as well as access to valuable information.

It's like Lennon said, we've gotta help keep the mindsets of our communities limber so that, when disasters like Hurricane Katrina or Sandy occur, people and organizations can adapt and thrive in their new surroundings. Emergency managers must engage with all walks of life to assist communities with preparedness activities in ways that are appropriate to that community's ethos or level of interest. To a degree, the needs of a quiet little beach community will differ from those of a family in North Hollywood near the In-N-Out Burger, or a group of loosely connected patrons of a family restaurant.

Sadly, being prepared, whatever the price, will resonate only with a small minority while too many will take a more nihilistic approach to having household emergency plan or even establishing relationships with their neighbors. Unfortunately these people don't care about anything, least of all the possibility of how they could be impacted by even a small scale disaster. Regardless, emergency managers have an obligation to try to engage and work with the whole durn human community to improve their resilience.

Despite the challenges, we can't drag a negative attitude into the tournament. The "scare 'em into preparedness" approach, promulgating Armageddon scenarios that are darker'n a black steer's tookus on a moonless prairie night doesn't work. That kind of unchecked aggression actually turns most people away from the simple preparedness steps and conversations they should have within their household. It's verrry un-Dude. We've gotta keep the messages positive and simple and encourage communities to own their preparedness and look after one another. We've got to take it easy, man. And, uh, *make* it easy to help people get prepared and connect with their neighbors.

Promoting a one-size-fits-all resilience model is fatuous. The various professional sectors involved with resilience must develop a range of activities that support varying levels of interest and engagement by diverse individuals, organizations and communities. Most initiatives should be community-driven where possible, even if most of the public's thinking about this can become very uptight. We must convince people to see themselves not just as "I" but "We." The Royal We.

This isn't 'Nam. This is community development, there are rules. If community planning gets too complex, there's always something that can go wrong. That wrong turn often occurs at the outset because those leading the project have not spent adequate (or any) time listening to the community they are trying to assist. It used to be that if you were an emergency manager, they gave you a beeper and a promise to call with instructions if the whole world decided to go crazy. Now it's clear that, if we're not listening to communities from the outset, we have no frame of reference in which to facilitate resilience or recovery. If we take the time to listen occasionally, we might learn something.

We can't solve your problems, sirs, only you can. One of the first steps is determining the issue a community is trying to solve. Before the facilitators down at the resilience office develop a list of any pre-defined solutions, they must first listen to and work with the community to determine what resources – physical and social – are available in their backyards and across their own networks. Then, they encourage their ideas and develop appropriate solutions based on their interests and needs. Granted, some ideas are like a child who wanders into the middle of a movie, and so require frames of reference and guidance. Perhaps most important is to remember to take 'er easy, maintain professional courtesy with the compeers. A far-out emergency manager must take the time to engage, listen and support those local networks, so their style will be dug and their notes will be taken with joy.

Throughout the process, there will always be a mix of strikes and gutters, ups and downs, and a lotta ins, outs, and what-have-yous that need to be considered along the way. In the end, when the process is community-driven, there is a much higher likelihood of the outcome being appropriate for and ultimately owned proudly by that community. If they will it, it is no dream. It's their roll. We're just here to help them make it to the finals.

....

Daniel Neely is the Manager of Community Resilience for the Wellington Region Emergency Management Office in New Zealand. He's a native of the Sonoran Desert, a former Peace Corps Volunteer and takes comfort in assisting communities to be better prepared and connected with one another. Between league games, he makes the occasional attempt to create a website for ideas that build adaptive and resilient communities at www.ideaptive.com

Alex Ruiz, *Woo*

A Psychological Analysis of Personality: "The Dude" in *The Big Lebowski*

BY JAMES KERR

Contained is a personality analysis of the character, The Dude from the film *The Big Lebowski* (Coen & Coen, 1998). The various aspects of The Dude's personality are addressed using psychoanalytic perspective, behaviorist perspective, a cognitive perspective and trait perspective. The Meyers-Briggs, Big Five and P-type personality surveys are conducted by James Kerr on the fictional character of The Dude.

To our knowledge, a psychological profile of Jeffery Lebowski (The Dude) has not been attempted before. This report will probe the personality of The Dude from the film *The Big Lebowski*. The Dude will be analyzed from a psychoanalytic perspective, a behaviorist perspective, a cognitive perspective and trait perspective. The report will conclude by discussing The Dudes personality as a whole and answer what impels so many to admire and sympathize with this character.

Psychoanalytic Perspective

It is fair to say The Dude lives very much in the present moment (his conscious mind). There are two aspects of his personality that encourage this, one is his laid back philosophy towards life and the other is his chronic smoking of marijuana. The Dude has limited access or use for his preconscious or available memory (Boeree, 2009). The Dude routinely has troubles retrieving memories and maintaining his train of thought. It is possible that this is a side effect of "adhering to a strict drug regimen" in order to prevent his thinking from getting "uptight."

The Dude operates primarily within the structures of the id and the ego. His desires are to bowl, to get high and to have his rug replaced. Each one of these id[1]-based desires are derived from the pleasure principle[2]: bowling relieves his boredom, getting high allows him to avoid unpleasant realities, and getting a new rug creates order in his home because as The Dude says, "that rug really tied the room together" (Friedman and Schustack, 2009).

The reality principle[3] takes form when The Dude needs to reconcile is id desires with the real world ego implications. The Dude unabashedly seeks reality-principle satisfaction. After his rug is soiled he does not hesitate to seek The Big Lebowski and demand compensation for his rug. The Dude is not put off by superego concerns such as class or wealth. He feels completely entitled as he saunters into the mansion based on conscious needs and principles. He is genuinely surprised when the other Lebowski refuses to replace the rug. The Dude says, "Come on, man, I am not trying to scam any one here." In The Dude's world his sound argument should be enough as he has little regard for (or awareness of) superego-based societal concerns.

After he is berated, accused of "looking for a handout", and called a "loser" and a "bum" he leaves the meeting and immediate lies to The Big Lebowski's assistant, saying "the old man said take any rug in the house." The Dude is not swayed by societal rules or norms. He is a complete non-conformist with a disregard for status and authority.

Psychosexually The Dude appears fixated in the oral stage. As Boeree asserts people with oral fixations, "often retain an interest in "oral gratifications" such as eating, drinking, and smoking" (Boeree, 2009). The Dude is overweight and rarely seen in the film without a drink (White Russian or Miller beer) or joint in his mouth. There is no information offered as to his upbringing or how his relationship with his mother factors in to this fixation. Friedman and Schustack (2009) suggest that the oral stage is place of security and pleasure were an individual must mature from in order to progress to the next stage. They write that individuals fixated at the oral stage may, "remain preoccupied with issues of dependency, attachment, and "intake" of interesting substances and perhaps even interesting ideas" (2009, p.

---

[1] The id, one of the three parts of consciousness in Freudian psychology, represents basic urges and desires. The others are the ego and the superego. The ego is the primary sense of self, driven by the id and governed by the superego which provides a sense of conscience or responsibility to others.

[2] The basic driving force of the id: to seek pleasure and avoid pain.

[3] Governed by the ego, the reality principle is employed to contend with the fact that we cannot always fulfill our immediate desires.

78). While the film does not offer any information in regards to The Dude's personality development in childhood there are two dream sequences which offer significant insight to his subconscious thoughts.

In the first dream sequence The Dude is flying over Los Angeles. This is an enjoyable experience for him. In the distance Maude Lebowski (daughter of The Big Lebowski) is flying away on The Dude's recently stolen carpet. The Dude pursues by doing a breast-stroke maneuver while flying. As The Dude is gaining upon her he soon discovers a bowling ball in his outstretched hand. The bowling ball causes him to plummet unpleasantly towards the ground. Next he finds himself as a miniature version of himself with a bowling ball rolling towards him. The Dude is rolled upon by the ball but instead of being crushed, he fortuitously enters one of the finger-holes of the bowling ball and is rolled inside the ball down the lane into a set of awaiting pins. We see through the rotating ball that Maude is the one who set the ball on its trajectory.

There are many psychoanalytic symbolic meanings within this dream. According to Freud flying in dreams symbolizes sexual excitement (Perron, 2008). This theory would hold true as The Dude does seem happy at this point in the dream and he does eventually have sex with Maude Lebowski. The recurring images of the bowling ball are symbolically interpreted by Joel Harker (2008):

> The act of bowling is an adapted symbol which I will take to be representative of the Myth of Sisyphus. Sisyphus tragic Greek hero who is damned to endlessly toil by repeatedly pushing a rock up a hill (and when it reaches the top, it rolls back down and he must start all over again)…as the bowling ball is to The Dude, thus is the epistemic rock to Sisyphus. This ceaseless labor is a metaphor for the absurd repetition and meaninglessness of everyday life.

Bowling as a symbol of the epistemic rock of Sisyphus fits well with what may be the subconscious (superego) thoughts of The Dude. The Dude's life is repetitive and meaningless, especially when viewed by an upper-class individual like Maude Lebowski. The Dude may be able to subconsciously fantasize about having her but despite his conscious refusal of authority and class structure, his superego understands these realities place her beyond his grasp. In the dream The Dude is hurtled back to earth by the weight of the bowling ball. Bowling is representative of his endless toil – his repetitive, unemployed, lower class lot in life.

The second dream sequence starts with Dude represented as a strong male. He is a cable TV repairman with magical gold and silver bowling shoes (the repairman being alluded to earlier in the film as a sex symbol in a porn film). He walks down a large staircase to meet with Maude Lebowski. She is symbolized as a Valkyrie; wearing a golden helmet with horns, holding a golden trident and wearing a dress with two golden bowling balls covering her breasts. The Dude again appears with a bowling ball, this time it is bright red. He holds it with strength and pride teaching Maude how to bowl. He then finds himself floating down the bowling lane between the legs of many women. Once he reaches the end of the lane he finds he is being chased by three German Nihilists in red spandex suits carrying enormous pairs of scissors.

Similar to the first dream sequence, this dream taps into the subconscious sexual desires The Dude harbors for Maude Lebowski. He travels down a tall staircase, also a Freudian symbol of sexual excitement (Perron, 2008). Through his control of the red bowling ball he metaphorically represents Mars, the god of war and a symbol of masculinity (universetoday, 2008). Maude is also a symbol of strength, though a female one represented by the Valkyrie (a Norse warrior goddess). The Dude must calmly pair with his mythological counterpart to attain his goals. Note that in reality, Maude has hired him to find out what happened to one million dollars in ransom money, offering him ten percent if he locates the money. In the end the Maude and Dude do "pool their resources" to figure out the missing clue that allows The Dude to solve the mystery of the missing money. Moreover, they also pool their genetic material, to give rise to a child. The Dude realizes both his sexual and intellectual goals in his union with the object of his desire.

Prior to his ultimate "achievement," sexual anxiety appears repeatedly to haunt The Dude. The image of the nihilists with scissors is a classic sign of one of Freud's more well-known complexes: castration anxiety. There are many instances where The Dude is consciously threatened with castration throughout the film. As Walter Kirn writes in Rolling Stone Magazine (2008):

> This phallic triumphalism spooks The Dude. Fears of castration assault his porous psyche like armies of chattering, wind-up, joke-shop teeth. A hungry ferret is tossed into his bubble bath. A fumbled joint nearly incinerates his pants. Mimes with gigantic scissors invade his dreams. In the meantime, Lebowski's performance-artist daughter, Maude, is plotting to discard him like a turkey baster once she's managed to water her parched womb with his precious bodily fluids. And then, of course, there are all the toppling bowling pins, scourging The Dude's subconscious with every strike.

Kirn points out factors that contribute to The Dude's fear of castration, and ultimately, fear of death. Subconsciously the dream is telling The Dude that his pleasure principle and reality principle have collided. He can only fantasize so long before his id and ego are overruled by his superego. Through various conscious and subconscious signs he is being warned that he may be castrated before he has attained his unconscious desire – to partner sexually with Maude Lebowski. Moreover, both dream sequences end with Dude being taken beyond his control to the end of the bowling lane. In the first dream he travels to the end of the lane alone, in the second he connects with Maude and throws the ball towards the pins together with her, but then his ego puts himself in place of the ball and Maude is replaced with a bevy of split-crotched chorines; the result of this impulsive betrayal is that he is cast into the dark void alone and at the mercy of the castrating Nihilists.

The Dude uses various coping mechanisms to aid his assaulted ego. As the dream sequences indicate The Dude is in a complex relationship with Maude Lebowski. He is in denial over his attraction to Maude not only because she is a threatening female, but because she poses a threat to his uncommitted youthfulness[4]. Maude is a feminist artist and a very opinionated, driven and outwardly sexual individual, as opposed to the lazy, unopinionated Dude who may be too indolent to actively pursue sexual relationships.

The first two encounters with Maude take place at her studio, where The Dude finds himself surrounded by images of female strength and paintings of giant scissors. Jean Cournut writes of how castration anxiety can be caused via contact with women, explaining how Freud's book, *The Taboo of Virginity* "deals explicitly with the castration anxiety precipitated in men by contact with women, universally recognized as a danger to male sexuality, that is to say, as always potentially castrating." (2008) It could be argued that The Dude is sublimating such dangerous sexual desires by engaging in uncharacteristically risky behavior in order to solve the case of the missing wife and the missing ransom money (Friedman and Schustack, 2009).

At the end of the film The Dude has returned to his original state, displaying the same oral fixation (his last act is to order beer at the bar), but with the satisfaction of having achieved his sexual goals, overcome castration anxiety, and dismantled any lingering concerns of the superego about his status in society.

Behavioral Perspective

From a behavioral perspective The Dude has learned a variety of responses in order to deal with daily life. Classical conditioning, operant conditioning and social learning would all serve to explain how The Dude's actions are learned responses to his environment. In The Dude's case the avoidance of many regular responsibilities (work, family, rent) can be explained as operant conditioning according to Skinner (Friedman and Schustack, 2009). If The Dude has had negative experiences in the past with such behaviors he will avoid them (Friedman and Schustack, 2009).

As a member of the hippie generation The Dude learned to not trust government, authority and the "square community." His lack of cultural conditioning might suggest that he has personally avoided such systemization, however, an ardent behaviorist might claim that either his earlier conditioning has been so strongly imprinted that natural extinction has not occurred, or that such behaviors have been reinforced throughout his life.

Behaviorists would also point out The Dude's dependency on drugs and alcohol. While The Dude demonstrates no withdrawal or craving symptoms during the film it can be assumed, based on the prevalence of his consumption, that he experiences compensatory responses (J. Dyce, personal communication, August 4, 2009). This concept suggests that as The Dude is exposed to triggers (bowling, relaxing at home) he will have increased cravings for marijuana or alcohol in accordance with the severity of the situation. Since The Dude consumes drugs and alcohol throughout the film, in times both of repose and of stress, the data is insufficient to generate a hypothesis.

Cognitive Perspective

The Personality type The Dude would most closely resemble would be the *Adventurous personality type* (J. Dyce, personal communication, August 4, 2009). Based on the work of Horney and Niebuhr, Dr. John Oldham (2008) expands on what it means to be an Adventurous P-type. Oldham lists eight categories that make up the Adventurous type: Nonconformity, Challenge, Mutual independence, Persuasiveness, Wanderlust, Wild oats, True grit, and No regrets (2008). In the interest of being succinct I will touch on the aspects of The Dude's personality that are represented in this theory but not recognized in other personality aspect theories.

Challenge at first does not seem to align with The Dude's personality. However, he was very daring and adventurous when he was an activist. The Dude is up for a challenge as is evident in his actions throughout the film. It appears that he has just become more selective (read: lazy) in his choice of causes.

Oldham (2008) describes Mutual independence in terms of people who "do not worry too much about others, for they expect each human being to be responsible for him- or herself." This is evident in the relationships the in which The Dude finds himself. His best friend is a Vietnam War vet and his "lady-friend" is a radical feminist: the beliefs of neither seem to concern The Dude so long as they do not aggress upon his own freedom to believe and live as he chooses.

When Persuasiveness proves an ineffective tool, The Dude's employs True grit instead. Despite his numerous attempts at persuasion The Dude is rarely successful because of his demeanor and appearance. He gets little respect throughout the film – for example, the police chief of Malibu refers to him as "some kind of sad-assed refugee from the fucking sixties."[5]

Oldham defines True grit as being, "courageous, physically bold, and tough. They will stand up to anyone who dares to take advantage of them." (Oldham, 2008) Though an avowed pacifist, The Dude is not afraid to speak his mind in the face of an adversary. He is not afraid of standing up to The Big Lebowski despite the imbalance of resources and power between them. He shows complete lack of deference to the various people who assault him, from the Malibu police chief to Jackie

---

[4] What psychoanalyst and Carl Jung protégé Marie Von Franz termed "Puer aeternus" – eternal child.

[5] This appears in the original, published script, but not in the final cut of the film.

Treehorn's thugs to Maude and her assistants, to the Nihilists.

Oldham defines the No Regrets category as: "living in the present. They do not feel guilty about the past or anxious about the future. Life is meant to be experienced now." (2008) This philosophy is central to The Dude's character and a part of what makes him a far more complex and estimable character than the prototypical "burnt out hippie" often found in ordinary comedies.

The Dude's philosophy will be discussed further but can be introduced by citing one of two exchanges with a character named The Stranger. This character acts as narrator of the film and appears in two scenes. He has a sort of omnipotent quality about him and may be an allusion to Albert Camus' existentialist novel of the same name. Harker says of their final exchange at the end of the film: "The Dude equates to an American version of The Stranger's Meursault in the sense that he lives without responsibility, contemplation, or regret . . . The Dude is merely acted upon and made to react (2008). The Dude realizes that life will be full of "strikes and gutters" but none of this fazes him because he feels it is out of his control and moreover that none of it really matters in the end. Hence, "The Dude abides" by his own self-made code which transcends good or bad, regret or anxiety.

Trait Perspective

The Trait perspectives of the Meyers-Briggs 16 Personality types and The Big Five model of personality type offer additional understanding into the personality of The Dude. Both tests were (obviously) conducted by proxy and are based on my interpretation of the character in the film.

The Meyers-Briggs personality survey concludes that The Dude is an Idealist or INFP (Appendix B) (personalitycafe.com, 2006). The Big Five found that he is mid-range in the domains of Extroversion and Agreeableness, while more extreme in the domains of conscientiousness, neuroticism and openness (Appendix C) (outofservice, 2009).

The Meyers-Briggs survey seems to address the aspects of The Dude's morals more fully than the other perspectives considered here. It states the Idealist is not concerned with, "hard facts and logic . . . they don't understand or believe in the validity of impersonal judgment . . . under stress may obsess about details that are unimportant to the big picture . . . [and] brood over a problem repeatedly" (personalitycafe.com, 2006). This description explains how The Dude at one time can be focused and calm but under certain circumstances comes completely undone. During the unusual stress of making the ransom hand-off The Dude panics after the kidnappers hang-up on him. He screams, "Shit, Walter, you fuck, you fucked it up! You fucked it up! Her life was in our hands, man!" To which Walter replies, "Nothing is fucked here, Dude. Come on, you're being very un-Dude. They'll call back." Though Walter's reaction suggests that this sort of brooding and worry is generally uncharacteristic of The Dude, it offers an explanation for his frequent (if brief) panic attacks during the course of the movie.

A second example of this is when the ransom hand-off goes wrong The Dude obsesses repeating over and over "they're going to kill that poor woman." Again Walter attempts to console him saying, "really, Dude, you surprise me. They're not gonna kill shit. They're not gonna do shit. What can they do? Fuckin' amateurs. And meanwhile, look at the bottom line. Who's sitting on a million fucking dollars?" As ludicrous as this situation may be, it shows The Dude is again acting out of character as he is unable to focus on the big picture. Generally The Dude is a man of inaction; in his new, unfamiliar situation he must play the part of hero which at times is too stressful and too far a departure from his actual personality.

As mentioned previously, The Dude is not afraid to stand-up to authority when he feels that an injustice has occurred. The Idealist is, "very aware of social injustice, and empathizes with the underdog . . . they will feel most useful when they are fighting to help people who have been misfortunate in our society" (personalitycafe.com, 2006). Certainly The Dude had such a fight when in his younger years he was a part of the Seattle Seven and co-author of the Port Huron Statement. However, The Dude has become less outspoken and radical as he has aged. Often he is the underdog and must fight to be heard or even taken seriously.

A key trait of The Dude's personality is faith. While The Dude is certainly a non-conformist and in some ways a radical it does not mean he is without a belief system. The Idealist is said to be, "more spiritually aware than most people, and are more in touch with their soul than others . . . most have strong Faith" (personalitycafe.com, 2006). To pinpoint The Dude's faith is not a simple task as it is not explicitly stated in the film. The theory that most aligns with The Dude's faith and personality would be existentialism – particularly the "phenomenological view" of existentialism. (Friedman and Schustack, 2009) The phenomenological view is supported by both Jean-Paul Sartre and Albert Camus.

Sartre believed in "the responsibility of all individuals for their own decisions, [that] . . . we need to see ourselves as free actors in order to achieve authentic human existence" (Friedman and Schustack, 2009, p. 318). A copy of Sartre's book "Being and Nothingness" is even seen on The Dude's bedside table.

Friedman and Schustack (2009) remark that though Camus was "concerned with the fundamental absurdity of existence, [he] nevertheless saw value in the individual's having the courage to attempt to correct injustice" (p. 318). Again these phenomenological beliefs are exemplified through The Dude's actions and personality test results. Both The Dude's P-type and Meyer-Briggs code type support such psychological/philosophical diagnoses.

While The Dude does not strictly adhere to anything in life, a website called Dudeism.com is one of many forums linking The Dude to Eastern religion. These teachings align well with the phenomenological viewpoint. Oliver Benjamin, founder of Dudeism.com writes:

> The Dude's lifestyle and attitude neatly mirror that of several Asian sages, particularly Lao Tzu, the founder of Taoism. Taoism's basic outlook is that aggression only begets more aggression, and that one lives in harmony with the world only when they "go with the flow" and not try to achieve too much.

A prime example of The Dude going with the flow occurs during an interaction with his landlord. Martin "Marty" Randall, is an awkward man who clearly looks up to The Dude, begins the conversation by asking for The Dude's help. He says:

> **Marty:** Dude, I finally got the venue I wanted, I uh, I'm performing my dance quintet – you know, my cycle? – at Crane Jackson's Fountain Street Theater on Thursday night, and uh…I'd love it if you came and gave me notes."
> **The Dude:** "I'll be there, man."
> **Marty:** "Uh, Dude, Uh – tomorrow's already the 10th."
> **The Dude:** "Far out."
> (pause for Dude to understand) " . . ."
> **The Dude:** "Oh, oh, alright. Okay."
> **Marty:** "Just, uh, slip the rent under my door."

The Taoist teaching to "act without action" (Friedler, 2009, Chap.63) is demonstrated through this interaction. The Dude is not attempting to dodge the man, he is simply oblivious to regular concerns such as days of the week, deadlines or rent payments. Furthermore, it should be noted how The Dude is admired – for some reason Marty looks to The Dude as a creative advisor. Seeking The Dude's guidance is the main reason for the interaction; the rent is more of an extraneous formality, one that causes The Dude no embarrassment or anger.

When The Dude is interrogated by the police chief of Malibu, one again witnesses The Dude's non-materialistic nature. The only form of identification The Dude carries with him, in fact the only item in his wallet, is a Ralph's grocery store discount card. The *Tao Te Ching* by Lao Tzu reads, "sages do not accumulate." (Friedler, 2009, Chap.81)

The Dude is not without his inconstancies despite his existentialist tendencies and support relating to Taoist beliefs. His Big Five profile ranks him in the 1st percentile of neuroticism. There would appear to be some discrepancy between The Dude being so low in neuroticism and his several outbursts during the film, however one could assert that it is the strange situations The Dude is placed in which challenges his inner peace. When The Dude decides to take action he strays from his Zen like middle-path and disharmony ensues. Benjamin (2009) observes, "when steered from his accustomed course by his friend Walter . . . his life falls into shambles . . . [then] he finds his "center" once more, offering the meditative-sounding mantra: "The Dude Abides." The Dude's decision to take action is the impetus of the film. Through the course of these actions The Dude's conditioning, personality and patience are challenged.

As has already been established, The Dude feels compelled to fight for the underdog and stand up for injustice. While Walter is an accomplice to many of The Dude's bad decisions The Dude makes his own choices and is responsible for his own actions. The Dude demonstrates growth through the course of the film. As Ralph Waldo Emerson states:

> It is easy in the world to live after the world's opinion; it is easy in solitude to live after our own; but the great man is he who in the midst of the crowd keeps with perfect sweetness the independence of solitude" (1942, p.36).

This is The Dude's challenge throughout the film – to be thrust back into a society that he has long ago rejected, and still remain true to himself. His journey is not without its stumbles, but in the end he is a stronger man for it. As The Dude reflects with Maude Lebowski's limo driver after losing the million dollar ransom:

> **Dude:** I was feeling really shitty earlier in the day, I'd lost a little money, I was down in the dumps.
> **Tony:** Aw, forget about it.
> **Dude:** Yeah, man! Fuck it! I can't be worrying about that shit. Life goes on!

Throughout the film, that world he long ago rejected conspires to pull him away from his gentle, unworried nature, and every time he proves his integrity and inner-strength by finding his way back to his established identity without a superabundance of effort or protracted search. For those seeking self-actualization themselves, there is much in this to admire.

Discussion

A cult following has developed since the release of this film in 1996. Since 2002 Lebowski fests have been held and what started as one random event with 150 participants has now grown into a multi-city festival (15 cities in 2009) with thousands of loyal attendees (Lebowskifest.com, 2009). What draws individual's to this film and The Dude?

The Dude represents a perfectly imperfect individual. An individual that is confident and content with himself. The Dude does not judge himself or others. He is at peace with both his capabilities and limitations. Good enough is good enough for The Dude.

One may say that The Dude is someone that everyone can relate to – an everyman, but this may not be true. In preparing this report I felt a kinship with The Dude but have come to realize that in terms of personality we are polar opposites. There are few out there who could handle the detachment, the hedonism, the apparent meaninglessness of The Dude's life; yet what may be attractive is the chance to witness a man so unapologetic and comfortable with himself, free from quotidian concerns or the need to prove anything to himself or anyone else.

The film begins by asking the question whether The Dude is a hero? This question is not answered directly because to do so would not being in keeping with the existential candor of the film. The Dude may not be a hero, but neither is he a loser, or a useless pot-head – The Dude simply is, or rather "abides." As the Stranger remarks, "Sometimes, there's a man, well, he's the man for his time and place. He fits right in there. And that's The Dude." Perhaps The Dude is the man for his time and place because he is immune to the specific dictates of any particular time and place. Perhaps he is a man for all times and all places.

....

James Kerr is a Registered Clinical Counselor from Victoria, British Columbia with an M.A. in Clinical Psychology. He currently runs a private practice: "A Counselor *for* Cannabis Users."

References:

Boeree, G. C. (2009). Personality theories: Sigmund Freud. Retrieved August 10, 2009 from http://webspace.ship.edu/cgboer/freud.html

Coen, E. (Writer/Director), & Coen, J (Writer/Director). (1998). *The Big Lebowski*. [Motion Picture]. United States: Universal Studios.

Cournut, J.(2009) International dictionary of psychoanalysis: Castration-complex. Retrieved
August 10, 2009. From:
http://www.enotes.com/psychoanalysis-encyclopedia/castration-complex

Emerson, R. (1952). The Works of Emerson. London: Tudor Publishing Co.

Friedler, R. (2009). thetao.info: All about the Tao Te Ching. Retrieved August 12, 2009, from http://www.thetao.info/english/english.htm

Friedman, H. S., & Schustack, M. W. (2009). Personality: Classic theories and modern research (4th ed.). Boston: Pearson Higher Education.

Harker, J. (2008). Literary cultural theory. Retrieved August 8, 2009, from
http://literaryculturaltheory.blogspot.com/2008/02/philosophy-of-absurd-in-big-lebowski.html

J. Dyce, personal communication, August 4, 2009.

Kirn, W. (2008, September 4). A Hero for Our Time. Rolling Stone, pp. 41. Retrieved August
10, 2009, from Academic Search Premier database.

Oldham, J. (2009). P-types: Adventurous personality type. Retrieved August 12, 2009, from
http://www.ptypes.com/adventurous.html

Lebowskifest. (2009). Retrieved August 12, 2009, from http://www.lebowskifest.com/default.asp

Outofservice. (n.d.). The Big Five personality test. Retrieved August 4, 2009, from http ://www. outofservice.com/bigfive/results/?oR=0.85&cR=0.222&eR=0.531&aR=0.639&nR=0.062&y=1960&g=m

Perron, R. (2008). International dictionary of psychoanalysis: Dream symbolism. Retrieved
August 4, 2009, from http://www.enotes.com/psychoanalysis-encyclopedia
dream-symbolism

Universetoday. (2009). Symbol for mars. Retrieved August 12, 2009, from http://www.universetoday.com/guide-to-space/mars/symbol-for-mars/

Personality Café: www.personalitycafe.com

Appendix A

Personality test for "The Dude" taken by James Kerr:

Your type is: INFP: Introverted (I) 62.07%, Extroverted (E) 37.93% Intuitive (N) 68.57%, Sensing (S) 31.43%, Feeling 51.72%, Thinking (T) 48.28%, Perceiving (P) 85.71%, Judging (J) 14.29%

Appendix B

The Dude's Big Five Profile taken by James Kerr:

Extroversion 42th percentile, Agreeableness 44th percentile, Conscientiousness 2th percentile, Neuroticism 1.

Johnee Fullerton, *The Lebowski Mortuary*

Spencer Nobles, *Whaddya Need That For, Dude?*

The Importance of Living:
Lin Yutang Meets The Dude

BY GUIDO MINA DI SOSPIRO

There are a few works out there like *The Big Lebowski*, be they novels, movies or even pieces of music, that manage to make the esoteric, exoteric. Such works rarely surface, though, because the shallow machinery of the publishing, movie and music industry is mostly allergic to them. Another is Lin Yutang's masterwork, *The Importance of Living*. As I was re-reading it, I found so many passages that seem custom-made for The Dude that I thought it might be fun to explore the points of departure and arrival of both works, in tandem.

Lin Yutang offers an approach that goes beyond life-renouncing religions, daring transcendental explorations, and clichés such as "enjoy yourself, it's later than you think." One thing was clear to him as it must be to so many of us: being alive, living, matters. The Austrian poet Rainer Maria Rilke suggests why in the ninth of his *Duino Elegies*, written between 1912 and 1922, and excerpted here in the translation of A. Poulin, Jr. To the question, "Why, then, do we have to be human and, avoiding fate, long for fate?" the poet replies: "Because being here means so much, and because all / that's here, vanishing so quickly, seems to need us / and strangely concerns us." And a few lines down: "To have been on *earth* just once – that's irrevocable."

How are we to celebrate, then, the plain yet miraculous reality of being alive? The poet surprises with "Praise the world to the angel, not what can't be talked about. / You can't impress him with your grand emotions. In the cosmos / where he so intensely feels, you're just a novice. So show / him some simple thing shaped for generation after generation / until it lives in our hands and in our eyes, and it's ours. Tell him about things. He'll stand amazed (. . .)"

So there it is, straight from the pen of one of the most mystical poets in western literature: an exhortation to speak to the angel not about grand emotions but about the world, about *things*. Some years after Rilke finished his elegies, Lin Yutang wrote in *The Importance of Living*: "As for philosophy, which is the exercise of the spirit *par excellence*, the danger is even greater that we lose the feeling of life itself. I can understand that such mental delights include the solution of a long mathematical equation, or the perception of a grand order in the universe. This perception of order is probably the purest of all our mental pleasures and yet I would exchange it for a well prepared meal." Years ago, when I first read this passage, I laughed out loud. It was liberating. But where is Lin Yutang coming from? In another book of his, *The Wisdom of China*, he remarks: "The Chinese philosopher is like a swimmer who dives but must soon come up to the surface again; the Western philosopher is like a swimmer who dives into the water and is proud that he never comes up to the surface again."

I'd tend to agree, but there probably is a linguistic reason for this. The Chinese never developed a proper alphabet, but rather ideograms, or Sinograms, or better yet, Han characters. The Kangxi Dictionary contains the astonishing number of 47,035 characters. Compared to the 24 letters of the Greek alphabet, the 23 of Classical Latin and the 30 of the German alphabet, it's evident that writing and reading in Mandarin is an effort in itself, which explains the emphasis placed by Chinese on calligraphy.

Ancient Greek, Latin and German have been used by most of the greatest philosophers of the western tradition, with Latin being the lingua franca of European scholars for centuries. Inevitably, intellectuals would be tempted to play around with words – and they did! Western philosophy is immensely more voluminous than its Chinese counterpart, but its value should always have been considered from an historical perspective. No one in his right mind should have argued over, say, St. Thomas Aquinas's five proofs of the existence of God – but that went on for centuries. The history of Western (theoretical/discursive) philosophy ought to have been read like the history of architecture: philosopher so-and-so built that castle in the air, while his opponent built this other castle. Western philosophy should be appreciated *aesthetically* rather than intrinsically.

Again in *The Wisdom of China*, Lin Yutang writes: "The Chinese can ask … , 'Does the West have a philosophy?' The answer is also clearly 'No.' … The Western man has tons of philosophy written by French, German, English, and American professors, but still he hasn't got a philosophy when he wants it. In fact, he seldom wants it. There are professors of philosophy, but there are no philosophers."

So, what exactly does Lin Yutang prescribe as a philosophy of life? And how does The Dude, our hero, happen to behave in accordance with so many of the philosopher's ideas?

A good point of departure is the stubborn persistence, even in our secularized western world, of Manichaeism. In short, Manichaeism is a dualistic religious system of the prophet Mani (c. 216-276 AD), a mix of Gnostic Christianity, Buddhism, Zoroastrianism, and other elements, whose basic doctrine is an unrenounceable conflict between light and dark, with matter being regarded as dark and evil, and the spiritual world as light and benign. Denis de Rougemont has written a seminal book, *Love in the Western World* (1939, revised 1972), in which he argues in my view convincingly that in the West there exists a single love story, that of the Tristan myth of the star-crossed lovers who cannot find love on earth but only in the afterlife. It is a purely Manichean theme that, incredibly, haunts us to this day. For example, the most popular love story ever filmed, *Titanic*, is a pure reenactment of the Manichean Tristan myth. It says explicitly that perfect love cannot be had in the world of matter, but only in the world of spirit. Tens of millions in the West believe this, whether or not they're aware of it.

In *The Importance of Living*, on the other hand, Lin Yutang entitles the sixth chapter *The Feast of Life*. It begins with some assertions that go very much against the grain: "Philosophers who start out to solve the problem of the purpose of life beg the question by assuming that life must have a purpose. (. . .) I think we assume too much design and purpose altogether. (. . .) Had there been a purpose or design in life, it should have not been so puzzling and vague and difficult to find out." Later on, in a brilliant twist, he adds: "Are we going to strive and endeavor in heaven, as I am quite sure the believers in progress and endeavor must assume? But how can we strive and make progress when we are already perfect? Or are we going merely to loaf and do nothing and not worry? In that case, would it not be better for us to learn to loaf while on earth as a preparation for our eternal life?" I can see The Dude smiling here. Human happiness, Lin Yutang continues, is "largely a matter of digestion. (. . .) if one's bowels move, one is happy, and if they don't move, one is unhappy. That is all there is to it." Take that, transcendentalists! If this sounds like a crass remark that may come out of Sancho Panza, it is not, and we shall see why.

Human happiness is sensuous, and there need not be a polarity between sensual and spiritual pleasure. Manichaeism, in other words, is really a bad habit. "My suspicion is, the reason why we shut our eyes willfully to this gorgeous world, vibrating with its own sensuality, is that the spiritualists have made us plain scared of it. A nobler type of philosophy should reestablish our confidence in this fine receptive organ of ours, which we call the body, and drive away first the contempt and then the fear of our senses."

In *The Big Lebowski* The Dude is rudely extrapolated from his habitual milieu and insulted, threatened, and beaten repeatedly. But in the brief interludes in which he's left in peace, we see him smoke weed; take a warm bath while enjoying the songs of the whales; lie on his carpet while listening to bowling sounds; sip his beloved White Russians; engage in Tai chi, and so on. All sensual pleasures that add to his spiritual enjoyment of life, too. "Only by placing living above thinking can we get away from this heat and the re-breathed air of philosophy and recapture some of the freshness and naturalness of the true insight of the child." Materialism should never be that of Sancho Panza, nor should spiritual yearnings negate our sensual enjoinment of life. According to Confucianists, the highest conception of human dignity is "when man reaches ultimately his greatest height, an equal of heaven and earth, by living in accordance to nature." In *The Golden Mean* the grandson of Confucius writes: "What is God-given is called nature; to follow nature is called Tao (the Way); to cultivate the way is called culture. (. . .) When a man has achieved the inner self and harmony, the heaven and earth are orderly and the myriad things are nourished and grow thereby."

The following chapter in the book seems, again, custom-made for The Dude. In the opening of *The Big Lebowski*, the cowboy narrator says as a voice-over: " . . . And even if he's a lazy man, and The Dude was certainly that – quite possibly the laziest in Los Angeles County . . . which would place him high in the runnin' for laziest worldwide." Yes, The Dude is far from full of zip, and Lin Yutang chimes in with another perfect chapter for him: *The Importance of Loafing*. Eventually we stumble on the following marvelous challenge to our assumptions, or rather the assumptions imposed on us by canonical western culture: "Time is useful because it is not being used." Forget "time is money"! And there's more. "On the whole, the enjoyment of leisure is something which decidedly costs less than the enjoyment of luxury. All it requires is an artistic temperament which is bent on seeking a perfectly useless afternoon spent in a perfectly useless manner. The idle life really costs so very little." We can think of countless afternoons The Dude must have spent bowling or enjoying any of the other activities he is fond of. The art of living should never degenerate into the mere business of living, and The Dude is a consummate artist. What if this earth were our only heaven? The Dude tries to make the best of it, but without hedonistic excesses. In fact, even under duress, he consistently comes off as balanced and level-headed.

And it is here that Lin Yutang finds it appropriate to explain that "the distinction between Buddhism and Taoism is this: the goal of the Buddhist is that he shall not want anything, while the goal of the Taoist is that he shall not be wanted at all." And that's exactly how The Dude was living until some thugs, because of a case of mistaken identity, did want him, and all his troubles began. Up to then, we assume, he was being a perfect Taoist, and a Taoist he tries to remain even through all the vicissitudes he didn't ask for.

Chapter Nine, *The Enjoyment of Living*, is yet another Dudeist delight: it begins with *On Lying in Bed*. "It is amazing how few people are conscious of the importance of the art of lying in bed." Lin Yutang goes on to describe in detail how many benefits can be found in this very natural non-activity, and I can't imagine The Dude disagreeing in the least. "It is amazing how few people are aware of the value of solitude and contemplation. The art of lying in bed means more than physical rest for you (. . .). It is all that, I admit. But there is something more. If properly cultivated, it should mean a mental house-cleaning."

When the Big Lebowski rudely asks, "Are you employed, sir?" The Dude is dumbfounded. "Employed?" he retorts. From the depths of his Taoist core, this must sound like the question from a being with a very low level of consciousness. Doesn't the Big Lebowski know, The Dude could be asking, that, for example, "a writer could get more ideas for his articles or his novel in this posture (i.e., lying in bed) than he could by sitting doggedly before his desk morning and afternoon"?

Other subchapters would delight The Dude: *On Smoke and Incense*; *On Drink and Wine Games*; *The Inhumanity of Western Dress* (The Dude certainly favors comfort over restrictive, choking garments).

The chapter *The Enjoyment of Travel* further enlightens us. When traveling in a strange land, as a Chinese nun put it, "not to care for anybody in particular is to care for mankind in general." Lin Yutang elaborates with one more startling concept: "There is a different kind of travel, travel to see nothing and to see nobody, but the squirrels and muskrats and woodchucks and clouds and trees." We do focus on human beings too much, don't we? "To be able to float about is already a special talent." And The Dude sure can float. "And to be able to wander about at ease is already to have a special vision." And in the film The Dude sure wanders from place to place, from hostile to hostile, always at ease despite the rude receptions.

We get the impression that The Dude is under so much pressure that he's forced to drink more White Russians than usual and smoke more weed, too. He tells Maude, after he's unwittingly "helped her to conceive": "Fortunately I've been adhering to a pretty strict, uh, drug regimen to keep my mind, you know, limber." Yes, it must have been very unpleasant to be insulted, threatened and beaten by so many people in such a short period of time. Normally The Dude probably wouldn't need such a "pretty strict drug regimen" because, as T'u Lung writes in *The Travels of Minglaiotse* (translated and excerpted in *The Importance of Living* by Lin Yutang) "The art of attaining happiness consists in keeping your pleasures mild."

Finally, we come to the subchapter *Art as Play and Personality*. We know The Dude is an avid bowler, so clearly playing is very important to him. "Now is characteristic of play that one plays without reason and there must be no reason for it. Play is its own good reason."

The book closes with a final exhortation to be reasonable. And The Dude certainly proves very reasonable before the very unreasonable events that befall him, as well as the very unreasonable temperament of his foil, his buddy Walter.

In the end he's shown smiling, "taking it easy for all of us sinners" and, in essence, abiding. Indeed, "The Dude abides." Much has been made about this closing statement, and much should have been made of it. But over the course of the film The Dude is shown under duress, not in his normal life. He does a terrific job in remaining balanced, level-headed and reasonable; he does abide, and how. But there is implicitly much more to The Dude. Too much of his lifestyle – the glimpses we catch of it amidst the turmoil – seems to be directly inspired by Taoism. Most of all, this: his having achieved transcendence within the limited sphere of his human *immanence*. Precisely in this lies the secret of life intended as heaven on earth.

> Look, I'm alive. On what? Neither childhood nor
> the future grows less . . . More being than I'll ever
> need springs up in my heart.
> – From Rainer Maria Rilke's Ninth Elegy, translated by A. Poulin, Jr.

....

Guido Mina di Sospiro is an award-wining novelist who was raised in Milan in a multilingual home. He trained as a classical guitarist before leaving Italy after university to attend USC's School of Cinema Production. He then became a journalist and correspondent from Los Angeles on the movie and music industries for two Italian and one German magazines. He now maintains a blog on the New York-based web-magazine *Reality Sandwich*. He has written various books that have been published around the world. His novel *The Forbidden Book* (http://amzn.to/1924zeK), co-written with Joslceyn Godwin, has just been released. Soon to the published is also *The Metaphysics of Ping-Pong* (http://amzn.to/17NBMfj). Mina di Sospiro lives in the Washington DC area with his wife and their three sons.

Eric Heatherington, *Room Decor*

Kate Radomski, *Nice Marmot*

That Rug Really Tied the Room Together

BY JOSEPH P. NATOLI

[A]ll the brothers' intelligence and skill can't make up for the sense of vacancy in their movies. Until they find a way to let a little real life in (grownup reality, that is), Joel and Ethan Coen will somehow seem stunted-no more than the brightest kids in the class.
Daphne Merkin, "Smart Alecks," *New Yorker,* March 1998

The Big Lebowski is an empty frame.
– Stuart Klawans, "Sex and Bowling," *The Nation,* March 30, 1998

Through this bewildering landscape . . . wanders our addled Philip Marlowe figure, taking herb, swilling White Russians and, truth to tell, looking increasingly heroic relative to the dysfunctional world around him.
– Andrew O'Hehir, "Everyman Must Get Stoned," *Salon*

I'm still running / Against the wind . . .
– Bob Seger

One of the consequences of friends knowing that I may be writing about films that they've seen and don't quite know what to make of is their asking me what do I make of this or that film. Now they know whether they like or don't like a film but times are such – postmodern I mean – that just what they especially don't like about a film may yet be their hidden access to the whole film. What unsettles us and holds us off could possibly provide an epiphany. A transformative moment. Hold on another second and maybe the opaqueness here will attach itself to the Dark Holes of our postmodern age, move us into new figments of old figments like cause and effect, linear time, noncontradiction, nonrandom order, external reference points, and grownup reality. I take it for granted that today everyone is holding on another second to see if their command of reality isn't going to be pulled right out of their hands, flung high in the air so that all the new movements, all the new revelations of an ever-changing us-and-reality relationship can be clearly seen.

That's not to say that everyone is ready to go along with the new swerve. Refer to our "culture wars" here: On one side you have an army digging in and ready to hold on to grownup reality in the finest tradition of family values as displayed on Nickelodeon cable TV, and, on the other side, you have any number of radical, guerilla-like factions more than ready to admit that reality has moved on, say, from adultery or suicide or same-sex marriages or abortion or transexuality as destructive on all counts to the same as new constellations being brought to recognition for the first time in the firmament. We are never at play on a planet rotating on its axis and spinning in the heavens when we belong to the conservative cultural army but quite seriously grounded in Truths, Laws, Imperatives, Explanations, Equations, and Investment Principles. Bend one knee, please. They are, of course, opposed by those who see themselves at play with reality, bending it, rather than a respectful knee, to fit the contours and dimensions of an infinitely flexible and varied human nature.

If you invest the spirit of one side with the spirit of the other, and vice versa, you get the sort of awareness each side needs of the other in order to have a really good intense cultural war. You also get a cultural climate in which the two attitudes are to be found at all settings on a good blender. And, ironically, market imperialism – which on one hand demands an inert social order which offers stability – makes its profits by pulping reality to push product. The market is at play with a pliable reality; Return on Investment is the only immoveable part.

When events – like Princess Di's death or Clinton's sex drive become like a movie we can't get control of, they now fall into this culture wars' miasma, à La Brea Tar Pit, which is our minds, in which white bones of all sizes swim about, and it's our job, as reconstructors, to put it all together. This is the sort of occasional acid-trip scene that Dude, of *The Big Lebowski,* might have. Which side is The Dude on? Why he's clearly at play with reality, skirting all the necessities that bind our present entrepreneurial society. Market players don't play the way The Dude does. They get into a competitive global arena and they make sure they come out winners. The fact that in getting to be winners they are willing to obey no laws but those of profit, no principles but those of profit, and no tradition but only what profit requires at that moment does not turn them into Dude. His disrespect is for self-aggrandizement, his unconcern is for being rich, his rebellion is against self-interest. And because he is so startlingly atavistic, so disturbingly nonentrepreneurial in 1998, after some twenty years of ascendant Dow, he activates a new clash of the culture wars but at the same time he and his crew of masterless men push the postmodern envelope a bit further. I mean to say that *The Big Lebowski* pushes us to wondering whether we can't command its subject because we're right and there is no subject, there is no rug that brings the whole room together, or that the fact that we can't command its subject and are wondering why is precisely what the film's subject has led us to.

Dude and his friends are bowling outside our lanes and we've already rented shoes and are trying out bowling balls in preparing to join them. I'm not saying that we're all prepared to score this game according to rules we can't even begin to fathom. Nor that once we see the kind of game the Coen brothers are rolling here, we don't try to close it down at once. All I'm saying – and I sound like The Dude when we can't wrap things up or follow all the in and outs of the "case" – is that at this moment in America, market imperialized as we are, this is a postmodern flaunting of reality making and we're all bowling on those lanes, just scoring the results differently.

Let's explore the "sense of vacancy" that the *New Yorker* film critic mentions. Who possesses this "sense of vacancy"? And does it arise from a "sense of realism"? And, indeed, don't we reveal what sense of realism we hold when we begin to talk about "grownup reality," whose antipode surely must be infantile reality? Within this particular "sense of realism;' a certain "sense of vacancy" arises when not enough "grownup reality" is let in. But what if, say, we adopted the "sense of realism" of an eighteenth-century fruitcake like William Blake, who, because he was a fruitcake, confounded the realms of Innocence and Experience, childhood and adulthood. Because he was a fruitcake – sang on his deathbed, for instance – his "sense of realism" wanted to "let in" to "grownup reality" the joy, imagination, spontaneity, exuberance, emotions, playfulness, the dreaming and irrationalism of childhood. None of this appears particularly appealing when viewed by those already in the realm of Experience; it all appears frivolous, childish, disorderly, lunatic, and ludic; and where there should be grownup thought there is only a failure to achieve cognitive grasp, a prepubescent assertion of the will, a bombardment of cognitive dissonance. In short, when time and space are not filled with the priorities of what now passes socially and culturally as "grownup reality," then the observer notes a "sense of vacancy."

This "sense of vacancy" is, however, a presence in this movie. It is not, therefore, the byproduct of *failure* to bring something into being but rather the result of the film *bringing* something into being. What does it bring into being? Well, from where I sit alongside you in our present "grownup reality," I'm not quite sure because it all first registers as unplotted, less than purposeful, fractured, disconnected, ludic, mazelike, discordant, surrealistic, incoherent, a jumble, a farrago. What does it appear like to the Coen brothers? I know from their film *Fargo* that they have a real grip on grownup reality as presently being manufactured in the Midwest. And they can't see the whole of it without seeing the ludic, farrago dimensions of that reality. For them it appears that grownup reality is always already filled to the brim with unstoppable mania, is always tending to bring its own sobriety and control onto the snowy drifts of the cockamamie where the hard, cold edges of grownup reality finally melt away in the sun. In *The Big Lebowski* all of the grownup reality The Dude becomes entangled in gives way to a musical number à la Busby Berkeley. And when The Dude is hit over the head and things grow dark as they do for Dick Powell in *Farewell My Lovely,* The Dude doesn't fall into a deep, dark pool and wind up running through a dark corridor of endless doors pursued by who knows what. Instead, he flies like Superman with arms spread wide over Los Angeles at night with all its lights fluttering below. He has a great, happy smile on his face; he surely dreams he can fly away. And then he's embracing a bowling ball, a look of surprise on his face, as he plummets downward, his flight canceled. He's weighted down and it's the weight of real-world gravity.

As in *Fargo*, all real-world gravity passes through human mediation, which gives it this role or that, assigning it wherever our "sense of real- ism" sees fit. Oddly enough, what the force of gravity is – often cited as an indisputable component of and proof of the "real world" – contributes to our "sense of vacancy." It is a vacant force in a realm of vacancy. It's so real we bring to it nothing in our daily lives, living as if it meant nothing and didn't exist. It is so powerful a force in the real world and at the same time lies unmediated in human life. We bring to it no meaning and no value, unless of course we are working for NASA. I am merely trying to point out that a "sense of vacancy" inhabits all the "hard" stuff we connect to the "real world." Observations of a "sense of vacancy" in a film which is – whether it's a film you like or not or the critics like or not – is a ludicrous claim, because all films film human mediations of reality. They film "worldliness," the movements of people within the world they are already part of. Electricity, nuclear fission, the synapse, photosynthesis, $E=mc^2$, LaPlace Transforms, and so on, are vacant lots in everyday human mediation of the world; we greet them with a "sense of vacancy," even on exams where the only human transformation they have is in terms of grades, a symbolic enterprise whose meaning and value are socially and culturally manufactured.

So the Coen brothers greet grownup reality with a "sense of vacancy" and rather than put on gravitas they try to take a look at things as if they themselves weren't obliged to obey the laws of grownup reality. And they literally film their attempt as a point-of-view shot from inside a bowling bowl. What sense of realism do we get from inside that moving bowling ball? If you're inside that bowling ball do you project a "sense of vacancy" out there in the lanes, with the bowlers and their world? Or, do you take your gravity-bound "sense of realism" in there with you and hold on to the notion that vacancy is here inside the bowling ball and anything from this perspective results in a "sense of vacancy"? Who's going to mark the frame empty? From inside the bowling ball every frame is filled with action, every frame is a roll down one or another lane, and the sights along the way vary-pace, time, and speed locked into a new equation each and every time.

The flight of the bowling ball, like The Dude's flight over LA, are metaphors of travel Coen brothers-style and it seems to me a profitless endeavor to object to their style of travel. Unless, of course, you are thoroughly convinced that grownups can and should travel only one way across a reality that allows for only that perspective of travel. Once you settle in for the ride on the Coen brothers' terms you can see that every character in the film, not just The Dude and his bowling buddies, are coming at reality from separate lanes. And every dude on every lane has his or her bowling style and perspective. Now I don't know about you but when I bowl, I'm glancing at who's bowling on the right and left of me. I watch the lanes on either side. I distinguish mature bowling styles from amateur ones. I engage in bowling chatter and listen to that around me. I am on lane four and way over to my right someone is bowling on lane fifty; noise and movement blur where I am from where that bowler is. You might say that the reality of lane fifty lacks interest for me, but that's only an effect of where I am on lane four. I don't know how much I could say about life on lane fifty without filling you with a sense of vacancy.

Let's find a way to wander from lane to lane, although this sort of lateral movement doesn't take place in a bowling alley because we stand side by side, lane by lane, focused on the pins in front of us, moving toward them, releasing, and then returning. If reality is only ahead in our lane and if we are the only ones with the proper bowling form, we're the only ones bowling like grownups, then the plot and perspective on lane fifty shouldn't mean a whole hell of a lot to us. On the other hand, if you take a postmodern view of things – and the Coen brothers do – then you're going to bowl laterally. Maybe your game will improve and your "sense of realism" expand; maybe your empty frame will get filled in and your "sense of vacancy" shifted back out to empty space.

Let's journey cross-alley in this film. Let's put The Dude in the center lane. The film opens with him strolling down the dairy aisle of Ralph's supermarket, stopping to sample from a carton of milk. The Dude is caught in a time warp: He experiences the occasional acid flashback, listens to whale song while soaking and taking in his bathtub, listens to the music of Creedence Clearwater Revival and passes time at the bowling alley with his buddies Walter and Donny. Reagan never happened for The Dude; he missed the film *Forrest Gump* so he doesn't know he's been declared extinct by Newt Gingrich, a wrong turn in American history. The Dude's misadventures begin when he is mistaken for another Lebowski, the Big Lebowski, the Lebowski who has won, who apparently has all the toys. The goons that piss on The Dude's rug have been sent by Ben Gazzara playing Hollywood's creation of the porn and drug sleaze-kingpin behind the sleaze. But The Dude doesn't cross his path until later. Now he is set on getting restitution for his rug because this rug really tied the room together, a thought not his own but his friend Walter's. Walter has the gift of all true paranoiacs: He can tie together the most disparate things and he certainly knows what the key piece is when trying to fit things together, trying to make sense of things. The counterpresence here is Steve Buscemi's Donny, for whom the whole world is just a series of sentence fragments and conversations only partially heard. His constant interrogations elicit the same response from Walter: "Shut the fuck up, Donny." Donny is not privy to the real workings of things and in Walter's view can't possibly be brought up to speed.

There is, however, a home base to Walter's thoughts: Vietnam. Everything, no matter how unrelated on the surface to that conflict, is inevitably linked to it. Nam is the rug spread out in Walter's mind which ties the room together. The discrepancy between that sense of order and what is in the world leads Walter and those who follow his "logic" into strange conflicts and many casualties, a sort of microcosm of Nam itself. But no Tet Offensive daunts Walter whose absolute certainty and determination never falter; no matter how distant the points may be on the map, Walter can connect them. He never experiences a sense of vacancy. Or, more precisely, he never experiences a sense of vacancy he can't fill.

Seduced by Walter's logic that he needs to be compensated for that rug which really tied the room together, The Dude pays a visit to the Big Lebowski. Lest we ourselves forget that it's the '90s and Dude is all that's left over from the Counterrevolution, the Lebowski of the '90s – the BIG Lebowski – a fatcat in a wheelchair, describes The Dude to The Dude's face early in the film. He tells The Dude how in spite of being crippled he has succeeded in becoming a winner, a success, and he did it because he was relentlessly, competitively entrepreneurial. In other words, he represents the shtick of the last twenty years to The Dude. He won't give The Dude a handout; did he personally piss on The Dude's carpet? No, then he's not responsible. The Dude insists that he's suffered a great loss by being mistaken for the Big Lebowski. But the Big Lebowski doesn't share The Dude's sense of order and throws him out. The Dude nevertheless leaves with a Persian rug, which gets taken back later by the Big Lebowski's daughter, Maude, for whom it holds cherished memories of her mother. Maude will later mate with The Dude because she wants a child but she doesn't want anyone connected to her life fathering that child. So she picks The Dude; the lane he's bowling on is so far removed from the one she's on that even sex can't really bring them together. She fills The Dude in on the real success story of her father, the Big Lebowski: He has no money of his own; the money was her mother's and now it's in a foundation administered by Maude. She once let her father invest some of the foundation's money and he lost it all. He's an incompetent, lying, vain man who bought himself a trophy wife. He is, in short, a fraud; he didn't earn millions; he can't take the high ground with The Dude. In fact, The Dude is his moral superior: He's down but he's not a hypocrite, nor is he vain and selfish. He doesn't make people trophies; a bowling trophy would suffice for The Dude.

On his way out of the Big Lebowski's, The Dude meets the trophy wife, Bunny, who later may or may not be kidnaped. As The Dude glances over at the pool, he asks "Who's that?" "He's a nihilist," Bunny responds. "Oh, a nihilist," Dude says, nodding, as if a nihilist sleeping on a rubber float in a swimming pool was per usual. Bunny has been painting her toenails and now she holds up a foot and wants The Dude to blow on it. "Oh, you want me to blow on it?" The Dude says. But then he drifts off, following his rug being carried out. When he visits Maude in her studio she isn't painting her nails; her own body isn't her art as it is for Bunny the porno star now trophy wife. Maude swings naked over a canvas below and splatters paint on it as she flies by. Some of that paint gets on The Dude who is as unperturbed with the expression of "high" art as he is with "low" art. Art is not his passion, nor lust, nor money, nor ambition, nor nothing itself. Neither a committed artist of life or of profit or of nothing, The Dude carries on at his own pace. There's something stubbornly heroic about the way The Dude feels called upon to not only attend to all the ins and outs of the plot he's wandered into but make some sense of it, come to some kind of conclusion. It's not a committed intent, a serious drive through the main street of this bewildering landscape. The Dude's command of the ins and outs of life's intricacies-and the bewildering landscape he's wandered into- never goes beyond his knowing the way to the In & Out Burger Shop. You might say that while everyone else has an abstracted sort of connection with the world, The Dude's remains concrete and particular.

But he does take it as it comes; I mean he takes it as serious as life gets. He doesn't dismiss it as vacancy on his way to nobler ground. He hasn't, for instance, adopted a posture of scornful and amused aloofness as David Thewlis does in a brief cameo. The Dude has come to see Maude and finds only Thewlis sitting there, amused by not only The Dude's appearance but seemingly by his very existence. Later, when Maude shows up and answers a phone call there's a three way "inside" joke that the phone caller, Maude, and Thewlis share. Theirs is a world in which avant-garde art and living life like art disdain the mundane, especially a figure such as The Dude, who represents all the messiness, disorder, and confusion that art seeks to transcend. Ironically, it's not aesthetic detachment that will impregnate Maude. For that she has to turn to The Dude. Quite interestingly, Thewlis is one of the only people in the film who provokes The Dude's wrath. "Who the hell are you anyway?" The Dude asks him after Thewlis has treated him to reeking condescension. Who indeed is Thewlis here but the aloof, scornful critic who will soon write about a "sense of vacancy" pervading the film?

Even though it is The Dude who has the occasional acid flashback, he lives without illusions. But he's surrounded by the deluded. Jesus, the Latino bowler, takes vanity to a new high; he is in his own mind the cock of the walk, all posture and braggadocio. He promises great harm but will never deliver; his delusion is harmless. But when The Dude winds up in the hands of a Malibu police chief he winds up smack in the middle of a law and order, "tough on crime" worldly outlook. It's suddenly "Giuliani time," allegedly the words New York City police used when they were brutalizing a hapless victim. This sort of neo-Nazi barbarity and brutality is part of the nihilists' approach also; they throw an attack marmot into The Dude's bathtub as he is soaking, toking, and listening to whale song. Their violence finally runs up against Walter's, the Vietnam vet, calmly telling the frightened Donny not to worry because these guys are amateurs. And Walter does go through them as if they were paper bags. A black leather, German skinhead, Sprocket look makes a good photo-op, but it's nothing but '80s and '90s hype compared to the violence Walter has seen. But the clash is too much for Donny whose weak heart gives out and he dies on the spot. Later, his ashes will be flung out of a two-pound coffee can into the wind and back into The Dude's face.

I can't help thinking: Who in this film is living as if they were mortal? As if they had one and not more lives to live? Do you counter mortality by committing yourself to something, like art or sex or wealth or power or anger or service? The Golden-age TV scriptwriter that The Dude and Walter visit, in the hope of getting back a million dollars from a fourteen-year-old thief, is in an iron lung set up like a casket at one end of the living room. Maybe every script he's written is now being replayed in his mind to the rhythm of the iron lung bellows. It's as if the reality of the present continues on unscripted. There was always life going on outside the script; and the script was less enduring than the life. Was mortality held off by a script, no matter how Golden Age? Or does that all inevitably lead you into thinking that you can't follow the ins and outs of life and world but that you are getting the most you can out of it? The Dude is not entrepreneurial; he's no symbolic analyst; and he's certainly not shaping his own destiny. He is in fact being led through a maziness that confounds grasp. But maybe he's here in a way that no one else in the film is. Maybe The Dude is leaving his frame empty and that's an accomplishment whose skillfulness we just can no longer recognize. But I see it as a reminder that while we may need to journey, the world doesn't journey. There is no journey but only movement, and that movement, foundationally, has no order or causality or time or speed or space. I am not claiming that The Dude is enlightened in the way of the Dalai Lama or has reconciled in himself the paradoxes of consciousness immersed in what merely exists, what is outside of what we humans make of it. And yet The Dude is a pause on our journey here; perhaps a pause, received as vacancy, but a pause in our entrepreneurial rush to "return on investment."

....

Books written by **Joseph Natoli** can be found on Amazon; forthcoming will be Travels of a New Gulliver, as well as a new website: www.josephnatoli.com with links to his online articles on film, TV, music, politics, food, sports, education and travel. He stopped looking for a rug to tie the room together long ago.

Joe Forkan, *Wanderer Above the Sea of Fog*

Joe Forkan, *Supper at Emmaus*

"Trapped By Their Pasts":
Noir and Nostalgia in *The Big Lebowski*

BY MARC SINGER

Although the Coen brothers routinely deny the possibility of any calculated meaning in their films, they nevertheless produce subtle and substantive works even in their most seemingly frivolous exercises. Perhaps no film better exemplifies this sly denial and assertion of meaning than their 1998 comedy *The Big Lebowski*. A parody of hard-boiled fiction and film noir–combined with Westerns, Cheech and Chong comedies, Busby Berkeley musicals, and of course bowling–the film nevertheless contains a serious treatment of the role of the past, particularly the antiwar tradition of the 1960s, in contemporary anxieties over politics, war, and masculinity. The Coens have appropriated the themes and conventions of crime fiction and film noir to produce a film about the disjunction between the counterculture of the sixties and the politics of the nineties, a film about the impassable gulf between past and present.

Not so much a nostalgia film, then, as a film about nostalgia, *The Big Lebowski* represents the past through a wide-ranging and voracious cultural pastiche. One of the most important referents in that pastiche is the Coens' appropriation of the plot and characters of Raymond Chandler's 1939 novel *The Big Sleep*. Superficially, this appropriation appears to be strictly parodic as the Coens update private eye Philip Marlowe into perennial stoner Jeff "the Dude" Lebowski. Yet their adaptation is also more scrupulous than it first seems, replicating many of Chandler's themes and creating a noirish narrative in which the characters are "trapped by their pasts" (Ethan Coen, qtd. in Robertson 99), gripped by an unshakable and often destructive nostalgia. This nostalgia renders the Dude, like Philip Marlowe before him, "an outsider in the modern world" (Phillips 249), a living relic of the sixties counterculture who has somehow survived into a world that vilifies him and his values.

The Dude's preservation of his countercultural past does not go uncontested, as several other characters struggle with him over the memory of the 1960s; it is no accident that the film is set during the Gulf War as the elder George Bush attempts to banish the spectre of Vietnam with a quick victory over Iraq. This conflict over the national memory highlights two related contests within the film, as the Dude and his fellow characters spar over the appropriate response to aggression and over the definition of manhood itself. The Coens repeatedly suggest, with facetiousness masking sincerity in the manner that has become one of their hallmarks, that *The Big Lebowski* revolves around the question of "What makes a man?" and that the Dude is "the man for his time n'place"–an unlikely representative of manhood and virtue who stands in stark contrast to, but cannot correct, the corrupted values of his era.

Chandler and the Coens

The Big Lebowski continues a Coen tradition of reworking the archetypes of hard-boiled crime fiction. Much as *Blood Simple* (1984) and *The Man Who Wasn't There* (2001) draw upon the sinister love triangles and frustrated middle-class ambitions of James M. Cain, and *Miller's Crossing* (1990) the elaborate double-crosses of Dashiell Hammett, so does *The Big Lebowski* invoke the sprawling plot structures of Raymond Chandler–specifically *The Big Sleep*.[1] Nearly every critic of *The Big Lebowski* acknowledges this debt to Chandler, although for some writers such as Carolyn R. Russell, the intertextuality is little more than "straight parody" (Russell 142). Fewer critics have examined how the film's themes–particularly its explorations of nostalgia, violence, and masculinity–gravitate around its noirish conventions and its evocations of *The Big Sleep*. Yet these parallels, which range from literal correspondences of plot and character to more elusive but fundamentally similar social critiques, point to many of the film's central concerns.

The Coens' screenplay both echoes and parodies Chandler's ethic of knightly manhood. Superficially, the Dude appears to be a parodic inversion of Philip Marlowe, a pot-smoking burnout who violates every tenet of Marlowe's code: he attempts to steal his employer's money rather than refuse it; he happily sleeps with his employer's daughter rather than refuse her; his few efforts at picking up a clue or ducking a tail or interrogating

---

[1] Erica Rowell also detects some allusions and similarities to Chandler's *The Long Goodbye* (1951), above and beyond those that came to the Coens by way of Robert Altman's 1973 film adaptation (229-33).

a suspect usually end in humiliation and failure. As Ethan Coen has said, the Dude is "the least equipped to deal" with Marlowe's style of detective work (qtd. in Mottram 133), turning the film into a mockery of Chandler's brand of heroism.

But the Coens also offer a more serious adaptation of Chandler's work, retaining many of the themes of *The Big Sleep* and even restoring the social criticism that had been muted in Howard Hawks's 1946 film adaptation. The Hawks film shifts the blame for Rusty Regan's murder from Carmen Sternwood and the Sternwood family to the gangster Eddie Mars; Peter Rabinowitz has noted that this transforms the plot from an indictment of corruption among the wealthy into a simple condemnation and punishment of organized crime.[2] As a result, Rabinowitz writes, "The moral universe of Hawks's film is consequently much more soothing than that of the novel" (128). The Coens do not opt for such moral simplification; in making the Big Lebowski the film's primary antagonist and greatest criminal, they reinstate and amplify Chandler's critique of wealth.

Sean McCann argues, in his book *Gumshoe America* (2000), that *The Big Sleep* "is an allegory of economic predation in which the vernacular energy of the white ethnic falls prey to the economic elite [. . .] a gothic tale of the way that the wealthy survive by leeching the vitality of the forthright and honest" (166). The primary example and victim of this predation is of course the missing Rusty Regan, who is slain by the vampish Carmen Sternwood and dumped in the family's dry, exhausted oil well; she plans to do the same to Marlowe. But Carmen isn't the family's only rotten apple. McCann challenges the common critical characterization of General Sternwood as a kind but ailing paternal figure, the Fisher King to Marlowe's knight-errant, a view typified by Ernest Fontana's description of Sternwood as both "the lord that Marlowe as knight serves [. . .] a sick, dying lord" (162) and "the masterful entrepreneur who develops socially beneficial, primary raw materials" (163). McCann disputes both the chivalric and economic aspects of this characterization, arguing that the General is just as predatory as his daughters (McCann 167-70), a parasite who depended on Rusty Regan for "the breath of life" (Chandler 11) and who seeks to replenish that breath with Marlowe. As if to confirm this interpretation, Chandler surrounds the General with orchids, whose "flesh is too much like the flesh of men," whose perfume "has the rotten sweetness of a prostitute" (9), signifying none too subtly Sternwood's decadence. As the General himself admits, neither of his daughters "has any more moral sense than a cat. Neither have I. No Sternwood ever had" (Chandler 13).

The Coens maintain a surprising fidelity to Chandler's critique of wealth in their depiction of the Lebowski family, restoring the moral condemnation that Hawks excised in his depiction of the Sternwoods. Carmen/Bunny is no longer a lone aberration, as the Lebowskis are rotten to the core. The Big Lebowski, in particular, is no kindly, ailing patriarch who inspires loyalty in his Marlowe–instead he berates and abuses the Dude until the Dude makes a key discovery about Lebowski's fortunes, leading to his only true deduction of the entire movie, when he realizes Lebowski has stolen the ransom money from his first wife's charitable foundation. The Big Lebowski is the ultimate grifter in the Coens' world, his charade of honest entrepreneurship masking a parasitic heart.

The other Lebowskis, it must be said, are little better. Bunny is no longer a murderer like her analogue, Carmen, but her negligence nevertheless initiates the plot when her massive debts to Jackie Treehorn accidentally entangle the Dude in her family's affairs; similarly, her sudden disappearance for a trip to Palm Springs opens the door for her faked kidnapping and her husband's subsequent embezzlement. Bunny, too, is every bit as rapacious as the Sternwoods when it comes to chasing after money. She not only makes porn movies for Jackie Treehorn, she also propositions the Dude at their first meeting with the offer of a thousand-dollar sex act–and she'll charge her husband's personal assistant a hundred if he wants to watch. According to Maude Lebowski this behavior stems from Bunny's nymphomania, another compulsion the trophy wife shares with the uncontrollable Carmen Sternwood.

But then, Maude hasn't fallen far from the family tree either. She also manipulates the Dude's sexual desire for her own gain, albeit with greater success, discretion, and control than Bunny. Much like Vivian Sternwood, who is more reserved and subtle than Carmen but ultimately just as predatory (McCann 168), Small wonder, then, that a disrobed Maude turns up naked in the Dude's apartment with the intention of seducing him – a scene that, in Chandler's novel and Hawks's film, features Carmen rather than Vivian Sternwood (Tyree and Walters 52-53).

Moreover, Maude's artistic activities are steeped in an aura of elitism that isn't far removed from her father's arrogant investment in his illusions of wealth and class. When she questions the Dude about his past, she is less interested in his authentically countercultural antiwar activities than in his supposed background in "the music business." (She becomes visibly disappointed when she discovers he was just a roadie for Metallica.) Much like her father, she treats the Dude as little more than a befuddled servant. For all that she presents the Dude with the highly engaging image of a sex-loving feminist and a bohemian artist, Maude proves to be as manipulative and elitist as her father, offering no serious challenge to the culture that the Dude has rejected. Her avant-gardism is little more than a socially acceptable

---

[2] As Rabinowitz rightly surmises, many of the changes in Hawks's plot were mandated by industry censors and studio dictates; original drafts of the William Faulkner/Leigh Brackett script stayed much closer to Chandler's story. Phillips provides a thorough account of these changes in Chapter 4 of *Creatures of Darkness*.

indulgence for the wealthy, leaving the Dude as the film's closest thing to a true radical.[3]

This political and cultural isolation points to one last, and perhaps most important, similarity between the Dude and Philip Marlowe. Gene Phillips describes Marlowe as "an outsider in the modern world" (249), a label that could just as easily apply to the Dude. Both men maintain their "sense of values in a decadent society that flouts them" (Phillips 249), adhering to older standards that their contemporaries despise. The Dude, like Marlowe, "sees modernity is in trouble" (Rowell 220) and becomes a caretaker of values his society has abandoned. In isolating the Dude for his "holdover sixties values" (Levine 143), the Coens recreate Marlowe's modernist alienation within a more contemporary political and historical context.

Notes on Nostalgia

The Big Lebowski operates in an atmosphere of social and temporal alienation typical of film noir. Paul Schrader's influential "Notes on Film Noir" (1972) cites this bitter nostalgia as one of the genre's signal traits:

> the narration creates a mood of *temps perdu*: an irretrievable past, a predetermined fate, and an all-enveloping hopelessness. In *Out of the Past* Robert Mitchum relates his history with such pathetic relish that it is obvious there is no hope for the future: one can only take pleasure in reliving a doomed past. (220)

Schrader finds this obsession with the past so central to film noir that he calls it "the overriding noir theme [...] Noir heroes dread to look ahead, but instead try to survive the day, and if unsuccessful at that, they retreat to the past. Thus film noir's techniques emphasize loss, nostalgia, lack of clear priorities, and insecurity" (221). These lines provide an equally apt description of the Dude and *The Big Lebowski*. While the Coens explicitly reject the expressionist visual style of film noir, they recognize that the film's pervasive focus on nostalgia links it to noir and hard-boiled fiction; Ethan Coen told Robertson that "noir seemed to be the flavor of the narrative, with all these characters trapped by their pasts" (Robertson 99).

Coen's comment about "all these characters" indicates that the Dude is not alone in his temporal alienation as Marlowe is in his. Nearly every character in the Coens' film is in some sense an outsider in the modern world, living in nostalgia for an earlier era. Ronald Bergan observes that "All the characters in *The Big Lebowski* live in the recent past" (199); most of them, in fact, are still fixated upon the culture or the events of the 1960s. Beyond the Dude's permanent habitation of that decade, his best friend Walter Sobchak is forever reliving his tour in Vietnam; Jackie Treehorn conjures images of Hugh Hefner in his heyday, the screenplay specifying that he plays "1960s mainstream jazz, of the Mancini-Brubeck school" (Coen and Coen 98) at his parties; Maude evokes the artists of the Fluxus movement. The film's antagonists, on the other hand, look back to a decade that repudiated the social changes of the sixties. J. M. Tyree and Ben Walters suggest that the Big Lebowski "is lost in the 1980s just as the Dude is lost in the 1960s" (67), while Robertson cites costume designer Mary Zophres's observation that Uli and the nihilists dress "like they're caught in a time warp from the '80s" (115). But allusions to the past extend far beyond these obvious references, and well into the film's gallery of minor characters: Maude's chauffeur listens to Dean Martin, Smokey is another aging Vietnam-era pacifist, Donny wears a collection of retro bowling shirts, and the film's sets, costuming, and production design are steeped in the "Brunswick look" of 1950s and 1960s bowling alleys and accessories (Robertson 102). Even in the midst of this pervasive mid-twentieth-century pastiche, the characters look back to the myths and archetypes of the Wild West, created by the dying television writer Arthur Digby Sellers and embodied in the cowboy Stranger.

Walter in particular latches onto these signs of the past. He scrupulously performs all the duties of his former marriage, including his conversion to Judaism; when the Dude tells him, with characteristic discretion, "You're living in the fucking past," Walter angrily proclaims, "Three thousand years of beautiful tradition, from Moses to Sandy Koufax – YOU'RE GODDAMN RIGHT I'M LIVING IN THE FUCKING PAST!" This fixation on the past also leads Walter to make an unwitting father figure out of Arthur Digby Sellers, as he claims that *Branded*, "especially the early episodes," was a source of inspiration to him. As Walter's ire at young Larry Sellers rises, the greatest insult or challenge he can issue is, "You're KILLING your FATHER, Larry!"–a statement that clearly holds more meaning and terror for Walter than it does for the boy.

Ironically, by adopting this personal mission to straighten out the recalcitrant son, Walter turns Arthur Digby Sellers into his own private General Sternwood in a parodic reflection of *The Big Lebowski*'s already parodic main plot. This plot-within-a-plot not only escalates the degeneration of Chandler's archetypes (this Sternwood analogue comes not in a wheelchair, but an iron lung), it also mocks the deepest symbolic resonances of *The Big Sleep*. Marlowe's intercession on behalf of an impotent and perhaps unworthy father figure, his scrupulous preservation of a decaying and morally bankrupt family, seems even more ludicrous when applied to the Sellers clan than it does with the Lebowskis; the patriarch's lost authority is no longer lamented or even subverted, but openly ridiculed. The complete debacle of Walter's self-appointed Chandlerian mission (he not only fails to redeem Larry Sellers, he also causes further damage to

---

[3] Even the Dude's radicalism proves awfully tenuous. Mottram observes that the Dude casually compromises his radical values throughout the film, whether it is through his "increasing Capitalist tendencies" (143) in his pursuit of the missing money or his easy, uncritical adoption of George Bush's (and Walter's) aggressive rhetoric.

the Dude's car) suggests that his fixation on the past is fruitless, dangerous, and humiliating. Walter is, like the Dude, another mock-Marlowe who attempts to preserve a personal code of honor; as he tells the hapless Smokey, holding him at gunpoint over a supposed scoring infraction, "This is not 'Nam. This is bowling. There are rules." But Walter's obsession with preserving the values of his past inevitably leads him into scenes of farcical and self-destructive violence, a dangerous consequence of his excessive nostalgia.

The Dude and Walter may engage in "a properly modernist nostalgia" (Jameson, *Postmodernism* 19) for a time when they believe their ideals were more widely upheld, but the film also represents that more postmodern process of nostalgia by which the sixties have become flattened into a convenient historical shorthand, a set of totemic clichés to be plundered by opportunistic artists or reviled by triumphant conservatives.[4] The film is, in part, about the national repudiation of the memory of the 1960s, and about two characters, both prisoners to their own pasts and ethical codes, who cannot forget them. While the Dude and Walter have diametrically opposed stances on Vietnam, their mutual preservation of their pasts becomes, by the early nineties, a common struggle against the national memory. In a film in which everyone else either hates the sixties (like the Big Lebowski) or is engaged in appropriating and commodifying that decade's countercultural chic (like Maude Lebowski or Jackie Treehorn), only the Dude and Walter attempt to guard what they see as its ideals.

By alienating the Dude and Walter for their attachment to the 1960s and to Vietnam, the Coens have worked a substantial change on Chandler's nostalgic template. Their characters are trapped not only by their personal pasts, but also by the ghosts of a national history that has almost, but not quite, been expunged from the culture. It is no accident that the film is set in the early nineties–"just about the time of our conflict with Sad'm and the Eye-rackies," as the Stranger says–as the Bush administration tries to use one war to efface another. The Gulf War was not just supposed to be a different kind of war; Bush framed it as a means of purging the Vietnam War and its legacy of antiwar protest from the national memory (Kendrick 59). Many characters in *The Big Lebowski* are similarly obsessed with erasing or denigrating memories of Vietnam and its legacy of antiwar protest. The Big Lebowski proudly proclaims, "Your 'revolution' is over, Mr. Lebowski! [...] The bums lost!" The Dude himself approaches the Big Lebowski, thereby becoming entangled in his embezzlement scheme, only because he listens to Walter's rhetoric of resisting "unchecked aggression," rhetoric transparently lifted from the clip of George Bush that plays in the film's opening scene.[5] Walter later characterizes Smokey's pacifism as an emotional problem and tells the Dude that "pacifism is not something to hide behind." Figures everywhere are pushing the Dude to abandon his pacifist principles and take aggressive action–although such actions usually backfire as the Dude is beaten and jailed and his car and apartment are destroyed.

The Coens offer no unproblematic response to aggression and no unambiguous code of manly behavior. Little wonder, then, that the characters settle into nostalgia, telling themselves the past offers the answers they cannot find in the present. Their struggles over the meaning of their past, particularly their various attempts to forget, preserve, or resolve the memory of the Vietnam War and the 1960s, inevitably return to conflicting definitions and strategies of masculinity. Generational struggle and masculine anxiety become inseparable as the film's most fundamental conflict.

Joel Coen has stated that *The Big Lebowski* is inspired by generation-gap movies of the 1970s, "Except that today the younger generations are almost reactionary in comparison with those of their parents. That's really the subject of the film–this idea of anachronism of incompatibility" (qtd. in Mottram 139). Even in their most mordant and ironic moments, the Coens can still hint at authentic subtexts in their films; and while the arch comedy of *The Big Lebowski* may prove especially resistant to interpretation, it delivers a grim commentary on the difficulty of responding to aggression, the challenges of defining contemporary masculinity, and the desperation of the American public to forget both the Vietnam war and its protesters. The Coens may ridicule the Dude and Walter for their nostalgic fixations, but they have also created something authentically Chandlerian in their protagonists' dogged preservation of memories and values that the rest of their culture would rather ignore.

---

[4] In his essay "On Raymond Chandler," Fredric Jameson defines this modernist mode of nostalgia as "an attachment to a moment of the past wholly different from our own, which offers a more complete kind of relief from the present" (76). By contrast, Jameson characterizes postmodern nostalgia as a "complacent eclecticism [...] which randomly and without principle but with gusto cannibalizes all the [...] styles of the past and combines them in overstimulating ensembles" (*Postmodernism* 18-19).

[5] The Dude is especially fond of reusing other people's phrases, but nearly every character repeats or is repeated by someone else, even if they never meet or hear about each other. Tyree and Walters note that "The overall effect is to suggest a kind of endemic recycling, as if the state's water or power shortages might also apply to thoughts and words" (35). The film's linguistic system is just as closed and impoverished as its economic one, as exhausted as the Big Lebowski's fortunes or General Sternwood's dry well.

....

Marc Singer is Associate Professor of English at Howard University in Washington, DC. He is the co-editor, with Nels Pearson, of Detective Fiction in a Postcolonial and Transnational World (Ashgate, 2009) and the author of Grant Morrison: Combining the Worlds of Contemporary Comics (University Press of Mississippi, 2012).

Works Cited

Bergan, Ronald. *The Coen Brothers*. New York: Thunder's Mouth Press, 2000.

The Big Lebowski. Screenplay by Ethan Coen and Joel Coen. Dir. Joel Coen. PolyGram, 1998.

The Big Sleep. Screenplay by Leigh Brackett and William Faulkner. Dir. Howard Hawks. Warner Brothers, 1946.

Chandler, Raymond. *The Big Sleep*. 1939. New York: Vintage, 1992.

Coen, Ethan and Joel Coen. *The Big Lebowski*. London: Faber & Faber, 1998.

Fontana, Ernest. "Chivalry and Modernity in Raymond Chandler's *The Big Sleep*." 1984. Rpt. in *The Critical Response to Raymond Chandler*. Ed. J. K. Van Dover. Westport, CT: Greenwood, 1995. 159-65.

Jameson, Fredric. "On Raymond Chandler." 1970. Rpt. in *The Critical Response to Raymond Chandler*. J. K. Van Dover, ed. Westport, CT: Greenwood, 1995. 65-87.

– *Postmodernism, or, The Cultural Logic of Late Capitalism*. Durham, NC: Duke University Press, 1991.

Kendrick, Michelle. "Kicking the Vietnam Syndrome: CNN's and CBS's Video Narratives of the Persian Gulf War." *Seeing Through the Media: The Persian Gulf War*. Susan Jeffords and Lauren Rabinovitz, eds. New Brunswick, NJ: Rutgers University Press, 1994. 59-76.

Levine, Josh. *The Coen Brothers: The Story of Two American Filmmakers*. Toronto: ECW Press, 2000.

McCann, Sean. *Gumshoe America*. Durham, NC: Duke University Press, 2000.

Mottram, James. *The Coen Brothers: The Life of the Mind*. Dulles, VA: Brassey's, 2000.

Phillips, Gene D. *Creatures of Darkness*. Lexington: University Press of Kentucky, 2000.

Rabinowitz, Peter. "Rats Behind the Wainscoting: Politics, Convention, and Chandler's *The Big Sleep*." 1980. Rpt. in *The Critical Response to Raymond Chandler*. J. K. Van Dover, ed. Westport, CT: Greenwood, 1995. 117-37.

Robertson, William Preston. *The Big Lebowski: The Making of a Coen Brothers Film*. Ed. Tricia Cooke. New York: W. W. Norton, 1998.

Rowell, Erica. *The Brothers Grim: The Films of Joel and Ethan Coen*. Lanham, MD: Scarecrow, 2007.

Russell, Carolyn R. *The Films of Joel and Ethan Coen*. Jefferson, NC: McFarland, 2001.

Schrader, Paul. "Notes on Film Noir." 1972. *Film Genre Reader II*. Ed. Barry Keith Grant. Austin: University of Texas Press, 1995. 213-26.

Tyree, J. M., and Ben Walters. *The Big Lebowski*. London: British Film Institute, 2007.

APPENDIX

Notes on *The Big Lebowski* Screenplay

BY WILLIAM ROBERT RICH

This is a film about a man who, in a case of mistaken identity, has his favorite rug micturated upon by one of his attackers. He doesn't learn anything new about himself. He's the same person in the end that he was at the beginning. Internally, he just wants to take it easy. That's what he's doing when we first see him at Ralphs, writing a sixty-nine cent check for half & half, and that's what he's doing as the film closes. Takin' her easy for all us sinners. Structurally, the film is driven by three strong external goals:

1. To be compensated for his soiled rug (Act I)
2. To act as a ransom courier and identify Bunny Lebowski's kidnappers (Act II-A)
3. To solve the mystery of Bunny's kidnapping before *The Big Lebowski* kills him or The Nihilists cut off his Johnson (Act II-B & Act III)

The first goal deals with his rug. He meets with The Big Lebowski to seek compensation for his soiled rug, as the men who attacked him and ruined his rug were really targeting The Big Lebowski. When The Big Lebowski refuses, The Dude tricks his assistant into giving him a rug from the mansion. The turn that gives us the new external goal, which happens when The Dude is called back to the Lebowski mansion. There, he discovers The Big Lebowski's wife, Bunny Lebowski, has been kidnapped and The Big Lebowski wishes to hire him to act as courier in the ransom drop-off. After a botched ransom drop-off and having his car stolen with the ransom money inside the trunk, The Big Lebowski puts a price on The Dude's head with the kidnappers, giving us the final external goal of the film. From that point forward, The Dude must solve the mystery of Bunny's disappearance before the kidnappers or The Big Lebowski have him killed.

The Big Lebowski Screenplay: The Characters

The characters bring this film to life. I would bet that this film has more memorable scenes than the mighty Casablanca and I don't say that lightly. Okay … I'm should probably speak for my generation, though generations on either side might agree, too. There's something special about the Coens. They understand that not everything needs to be taken seriously. They spend time with characters who do nothing to influence or antagonize their protagonist because they help paint a unique world. It's a risk most don't pull off and they seem to make look easy.

Theodore Donald "Donny" Kerabatsos

Donny's around in some major scenes. He rides with The Dude and Walter to shake down Little Larry Sellers, but Walter makes him wait in the car. Poor Donny escapes mere seconds before any angry Corvette owner takes a crowbar to it. He fights off Nihilists with The Dude and Walter, only to die of a heart attack after the altercation. His funeral takes up over half of the epilogue. All that, and Donny's total significance to the plot equals zero. You could take Donny out and it would still be the same story, but it wouldn't be the same movie.

Jesus Quintana

Jesus Quintana is a one helluva bowler. His bowling team stands in the way of Walter, Donny, and The Dude surviving the semi-finals. He also happens to be a registered sex offender who served six months in Chino for exposing himself to an eight-year-old. The Coens give us one of the most memorable and quoted characters in the film, and he has less than five minutes of screen time. With all that character, what does Jesus have to do with the plot? Nada, folks. Nada.

The Stranger

Voice-over narration has developed a bad rap from its use of telling audiences the thoughts of a particular character, something that should be revealed through subtext and action. I've taken a ride on that boat before, but it didn't take me long to realize some of my favorite films use it (The Shawshank Redemption, Network, Taxi Driver, Goodfellas, Memento, Annie Hall, Fight Club, Risky Business, Adaptation, The Royal Tenenbaums).

The Stranger is just another fine example of The Coen Brothers' brilliant use of character. He's a third-party perspective to the story, similar to Red in The Shawshank

Redemption, but without major scenes that influence the protagonist. He's another color that paints a more vivid picture. Like with Donny and Jesus, you could take The Stranger out and have the same story, but you sure wouldn't have the same film.

BASIC SCREENPLAY ANALYSIS

Protagonist: Jeffrey "The Dude" Lebowski, aging pothead and avid---bowler.

Characterization/Main Misbehavior: Unemployed, lazy.

External Goal: To be compensated for his soiled rug / To act as the ransom courier and identify Bunny Lebowski's kidnappers / To solve the mystery of Bunny's kidnapping before The Big Lebowski kills him or The Nihilists cut off his johnson

Internal Goal: To take 'er easy for all us sinners out there.

Main Dramatic Conflict: The Big Lebowski, The Nihilists, Walter

Theme: Life is a series of strikes and gutterballs.

Central Dramatic Question: Will The Dude solve the mystery of Bunny's kidnapping before The Big Lebowski kills him or The Nihilists cut off his Johnson?

Ending: The Dude and friends defeat the Nihilists.

STORY ENGINES

ACT I

In a case of mistaken identity, The Dude's favorite rug is micturated upon. When his attackers' original target, the wealthy Big Lebowski, refuses to compensate him for his soiled rug, The Dude steals another rug from him. Later, The Dude is hired by The Big Lebowski to act as a ransom courier when his wife is kidnapped.

ACT II---A

The Dude, along with his best friend Walter, mess up the ransom drop and the kidnappers do not get the money. Before The Dude can return the money, his car is stolen with the money inside the trunk. The Big Lebowski later confronts The Dude with a severed toe, presumably belonging to his wife. He tells The Dude he has instructed the kidnappers to do whatever they need to recover the missing money from him.

ACT II---B

After police locate his missing car, The Dude discovers a clue from the car thief that doesn't go anywhere. Later, he sleeps *with The Big Lebowski's daughter, Maude Lebowski. When* she informs him that her father doesn't have any money of his own, it gives The Dude *TBL's* potential motive for keeping the ransom money.

ACT III

The Dude confronts The Big Lebowski about the money and discovers Bunny is alive and well at his house. Later, The Dude faces off against the kidnappers and is lucky enough to have his buddy Walter defeat them.

EPILOGUE

The Dude and Walter spread Donny's ashes in the Pacific and get back to what they love the best: bowling.

FULL SCREENPLAY ANALYSIS

ACT I

1. **Opening Images:**
A tumbleweed makes its way through the desert to Los Angeles, all the way to the Pacific Ocean.

4. Wearing a robe and sunglasses, THE DUDE –a.k.a. Jeffrey Lebowski – buys half and half at Ralphs. He writes a check for sixty-nine cents.

5. **INCITING INCIDENT:**
Arriving at his apartment, The Dude is attacked by men hired by Jackie Treehorn who are looking to recover a debt owed by his wife, Bunny Lebowski. One of the attackers, an Asian-American, pees on his rug. Sadly, it's just a simple case of mistaken identity. The Dude is not married.

10. At the bowling alley, WALTER, The Dude's best friend, insists "the other Jeffrey Lebowski" compensate him for his soiled rug.

15. The Dude arrives at the mansion of THE BIG LEBOWSKI and asks him to replace the rug. The Big Lebowski becomes furious. The Dude says "fuck it" and leaves.

16. **STRONG MOVEMENT FORWARD:**
The Dude lies to The Big Lebowski's assistant, BRANDT, saying The Big Lebowski told him he could have any rug he wanted.

17. Outside, The Dude finds BUNNY LEBOWSKI lounging by the pool. She offers to suck his cock for a thousand dollars.

22. The Dude is late on his rent. He listens to voicemails from Brandt, insisting they are not
concerned about the rug and to call back immediately.

24. **END OF ACT TURN:**

The Dude meets with The Big Lebowski again to discover his wife Bunny has been kidnapped for a heavy ransom. They want to pay The Dude $20,000 to act as courier for the money because they suspect the kidnappers might be the same folks that soiled his carpet and he could identify them, linking the kidnapping to Jackie Treehorn.

ACT II-A

30. Resting on his rug, The Dude looks up to find two men and a woman standing above him. One of the men knocks him out. A dream sequence begins to Bob Dylan's "The Man in Me."

32. The Dude wakes and discovers his new rug gone.

32. Brandt gives The Dude Bunny Lebowski's one million dollars in ransom. Brandt repeatedly tells The Dude "her life is in your hands."

33. The Dude picks up Walter to help with the ransom drop off, even though the kidnappers instructed only one person's involvement.

37. **FIRST TRIAL/FIRST CASUALTY**:
Walter throws a ringer over a bridge and chaos ensues. The kidnappers escape without the ransom money or anyone seeing them.

40. **COMBAT**:
The Dude's car, with one million dollars in the trunk, is stolen.

43. The Dude receives a call from Maude Lebowski, claiming she is the one who took his rug.

48. MAUDE LEBOWSKI, The Big Lebowski's daughter, believes Bunny kidnapped herself. She hires The Dude to recover the lost money for a fee of ten percent.

53. **MIDPOINT**:
Outside his apartment, The Dude is manhandled into a waiting limousine. Inside, The Big Lebowski accuses The Dude of stealing the ransom money, and gives him an envelope sent to him by the kidnappers which contains one of Bunny's severed toes. The Big Lebowski promises to direct the kidnappers to visit "ten-fold" harm upon The Dude in order to recover the money.

ACT II-B

54. The Dude meets Walter for coffee. Walter insists the toe wasn't Bunny's and that Bunny kidnapped herself.

57. The Nihilists – presumably Bunny's kidnappers – break into The Dude's apartment, demanding the ransom money within twenty-four hours or they will "cut off his Johnson."

58. The Dude's car is found by the police, but the money is still missing.

65. The Dude meets with Maude again. She insists he see a doctor regarding the bruise he sustained when she took the rug from him.

66. The Dude visits Maude's doctor.

67. **ASSUMPTION OF POWER**:
After dropping a joint in his lap, The Dude wrecks his car. Attempting to get out of the car, he discovers evidence from the car thief: a high school essay on The Louisiana Purchase.

69. Walter and The Dude locate the author of the essay, LITTLE LARRY SELLERS, and question him at his home.

71. Larry won't talk and Walter becomes furious.

74. Assuming Little Larry is the owner of new Corvette, Walter smashes up the car with a tire iron. The car's real owner appears out of nowhere, an emotional wreck and yanks the tire iron from Walter. Believing The Dude's car belongs to Walter, he smashes the hell out of it in a fit of rage.

78. The Dude is summoned to JACKIE TREEHORN's mansion. Bunny Lebowski owes Jackie a sizable debt and Jackie wants his cut from the ransom money The Dude collected from The Big Lebowski.

79. The Dude gives up Little Larry Sellers as the thief of the one million dollars, but Jackie doesn't believe him.

80. The Dude passes out moments after he realizes Jackie drugged his drink.

81. Dream sequence to Kenny Rogers' "Just Dropped In (To See What Condition My Condition Was In)."

86. The Dude is arrested outside Jackie's party. The Malibu police chief roughs up The Dude and demands he "stay out of Malibu!"

88. We glimpse Bunny Lebowski, alive and well . . . with all ten toes.

89. The Dude comes home to find Maude Lebowski in his apartment. She drops her robe and says "love me, Jeffrey."

91. **END OF ACT TWO TURN**:
In bed with The Dude, Maude reveals her father doesn't have any money of his own. The money belonged to her mother. Maude has provided him "a reasonable allowance" to live.

Discovering The Big Lebowski has no money gives The Dude a potential motive for The Big Lebowski to pocket the ransom money for himself.

92. Maude informs The Dude she wants to have his child, but doesn't want him active in the
child's life. The Dude is fine with that.

93. **DECISION**:
The Dude calls Walter to drive him to The Big Lebowski's mansion.

ACT III

95. The Nihilists dine on pancakes. One of their girlfriends is missing a toe.

96. The Dude tells Walter The Big Lebowski never put the ransom money in the briefcase and kept the money for himself.

97. The Dude and Walter arrive at The Big Lebowski's mansion and find Bunny running around, completely naked and completely unharmed.

99. **POINT OF NO RETURN**: The Dude and Walter confront The Big Lebowski about the missing money. He does not confess, only saying "you have your story, I have mine."

102. Outside the bowling alley, The Nihilists have torched The Dude's car. They demand the
ransom money.

104. **CLIMAX**: The Nihilists attack and Walter kicks all of their asses.

The Dude does absolutely nothing here. Along with Donny, The Dude's just trying to give The Nihilists all his cash and pray they go about their business. It's Walter that defeats the bad guys in the end.

105. Donnie suffers a heart attack during the fight with the Nihilists and dies.

EPILOGUE

109. Walter spreads Donnie's ashes over the Pacific, but thanks to a strong gust of wind, most
of it ends up on The Dude.

110. The Dude becomes furious with Walter, but they make up when Walter hugs him.

112. Back at the bowling alley, The Dude talks to The Stranger. He leaves and The Stranger talks
to us about the story being all wrapped up and his fondness for The Dude and his lifestyle, and alludes to the offspring of The Dude and Maude, closing the film.

112. **THE END**.

....

William Robert Rich is a lazy man. He's also a Lebowski enthusiast and story analyst, known worldwide as the Founder and Chief Editor of ScreenplayHowTo.com and co-author of *Story Maps: The Films of Christopher Nolan*. On any given day you can find him walking his dog, McFly, a beautiful yellow Labrador, down Congress Avenue in Austin, Texas. Though the sunglasses and service dog harness may throw you off, rest assured, Rob is not blind and McFly is not a guide dog.

Biographies of the Illustrators

Mauro Antonini was born in Rome, where lives and works. He is a critic for various Italian magazines and author of various books about cinema, comics and drawing techniques. In 2010 he collaborated with special effect master Sergio Stivaletti as cartoonist of "The Invisible Man" comic book sequence that appears in the short movie *Halloween Party*. In 2011 he created the Piccion character and the single panel web-series *Piccioncinema*. Under the nickname Manthomex, he posts projects on Deviant Art and other sites like FurryAffinity. His most prominent work on Deviant Art is the *Crimson Comics* series featuring the character he created, Lil Crim.
http://manthomex.deviantart.com/
http://piccioncinema.deviantart.com/

Alberto Barina is 26 years old and from Italy. His Deviant Art page can be found at:
http://alberto-b.deviantart.com/

Christopher Berge is the lead graphic designer at a commercial printing plant in Sacramento, CA. He is also a freelance illustrator and artist. Please contact him at aggrokulture@gmail.com for inquiries. You can also see more of his work or order prints at aggro-kulture.deviantart.com

Hyndira Borba is 22 years old and lives in Santa Catarina, Brazil. She has a degree in advertising, but her true love has always been illustration and all kinds of works that are meant to be appreciated visually. The Big Lebowski T-shirt was a personal work she designed for herself and a few friends by hand at home. You can see her work here: http://hyndiraborba.deviantart.com/

Matt Camp is an artist from Portland Oregon who has drawn for DC, Dark Horse, Marvel and Image. Now he draws for deadline-free enjoyment.

Vincent Carrozza is an artist/illustrator with a taste for popular culture and a sense for the absurd.
He lives in Australia with his wife and children and is still terrified of The Lollipop Guild.
Website: www.6amcrisis.com
Facebook: www.fb.com/vincent.carrozza

Koen Cassiman: Koen Cassiman is young visual artist, located in Gent, Belgium. You can view his work at www.kocas.be

Brandon Chapman is currently a student living in Michigan and studying Illustration. He's an amateur comic writer/illustrator and part-time deep sea crab fisherman. Actually the last part isn't true, but he did watch part of an episode of *Deadliest Catch* once.
You can check out his work at waterloggedcomic.com & bchapman.deviantart.com

By day, **Steven Cote** produces local television commercials deep in the frozen Canadian wilderness. By night, he is a lone outlaw – a hired gun of blazing creative glory, living vicariously through graphic design and animation. Feel free rattle his chain and check out his work at panicbuttondesign.wordpress.com.

Giuseppe Cristiano is a former comic artist and scriptwriter has been drawing storyboards for almost two decades. He freelances for advertising agencies and film production companies in Europe and USA.
Website: http://www.framingfilms.com
blog: http://giuseppecristiano.tumblr.com

Camille Custard is a Russian architecture student. She's an illustrator amateur and a big cinemaholic. Jeff Bridges became her first movie-crush when she saw "Tron" at eight years old. You can find her works on DeviantArt (~toweliekam), or send an email (towelie_kam@mail.ru).

Brian "Scoop" Diehl was a Dudeist even before the dude hit the silver screen. He's a bowler who would rather have an oat soda with friends than deal with the corporate world (for which he spent 10 years in as a director of marketing for NEC). Growing up, he studied art through private lessons, then at Kent State. His knowledge of computer graphics, however, came from the school of hard knocks. Brian is most comfortable around the dudes of the world and is always happy to share his vision of the universe through pen and paper. He draws and writes for a living in Hudson, Ohio – and for a beer or two will be happy to sketch something for you on a bar coaster. You can see more of his stuff at www.thinknik.com

James Duncan has been illustrating his entire life, and posting his art on the internet for over the past twelve years, sharing his thoughts with a world that hasn't slowed down enough to take the time to read them. Living in Montreal, Quebec, Canada, James is a hardworking husband (though his wife might disagree), and a loving father to his two greatest accomplishments, Kaesye & Finnegan. *The Big Lebowski* has always had a place on his top 5 movie list, but it's taken a bigger hold of his life ever since he became an ordained Dudeist Priest in 2009, and the author of *Am I a Dude*, the first children's book for all the little achievers out there! www.kaesye.com.

Gregg Firestone is a hobbyist whose doodles can be found on a hometown pizzeria box, a documentary film, sticky notes all over California, and a friggin' book! He also draws a ton of cats and fakes terrible European accents. He sends huge thanks to family and friends for not smothering him with a pillow in his sleep. http://beefteriyaki.deviantart.com/

Joe Forkan is a figurative and landscape painter who lives and works in Southern California. He was born in Walden, New York. He received his BFA in Studio Art from the University of Arizona in 1989, and an MFA in Painting from the University of Delaware in 2002. He is currently Professor of Art at California State University Fullerton.

Manu Jurado Garrido is a young illustrator and graphic designer from Córdoba, Spain. He has illustrated various publications, and participated in collective exhibitions and artistic festivals in his country. Since 2007, he has participated in exhibitions with the artistic collective *PaOctubre*, a group that experiments with modern illustration techniques.

Individually, he had his first exhibition of watercolors "11 Pasos" in 2010, which was followed by "Concepts" and "Devaneos Literarios" (2011). Now, he is working on "Hasta el cuello", which he hopes to exhibit in 2013 in various cities in Spain.

For more info of Manu Jurado's works, please visit www.manujurado.tumblr.com

James Grange is a writer and artist living in Seattle, Washington. His website, Coloropolis.com, features art and pop culture coloring pages for adults.

Kyle Hellkamp first saw The Big Lebowski on April 20th, 2006, and honestly did not care for it at the time. As he grew older and more mature, his tastes also developed and he discovered what an awe-inspiring experience The Big Lebowski is. Kyle is a student of physics, an avid artist, owner of two cockatiels (Arlow and Jewel), and author of the book "Our Electric God" (http://amzn.to/13GYlzz). He also has a large poster of The Big Lebowski on his wall, which really ties the room together.

Eric Hetherington has dabbled in illustration since he could hold a pen (and still has his very first picture to prove it!). He considers himself a bit of a comic entrepreneur (and by entrepreneur, he means never made any money off of it). You can follow his latest venture into the world of sequential art at: www.facebook.com/Groompish

Chris Hoffman has 20 years experience as a professional illustrator in the DFW metroplex area. He works full time at a successful studio in Arlington TX where he creates imaging for toy packaging and video game covers. He also does personal portraits and sketch cards for companies such as Cryptozoic, Breygent and Versicolor. He works primarily with markers, paint and colored pencils, as well as digital programs like Adobe Illustrator and Photoshop. laklun@aol.com

The right Reverend **Dave Johnson**'s bio cannot be contained on one page. Besides bringing down the former Soviet Union with his manly facial beard, he's been drawing comic book junk for over 20 years now. Raised by Masonic Shriners, he learned early on that small cars are terrible to bang chicks in. But they did instill a burning desire to wear funny hats and ask for money on street corners. Which you can find him doing when he's not doing covers for Marvel. DC Comics, DarkHorse Comics, Valiant and more. On titles like Punisher, 100 Bullets, Deadpool, Shadowman, BPRD, Spaceman, Unknown Soldier etc, etc. He also did some interiors a while back, like SuperPatriot and Superman: Red Son. In addition to all that he worked in animation for over 10 years on shows like Batman Beyond, Justice League, Legion, G.I. Joe Resolute, and designed/art directed the original Ben 10 series for Cartoon Network. What will he do next? Who really gives a crap? Reverend Dave just wants to sit in a bar with the Original Drink and Draw Social Club crew, getting hammered with drawing on beer coaster in downtown Los Angeles. So if you see him on the street, throw a dollar his way. It will go towards a good cause. Liver failure.

Matthew Killorin is a wellness consultant and blogger, and he abides in Richmond, Virginia. You can share your favorite Big Lebowski quotes with him on Google+: http://bit.ly/13s7kGB

Jane Labowitch is a freelance illustrator based in Chicago. When she's not illustrating, she's etch-a-sketching anything to her heart's content. You may contact her at janelabowitch.com or princessetchasketch.com, or email her at janelabowitch@gmail.com

Lama Under the Hat
Gmail - eldron005@gmail.com
Last.fm - OMFG-IM-A-CAT
Flickr - acid_lama
DeviantArt - lamaunderthehat

Rich Nairn is an artist based in Kent, England who goes by the nickname of "The Artful Doodler". He feeds the monkey by drawing cartoons and caricatures…quite a lazy occupation, quite possibly the laziest of all artist's occupations, which would place it high in the runnin' for laziest worldwide.

You can see Rich's regular, "Ruminations of a Dudeist Cartoonist" and other creations at www.theartfuldoodler.co.uk

Paul Niesen teaches English at the University of Wisconsin-Oshkosh and doodles during monthly Department meetings.

Spencer Nobles is a comic book artist from a small town in Minnesota that just happens to be the very hometown of the Coen brothers. He has always been a fan of their work and has been uniquely inspired by their outrageous characters and indefatigably compelling stories. In fact, his parents went to high school with Ethan Coen, which he considers a pretty cool thing.

Erol Osman is a good man and thorough artist from London UK who goes by the alias eos vector. His art has been commended as being "strongly vaginal" which doesn't bother him at all. For recreation he does the usual: bowls, drives around, and has the occasional acid flash-back. You can view more of his artwork and perhaps give him some notes at www.eosvector.com.

Jeffrey Peterson is also known as "The 420 Comic" He has appeared on TMZ, E!, Inside Edition, VH1, PBS and Spike TV. He has been a Cannabis Activist since 1991, 7 x Host of Hemp Con, 3 x Host of Kush Expo, Co-Host Sacramento Hemp Fest 2012, MC for Wasteland Weekend 2012, MC for LA Harvest Cup 2011, Host of Adultcon LA 2011, Host of Love Letters to Mary Jane. He has headlined Treating Yourself Expo in Toronto, Produced The Dopest Show On Earth Since 2006, was a producer for The Interview w/ Frazer Smith Podcast on The Toadhop Network and Go Cast Network, was the Official Comedian for Los Angeles NORML, and a Stand-up Smack Down Champion. Since 2003 he has been a headlining stand-up comic/host performing around in Las Vegas at Orleans, The Green Door, The Double Down and Lucie's Lounge and in Los Angeles at The Comedy Store, The Laugh Factory, The Improv, The Jon Lovitz Comedy Club, Flappers Comedy Club, The Ha Ha Cafe, The Whisky, The Roxy, The Viper Room and The Ice House. Jeffrey was recently featured on TMZ for the 2nd time, E!, Inside Edition and California's Gold with Huell Hauser for PBS. When not promoting or partying or working on his comic book for the Cannabis Culture called Cali Chronic ComiX (from the Creators of California Chronicle XXX), he can be found performing stand-up on stage around the Southwest or entertaining the open minded sex fiends, barflies and stoners of Las Vegas, Nevada

Kate Radomski is a freelance illustrator, character designer, and chronic daydreamer with a cheesecake addiction. Though a frequent wanderer, she currently lives in Baltimore, MD.
www.kateradomski.com

Dany Rand (Dan Winterbottom) has worked on various artistic commissions and t-shirt designs. To see more of his work or request a design, check him out at http://nastyd13.deviantart.com/

Riccardo Rosanna is an Italian comic book illustrator and graphic professional. He studied at the School of Comics in Milan. His deviant art page is http://ozzie325.deviantart.com/, his email is: marvi-riki@hotmail.it.

Alex Ruiz began his professional art career as a character animator on *The Simpsons* at the age of 19. He then became an assistant director on the hit series, taking on more responsibilities on the creation of the show, ultimately receiving an Emmy nomination for his work. Eventually, Alex realized his passion for making still images rather than animating scenes, and shifted into a career as an illustrator. He then moved into the position of Director of Illustration for 20th Century Fox's License and Merchandise department, working on properties including James Cameron's Avatar, Aliens, Halo 3, Eragon, Family Guy, the Simpsons, McFarlane/Spawn Toys and many more properties.

Alex is currently a freelance concept artist/illustrator lending his talents to the film, television, video game, and music industries. Clients include 20th Century Fox, Activision, The Workshop, Universal Studios, Sony, Radical Comics, Virgin Comics, and visual effects houses Frame Machine, Perspective Studios, and The Picturemill. He is also an art instructor at the Los Angeles Academy of Figurative Art, the Computer Graphics Master Academy, and Studio Arts in Los Angeles, teaching classes in conceptual design, architecture, digital painting and anatomy. Website: http://conceptmonster.net/ Facebook: http://www.facebook.com/alexruizdesign/ Twitter: http://twitter.com/alexruizart

Anthony Sims is a multimedia artist that currently works out of the greater Tampa Bay area in Florida, with dreams of relocating his family of four to the urban paradise of San Francisco. He grew up in the suburbs of Maryland, where he attended Montgomery College for certifications in graphic design and animation. Later, upon moving to FL, he obtained his BFA degree from The Art Institute of Tampa in "Media Arts and Animation." He has operated a small freelance art studio since 2002, and currently teaches Digital Design and Animation at Rasmussen College, based out of New Port Richey, FL. He is currently working towards his MFA in Animation and Visual Effects, with a specialization in 3D Modeling. He is a multimedia artist that is both traditionally trained in the classic arts of drawing, painting, and sculpture, as well as digitally trained in graphic design, digital painting/photo manipulation, video, and of course, animation. He lives with his beautiful wife Lacy, and his children Christopher and Rhiannon. Outside of his family, his most prized possession is his Wacom Cintiq 22HD art monitor, which was a huge boon to his digital art workflow. You can see his recent work collected at http://facebook.com/AnthonyPhillipSims and http://www.ronindms.com.

Will Staub is an active member of the Church of the Latter Day Dude. Well, as active as anyone can be while taking 'er easy. He hopes to contribute more works and ideas to the church, since it has contributed much to his daily life and philosophy.

Eric Streed is a recent graduate of VCU Arts in Richmond, Virginia with concentrations in Concept Design, Video Game Design, and Illustration. He is a great lover of all things dude, and was thrilled at the chance to be a part of this book. You can find more of his work at http://be.net/streedes.

Though he doesn't consider himself an artist, **Bryan Thornsberry** creates art as a means of an outlet to his real life's frustrations and fallacies. He picked The Dude of Los Angeles County as an homage piece, to a lazier time in his life…to tell you the truth, he doesn't remember much of it.

Lanny Tunks used to draw a lot as a kid, and has only been taking it seriously in the last 6 months. It has been a productive 6 months, and he hopes this is something that will continue to grow and build on in the years to come. http://www.facebook.com/MacabreDepictions

Bas de Voogt Bas de Voogt was born on May 30, 1993 in Rotterdam, where he currently still lives. He has just finished studying Game Art at Grafisch Lyceum in Rotterdam. Drawing portraits has always been a passion of his. He used to work only with paper and pencils but for the last couple of years has found himself more comfortable with a drawing tablet and Adobe Photoshop as he finds he can work a lot faster and add more details. Besides drawing he also enjoys gaming, jamming on his piano and reading about human psychology, Buddhism and stuff like that.Portfolio website:
http://basdevoogt.wordpress.com/
E-mail: basdevoogt@gmail.com

Josua Waghubinger is a 23-year old graphic design student from Germany. His work can be enjoyed at http://montoria.deviantart.com/

Joe Ward is a comic artist, illustrator and mammal. He happily accepts commission work, enjoys white Russians and tends to abide. You can find his work at http://captainsnikt.deviantart.com.

Self-taught illustrator and freelance writer **Daniel J.S. Webb** grew up in London, England, a city whose vibrant characters and ever changing landscape keeps him entertained every day. A lifelong passion for film runs through his work and keeps the flat he shares with his always patient girlfriend full to the ceiling with movie memorabilia and collectable Mr. Potato Heads.

Brandon Yarwood is a 15-year professional with a passion to do work he's proud of. He likes his art to have character while being clean and stylized. He lives in Indianapolis with his lovely wife, two sons and two really spoiled dogs. http://yarwoodart.com

Printed by Amazon Italia Logistica S.r.l.
Torrazza Piemonte (TO), Italy

56054165R00118